Jewish Civilization

SUNY Series in Israeli Studies

Russell Stone, Editor

Jewish Civilization

The Jewish Historical Experience in a Comparative Perspective

S. N. Eisenstadt

State University of New York Press

Published by
State University of New York Press, Albany

© 1992   State University of New York

For information, address State University of New York
Press, State University Plaza, Albany, N.Y. 12246

Production by M. R. Mulholland
Marketing by Bernadette LaManna

Library of Congress Cataloging-in-Publication Data

Eisenstadt, S. N. (Shmuel Noah), 1923–
    Jewish civilization : the Jewish historical experience in a
comparative perspective / S. N. Eisenstadt.
        p.   cm. — (SUNY series in Israeli studies)
    Includes bibliographical references and index.
    ISBN 0–7914–1095–1 (alk. paper). — ISBN 0–7914–1096–X (pbk. :
alk. paper)
    1. Jews—Civilization. 2. Jews—History. I. Title. II. Series.
DS117.E37   1992
909'.04924—dc20
                                                                91-25562
                                                                CIP

10 9 8 7 6 5 4 3 2 1

To the memory of my teachers
at the Hebrew University

Itzhak Baer
Ben Zion Dinur
Arthur Ruppin
of
Yehezkel Kaufmann
and of
Arnaldo Momigliano

Contents

Introduction

This book presents a somewhat new approach to the analysis of the Jewish historical experience. The major argument of this book is that the best way to understand this experience is to look on Jews not just as a religious or ethnic group, nation, or "people," although they have been all of these, but as bearers of a civilization.

The term *civilization* will be used here in a rather specific way with special emphasis on its difference from religion, if we define *religion* as a set of beliefs, especially about various transmundane matters, patterns of worship, of ritual observances and the like. *Civilization,* in the sense used here, entails the attempts to construct or reconstruct social life according to an ontological vision that combines conceptions of the nature of the cosmos, of transmundane and mundane reality, with the regulation of the major arenas of social life and interaction of the political arena, authority, the economy, family life, and the like. Although in the history of humankind civilizations and religions were very closely interwoven—at the same time many religions have been only a part of the component or not necessarily the most central component of civilizations. This distinction, which can be found already, even if in a muted way, in many preliterate and archaic societies—such as those of the Ancient Near East—becomes clearly visible in the "great" Axial Age civilizations, in ancient Greece and especially the Hellenistic civilizations, in the monotheistic religions and civilizations, in Hinduism, Buddhism, and Confucianism. In these civilizations religion constituted basic components of civilization, but in some places they constituted religious working within the framework of other civilizations. The clearest illustration of such a case is probably the fate of Buddhism and Confucianism in Japan, where Buddhist (and Confucian) beliefs and cults thrived, without however creating a distinct civilization (as was the case with respect to Buddhism in Southeast Asia, or with Confucianism in China, Korea, and Vietnam). In Japan these cults and belief or ethical systems operated within the framework and basic premises of a distinct Japanese civilization. Similar illustrations can be given from the history of expansion of Islam or Christianity. At the same time these illustrations attest to the fact that different people, different societies, or different polities may belong to the same civilization, especially to one of these "higher" civilizations.

It is our claim that the best way to look at the Jewish historical experience is to analyze it as the history of a civilization in the way we have defined it here, and not only as a history of a people, religious, ethnic, or national group. Indeed, the very fact that all these terms can be applied to the analysis of the Jewish historical experience indicates that none of them is sufficient. Moreover, it seems to us that only if one looks at this experience in civilizational terms may one begin to cope with the greatest riddle of that experience; namely, with its continuity despite destruction, exile, loss of political independence, and loss of territorial continuity; despite exile and dispersion and concomitant far-reaching changes not only in the concrete ways of life but also in basic religious orientation and practices. Accordingly, in this book we shall examine selected aspects of the Jewish historical experience from such civilizational perspective.

In the first part, the first three chapters of the book, we examine some of the basic characteristics of the Jewish civilization as they have crystallized in its formative periods, those of the First and Second Temples and later, and in the long exilic medieval period. In these chapters we shall show that throughout these periods the Jews behaved not only as a national group or religious sect, but as bearers of a distinct civilization; and they also were so perceived by their neighboring or host civilizations. We shall indicate in what way they differed from "people," nations, or religious sects or groups that were not bearers of a distinct civilizational vision but usually parts thereof. We also point out some of the major differences, both in terms of their respective premises and historical experience, between the Jewish and the other civilization: the pagan civilization, in the framework of which the ancient Israeli civilization arose; the Hellenistic and Roman civilizations of antiquity; and above all the two other monotheistic civilizations, Christianity and Islam, the encounter with which constituted a basic component of the Jewish historical experience.

In the second and largest part of the book, we continue our analysis into the modern period, in which the basic relations between the Jews and their host societies or civilizations have changed drastically. The focus of our analysis here will be the question whether during this period the Jewish people have continued to exhibit some of their specific civilizational characteristics or whether they became dissolved into "simple," religious, ethnic, or even national groups.

We approach this problem by an analysis of several modes of the Jewish modern historical experience. First, we examine the different patterns of incorporation of Jewish communities in some of their host societies in Western and Eastern Europe, and the United States, in the nineteenth and first four decades of the twentieth century. Second, we analyze the national movements that developed among the Jews from the end of the nineteenth century, especially the Zionist movement. Third, we analyze some of the specific characteristics of Israeli society—the most concrete outcome of the revolutional ideological orientations of the Zionist movement and some central aspects of its political culture in their relations to the Jewish one.

Throughout our analysis, in all these chapters, we ask ourselves to what extent some of the crucial aspects of Jewish experience in each of these cases is similar to that of comparable groups—such as the incorporation of other ethnic and religious minorities in the modern nation-state; other modern national movements; and other revolutionary ideological settlers societies. With respect to the last problem we compare Israeli society with the United States. In all these cases we ask to what extent such experiences have exhibited some distinct—and common—characteristics that can be attributed to some of the specifically Jewish civilizational characteristics analyzed in the preceding chapters.

Already, the very titles of these chapters point to a very specific characteristic of the Jewish modern historical experience that distinguishes it from that of other groups. This characteristic is the very heterogeneity of modern Jewish life, the simultaneous existence of all these different patterns of Jewish-historical experience: those of incorporation into modern societies; the development of multiple national movements; the establishment, for the first time after the period of the Second Commonwealth, of an independent Jewish state in the land of Israel. At the same time between these various Jewish communities and movements there have existed continuous interrelation—the like of which probably cannot be found in most other ethnic, national, or religious groups.

This very heterogeneity of Jewish modern and contemporary experiences poses new challenges, and in the final chapter we bring together these different lines of analysis by asking about the possible directions of Jewish experience in the contemporary world.

It is obviously not our intention to present detailed historical analyses of the different periods of Jewish history analyzed in the various chapters of this book—and accordingly we shall not be able to do justice to the very rich harvest of research and interpretation of all these periods that have burgeoned lately. Given the major purpose of the book we shall concentrate on the aspects of these periods which are most relevant to our argument.

The major arguments of this book were initially presented at Stanford University where in fall 1984 I served as the first Professor of Jewish Studies and at the Henry Jackson School at Washington University, Seattle, where in spring 1986 I was the first Stroum Visiting Professor of Jewish Civilizations.

The core of the book—Chapters 1–4, 6, and 7—initially were given as the Bloomingdale Lectures at Brown University and the Evans Lecture at Duke University in 1987. I am indebted to Professor J. Neusner for extending to me the invitation to give the Bloomingdale Lectures and for the constructive comments on them by him and Professor C. Goldscheider. I am grateful to them and Professor E. S. Frerichs for their generous hospitality at Brown and to Professors E. Meyers and E. Tiryakian at Duke. I am also grateful to Professor J. S. Migdal for the invitation to the University of Washington and to Professor J. Kieval and Dorothy Becker for their hospitality during my visit there. Chapter 8 was initially given as the 1986 memorial lecture at Princeton University. The chapter on the United States and Israel has been presented on several occasions in Israel and the United States, especially the introductory lectures for Fullbright Scholars in Israel.

I would like to thank Professor M. Abitbol, Dr. S. Crosby, and Mr. Justice M. Shamgar, President of the Supreme Court of Israel and anonymous readers for SUNY Press for very useful comments on drafts of several chapters, also Len Shram and Janet Shaw for editorial help and M. Levy, Minnie Pasin, Barbara Cotton, and Kristine Ilani for typing parts of the manuscript, and Kathleen Bruhn for very helpful research assistance.

1

Jewish History as the History of Jewish Civilizations

Introduction: The Problem of Jewish Continuity

The major theme of this book is that one of the best ways to approach the study of Jewish society and history—from its beginnings up to the contemporary scene in general, and Israel in particular—is by analyzing it as the history of a civilization.[1] I use the term *civilization* because I wish to stress explicitly that such concepts as "religion," "nation," and "people" are not adequate for an understanding of Jewish history, although, needless to say, they all refer to important aspects of the Jewish historical experience.

Even though throughout the ages the Jews have constituted a distinct religious community, with specific beliefs and patterns of worship, *religion* is inadequate to explain all aspects of their historical experience, because there is more to it than religion. Two examples will suffice at this juncture: The Jews' ideological and metaphysical attitudes toward the land of Israel, from which they were exiled for so long, and the ways in which their relationship with other religions and nations were mutually defined cannot be explained solely in terms of religious belief, as we shall see in greater detail later on.

The same structure applies, in different ways, to such terms as *nation* and *ethnic group*. These terms are inadequate to explain the Jewish historical experience, because most of them refer to types of collectivities that have developed in the modern era. They easily cannot be applied (though in fact they often are, for lack of better terms) to the collectivities of earlier periods. Instead, terms like *tribal communities, holy community,* or *people,* in themselves quite vague, better denote the nature of the specific early Israelite and Jewish collective identity.

Similarly, because the modern Jewish historical experience is closely related to these older patterns, the modern terms, derived chiefly from the modern European experience, are not fully adequate for the analysis even of the modern Jewish case. Later we shall see that for the same reasons we should not refer to the Zionist movement as just another modern national movement.

Though all these terms contain important elements of truth, their inadequacy becomes apparent when we attempt to explain the great variety of Jewish historical experience from the early Israelite era up to modern times, and above all when we consider what probably is the greatest riddle of the Jewish historical experience: its continuity through some three millennia.[2]

The external facts of Jewish history are well known. Jewish history emerged sometime in the middle of the second millennium before the Christian era (BCE). Its first decisive encounter was the conquest of the land or infiltration of Canaan by the Tribes of Israel, according to biblical tradition, and the leadership of Joshua, presumably already bearing the stamp of legislation attributed to Moses; and then the settlement of these tribes in Canaan. Such conquest, quite natural in those times in that part of the world, necessarily entailed a continuous encounter and conflict with their neighbors, the various nations or tribes that also had settled in that territory. This settlement was initially, in the period of the Judges, a relatively dispersed one, with the different tribes leading relatively separate existences, yet with some common sacred places, coming together to some degree in times of war, and maintaining some continuous common transtribal identity.

From the very beginning of this period the Israeli tribes were characterized by several special social characteristics, which we shall analyze in greater detail later on. At this stage of our discussion suffice it to point out that the most important of these characteristics were their relative profusion and the heterogeneity of social, economic, and cultural forms and elements of which they were composed. Most important among the latter, of course, were the priests and prophets who, as we shall see, had acquired some very outstanding characteristics that distinguished them from their seeming counterparts in neighboring societies.

In the tenth century BCE came the period of the monarchy established first under Saul, then David and Solomon. Attempts to centralize the cult took place and the First Temple was erected under Solomon. After the death of Solomon, under his son Rehoboam, the realm was divided into the two Kingdoms of Judah (composed mostly of the tribes of Judah and Benjamin) and of Israel (composed of the other ten tribes). These kingdoms were continuously involved in the international conflicts of the region, especially the conflicts between the great empires—Egypt, on the one hand, and Assyria and Babylonia, on the other—as well as various kingdoms in the north, such as the Aramaeans. When the Assyrians destroyed the Kingdom of Israel in 722, the ten tribes almost totally disappeared as a distinct cultural and political entity. The Davidic monarchy, the priestly cults, and the prophetic tradition in Judah with its center in Jerusalem faced ultimate destruction in 586. Large parts of the population, especially its leaders, were exiled to Babylon, and the dispersion to other lands, especially to Egypt, began.

Up to this point, the story, although very dynamic and to some degree dramatic, was not unique, and the Israelite nation would have disappeared from the face of subsequent history as did so many other nations in this region at that time. But they did not disappear, and in this they are unique. Large parts, and probably the more active leadership elements, of the population of Judah went to Babylon. Many of course remained there, but many of the exiles in Babylon kept the dream of returning to Zion. After the Persian conquests of Babylon under Cyrus (550–530 BCE) and later in 525 of Egypt by Cyrus's son Cambyses, they—or rather some of them—started to return to Eretz Israel and joined those who remained there in a state of decline. They came here first in rather small dispersed groups. Then under the vigorous leadership of Ezra and Nehemia they reestablished and reconstructed their religious and communal-political institutions, rebuilt the Temple, and forged a new national identity (yet one based on continuous reference to the former period and its symbols) and new political organizations. From this, a new, independent political entity emerged after the Hasmonean revolt. The external story of this period is very well known and needs no more than a brief recapitulation.

With the fall of the Persian Empire in 330 BCE and the rise of the Hellenistic monarchies in the Middle East, the Jewish people developed a much stronger confrontation with the new expanding civilizations. The Jewish communities in general, and that in Eretz Israel in particular, became increasingly entangled in the political struggles of the region. At the same time Jewish settlement expanded beyond the Temple city-state of Jerusalem, with the consequent possibility of confrontation between the Jews and the Hellenistic, and later also Roman, rulers.

This culminated in the second century BCE in the first dramatic encounter with the Seleucid King Antiochus IV, giving rise to the Hasmonean (Maccabean) revolt and the Hasmonean theocratic monarchy in which the office of High Priest and ruler (ethnarch-Nasi) were combined. This dynasty lasted till about the middle of the first century BCE. It was characterized, especially during the reign of Alexander Iannai (Ianneas) (103–76 BCE) and his successors, by a policy of far-reaching expansion, bringing the Jews into continuous encounter with both various local populations and the "super powers." During Alexander Iannai's reign an intensive civil war broke out, led by groups of the Pharisees. After his death Judea became strongly entangled in the Roman expansion in the Near East and Roman-Parthian wars. The end of the Hasmonean dynasty came about 37 BCE, when Herod, the son of the Edomite adviser to Hyrcanos, Alexander's son, was declared King of Judea by the Romans and reigned till 4 BCE as a Roman client—and as a secular king.

Under Herod's successor the kingdom was divided among his three sons, and in year 6 of the Christian era (CE) the Roman government assumed direct rule in Judea—a change even welcomed by those more religious sectors of the Jewish population who strongly opposed the reign of a non-Jewish king. This direct subjugation to the Romans was interrupted under the brief reign of Herod's grandson Agrippa (41–4 CE), a friend of the Roman emperor Caligula. Agrippa attempted to reestablish some sort of a unified Jewish monarchy and on the whole was accepted by most sectors of the Jewish population. But with his death a continuously growing tension developed between the Roman procurators and the Jewish people, as well as increasing division within the latter, giving rise to the great war or rebellion against the Romans (66–7 CE), the destruction of the Second Temple in 70 CE, and loss of political autonomy. and the move of the Sanhedrin under the leadership of Rabbi Yohanan Ben-Zakai, the leader of the Pharisees, to Yavneh.

But the period of the Second Temple did not only see the emergence and crystallization of a new independent political entity. It was also a period of great cultural transformations. The Prophets, so predominant in the period of the First Temple, gradually disappeared; the priests, at least in the beginning of this period, became much more predominant; kings from priestly families emerged and also, perhaps most important, some entirely new types of leaders, based to a large degree on new traditions of learning as well as a multiplicity of sects.

Externally, the Jewish nation continued its encounters with mighty pagan Empires and nations, and also with a new type of civilization, the Hellenistic, and with the Hellenistic and Roman Empires whose claims to some universal validity were rooted not just in conquest or the mightiness of their gods but in their philosophical and legal traditions. At the same time there was great internal cultural creativity, giving rise within the Jewish nation to many new religious, cultural and social visions. One of them, connected with Jesus, was destined in the form of Christianity to reshape the whole course of history in the West and later in the world.

The combination of internal and external turbulence culminated, as we have seen, in the destruction of the Second Temple in 70 CE, the loss of political independence, and, ultimately, dispersion. At the same time a new institutional mold emerged that evinced rather special frameworks of civilization, religion and collective identity despite loss of independence and continuous dispersion. Later on these continuous frameworks were to be confronted with Christianity, then Islam, as the dominant religions in most of the lands in which the Jews lived.

These developments created a situation in which the Jews were not just a national or religious minority in some "alien" environment. They became such a minority in civilizations whose historical roots and basic premises were closely interwoven with Jewish history and faith, which not only developed historically out of the Jewish fold, but for whom continuous Jewish existence always constituted an ideological challenge and an ambivalent and negative reference point, for whom the Jews' adherence to their faith and mode of life was not just curious and strange, but an ideological threat to the very legitimacy of their own civilization.

There were two poles to the continuity of Jewish civilization: first, the development of international and cultural frameworks and social networks that made possible the continuity of the Jewish people and civilization in a situation of dispersion of Jews in many lands; and second, the strong, ambivalent attitude of the "host" civilizations, reciprocated by a parallel ambivalent attitude among the Jews toward these civilizations. These poles shaped the course of the Jewish history of exile.

The riddle of this continuity begins at the end of the First Temple period. Alone of the many exiled and dispersed peoples of antiquity, including those of the Kingdom of Israel (Samaria), the people of the Kingdom of Judah, having been exiled to Babylon after the destruction of their Temple and kingdom, returned to their homeland. There they established, albeit in a new pattern, their particular way of life and religion and their political and collective identity, defining themselves as a continuation of their earlier preexilic period.

The continuity of the Jews after the destruction of the Second Temple is an even greater enigma, although in a sense the Jews—and Christian and Muslim civilizations—have accepted it as a given. Obviously this was more than just the continuity of a small religious sect, although even in such terms it would be unique.

It is possible of course to speak of the continuity as that of a "people." But what kind of people has no territory, only memories or hopes of return to a territory, and a strong political orientation, but no autonomous or independent political entity or political-territorial continuity?

These examples—many more could be given—illustrate that certain elements of the Jewish historical experience transcend the categories of religion (taken as merely a system of belief and worship), nation, and ethnic group. It seems to me that the term *Jewish civilization,* as I define it in this book, is the most appropriate rubric for our purposes.

The Civilizational Approach to Jewish History

The term *Jewish civilization* also is appropriate because it helps us examine critically some prevalent views of the nature of Jewish historical experience, which have been extremely influential in modern historiography and social science. I shall refer to only two such views: one, rather unsympathetic—some would say even anti-Semitic and certainly anti-Zionist—is that of the eminent British historian Arnold Toynbee;[3] the other view—earlier, much more "philo-Semitic," even sympathetic to the beginnings of Zionism—is that of the great German sociologist Max Weber.[4]

Both scholars analyzed the Jewish historical experience from a comparative perspective that can best be called *civilizational*. Toynbee used this term advisedly: civilizations constituted the basic units of his comparative historical analysis. Weber used the term *world religions;* his analysis focused on the systems of belief and worship prevailing in these religions as well as on the ways in which some aspects of such systems shaped the institutional contours and historical experience of the societies in which they become predominant and institutionalized.

Toynbee did not deny that the Jews constituted a civilization; indeed, he included them in his monumental, though often criticized, *Study of History*.[5] Max Weber included his brilliant "Ancient Judaism" in his *Sociology of Religion,* in which he analyzed the great or world religions: Judaism, the religions of China (Confucianism and Taoism), Hinduism, Buddhism, and Protestant Christianity.[6]

Thus both Toynbee and Weber indicated—or at least intimated—that the best way to explain this historical experience is by comparing it with those great civilizations that were closely linked with religions but cannot be understood solely on the basis of patterns of belief or worship. These civilizations constituted something more complex than religious communities or belief systems: the construction of the way of life of entire societies; that is, the organization of their ways of life in some distinct way according to some vision or premises. Both Toynbee, explicitly, and Weber, implicitly, were talking in terms of civilizations.

It is true that they both saw the Jewish historical experience as exceptional. Both were perplexed by the riddle of Jewish continuity, and both were naturally influenced, though in different ways, by the Christian view of a radical break between the earlier biblical Jewish experience and the later, post-Christian one.

Toynbee characterized the exilic rabbinic Jewish civilization as a fossilized civilization. According to him, its fossilization was manifested above all in its exclusive emphasis on law and ritual, and in its almost total self-segregation from other civilizations.[7]

Weber claimed, on similar grounds, that after the period of the Second Temple the Jews became a religious community, as distinct from a political one, or a full world religion or civilization. They also became, almost of their own volition, a pariah people, that is, a segregated group, ritually unclean and of low economic status, with the concomitant loss of their civilizational momentum.[8]

It seems to me that Weber and Toynbee were correct to apply the civilizational perspective to the Jewish case, but erred in characterizing its uniqueness from a comparative civilizational point of view. They erred in their implication that the post-Christian Jewish historical experience ceased to be civilizational in the full meaning of this term, as explicitly or implicitly used by them. Consequently they were unable to explain the riddle of the continuity of the Jewish historical experience.

A closer look at some of the historical evidence will show the inadequacy of both views, whatever elements of partial truth they may contain. Of course it is true that ritual, prayer, legal exegesis, and communal organization were the major arenas of Jewish cultural activity from the loss of political independence (broadly speaking, from late antiquity) through the Middle Ages and early modern period. But there were other arenas as well. We need mention only philosophers like Maimonides and Saadya Gaon, or mystics like the Kabbalists of the early Renaissance, to see the inadequacy of viewing Jewish civilization as fossilized.[9] The mere fact that there were important philosophers, mystics, and the like among the Jews in the Middle Ages is not the point. What is of crucial importance are three closely interrelated aspects of their activities.

First, these were not isolated or marginal figures. Their activities constituted an integral component of Medieval Jewish cultural creativity. Hence, we see that this creativity was not limited to the field of laws and rituals—a field that, full of different orientations and tensions, itself was constantly changing and developing. Moreover, like some of the Jewish poets of the Spanish period who created a vast secular poetry, of a kind unknown in Jewish life until the modern times, most of these scholars usually also were engaged in talmudic exegesis, again attesting to the close if often tense relationship between these different areas of Jewish cultural creativity in this period.

Second, all these activities and studies—and sometimes the more ritual and legal ones as well—were not tightly enclosed in the framework of the Jewish community, but constituted a part of the general Medieval cultural scene. This is true not only of such towering figures as Maimonides, but of almost all of them—philosophers, mystics, and to some degree legal scholars. They often wrote in Arabic; they had close relations with non-Jewish scholars; and the scholars of the three monotheistic civilizations often provided mutual reference points for one other. Moreover, these scholars' definition of what is specifically Jewish, Christian, or Muslim frequently emerged from the continual controversies among them. Such controversies usually were not just academic exercises; they bore the hallmarks of heated and intense intercivilizational or interreligious competition.[10] Needless to say, most Jews, like most Christians, did not participate in these activities; however, the activities of these scholars and the disputations among them greatly affected, not only many aspects of the daily life of their communities, but often also their fate in the countries in which they lived.

Truly enough, and this is our third point, these relations were not always very amicable—to put it mildly. The history of persecutions, expulsion, and martyrdom—*Kiddush Hashem* ("Sanctification of the Name")—is too well known to require full documentation here. Also familiar are the disputations between Jewish and Christian (and to a lesser extent Muslim) scholars, usually staged by the authorities—kings or the Church, in order to demonstrate the superiority of the Christian religion.

Although the stories of the persecutions, attempts to convert the Jews, and disputations are indeed very well known, we may not always be aware of their full implications for Toynbee's view of Jewish civilization as fossilized and Weber's view of the Jews as merely a religious community and a "pariah people."

The term *pariah people* derives from the analysis of Indian society and refers to the Untouchables beyond the caste system, who are outcast, ritually segregated, and of low economic status (although in many ways Weber went beyond these connotations). Although these connotations do indeed apply to some degree to the Jews in the Middle Ages, the analogy with India is poor at best. We do not find there disputations aimed at public confirmation of the superiority of the Brahmins. Brahminic superiority was never questioned; above all it needed no active affirmation by the pariahs.

The very existence of these dispositions indicates that this was not the case with respect to the relations between the Jews and their "host" civilizations. Otherwise these host civilizations would not have needed to keep proving their superiority, nor would they have constantly attempted to convert the Jews.

These illustrations also indicate that Weber and Toynbee's view of a change in the nature of the Jewish historical experience after the rise of Christianity was not fully shared by the Jews' host civilization—even if, politically speaking, the official Christian (and to some extent also Muslim) position denied Judaism a status equivalent to that of the host religion.

To give one illustration, Weber stressed that after the period of the Second Temple the Jews became a purely religious, a political community, in contrast to Christianity's development into a dominant political religion or full world religion. As we shall see later, the contrary is true—at least with respect to the first period of Christianity. Here it suffices to point out, as both I. F. Baer and Arnaldo Momigliano have indicated, that there always has been a political component to the Jewish collective identity, although it was not the only one. This component frequently was couched in highly metaphysical terms and claimed to have universal significance.[11]

All these illustrations demonstrate the inadequacy of the views of Toynbee or Weber of the nature of the Jewish experience. Moreover, they show the inadequacy of analyzing the Jewish historical experience solely or mainly in terms of religion, people, nation, or the like. Although, let me reiterate, all these terms designate important components of this experience.

The Presupposition of a Civilizational Perspective— Culture, Ontology, and Social Dynamics

For all these reasons, then, the civilizational perspective seems to have the best potential for explaining the Jewish historical experience. What is meant by civilizational as distinct from religion or people or nation? As already indicated in the introduction, civilization, in the sense used here, entails the attempts to construct or reconstruct social life according to ontological visions that combine conception of the nature of the cosmos, or transmundane and mundane reality, with the regulation of the major arenas of social life and interaction—the political arena or authority, the economy, family life, and the like. Although in the history of humankind civilizations and religions were very closely interwoven, at the same time many religions have been only a part or a component of civilizations and not necessarily the most central component. This distinction, which can be found clearly in many preliterate and archaic societies, even those of the ancient Near East, becomes clearly visible in the "great" Axial Age civilizations, in the monotheistic religions and civilizations; however, in some places they constituted religious working within the framework of other civilizations. The clearest illustration of such a case is the fate of Buddhism and Confucianism in Japan, where Buddhist (and Confucian) beliefs and cults thrive, but without a distinct civilization, creating as Buddhism did in Southeast Asia or Confucianism in China, Korea, and Vietnam. In Japan these cults and belief systems operated within the framework and basic premises of a distinct Japanese civilization. Similar illustrations can be given from the history of the expansion of Islam or Christianity. At the same time these illustrations attest to different people being able to belong the same civilization, especially one of these "higher" civilizations.[12]

Such civilizational perspective is based on several assumptions. The first is that, as already implied, it is important to distinguish analytically between, on the one hand, those aspects of these religions that constituted components of the basic cultural or premises of these societies and, on the other hand, those aspects that from a later "secular" perspective could be designated as specifically religious, above all patterns of belief, rituals and worship.

The second assumption is the recognition that such premises grounded in ontological vision are of great importance for understanding many central aspects of institutional processes. The definition of any institutional complex, be it of the state, political institutions, or class formation, cannot be taken for granted, by defining them in terms of political power or political and administrative activities of the different, seemingly universal, political, and administrative agents, or in terms of universal status differences and the relative strength of different classes or various interest groups within a society.

In addition to these variables or aspects of the institutional processes—the importance of which nobody could deny, of course—it is of central importance to analyze the very definition and evaluations of the respective institutional arenas (the state, the economy, the family, and so on) in the broader context of the civilizations in which they develop and within which they also necessarily change through the historical experience of their respective societies. Thus a civilizational perspective strongly emphasizes the interrelations of the cultural and institutional aspects of the historical experience of different peoples, the interrelation between ontological visions or conceptions of the world, on the one hand, and the major arenas of institutional life patterns of social stratification on the other.[13]

The first crucial aspect of this interrelation is the formulation, on the basis of such visions and beliefs, of the fundamental conceptions of ontological visions and premises about the nature of social life, authority, and the like. The second aspect is the attempt to implement these premises in social life—or, in sociological parlance, to institutionalize them in specific ways. Thus, in greater detail, and in somewhat abstract and theoretical terms, the first component of a civilization is the formulation, promulgation, articulation, and continuous reinterpretation of the basic ontological vision of a society or sector thereof, its basic ideological premises, and its core symbols. The second major aspect of the interrelation between ontological visions and institutional formations and dynamics is the symbolic and ideological—i.e., cultural—definition of the different arenas of human activity in general and the political arena in particular.[14]

Culture mediates in the definition of sex, growth, and aging; mental and physical capacities; and the importance of time. It mediates definitions of the major arenas of social activity as well, specifying the ground rules that regulate social interaction and the flow of resources. Such definitions and regulations construct the broad contours, boundaries, and meanings of the major institutional formations and their legitimation and shape the major contours and boundaries of the major institutional arenas. First of all, culture structures the boundaries of major collectivities and the symbols, their centers and center-periphery relations; patterns of political authority; the modes of dominance and organization, and economic formations of structuring of social hierarchies; conceptions of authority and its accountability; various forms of conflictual behavior and challenges to authority; and the structure and symbolism of the different manifestations and movements of protest.

The impact of such premises and their institutional derivatives on institutional formation is effected through the activities of major elite groups and influential persons, especially through the various processes of social interaction and control that develop in a society. Such processes of control—and the opposition to them—are not limited to the exercise of power in the "narrow" political sense; they, as even sophisticated Marxists have stressed, are much more pervasive, activated not only by class relations or "modes of production." Rather, they are activated by the major coalitions of elites in a society, who have different cultural visions and represent different types of interests.

In connection with these ontological visions and their respective transformation into basic premises of the social and political order, these elite groups tend to exercise different modes of control over the allocation of basic resources in the society, thus shaping many crucial aspects of institutional formations and social life in their respective societies.

There are several such elite groups and centers of influence in a society. The political elites deal most directly with the regulation of power. Others articulate the models of cultural and of social order and the solidarity of the major groups. The structure of such elite groups is related closely to the basic cultural orientations prevalent in a society; in other words, different ontological visions.

The modes of control exercised by such coalitions combine the structuring of the basic ontological visions of societies with the control of several central aspects of the flow of resources in patterns of social interaction. Such control of the flow of resources is focused on the regulation of the access to the major institutional markets (economic, political, cultural, etc.) and positions, the conversion of the major resources among these markets, the patterns of investment and distribution of such resources in space and time, and the regulation of such spatial and temporal organization of the resources and of their meaning.

A central link connecting these two aspects or dimensions of control—that is, the construction of the basic assumptions and premises of society and the regulation of flow of resources—is the construction and regulation of the flow of different types of information, especially of that information crucial to the continuity of social life, of social order.

Therefore, in more general terms, the structure of such elite groups is closely related, on the one hand, to the basic cultural orientations prevalent in a society; that is, different types of elite groups bear different types of orientation or visions. On the other hand, and in connection with the types of cultural orientations and their respective transformation into basic premises of the social order, these elite groups tend to exercise different modes of control over the allocation of basic resources in the society. At the same time, the very implementation or institutionalization of such premises, together with the construction of a social division of labor, generates movements of protest and processes of change.

No institutional formation, no system or pattern of social interaction whether micro or macro sociological, however, is, or can be, very stable. The very processes of control, symbolic and organizational alike, through which such patterns are formed also generate tendencies to protest, conflict, and change.[15]

Because every social order always contains a strong element of dissension regarding the distribution of power and the values upheld, no institutional system is ever fully "homogeneous", in the sense of being accepted either fully or to the same degree by all those participating in it. Even if, for very long periods of time, a great majority of the members of a given society identify to some degree with the basic premises and norms of a given system and are willing to provide it with the resources it needs, other tendencies that develop in connection with the processes analyzed earlier may give rise to change in the initial attitudes of any given group to the basic premises of the institutional system.

Therefore, there exists the possibility that "antisystems" may develop within any society. Although antisystems often remain latent for long periods of time, under propitious conditions they also may constitute important foci of systemic change. That such potential antisystems exist in all societies is evinced by the potential in all of them for themes and orientations of protest, as well as of social movements and heterodoxies that often are led by different secondary elite groups.

Such latent antisystems may be activated and transformed into processes of change by several processes connected with the continuity and maintenance, or reproduction, of different settings of social interaction in general and the macro-societal order in particular. The most important of these processes are (1) shifts in the relative power positions and aspirations of different categories and groups; (2) the activation in the younger generation of the potential rebelliousness and antinomian orientations inherent in any process of socialization, particularly in those who belong to the upper classes and the elite groups; (3) several sociomorphological or sociodemographic processes that change the demographic balance among different sectors of the population; and (4) the interaction between such settings and their natural and intersocietal environments, such as movements of population or conquest.

The crystallization of these potentialities of change usually takes place through the activities of secondary elite groups who attempt to mobilize various groups and resources to change aspects of the social order as it was shaped by the coalition of ruling elite groups. Although such potentiality for conflict and change are inherent in all human societies, their concrete development—their intensity and the concrete directions of change and transformation they engender—vary greatly among different societies and civilizations. They differ according to the specific constellations within them of the forces analyzed earlier; that is, the different ontological visions, different types of elite groups, patterns of the social division of labor, and political-ecological settings and processes.

These constellations shape the different patterns of social conflict, social movements, rebellions, and heterodoxy that develop in different societies, as well as the relation of these movements to processes of institution building. They shape the direction of institutional change, the degree to which changes in different aspects of the institutional order coalesce, and their consequent transformation patterns.

The Axial Age Civilizations

All these formulations may sound rather abstract and general—as indeed they are. I therefore shall proceed to some more concrete illustrations and analyses, the starting point of which is the place of Jewish civilization among the so-called Axial Age civilizations.[16]

The term *Axial Age civilizations* was used by Karl Jaspers to describe those great civilizations that developed during the first millennium before the Christian era: in China in the late pre-Imperial and early Imperial period, in Hinduism and Buddhism, and much later, beyond the Axial Age proper, in Islam. The distinctive characteristic of these civilizations was the development and institutionalization of basic conceptions of a tension, a chasm, between the transcendental and the mundane order.

The conceptions of a basic tension between the transcendental and the mundane order developed primarily among small groups of "intellectuals," the elites in general, and the shapers of models of cultural and social order in particular. Ultimately, these conceptions were institutionalized in all these Axial Age civilizations; they became the predominant orientation of both the ruling and many secondary elite groups, fully embodied in their respective centers or subcenters, transforming the nature of the political elite groups and making the intellectuals into relatively autonomous partners in the central coalitions. Thus the diverse groups of intellectuals were transformed into more fully crystallized and institutionalized ones, often into clerics, whether the Jewish prophets and priests, the Greek philosophers, the Chinese literati, the Hindu Brahmins, the Buddhist Sangha, or the Islamic Ulema.

The development and institutionalization of such a conception of a basic tension, of a chasm, between the transcendental and the mundane order and the search to find ways to bridge that chasm, to implement some components of a transcendental vision in the mundane world, in all these civilizations, gave rise to attempts to reconstruct the mundane world according to the appropriate transcendental vision, the principles of the higher metaphysical or ethical order. The given mundane order was perceived as incomplete, often as faulty and in need of at least partial reconstruction according to the conception of how this basic tension could be resolved, how the transcendental visions are to be implemented in the mundane world. Among the most important, institutional derivatives of such ontological vision were the tendencies to the construction of distinct civilizational frameworks and distinct types of conceptions of accountability of rulers.

Some collectivities and institutional arenas were singled out as the most appropriate arenas for the institutionalization of the required resolution of the tensions between the transcendental and the mundane. As a result, new types of collectivities were created or seemingly natural and "primordial" groups—like tribes, territorial or kinship groups—were endowed with special meaning couched in terms of the perception of this tension and its resolution. The most important innovation in this context was the development of "cultural" or "religious" collectivities—such as Christian, Islamic, or Confucian—as distinct from ethnic or political ones. In these collectivities there tended to develop—albeit in different degrees in different civilizations—a strong insistence on the exclusiveness and closure of such collectivities and the distinction between inner and outer social and cultural space defined by them. This tendency became connected with attempts to structure the different cultural, political, and ethnic collectivities in some hierarchical order; and the very construction of such an order usually became a focus of religious ideological and political conflict.

Closely related to this construction of special civilizational frameworks, in all these civilizations, a far-reaching restructuring took place of the relation between the political and transcendental orders.

The political order as the central locus of the mundane order usually has been conceived as lower than the transcendental one and therefore had to be reconstructed according to the premises of the latter. The rulers usually were held responsible for implementing this restructuring of the political order. Consequently, it was possible to call a ruler to judgment in the name of some higher order to which rulers are accountable.

At the same time, the nature of the rulers was transformed. The God-King, the embodiment of cosmic and earthly order alike, disappeared, to be replaced by a secular ruler, in principle accountable to some higher order. Thus the conception emerged that rulers and the community are accountable to a higher authority—God, Divine Law, the Chinese conception of the Mandate of Heaven, and the like. The first and most dramatic appearance of this conception was in Ancient Israel, in the priestly and prophetic writings. A different conception of such accountability, an accountability of the community and its laws, appeared in Ancient Greece. In fact, this conception appeared in different forms in all these civilizations.[17] Concomitant with the emergence of conceptions of accountability was the development of autonomous spheres of law and conceptions of rights, relatively distinct from ascriptively bound customs. Closely related to these changes in basic political conceptions was the far-reaching transformation of the conceptions of human personality. The interpersonal virtues such as solidarity and mutual help were taken out of their primordial frameworks and combined, in different ways, with the modalities of resolving the tension between the transcendental and the mundane orders. This generated a new set of internal tensions within human personality; and through the appropriate reconstruction of the personality the chasm between the transcendental and mundane orders could be bridged and salvation attained. This was closely connected with the development of conceptions of the individual as an autonomous entity, often out of tune with the political order.

The general tendency to reconstruct the world with all its symbolic-ideological and institutional repercussions was common to all the post-Axial Age civilizations. But their concrete implementation, of course, varied greatly. No one homogeneous world history emerged nor were the different types of civilizations similar or convergent. Rather, a multiplicity of different, divergent, yet continuously mutually impinging world civilizations emerged, each attempting to reconstruct the world in its own mode, according to its basic premises, and attempting either to absorb the others or consciously to segregate itself from them.

It would be beyond the scope of this discussion to analyze either these differences or to attempt to explain them—all this has to be left to further publications. It might be worthwhile, however, to point out that some of the most important sets of conditions that provide the clues to understanding these different modes of institutional creativity are given in the way the premises of these civilizations are crystallized and institutionalized in concrete social settings. Two such sets of conditions can be distinguished. One refers to variations in the basic cultural orientations, in the basic ontological visions of the respective civilizations with their institutional implications. The other set of conditions refers to different concrete social arenas in which these institutional tendencies can be played out.

First of all, among the different ontological visions are crucial differences in the very definition of the tension between the transcendental and mundane orders and the modes of resolving this tension; for the implementation of the transcendental vision. There is the distinction between those cases in which the tension was couched in relatively secular terms (as in Confucianism and classical Chinese belief systems and, in a somewhat different way, in the Greek and Roman worlds) and those cases in which the tension was conceived in terms of a religious hiatus (as in the great monotheistic religions and Hinduism and Buddhism). A second distinction, within the latter cases, is that between the monotheistic religions in which God was conceived as standing outside the universe and potentially guiding it and those systems, like Hinduism and Buddhism, in which the transcendental, cosmic system was conceived in impersonal, almost metaphysical terms and in a state of continuous existential tension with the mundane system.

Another major distinction refers to the focus of the resolution of the transcendental tensions—in Weberian terms of salvation, or to put it in more general terms, the focus or the arena of the implementation of the ontological visions with its strong emphasis on the chasm between the transcendental and the mundane order. Here the distinction is between purely this-worldly, purely otherworldly, and mixed this- and otherworldly conceptions of salvation or implementation of the ontological vision. It probably is no accident that the "secular" conception of this tension was connected, as in China and to some degree in the ancient world, with an almost wholly this-worldly conception of implementation of the ontological vision, that the metaphysical nondeistic conception of this tension, as in Hinduism and Buddhism, tended toward an otherworldly conception of emphasis, whereas the great monotheistic religions tended to stress different combinations of this- and otherworldly conceptions of salvation, seen in the activities oriented to the "otherworld" as well as to the mundane world as the major arenas of implementation of their respective ontological visions.

Another set of cultural orientations that are of special importance to the ordering of the broader ranges of solidarity and connecting them with the broader meanings generated by the transcendental visions can be distinguished. First, of central importance here is the degree to which access to the central attributes of cosmic or social order is given directly to the members of any social category or subcategory—kings, priests, scholars and the like—enabling them to act as mediators between these attributes and the broader groups.

Second is the nature of relations between the attributes of cosmic and social order and the basic attributes of the major primordial ascriptive collectivities—like tribes or kinship or territorial groups. Here three possibilities can be distinguished. One occurs when the access to these broader attitudes is vested entirely within some such ascriptive collectivity. The second one occurs when there is a total distinction between the two. The third possibility arises when these respective attributes are mutually relevant and each serves as a referent of the other or a condition of being a member of the other without being totally embedded in the other. Such a partial connection usually means that the attributes of the ascriptive collectivities are seen as one component of the attributes of salvation or, conversely, that the attributes of salvation constitute one of the attributes of such collectivities.

The different combinations of these two sets of cultural orientations have been most important in shaping the broad institutional contours and dynamics of the different post-Axial Age civilizations. But the concrete working out of all such tendencies depends on the second set of conditions— the arena for the concretization of these broad institutional tendencies. These conditions included, first, the economic structure of these civilizations (although they all belonged to economically relatively developed agrarian or combined agrarian and commercial societies). Second, they varied greatly according to their respective political-ecological settings: whether they were small or great societies, whether they were societies with continuous compact boundaries or with cross-cutting and flexible boundaries. Third was their specific historical experience, especially in terms of encounters with other societies and in terms of mutual penetration, conquest, or colonization. The interplay among the different constellations of the cultural orientations analyzed earlier, their carriers, and their respective visions of restructuring the world and the concrete arenas and historical conditions in which such visions could be concretized has shaped the institutional contours and dynamics of the different Axial Age civilizations. The subsequent courses of world history, and their systematic exploration, should be the objects of further systematic analysis.

We now turn to an analysis of the initial premises of the ancient Israelite civilization, the seedbed of Jewish civilization, and on the basis of this analysis support our claim that the best way to look at the Jewish historical experience is to analyze it as the history of a civilization in the way which we defined it here and not only as a history of a people, religious, ethnic, or national group. Indeed, the very fact that all these terms can be applied to the analysis of the Jewish historical experience indicates that none of them is sufficient. Moreover, it seems to us that only if one looks at this experience in civilizational terms may one begin to cope with the greatest riddle of that experience, namely, that of its continuity.

2

The Distinctive Characteristics of Jewish Civilization in a Historical and Comparative Perspective

The Ancient Israelite Civilization

The ancient Israelite civilization was the first monotheistic religion and civilization that proclaimed and promulgated the conception of a universal and transcendent God who created the universe and imposed His will and Law upon it, who claimed to rule over all the nations, and who has designated the people of Israel as His chosen people. This first monotheistic civilization crystallized in rather specific historical circumstances—in connection with the transition from the various tribal federations to the more centralized kingdoms and the consequent attempts at the consolidation of these kingdoms—alluded briefly to in the first chapter.[1]

The actual crystallization of these tribal federations, various settlements, and kingdoms probably resulted much less from one or series of one-time acts (exodus from Egypt, conquest under Joshua, etc.), and rather was a much more continuous and to some extent haphazard process. From this process the ancient Israeli civilization emerged and, with it, some of its distinct characteristics and collective consciousness—a collective conscious that focused around the several aspects of the biblical tradition, as they were promulgated by various cultural elite groups.[2]

The basic monotheistic conception of God the Creator was common to all three major monotheistic religions and civilizations. But beyond this common core some very important differences developed among them. Among the most important components of the ancient Israelite, and especially later of the Jewish, monotheistic conception, were the following. First, a very strong emphasis developed on the covenantal, semicontractual relationship between God and the tribes of Israel, the people of Israel. The covenant with God was seen as the central focus of the tribal confederation, the forging of the Israelite tribes into a distinct nation as God's chosen people. This covenant between God and the people of Israel established a semicontractual relation between them, based on God's selection of the people of Israel, of His own free will, as His chosen people—but contingent on their acceptance of His commandments. The covenantal relationship made the people of Israel not just a passive object of God's will, but also an active, responsible agent in shaping its destiny, responsible before God, but seemingly able to make demands on God as well.

According to the accepted Jewish tradition this relationship with God began with the Patriarchs, with His covenant with Abraham. But its full impact on shaping the Israelite nation occurred only with the exodus from Egypt and the tribes' albeit reluctant acceptance of the Ten Commandments and the Torah. This event created the Israelite nation, establishing its identity in a number of primordial, religious, and historical senses. It imbued the Jewish collective self-identity with a strong combination of a universal religious consciousness and a collective historical consciousness—best epitomized in the conjunction, in later Hebrew prayers, of Zecher leMaaseh Bereshit ("The Memory of Creation") and Zecher leyetsiat Mitzraim ("The Memory of the Exodus from Egypt"). It combined also primordial and universalistic orientation. The later Israelite God, the God of the Israelite and certainly of the later Jewish tradition, was both the creator of the Universe and the God of Universe as well as the God of "our Fathers, of Abraham, Isaac and Jacob."

The combination of this specific type of monotheism with the covenantal dimension transformed various cultic traditions, legal precepts, and ethical commandments from traditional customs into God's commandments to His chosen people. These commandments indicated how the world should be restructured and also denoted the distinctiveness of this chosen people—giving rise to an emphasis on the legal sphere, the elaboration of legal codices and texts as one of the major expressions of the will of God and His commandments to the people of Israel.

This new religious conception had changed, in a far-reaching way, many of the contours prevalent in various tribes and nations of the ancient Near East. Thus, to give only one illustration, a periodic day of rest existed in a great number of these tribes and nations, as did also many other customs that became legal injunctions in the Old Testament. The special contribution of the Israelite religion was not the invention of the Sabbath, but rather its transformation from a custom into a principled legal universalistic commandment rooted in transcendental visions manifest in God's own behavior (...Because God rested on the seventh day...) and being, in principle, applicable to all people—even to animals.

The legal codes of the Pentateuch were fully crystallized only in the period of the Second Commonwealth. Many elements of the full codification—including probably the Torah of Moses, the presumed core of Deuteronomy, found during the reign of Josiah (640–609 BCE), and constituting the nucleus of religious reforms and centralization of the cult in Jerusalem—however, were of much earlier provenance.[3] All of them were characterized by an unusual combination of civil, communal, and cultic law and calendric prescriptions, religious and ethical commandments together with civil laws, with a very strong emphasis on social legislation—like the laws of the Sabbath and of the Sabbatical Year, in which all debts are canceled. These laws were given a religious and ethical connotation, giving rise to what David Weiss Halivni called "justified law."[4] They were not confined to a small group of priests, but increasingly accessible to the general public. All these elements were most fully epitomized in the figure of Moses—the great prophet-legislator and the formulator of the Covenant between God and the people of Israel.

It is a moot question exactly when these basic conceptions and orientations developed and became fully institutionalized and to what degree they were known and accepted by the different sectors of the Israelite tribes. Whatever the answers to these questions—and historians will probably discuss them forever, it is this crystallization that created the distinctive cultural identity of the Israelite nation, the Jewish people, and its civilization.

In connection with these developments there crystallized some of the ancient Israelite and later Jewish institutional and symbolic responses to the basic problems of all Axial Age civilizations; that is, definition of the relationship between the universalistic religious and the earlier primordial orientations, with the concomitant definition of the civilizational collective, and the specification of the major institutional arenas in which the dominant transcendental visions were to be implemented. Thus, first of all, the sociopolitical arena was designated as the major domain in which the vision was to be implemented. However, unlike Greece, where such designation occurred partly, and above all China, this did not lead to a semisanctification of this realm, although it generated a certain potential in this direction. Instead, it connoted a strong drive to structure, to organize this arena according to the ethical and legal-ritual precepts that in principle apply to all nations. This attitude was rooted in Judaism's claim to universalism as the first monotheistic religion and in its attempts to separate itself from other groups by claiming to transcend their particularistic religious symbols. Such segregation entailed the continuous bringing together of the symbols of primordial, ethnic, national, political, and religious identity. Because of the growing tendencies toward universalism and the strong competition of other religions, this solution was not purely particularistic, but contained a strong universalist orientation, in contrast to the solution developed for instance by the Samaritans, among whom the universalistic orientations disappeared almost entirely. It exhibited strong tendencies to proselytization, which often were in tension with the more particularistic primordial emphasis.[5]

These proselytizing orientations were closely related to the ambivalent attitude toward the various neighboring nations. Such ambivalence veered between, on the one hand, the fear of their political and military power and the cultural threat they posed to the newly emerging ancient Israelite collectivity and, on the other, the denial of their religion; between the concomitant tendency to dissociate from the pagan nation and the conception of the God of Israel as God of the Universe, hence potentially of all the people, and the closely related liberal attitude to the "stranger in your gates," so characteristic of the Old Testament.[6]

Due to these factors, a continuous tension between the universalism of the religious orientation and the particularism of a primordial community that defined itself by its ideological and symbolic distinctiveness from its neighbors, through the combination of religious and primordial symbols, was built into the structure of Jewish identity from the dawn of Jewish history. Parallel to the tension between universalistic and particularistic in the construction of the Israelite collective identity also arose a tension between its primordial and sacral-transcendental components. The basic identity of the Israelite tribes probably was rooted in the primordial tribal attachments, but such attachments as the attachment to the land, the territory of Eretz Israel, from early on, although it is difficult to ascertain from how early, probably was closely interwoven with more transcendental orientations. Just as the nation was constructed as stemming from Abraham, Isaac, Jacob, but also constituted through the Covenant at Sinai. Similarly, the attachment to the land was based not only on concrete tribal-historical memory but also on the (conditional) promise of God—and this promise sanctified the promised land and the national community alike.

Among broader sectors of the society, especially in the period of the First Temple and before, the primordial components of their collective consciousness probably were most prominent, taken for granted. The more universalistic components of these conceptions and the different modes of interweaving them within the primordial components were promulgated above all by the various autonomous elite groups predominant in these societies, and also evinced some specific characteristics. Many specific types of autonomous elite groups developed, each a carrier of one of these major cultural orientations. The most important of them were the priests, the prophets, and the various representatives of the community, such as the elders and later the rulers (the judges and kings) who also attempted to play this role. They all saw themselves as carriers of the monotheistic vision and the Covenant between God and His people, and a continuous competition developed among them in a variety of different coalitions.

Three aspects of the elite groups are of special importance for understanding the institutional dynamics of Israelite society. First is their profusion, heterogeneity, and volatility. Second is that they were not embedded in the various ascriptive tribal or territorial units, but were symbolically and organizationally autonomous, recruited and defined by themselves—even if, as with the priests, in ascriptive hereditary terms—and legitimized as representing visions and values that were not part of the primordial symbols of the local or tribal groups but nevertheless were accepted among these groups. Third, these major carriers of the common political, national, and religious bonds seemed to cut across the tribes and were at least potentially common to all or at least to several of them.

The elite groups developed in a rather special political environment, which was of crucial importance for shaping the Israelite and Jewish historical experience. The most important aspects of this environment were the absence of compact political boundaries and the continuously volatile micro and macro political situation. The micro situation, of course, was the repeated encounters with other settled and migratory peoples within Palestine; the macro situation was that of Palestine itself, the perennial crossroads of the great empires of antiquity. The result was the continuous fluidity and openness of political boundaries, a constant flow and mobility of people, and difficulties in maintaining a stable, compact political entity and even a distinct cultural identity.[7]

These basic religious beliefs, cultural and political orientations, and conceptions and characteristics of elite groups, which emerged in Ancient Israel during the period of the First Temple, probably in the last century before its destruction, but possibly even earlier, shaped the specific contours of Jewish civilization and history and facilitated the development of the unique pattern of continuity that has characterized this civilization. The most important of these beliefs and orientations, as already mentioned, was the Covenant between God and the people of Israel, a semicontractual relationship based on God selecting the people of Israel as His chosen people by His own free will but contingent on their acceptance of His commandments.

Constituting a chosen people denoted not just (as was the case, for instance, in the Japanese conception) being a divine nation, naturally, automatically protected by God, rather it meant being chosen by God to perform his mission, being protected by Him when performing that mission and abandoned or punished when abandoning it.

Second was the emphasis that all members of the community had potential access to the realm of the sacred, the accountability of rulers and the community to a higher authority—God, Divine Law, or the like—and the emergence of concrete autonomous social groups or categories that represented, as it were, such higher authority and among whom there was continuous competition. Third, a continuous tension developed between the cultic and ethical-religious conceptions, with a strong emphasis on the legal tradition that combined these different elements. Fourth was a tension between the universalist religious and ethical and particularistic primordial orientations and a continuous combination and tension among political, ethnic, national, and religious elements in the construction of the Jewish identity, accompanied by an ambivalent attitude to neighboring nations.

Further, a very strong and unusual combination developed of the mythical and historical time perspectives, with a continuous tension between them. The strong mythical components that probably existed in the earlier periods of the tribes were not totally obliterated. They were superimposed by the very strong historical component in the Israelite and Jewish collective consciousness, manifest in the emphasis on the exodus from Egypt and the Covenant in Sinai and the conquest, by God's command, of the land of Israel. This historical consciousness superimposed as a mythical one has become the paradigmatic framework of the conception of collective timing in the Israelite and Jewish collective consciousness.

Out of these conceptions developed a very special type of self-definition of the collective, namely, as constituted through the covenant with God and not as just given by the primordial givens. Within the construction of this collective consciousness through the Covenant, the primordial components were given their proper, certainly not primary and sometimes problematic, place in the construction of the Israelite and Jewish collective consciousness. The same is true with respect to the relation to territory. The land of Israel, Eretz Israel, was the promised land, the land promised by God as part of the Covenant; and the attachment to it has been continuously moving between the ideological, thus transcendental, and primordial dimensions.[8]

These general orientations were continuously promulgated by various elite and active groups that, in their general form, have persisted, along with their orientations, throughout Jewish history. There were many autonomous elite groups in general and promulgators of models of cultural and social order in particular, with a strong orientation toward the mundane—especially political and social—fields. These elite groups shared the major religious and legislative functions and orientations; even when they specialized in one, like the priests who specialized in ritual, they maintained strong orientations to the others, the legal or ethical ones. Although they generally had no permanent center or organization, they maintained some identity and continuity of orientation and networks and continuously emerged anew, even if in altered organizational constellations. A great heterogeneity developed within all these elite groups, such as the priests or the prophets. Conflicts and tensions arose among these elite and subelite groups, connected not only with the representation of different specific interests but also with different interpretations of the tradition and different emphases on its major components: cultic, legal, ethical. All these groups competed for acceptance as the representatives of the higher authority to which rulers and community were accountable. Some of the major structural and institutional characteristics of the Jewish people and civilization grew out of the combination of these structural elements and religious-ideological orientations. The most important of them are structural heterogeneity, the existence of many different types of groups (peasants, tribal elements, urban groups, and the like), continuous differentiation and conflict among various social groups within a framework of common but not fully crystallized boundaries, the volatility and heterogeneity of the centers, multiple elite groupings (political, social, and religious), and the concomitant restructuring of the bonds between the leaders and the people; often leading to diverse social movements.

Of course, the concrete characteristics of these political, social, and religious groups varied greatly in different periods: between the time of the Judges and that of the monarchy, between these earlier eras and the Second Commonwealth, and between all these and the period of exile and dispersion. But the basic structural characteristics indicated earlier continued throughout Jewish history. The concrete form of government that developed in ancient Israel was some combination of tribal, communal, priestly, and monarchic principles and elements; and the concrete form in any specific period depended on the balance of internal forces as well as on the vicissitudes of the international situation. In this, the ancient Israelites were not radically different from their various neighbors. What was distinctive about them was the fact that the major sections of society and the different elite groups—be they the priests, prophets, leaders of tribes or communities, or the monarchic element—all made claims to have the right to autonomous access to the central political and cultic arena and to participate in some crucial activities of this arena, especially, but not only, the legislative ones. The extent to which various groups were successful in such claims again depended greatly on the changing internal and external circumstances, but the claims to such autonomous access and participation were always there.

These different groups and sectors did not just claim to have their own distinct, separate domains; rather they aimed to participate in the common political, legislative, and cultic framework. Such claims were rooted in some combination of older tribal tradition with the basic assumptions of the covenantal ideology that in principle emphasized that all members of the community were partners to the covenant. It is rather doubtful whether there indeed have developed, as claimed by Cohen and Elazar,[9] clear constitutional regulations about the rights of access to the center and participation to it of different sectors. In fact such claims—albeit of different groups—to some degree were accepted, providing some basis if not of consensus then at least of a common framework. They would constitute the bases, as we shall see, for newly emerging groups in the period of the Second Commonwealth and afterward. These characteristics, orientations, and social elements provided the setting for the constant restructuring of this civilization and the Jewish collective identity, usually by incorporating the older symbols within the new ones, and made it possible to maintain its continuity.[10]

The Crystallization of Jewish Civilization
in the Period of the Second Commonwealth

As already indicated, the first far-reaching combination of change and continuity developed in the period that began with the return to Eretz Israel after the Babylonian captivity and persisted throughout the period of the Second Commonwealth.[11] Also during this period, the characteristics of this civilization took full shape, along with the historical experience that distinguished it from other "great" Axial Age civilizations in general and the other later monotheistic ones in particular.

New orientations, new types of carriers, and new patterns of collective identity crystallized during the period of the Second Commonwealth—albeit through a continuous reference to the older ones and evincing marked continuities with some of the basic characteristics and symbols that had crystallized during the preceding period. The first of these new orientations was the apocalyptic and eschatological, with strong though not exclusive otherworldly connotations. Apocalyptic and even otherworldly orientations emerged above all in close relation to the experience of exile and return and the growing tension between the present and the future, which began to be stressed at the end of the First Temple period. These orientations were incorporated into the Jewish religious tradition, even if slowly and only partially.[12]

A more contemplative, ethical or philosophical orientation emerged from the encounter with Hellenism, especially in the wisdom literature.[13] This particular orientation was limited to small circles, although it was probably more widespread in the Egyptian diaspora. Finally, the covenant ideology, according to which all members of the community had direct access to the sacred, was reinforced—possibly only then was it fully crystallized. This, in a sense, caused a return to some of the original premises of the early tribal confederacy, but in a new, nontribal setting.

The changes in cultural orientation were closely related to those in the composition of the elite groups and the geopolitical and intercivilizational situation of the Jewish people—changes that were to continue, in one fashion or another, throughout subsequent Jewish history. One of these changes was the disappearance of the Davidic monarchy and its replacement by new types of political leadership, consisting of communal, although no longer tribal, leaders—the "elders" of the community and perhaps the members of the Great Assembly—of the priests, and new monarchs, especially the Hasmonean dynasty. Concomitantly the status of the priesthood was at least potentially elevated (the Hasmoneans were a priestly family). Thus, possibilities opened up for new types of political links between the political elite groups and the broader strata of the people.[14]

The new historical experiences naturally sharpened the tensions between the different components of Jewish collective identity, especially between the universalistic and particularistic ones. But above all it sharpened the awareness of the meaning of exile and made the search for the understanding of this experience in terms of the covenant between God and the people of Israel a central one in Jewish collective self-definition and self-awareness.

The major response to this problem was the heightening—building of the older prophetic ones—of the apocalyptic-eschatological orientations. To quote Paula Frederiksen:

> *Apocalypse* means the "revelation of hidden things." *Eschaton* means "the end." *Apocalyptic eschatology* thus means the revelation of knowledge concerning the end of time, which will bring God's definite, and ultimate, intervention in history. Certain key items associated with this event appear variously, and in various combinations, in Jewish apocalyptic literature. Chief among these are that God will establish His Kingdom; that Jerusalem, and thus the Temple, will be rebuilt or restored; that the exiles will be gathered in; the unrighteous punished; idolatry vanquished; and suffering and travail will be replaced by an everlasting peace. The reader will recognize in this list major themes from the prophetic response to Israel's experience under Assyria and Babylon. Indeed, at the heart of apocalyptic is the same conviction that inspired the prophets. God's covenant with Israel is everlasting, the apparent counter-evidence of present events notwithstanding, and therefore God will surely redeem and restore his people. But something crucial has changed here. The "restored" Israel is an idealized Israel, one that the scriptures never claimed to have been: a people entirely dedicated to Torah, with a priesthood and a Temple universally recognized as pure, under a perfect monarch, living and left in peace. And its perfections are universalized: what for the earlier prophets was to be a historical event in the life of Israel becomes, in apocalyptic writings, what God will bring about at the end of time,

changing the nature of historical reality itself. Apocalyptic eschatology thus projects onto the universe the experience of the Exile and Return from Babylon. The entire world will experience Israel's redemption, for it will signal the redemption of the entire world.[15]

The primary actualization of these possibilities was through the emergence of a new leadership element, a new type of political and cultural elite. Its major constituents were the scribes (sophrim), the members of the Great Assembly, and the leaders of a host of religious-political movements, the best-known of which probably were the various groups that identified themselves, or were identified by other groups, as the Pharisees—who, together with some of the scribes, may have been the predecessors of the sages. At the same time, a number of semiheterodox sects were emerging.[16]

After the return from Babylonia, and probably already in Babylonia itself, these new types of elite groups became the most active and innovative, although certainly not the only ones. They emerged as the new representatives of the higher authority to which the rulers and the community were accountable. They were not homogeneous, however, as later historical interpretations based on rabbinical literature suggest. For a long time they probably consisted of quite distinct elements that were continually evolving, being modified, and interacting with one another in various ways, often struggling over the proper interpretation of the law and access to the central political and legislative arena.

For the most part these elite groups developed outside any ascriptive structure or group and by recruitment according to criteria that in principle were open to all. Although intellectuals, they were oriented toward the articulation of basic models of the social and cultural order of the higher law, from which came their intensive involvement in political life, whether in the judicial halls of the Sanhedrin or Sanhedrins, in their own centers of learning and judicial institutions, or in coalition with other groups who were more concerned with communal prayer and popular learning. These different groups of elites provided leadership in the various sects, especially of the different elements that later came together in the institutional mold of the oral Law (Torah she-ba'al peh), characterized by an increased emphasis on legal and ritual prescriptions based on exegesis and continuous elaboration of the holy texts and communal prayer.

All these new elite groups shared some of the characteristics of those of the First Temple period, outlined earlier, especially their relative symbolic and organizational autonomy and the strong interweaving of political and religious orientations. They, too, developed a flexible social structure and they lived in a volatile geopolitical situation. But they differed from the elite groups of the earlier period, as well as from the priestly families of their own period, in the relative weakness among them of ascriptive and individual-charismatic ("prophetic") components.

Another crucial structural development in the postexilic period was the appearance of the Diaspora as a permanent feature of the Jewish experience, giving rise to the emergence of a multiplicity of centers or, to use S. Talmon's expression, to a multicentric situation. This added a new dimension to the heterogeneity of the structural elements in Jewish life and the volatility of the geographical or geopolitical situation of the Jewish people.[17] This situation became even more pronounced with the final disappearance of Jewish political independence and hastened the crystallization of those aspects of the relationship between the Jews and their neighbors that led Weber to characterize them as a "pariah people."

During the Second Temple period several basic ideological premises, the nuclei of which already existed, began to emerge from the continuous interplay among the activities of the new elite groups, the new geopolitical situation, and the new cultural orientations. These premises were connected with the development of a new institutional mold, a new institutional pattern and cultural patterns—or rather of several incipient cultural-institutional molds—promulgated and crystallized by the various elite groups and their coalitions. In many respects these molds persisted throughout subsequent Jewish history and are of crucial importance for understanding its course.

One result was the weakening, although not the full obliteration, of the monopoly of access to some of the attributes of holiness, sacrality, and sacredness held by ascriptive groups—priests and sometimes kings—and, paradoxically enough, also by the more individual and charismatic elements such as the prophets. A second result of the opening of the central sacred arena to all members of the community was a growing stress on the potentially free access by all members of the community to these attributes of holiness. There was a concomitant increased emphasis on a new type of communal cohesion, based on the "holy community" as a constituent element of the collective religious-political identity.[18] New criteria of leadership and elite status were articulated. They consisted of a strong elitist orientation based on study of the law and a broad populist base that emphasized prayer, observing the rules, and membership in the holy community. The channels of mobility into the upper religious and civic positions and political leadership thereby were opened to all members of the community—though this was probably truer when the sages were not in power than during the period after the destruction of the Second Temple, when they had to confront actual rulers and groups. Closely related to this, the idea of the accountability of the rulers to a higher law was more fully crystallized—albeit in connection with fierce competition among the different elite groups as to which was the true representative of this higher law. Finally, a more diversified scope of political-religious leadership developed, creating the basis for new and more intensive type of communal conflict. Within the context of all these developments the new mold, the new overall ideological and institutional pattern of the Oral Law became the central, and ultimately—but only ultimately—predominant pattern, but never the only such pattern.

This new mold brought into the open some components of the Israelite and Jewish tradition that were latent or secondary in earlier times, gave rise to a more reflexive articulation of these themes, and combined them with new ones in a distinct new pattern. This new mold evolved from the combined activities of the various communal leaders, the sages, and their precursors. An increased emphasis on legal-ritual prescriptions, based on exegesis, study, and continuous elaboration of the holy texts, along with communal prayer, became the new and eventually dominant components of the tradition.[19]

All these developments—and also, as we shall see, the evolution of Christianity—can be seen as secondary axial breakthroughs from the initial ancient Israelite one. The possibility of the development of such secondary breakthroughs was rooted in some of the specific institutional and cultural characteristics of ancient Israel, as well as in the new international or inter-civilizational relationships that developed during this period. These secondary breakthroughs developed in connection with the political ecological conditions identified in the early Israelite Axial Age. Of special importance were the continuous international competition among different empires, population movements, and great internal heterogeneity and perhaps above all the international and intercivilizational contacts.

From the point of view of our analysis special interest attaches to the development of competition between two different "great" Axial Age civilizations—Ancient Israel and the Hellenistic-Roman civilization. This was probably the first such encounter in history (at least in "Occidental" history) and certainly facilitated the development of secondary breakthroughs.

This encounter was a crucial importance for the new developments in Jewish civilization. Sectarianism and potential nuclei of heterodoxy appeared for the first time in Jewish history, leading after time to the emergence of Christianity. Indeed, as Alan Segal, among others, has recently shown, the development of Christianity from within Judaism and its ultimate separation from it cannot be understood except against the background of internal developments in Judaism, mainly those entailed by its encounter with the Hellenistic and Roman civilizations.[20] But Christianity's breaking away from the fold of Jewish civilization did not obliterate their common reference point, Ancient Israel, a reference point that was of crucial importance in their ongoing intercivilizational relationship.

Some Comparative Indications:
The Crystallization of Christianity and Christian Civilization

At this stage of our analysis it might be worthwhile to briefly compare some of the major characteristics of Jewish civilization with the other two monotheistic civilizations: Christianity and Islam. Such a comparison is of special interest because both these religions, and especially Christianity, developed out of Judaism or in close relation and reference to it and later constituted the major host civilizations for the Jewish people. These civilizations can be compared on two dimensions: their basic ontological conception and their respective historical experience. At this stage we shall concentrate on the first dimension.

Originally, Christianity shared the religious and institutional molds of the Second Commonwealth and its various later developments. At least at the outset Christianity was part of the first of the secondary breakthroughs—the continuous reconstruction of Jewish civilization in the period of the Second Temple—and broke away from the fold of Jewish civilization only at a somewhat later stage. The ultimate development of Christianity went in directions other than those taken by the Hellenistic civilization and by Second-Temple and later Judaism.[21]

The Jewish religion and people ultimately failed in the great competition among different religions that characterized late antiquity. This led to the victory of Christianity and the crystallization of Medieval Christian civilization in general and its Western European (Catholic) variant in particular. This failure occured only ultimately, for the competition between Judaism and other religions, including Christianity and later Islam, lasted for much longer than historians are wont to acknowledge. This failure did not occur because the Jews became a purely religious community, as Weber supposed, but in many ways for just the opposite reason, and above all because the self-perception of the Jewish collectivity and the symbols of its collective identity continued to combine primordial national and political components with religious and ethical ones.[22] The fact that even its ascetic elements and various sects were closely bound to this view of the close relationship between the Jewish civilization and the Jewish people and political community has been of crucial importance in this context.[23]

Early Christianity's break with Judaism, whether it occurred in early Pauline Christianity or somewhat later (the process of breaking away from Judaism in any case must have gone on for much longer than has been usually supposed), focused not only on the role of law versus faith, as has been very often claimed, but also, and perhaps above all, on three basic changes with regard to the Jewish faith and religion.[24] The first of these was the removal of the political and primordial elements of religious belief and collective identity from their connection with a specific people and their transformation into more universal, less specifically national or ethnic elements. This dissociated the religious from the "ethnic" components—although without necessarily negating them totally, as was later and even in a sharper way the case in Islam.

Second was the emphasis on mediation through the person of Christ, a mediation expressed in many rituals, combining an emphasis on the bodily image of God with a strong otherworldly transcendental orientation—in opposition to the Jewish emphasis on an incorporeal God, on law, and on primordial ideological ties to the land and a distinct people constituted as a holy community.

Third was a growing difference between Judaism, especially rabbinic Judaism, and Christianity, which crystallized in a somewhat later period, with respect to the mode of access to the realm of the sacred: "For the Rabbis...the primary reality was linguistic; true being was a God who speaks and creates texts , and imitatio deus was not silent suffering, but speaking and interpreting." By contrast,

> [T]he Christian tradition—whose philosophical roots, despite Tertullian's best efforts, became deeply embedded in Greek thought—also ultimately calls for transcendence of the world and language together. The central doctrine of the Church—Incarnation—celebrates not the exaltation of the word, but its transformation from the linguistic order into the material realm, its conversion into the flesh.[25]

In Judaism this special emphasis on the continuous interpretation of the text was very closely related to the weakening of any mediation of the sacred—in contrast to the reinstallation of mediation by the emphasis on Incarnation.

The combination of these three transformations of the original Jewish religious orientations was one of the most important reasons for Christianity's success in the great religious competition of late antiquity. It was the combination of all these elements that characterized early Christianity in the religious competition of antiquity. Only much later, in Protestant Christianity, did some of these tendencies weakened significantly, with a return to Old Testament symbolism. Needless to say, however, Protestant Christianity also retained the central mediating figure of Christ and did not share with Judaism the strong emphasis on access to the sacred through textual exegesis. But perhaps the most important reason for the success of Christianity was its transformation of Jewish apocalyptical eschatology by taking it out of the confines of the Jewish framework. To quote Paula Frederiksen again:

> For apocalyptic eschatology has been born of the historical experience of the Jewish people. It expressed Israel's faith in God's justice and

mercy, most especially as these were manifest in His covenant with Israel. Present miseries were seen to confirm God's commitment to his people; He intended adversity to turn them back to Torah. Thus exile ultimately could only mean return; destruction, rebuilding; depletion, renewal; oppression, liberation....

The redemption, further, of this world. Apocalpytic redemption affirms creation. When the Kingdom came, it would come on earth, which God had made. Hence the Pharisees, and later the rabbis, insisted that the dead who participated in the Kingdom would be raised with physical bodies.... God's Kingdom on earth could gloriously recapitulate the idealized features of the Davidic monarchies: the nation would be reconstituted, the lost tribes restored, and the "word of the Lord" would go forth from Jerusalem to all the peoples of the earth, who would gather to worship at the Temple.

Paul's vision, too, is Jewish. He sees God intervening definitively in history to redeem His creation, and he describes this vision in terms drawn directly from scripture. But we search in vain to find Paul praising the future Jerusalem or the eschatological Temple. Images of earthly fecundity or social harmony do not figure in his presentation. The coming Kingdom will be "in the air" (I Thes. 4:16), in the heavens (Phil. 3:20) where no flesh can dwell (I Cor. 15:50). The resurrection is spiritual, not physical (I Cor. 15)...

Jewish history and the Jewish commitment to God's nature as revealed in Torah created the dynamics of apocalyptic eschatology. Paul retains these dynamics but renounces their particularity. His vision of the End is no drama of national liberation writ large. On the contrary, in Christ and therefore in the coming Kingdom, such earthly distinctions between peoples and persons dissolve.... God's to promise to Abraham stands: it is irrevocable. "In you shall all the nations be blessed" (Gen 12:3; Gal. 3:8; Rom. 9:4ff.; 11:2, 20). But the heir to this blessing is Christ (Gal. 3:16), and Abraham is the father of all who believe, whether Gentile or Jew (Rom. 4:12). In brief, Paul denationalizes Jewish restoration theology.

Accordingly, Paul also denationalizes Christ. Only in Romans, where he briefly introduces Jesus as "descended from David according to the flesh" (1:3; cf. 15:12), does Paul present the messiah of Jewish tradition. Otherwise, Christ's significant point of origin is not the flesh (his putative Davidic descent) but the Spirit, which reveals him at his resurrection as the divine preexistent Son (1:4)....

Thus Paul radically redefines the concept of redemption as he does the concepts of Kingdom and Christ: through the originally political vocabulary of liberation, he praises a reality that is utterly spiritual. And his vision so shrinks the significance of contemporary politics that Paul, fully aware of the human agents of Jesus' execution, nevertheless can tell Christians at Rome to honor all governing authorities since they, appointed by God, "are not a terror to good conduct, but to bad" (13:ff.). Pilate, Felix, Festus, Caligula, Nero...the rapid approach of the Kingdom paradoxically allows Paul to take a long view (13:11).[26]

Thus we see that the crucial difference between Christian and Jewish religious orientations and civilizational premises was not the contrast between the purely religious almost sectarian character of the Jewish civilization and the purely "spiritual" character of Christian religion, as claimed by Weber. Christianity took over from Judaism some of the strong this-worldly political orientation that the Jewish civilization never really gave up, although it stressed more otherworldly orientations than did Judaism.

The political success involved in the crystallization of the medieval European (and Byzantine) civilizations was possible only because the strong otherworldly orientations of early Christianity did not exclude any this-worldly or potentially political orientations—even if, owing both to its dissociation from the Jewish people as well as the political circumstances of the late Roman Empire, these latter were quite subdued in early Christianity.

It is true that the strong depoliticization of early Christianity and its strong otherworldly orientations as compared with Judaism may seem to contradict the later political involvement of Christianity and the crystallization of Christian civilizations in Europe that had a strong civilizational and political orientation. Yet despite some views (e.g., that of Louis Dumont) that stress the basic otherworldly orientations of early Christianity, a closer look at the evidence indicates that Christianity in general, and its monastic and ascetic groups in particular, show indications of the crucial differences between the otherworldly orientations of Christianity and Buddhism—the exemplary otherworldly civilization.[27]

These differences are based on differences in their respective predominant cultural orientations, in the conceptions of salvation that became predominant in each of them, and in the specific ideological and institutional dynamics that they generated. These differences also explain the different impact and transformation of the seemingly similar otherworldly orientations that developed in these civilizations.

The difference between the Hindu (and Buddhist) otherworldly orientation and renunciation indeed does stand out in comparison with the Jewish and Christian (and to some degree Greek or Hellenic) orientation. For Hinduism and Buddhism, the purely otherworldly orientation of the renouncers was an extension, even if a dialectical one, of the otherworldly concept of salvation that constituted the basic premise of these civilizations and generated a distinct civilizational pattern. The very institutionalization of such a pattern gave rise to the dialectical extension of the ideal of renunciation as the purest embodiment of this orientation. In Christianity, too, a very strong otherworldly orientation developed from the very beginning. But in Christianity this otherworldly orientation was part of the attempt to crystallize a new transcendental vision from the outset that included both a melding of and a tension between this-worldly and otherworldly orientations.

Christianity's inherent this-worldly orientation, that is, the vision that reconstruction of the mundane world is part of the way to salvation, that the mundane world constitutes at least one arena for activities relevant to salvation, which stands in marked contrast to Buddhism, of course is rooted in its Jewish origins. Such a this-worldly orientation, in constant tension with the otherworldly orientation, has been manifested in Christianity's basic orientations and dogma as well as in its institutional settings. It already was evident in the central role of Christ, who, unlike the Buddha, was to be both the carrier of an otherworldly vision and also the earthly embodiment or at least aspect of God.[28]

In parallel, Christianity placed a strong emphasis on the lack of complete separability—or even opposition—between body and soul in general and on resurrection in particular (a concept that in itself already contains a strong otherworldly element or emphasis and was strongly disputed by the Platonists).[29] Another strong this-worldly orientation, in constant tension with the otherworldly one, is manifest in the Christian conception, inherited from Judaism, of God as Creator of the Universe and in the centrality of eschatology and particularly the historical dimension of this eschatology, that is, in the conception of salvation as occurring in history for the whole of humanity.

The relatively strong this-worldly orientation of Christianity was evident in its polemics—even those of its extreme ascetics—with the Platonic and gnostic schools, in various degrees displaying a strongly negative attitude to the body and to the physical world. Christianity's difficulties with neo-Platonism, despite the strong attraction Platonic thought had for patristic writers, also are important indications of this tendency. This strong orientation to activities in the mundane world can be found within Christian ascetic and monastic communities as well. Unlike Buddhist and Hindu renunciation, Christian monasticism of the early centuries was oriented toward this world, not as an attempt to escape from it.

Indeed, as C. Bowersock indicates, one of Christianity's great advantages in the religious competition of Late Antiquity was that its otherworldly orientation and ascetic activities ultimately enabled it to return to the world bearing a transcendent vision, a vision to no small degree toward reconstruct-ing the world, inherent in early Christian asceticism and monasticism.[30] This strong orientation to the structure of the community and the Church and to the relation between the ascetic orientation and more mundane activities explains the great concern with the problems of authority and organization among the early Christian ascetics.[31]

The strong predilection to a conception of salvation that combined this-worldly and otherworldly orientations within itself was inherent in Christianity from its very beginning. It was a part of Christianity's Jewish roots and its close relationship, almost from the very beginning, with Hel-lenistic civilization. Historical circumstances, the initial lowly status and per-secution of Christianity, submerged but did not obliterate these concerns in the earlier period of Christianity. More propitious historical circumstances, the conversion of Constantine, brought out these this-worldly ideological ori-entations in full force. Although the conversion of Constantine indeed was a turning point in the emergence of medieval Christian civilization, it was built on potentialities that already existed in the initial stages of Christianity. The tension between the this-worldly and the pure otherworldly orientation since has become a permanent part of the history of Christianity.

These tensions developed in different ways in different parts of Chris-tian civilization—Catholic, Eastern, Byzantine, and later Russian Christiani-ty—depending on the specific combination of this-worldly and otherworldly orientations that emerged in the respective centers and on the geopolitical circumstances and structure of political power and elite groups in each of them. A special mode of otherworldly asceticism developed in each of them and maintained a tension with this-worldly orientations.[32] The ways in which these ontological conceptions and the tensions that developed within them worked out in close relation with the concrete historical experience of these civilizations are some aspects we analyze in the next chapter.

The Distinctive Characteristics of Islamic Civilization

The distinctions that divide Judaism from Islam lie in other directions than those that divide it from Christianity. Let us first examine some of the basic premises of Islamic civilization. In Islam the most important cultural orientations were the deep chasm between the "cosmic" transcendental and the mundane realms and the emphasis on overcoming the resulting tension by means of total submission to God and by this-worldly political and mili-tary activity, the strong universalist element in the definition of the Islamic community; the autonomous access of all members of the community to the attributes of the transcendental order and to the implementation of this vision in this world through submission to God; the ideal of the ummah, the political-religious community with strong unitary components of all believers, distinct from any ascriptive, primordial collectivity; and of the ruler as the upholder of the Islamic ideal, the purity of the ummah, and the life of the community.[33] Closely connected to these is the emphasis on the political equality of all believers and the accountability of rulers and community to the Islamic ideal. New institutional formations developed, such as distinct "centers" throughout the periphery. There was a strong tendency for new types of ruling elite groups to evolve, particularly autonomous religious elite groups and institutions. Specifically Islamic patterns of urban life emerged.[34]

As Maxime Rodinson has emphasized, Islam evinced the characteristics of a "totalitarian movement," as if it were a political party strongly oriented to the militant reconstruction of the world. This ideology entailed a fusion of political-religious collectivities, collective identity, and elite groups. The original vision of the ummah assumed a complete convergence between the sociopolitical and religious communities. Many of the later caliphs (e.g., the Abbasids and Fatimids), as well as other Muslim rulers, came to power on the crest of religious movements that upheld this ideal, legitimized themselves in religious-political terms, and sought to retain popular support by stressing the religious aspect of their authority and courting the religious leaders and religious sentiments of the community. Political problems were a central dilemma of Islamic theology.[35]

Islam connected the reconstruction of a combined political-religious collectivity with a strong ideological negation of any primordial element or component within this sacred political-religious identity. Indeed, of all the Axial Age civilizations, particularly the monotheistic ones, Islam was the most extreme in its denial of the legitimacy of such primordial dimensions within the Islamic community—although in practice the story was often markedly different, as Bernard Lewis has shown.[36] In this respect it stood in opposition to Judaism, with which it shared other characteristics, such as the emphasis on the direct unmediated access of all members of the community to the sacred. It also differed from Judaism in its basic conception of the relationship between human and God, in the strong emphasis on total submission to God—as the name Islam connotes—and in the absence of the possibility of a contractual relation between God and human.

From the very beginning Islam's strong universalistic ideology was torn by the tension between the particularistic primordial Arab elements, which were the initial carriers of the Islamic vision, and the universalistic orientation that gained importance with the continual incorporation of new territories and ethnic groups.[37] It is true that two primordial aspects have persisted—the legitimation of rulers by virtue of descent from the Prophet and the emphasis on Arabic as the sacred language of Islam, the Koran, and prayer, and also to a large degree legal exegesis. This contrasts with Judaism,

where the Jews of Alexandria read the Bible in Greek (just as many synagogues in the United States pray in English), and Christianity, where the
liturgy was conducted in Greek (or other languages) in the East, in Latin in
the Catholic world, and in the vernacular in Western Europe after the Reformation. Beyond these two primordial elements, however, Islam did not sanctify any "ethnic" primordial communal elements or symbols. Rather, the universalist ideology of the ummah became predominant. Islam's mode of
access to the sacred also differs from that of Judaism. Islam emphasizes the
importance of God's word as text; but in principle—though of course not in
practice—the text is fixed, and not open to continuous interpretation.

These differences between the Jewish, Christian, and Islamic civilizations are of interest for an understanding of the development of Jewish
medieval civilization as it evolved within the sociological and political
framework of the other two monotheistic civilizations.

They point to the very important fact for understanding the interrelations between these three civilizations, namely so that they shared both common background as well as some of their basic ontological premises while at
the same time that they differed with respect to the interpretation of the
meaning of this common background as well as with respect to several components of their basic premises.

For all three religions and civilizations it was the Jewish civilization,
above all the ancient Israeli one that served as the common starting point of
their special relations to God, of their being chosen by God. While the bearers of the Jewish civilization continuously saw themselves as God's chosen
people both Christianity and Islam saw themselves as superseding post-bibli-
cal Judaism, and they both promulgated elaborate theological formulations to
justify this attitude of theirs. This attitude to Jewish civilization was much
stronger in Christianity than in Islam—as the latter saw itself also as superseding Christianity.

At the same time each of these civilizations did also emphasize very
strongly those of its premises which differentiated it from the other two, as
indicating its relative superiority to the other two.

These mutual attitudes were not purely intellectual or academic—
although their promulgation constituted a very central concern of the theologians and other scholars of these civilizations. These attitudes constituted
central components in the self-legitimation of these civilizations, in the legitimation of their institutions and in their claims to universality. And it is these
attitudes that constituted also the ideological core of the relations between
these civilizations, of the intercivilizational relations that developed among
them.

But the concrete contours of these interrelations were shaped by the
combination of this ideological core with the concrete historical circumstances.

3

Basic Themes and Institutional Formations of Exilic Jewish Civilization: The Inter-Civilizational Perspective

The Historical Setting

Jewish postexilic, Medieval civilization crystallized within the framework of Christian and Islamic civilization, transforming the contours of Jewish life yet again. This most enduring Jewish civilization probably started to develop during late antiquity, following the destruction of the Second Temple and then with the development of the Christian and Islamic civilizations.

During late antiquity and early Christianity most Jews lived in the Near and Middle East: in Palestine, Syria, Mesopotamia, Egypt, and the Byzantine Empire. Very few moved into Western and Central Europe. During the expansion of the Muslim Empires, from the seventh till the twelfth centuries, most Jews lived under Muslim rule in the Near East, Spain, and North Africa. An increasing number (but still a minority of the Jewish people) started to settle in Christian countries: Christian Spain, France, England, and Germany (Ashkenaz). After the expulsion from Spain and until the beginning of the seventeenth century, most Jews continued to live under Muslim, in this case Ottoman, rule in the countries of the Mediterranean and Near and Middle East, but there was a continuous migration into Christian countries: Italy, the Netherlands, and especially Germany, Poland, and other Eastern European countries. From the seventeenth century onward, the Jewish communities in the "Ashkenazi" countries expanded and became the major centers of Jewish life.

Notwithstanding the great differences between these three subperiods (detailed analysis of which is beyond the scope of this work), they shared some basic characteristics that are of great importance for our analysis.[1] The Jewish community in Palestine, still numerous during the first three centuries after the destruction of the Temple, continued to dwindle throughout this long period, giving rise to increasing dispersion and growing political passivity and subjugation. By the end of the seventh century of the common era (CE) Jews everywhere became a political minority, tolerated only by virtue of special permits (which could be easily abrogated). They were communities of strangers, living by the grace of rulers who were interested in them for fiscal reasons. They engaged mainly in middleman economic activities—as traders, artisans, and financiers—and only to a much smaller degree in agriculture. Their legal and economic rights were relatively circumscribed. They were in continual danger of serving as the object of popular discontent or of earning the displeasure of the rulers or ecclesiastical authorities, with the looming menace of riots and expulsion. Continuous dispersion and migration, with the concomitant multiplicity of different centers and shifts in their respective strength, became a basic part of Jewish existence.

Institutional Changes

In parallel with these developments a marked shift took place in the social and institutional organization of Jewish life—a shift to communal organizations, rabbinical and communal courts and centers of learning—and in the networks, contacts, and economic relations among them. These structures became the major institutional-organizational nexus of Jewish life. In the first two subperiods there developed in Eretz Israel and in Babylon, the preeminent exilic community of this period, strong centralized Jewish political institutions under the President (Nasi) in Eretz Israel and the Exilarch (Rosh Hagola) in Babylonia, which spawned many organs of internal administrative and juridical groups. With growing uniqueness and dispersion these organizations became weakened and ultimately disappeared, although the tendency to establish political autonomy and acquire the symbols of political status was very strong and would erupt in appropriate circumstances.

The dominant institutions were those of the communities and their courts, to which the gentile authorities usually granted some corporate rights, along with supervision of the Jews and control of access to at least some of the economic activities and rights of domicile open to Jews.[2] The kernel of the Jewish community included the family and networks of families, the synagogue and various communal organizations, and centers of study and learning.

The various institutions that evolved in this period constituted both a continuation and a break with the Second Commonwealth. There is no doubt, of course, that, after the return from Babylon, political independence was always precarious—much more so than during the First Temple era; even that degree of political independence and continuity enjoyed by the Davidic monarchy was lacking. Moreover, by the time of the Second Commonwealth many Diaspora communities had evolved—primarily in Egypt, Mesopotamia, and Syria—and created multiple centers as a permanent feature of Jewish existence. But the destruction of the Temple and loss of political independence represented a sharp and traumatic break with the past. Autonomous political power had been lost; thereafter, relations between the center and the Diaspora changed, as the very nature of the Diaspora, being exiled and a minority, became both a permanent fact and a continuous problem in Jewish life and collective consciousness.[3]

New types of leadership developed within these institutional frameworks.[4] The structure of this leadership necessarily underwent far-reaching changes after the destruction of the Second Temple. Yet here we encounter a rather paradoxical situation: these extensive changes in the structure of the leadership were accompanied by a striking continuity in its basic analytical characteristics.

The changes connected with the loss of political independence and dispersion were obvious. They were manifested above all in the progressive weakening of any relatively centralized political leadership. Whenever external circumstances were favorable, however, such a leadership still tended to emerge: the Exilarchs in Mesopotamia and their equivalent in other places, such as southern France in the tenth to twelfth centuries.

At the same time, and again under favorable circumstances, there was a shift to local or translocal organizations, the famous Va'ad Arba ha-Aratzot (Council of the Four Lands) in Poland and similar bodies in Moravia and elsewhere. But in general the communal leadership consisted of the leaders of individual communities and sometimes also included the rabbis and students in the major institutions of learning. In its composition and internal relationships this leadership displayed some striking similarities to the elite groups of earlier periods.[5]

The major elite groups in most Jewish communities always comprised some combination of three elements: the stronger, wealthier, oligarchic stratum; would-be popular political leaders; and the learned class of rabbis, scholars, and mystics. They usually composed the ruling coalitions that controlled community life. The last of these elements tended to develop a degree of specialization and autonomy in supracommunal and even transnational networks.

These different elite and subelite sectors always included numerous elements; continuous tensions developed among them and within each of them as well. These tensions were rooted in the fact that despite all the change in the composition of these elite sectors, as compared with earlier periods, they all still shared the basic beliefs and orientations of the Jewish civilizations analyzed earlier, and, above all, a strong commitment to the belief that all members of the community had access to the sacred realm, to the central arenas of the sacred, and in the covenantal relationship between God and the people of Israel.

The Predominance of the Oral Law (Halakhah)

These developments in the external organization of the Jewish people were connected with the growing predominance in Jewish life of the rabbinical mold of the Oral Law, the Halakhah. This gradually, by the fourth or fifth century CE, became the major hegemonic mold or the major institutional and cultural framework of Jewish civilization. By that time this mold had partially displaced the other institutional molds, both the priestly and political orientations connected with the Temple and an independent polity as well as the various sectarian tendencies propagated by the numerous sects and movements and especially by emerging Christianity.

During the first two or three centuries after the destruction of the Second Temple these sects and groups were still conspicuous in Judea and Galilee, and probably predominated in the desert in the form of various Hagarist or Samaritan groups. Some of the former later became closely related to a new and powerful universal civilization: Islam.

The competition among these groups and sects (who all still related to their common origin in Jewish civilization) was quite bitter and intense. From this competition the predominance of the rabbinical mold gradually emerged—a predominance that would continue up to the modern period. Even then, however, many of the sects and sectarian orientations were not obliterated; they were merely forced underground, as it were, into the margins of Jewish society or the interstices between Jewish, Christian, and Islamic civilizations.[6]

In the first centuries after the destruction of the Temple, the priestly families continued to enjoy a very high standing in the communities, in some places, such as the Galilee, constituting part of the upper stratum of Jewish society. But later on, from the end of the third century, their influence dwindled; and it disappeared almost entirely (except for performance of marginal ritual functions in the synagogue) with the increase of emigration from Eretz Israel.

As we have seen, in the Second Commonwealth period, the Oral Law, the later rabbinical mold, began to emerge from the combined activities of the communal leaders, the sages and their precursors, and the leaders of the major sectarian religious-social movements. It was characterized by increased emphasis on legal-ritual prescriptions, based on the exegesis, study, and continuous elaboration of texts, or on communal prayer as the focus of Jewish religion and tradition. Here, the emphasis on textual exegesis as the chief mode of access to the sacred developed.

This mold, this overall institutional and cultural framework, was guided by a combination of this-worldly attitudes and premises together with some of the otherworldly, ascetic, and eschatological ones that had developed earlier. However, within this mold, within this framework, the latter did not attain the same distinctiveness that they acquired in other monotheistic or otherworldly religions. The potentially revolutionary and universalist implications of these attitudes—most visible in some of the sects and later on in Christianity—were reinterpreted and hemmed in within the tradition of the Oral Law.

Also in the period of the crystallization of the hegemony, and in close connection with such crystallization, a full-fledged heterodoxy emerged and crystallized in Jewish history: the Karaites.

Numerous sects developed in the period of the Second Temple and the first centuries following it, as we have seen. Many of which, of course, had heterodoxical potential. The most extreme of them was Christianity, which, however, left the fold of the Jewish tradition. So long as no clear, regnant orthodoxy existed within this framework, various sects could see themselves as belonging to the Jewish collectivity and exist in different margins thereof—or even close to the center.

The situation changed drastically with the crystallization of the rabbinical orthodoxy. The Karaites developed as a full-fledged sect, against the background of many less organized ones and Messianic movements, first under the leadership of Anan Ben-David in ca. 760 from the very center of the rabbinical framework of the Oral Law. Their basic tenet was oriented against the very promise of the rabbinical; namely, the legitimacy of continuous reintegration of the Written Law through the Oral Law. Against this basic tenet of the rabbinical traditions, the Karaites developed what today would be called a fundamentalist stand: the total supremacy of the Written Law of the Old Testament, especially of the Pentateuch (the five books of Moses) and its literal interpretation.

To give only one illustration contrary to rabbinical injunction, they did not allow lights on Sabbath, promulgating in general a very ascetic line, legitimized by the necessity to maintain continuously the destruction of the Temple and rationalist interpretation and justification of the Jewish tradition. The last stance was closely interwoven with intensive discussions with Muslim philosophers.

The confrontation between the "rabbanites" and the Karaites continued as did at the same time social interaction between them. Slowly, especially with the gradual cultural and economic decline of many Islamic communities (in the Middle East), and with the shift of the center of Jewish communities from the lands of Islam to Europe, the importance of the Karaites diminished; many of them emigrated to Eastern Europe, where they did not play such a prominent role as in the lands of the Middle East.[7]

The predominance of this mold, and its acquisition of hegemony in the Jewish world, was promulgated and affected by its bearers—the rabbis and the sages, both through control of the institutions of learning and the synagogues. It was symbolized in elocution and the order in the synagogue and in making its symbol, the "crown of learning" (keter Torah), superior to the crowns of priesthood and of monarchy.[8]

Special attitudes developed toward the prophetic tradition. On one hand, the ethical, and even eschatological orientations and traditions were incorporated into the newly emerging paradigm through a process of codification and canonization of the scriptures; on the other hand, the possibility of further independent prophecy was denied. Revelation was replaced by the more structured process of study, legal exegesis, and collegial decisions by the courts and community organizations.

This new tradition of the Oral Law marked a shift from the predominance of ritual cultic elements and prophetic visions to the elaboration of canonic scripture, the interpretation and elaboration of the evolving Oral Law, and prayer. Interpretation itself was based on an increasing systematization of the legal-ritual precepts according to more abstract systematic principles. This systematization was codified first in the Mishna and the Tosefta and later in the two Talmuds, the Jerusalem and the Babylonian, that served as the bases for all later interpretations and the rabbinical literature that continues to this day. This literature was very rich and heterogeneous. The earlier works included more interpretative literature of the Midrashim, containing both legal and "legendary" (aggadic) elements, some of which was incorporated into the Talmud. Later came the She'elot u-Teshuvot (Questions and Answers), the combined commentaries and exegeses of the law, and the secondary codifications: the most important of which were Maimonides's *Mishneh Torah* (composed about 1178 CE), the *Arba'ah Turim* of the fifteenth century, and—the last great codification—the *Shulhan Arukh* of Rabbi Joseph Karo (1488–1575). Still later came the rich literature of commentaries on the Bible, Mishna, and Talmud: the most famous and popular being that of Rashi (Rabbi Shlomo Yitzhaki) of France (1040–1105). Finally, there emerged the widespread "ethical" (Musar) literature.[9]

This vast literature aimed at the systematic regulation of most aspects of the Jews' daily life: in the religious-ritual field, with special emphasis on dietary restrictions and to a smaller degree on dress; in the field of interpersonal relations in general and economic ones in particular; and also to some degree, as we shall see, in matters of communal organization and the relationship with the host nations. Thus it structured the specific contents and boundaries of Jewish collective life and civilization, while justifying and explaining these injunctions in religious and ethical terms. Throughout this period the mold of the Oral Law, with its combination of "ritual," "study," and purely legal aspects, became the common sociocultural framework that held the Jewish people together and provided the symbolic institutional continuity of the Jewish national and cultural identity.

The Hebrew language was of special importance in maintaining this framework, for it bound together the different Jewish communities. Like Latin in Catholic Christianity and Arabic in Islam, it was the language of prayer and philosophical discourse. But it surpassed Latin, and to some degree Arabic in the Islamic periphery, by also being the language of ritual-legal discourse and correspondence dealing with more mundane matters, such as commercial or family transactions.[10] Although Jews naturally learned the vernacular of their respective countries and although, at least in the Muslim world, a large proportion of Jewish philosophical treatises were written in Arabic (if frequently in Hebrew script), still the multiple uses of the Hebrew language greatly facilitated the maintenance of close relations among different Jewish communities and the common framework of Jewish civilization focused around the Halakhah.

Within this mold the major symbols of Jewish identity—couched in basic primordial, national, ethnic, and religious terms—were continuously articulated and regulated. These symbols were expressed in the various communal organizations and networks that provided the major institutional framework in which the continuity of Jewish culture was maintained and in which all the different elements or components of Jewish collective identity—"national," primordial, "ethnic," and religious, cultural, and political—were brought together.

Most Jews probably did not differentiate between these different strands of identity. They assumed that all these strands naturally came together and were bound by the law, and that their basic belief system was based on monotheistic and covenantal orientations. The fact that they were the chosen people provided the ultimate legitimacy of the entire structure of the law.

Toynbee saw in these characteristics of the medieval Jewish civilization evidence of its fossilization. To Weber they demonstrated that the Jews were a religious, and not a political, community, acquiring some of the crucial attributes of a pariah people. As mentioned in the first chapter, however, both views were partial and distorted.

The relationship between the Jews and their host civilizations were very different from those of other minorities. Indeed, many of the characteristics of a pariah people depicted by Weber were not peculiar to the Jews; during the historical period under consideration they applied to many nations and religions. In a sense, pariahhood and dispersion were the fate of minorities in most of the empires of antiquity. It would be wrong, however, to see these attributes as the most important aspect of the Jews' relationship to their host civilizations. Unlike many other minority peoples, the Jews attempted to maintain some more general civilizational role for themselves in the tumultuous politics of the period. They also persisted in claiming a universal validity for their religion and tradition—claims that were taken seriously, if hardly sympathetically, by their host civilizations.

During the Second Commonwealth the Jewish situation was already characterized by the combination of a rather precarious political and economic situation with attempts to participate fully in the political and cultural life of the period. This participation was based on attempts to forge an identity and institutional framework that would enable the Jews to maintain their political, religious, and primordial identity, while at the same time sustaining their claims to universal validity.

In the long period of the exile this situation changed dramatically; yet the Jews' belief in the universal significance of their religion did not abate. They no longer could compete openly with other civilizations and had to invest almost all their energy in maintaining their own cultural-religious framework, their segregation from the host nation, and the construction of relatively closed collective boundaries.

Even in these circumstances the legitimacy that the Jews claimed for themselves was not only religious or "cultic," but continued to contain strong political and "national" elements. This was evident in the emphasis on collective salvation and political redemption and in the metaphysical definition of both the exile and the primordial relationship between the land of Israel and the people of Israel, unique among dispersed peoples. There also were very definite universalist-civilizational components and premises to this claim of legitimacy.

Even in this period, then, the Jews were not merely a pariah minority who often performed the functions of middlemen. Their basic relationship with the host civilizations were not defined by these "pariah" attributes, but rather in terms of a common historical-religious origin: the Christian, and to a smaller degree Muslim, denial of the legitimacy of the Jews' refusal to accept Christianity and Islam. This refusal, accompanied by the specific historical relations with their host civilizations, caused their host civilization to view the Jews as potential competitors and even as a threat.

This attitude started to develop in the Roman Empire. It crystallized as Christianity became the predominant religion of the Roman Empire and again later, if to a lesser extent, with the Islamic conquest of the Near and Middle East. Christianity and Islam were "axial" monotheistic religions with claims to universality, attempting to construct civilizations that naturally encompassed all with whom they came into contact—including, of course, the Jews. Both were historically related to the Jewish religion and people, especially Christianity, but, in a somewhat milder version, Islam as well.

This historical relationship was a basic element of their self-definition. The Christians saw themselves as the true Children of Israel, while the Jews, persisting in their own faith, were deviants, practicing an aberration of the "true faith" of Israel. For the Muslims, Muhammad was the ultimate prophet, superseding if not necessarily totally negating the validity of his predecessors; here, too, the Jews' failure to accept him was seen as an aberration, even if they, and the Christians who were seen as the "people of the book," were granted a higher theological status than pagan people and, in benign periods, enjoyed some tolerance.[11]

Because the Jews were seen as an ambivalent reference point and potential threat to the legitimacy of their hosts' own creed, tense relations developed between the host societies and the Jewish communities, with each asserting the legitimacy of its own civilization. Both Christianity and Islam thus displayed an ambivalence toward the Jews that they did not feel toward other minorities. This ambivalence was expressed not only in pogroms, persecutions and expulsions, but also in the ideological dimensions ascribed to these actions. The manifestations of these dimensions included the frequent debates between Christian priests and theologians and Jewish rabbis and theologians, which formed a regular part of the medieval cultural scene in each of these civilizations;[12] it also could be seen in forced conversions, massacres, and the infamous blood libels in which Jews were accused of killing Christian children and drinking their blood. All of these led to Jewish martyrdom in sanctification of the Name of God (*Kiddush Hashem*). This ambivalence added a new dimension to the facts of the Jews' political subjugation and dispersion. For the Christians and Muslims these facts were seen as evidence of their own superiority; for the Jews, they constituted an important ideological challenge. It is significant that in civilizations like China or India, where this civilizational competition was nonexistent, the small Jewish communities indeed became a sort of religious-ethnic minority.

The Transformation of the Basic Themes of Jewish Civilization and the Crystallization of New Themes

The ambivalent relationship between the Jewish people and the two other monotheistic civilizations, especially Christianity, became closely interwoven with the internal fabric of Jewish life and civilization that developed during the long period stretching from the destruction of the Second Temple up to modern times and continues, in a new way, in the modern period itself. The civilizational, not only the political or economic, relationship with the host civilizations, rulers, and people and the tensions between the host and Jewish communities were of continuous relevance for the construction and maintenance of the boundaries of Jewish civilizations and for Jews' continuity as a distinct people.

As in the former periods, the Jews developed many new patterns of cultural and institutional formations and activities, which were seen as the "natural" continuation of the old patterns. There was an important difference from the period of the Second Temple, of course. With the ultimate decline of the center in Palestine, the dispersion and almost total loss of independent political power by the Jewish communities in Christian and Islamic lands, and the concomitant predominance of the legal-study-and-prayer mold, the institutional arena in which these various tendencies could be worked out became more limited. This restriction applied particularly to those tendencies connected with building political and economic institutions. Most of the basic ideological attitudes and tensions characteristic of Jewish civilization could not be implemented in a concrete institutional framework. Among the many changes that occurred, I would like to stress the transposition of the loci of many of the perennial themes of Jewish civilization and the crystallization of several new themes.

Although official halakhic Judaism never gave up its claim to be a civilization of universal significance, in fact Jews no longer really competed actively with other civilizations—even if these civilizations continued to fear such competition. The Jews concentrated mainly on their own frameworks, minimizing their aspirations to one specific construction of the real world while consciously opting for nonparticipation in contemporary political and civilizational history.[13] The only institutions that were constructed according to the basic tenets of their tradition were those of learning, ritual observance and prayer, and communal organization. By the very nature of the circumstances in which they lived, the Jews could not affect the economic arenas.

Their basic attitude to the mundane world—to economic life and communal organization—remained positive. But these arenas were not seen as arenas in which the basic premises of Jewish religion and civilization should, or could, be implemented. The internal and above all the international political arena, so predominant during the Second Temple period, disappeared almost entirely as such an arena. The fact of dispersion and political subjugation, of having become strangers and usually a persecuted minority, made this arena meaningless from the point of view of the basic tenets of the tradition, but not necessarily of their own natural communal interests. Life in Galut was seen as basically temporal—in many ways as a negative, even if necessary or given, existence. The Jews in the medieval world lived, as it were, outside history, opting out of concrete contemporary history and defining their existence outside its flow.

Assertions of the universal significance of the Jewish religion and the quest for political redemption were transposed into the distant Messianic future, beyond the scope of the Jews' daily activity. In principle they could hasten the redemption by proper observance of the law, but not by any direct political activity. The present existed in the confines of a narrow particularistic solidarity, as it were, outside history. Thus the tension between the universal and the particularist elements in Jewish culture was resolved, in a sense, by deferring the former to some future time when it might be possible to realize them, to conduct a truly open dialogue and encounter with other nations, religions, and civilizations. It was perhaps only, or above all, in the philosophical works and disputations that very strong elements of such dialogue was continuously promulgated.

The reality of Jewish life became particularistic, though with a strong tie to universal orientations and hopes. Given the realities of pre-Medieval and Medieval exile, the nature of the relations with the broader society within which the Jews were living, this universal orientation could not take on any real institutional dimension, as opposed to a purely intellectual one. The universal ethical orientations inherent in Jewish civilization remained latent, the focus for theological disputes, or a dream. This latency was connected, of course, with the solution of another dilemma, that between concrete reality and eschatological orientations and hopes. Here, too, the eschatological orientations, both universal and particularistic, together with their strong political elements were deferred to some unknown future, only tenuously related to the temporal, concrete reality. The religious and lay leaders of the Jewish community, although always emphasizing the Messianic hope, perceived any attempt to realize them, as for instance in Messianic movements, as a danger to Jewish existence and contrary to the basic premises of the halakhic mold.[14]

Therefore, most of the basic themes of Jewish civilization that developed in this period were ideological, cultural, or intellectual, with little application to the international institutional reality. But this irrelevance to institutions did not obliterate the potential institutional implications of many of these themes; they persisted and were articulated as the intellectual, ideological, and symbolic themes defining the symbolic boundaries of Jewish existence. Their potential institutional applications were always latent or dormant. Moreover, as we shall see in greater detail, they did influence the institutional arrangements of the Jewish community, especially their internal communal arrangements.

The Ideology of Galut and Eretz-Israel: Messianic Redemption and Martyrdom

Several additional themes, which could be discerned to some extent during the Second Temple period, became more fully articulated and more closely connected with the tensions between the particularistic and universal orientations of the Jewish tradition. These themes became an inherent part of Jewish tradition and collective self-definition, though, significantly enough, the halakhic tradition did not allow most of them to become autonomous or predominant. Several closely related yet not entirely identical themes were the most important: the metaphysical and ideological evaluation of Eretz Israel; the fuller articulation of Messianic visions; and the solidarity of the Jewish people.

Dispersion was not unique to the Jews, although probably its scope and continuity were. What was unique and specific to them was the tendency to a strong metaphysical or religious negative evaluation of Galut. Explaining the fact of Galut became, as the late Professor I. Baer has shown,[15] a major concern of many, if not most, Jewish philosophers and scholars. Whatever the details of these philosophical expositions, in most cases Galut was seen as basically negative, explained in terms of sin and punishment. Life in Galut was defined as a partial, suspended existence, but at the same time an existence that had to be nurtured to guarantee the survival of the Jewish people until the Redemption.

This negative evaluation of Galut focused on two closely connected but sometimes antithetical themes: the lack of political sovereignty (Shiabud Malchuyoth), and the partial and distorted spiritual or religious existence that was seen as the metaphysical or religious negative evaluation of Galut. These two themes were often combined, but different scholars or groups emphasized them in different degrees.[16]

The political and the metaphysical or redemptive themes were also central in the attitude toward Eretz Israel and in the articulation of Messianic visions. The attitude toward Eretz Israel, in a sense, was the counterpoint to that toward the Galut, often enunciated by the same thinkers, but with some autonomy. Eretz Israel was defined in both primordial and political terms; but—and this was the great innovation, even if built on earlier foundations—there was also a growing metaphysical attitude to it. Eretz Israel was seen first of all as the national patrimony from which the Jews had been expelled; but it was also seen as having a special metaphysical and religious meaning through which the Jews were constituted as a distinct people. The full realization of this meaning could come only with full Redemption. The attitude to Eretz Israel in a way became a mirror image of the political-primordial and metaphysical evaluation of life in Galut, and these attitudes about Eretz Israel became a basic component of the Jewish collective consciousness in the Diaspora. They imbued this identity with a seemingly nonrealistic, yet very strong and articulated focus, again combining in a unique way the particularistic and universal orientations.

These orientations toward Galut and Eretz Israel, of course, did not necessarily shape the daily life of most Jews throughout this long period. Their life focused on daily existence and survival, on the one hand, and on the maintenance of legal-ritual observances and prayer, on the other hand. Moreover, the halakhic authorities did not allow these orientations to become actualized beyond the sphere of the Halakhah and its apolitical and ahistorical attitude to existing reality. They did constitute a latent component of daily existence, however, especially as defined in the specific terms of Jewish tradition; and they were a fundamental constituent of the symbolically articulated expression of this tradition.

These attitudes toward Galut and Eretz Israel converged around the third theme, which, in a sense, subsumed them: the Messianic and eschatological theme and vision. Its roots lie in the early Second Temple period, even in the Babylonian exile, and found expression in the various sects of the Second Temple period as well as in Christianity. The proper interpretation of the Messianic vision, the vision of the Messiah who would come at the end of days, became the central focus of controversy between Judaism and Christianity. The salience of this point was intensified by the loss of political independence, dispersion, and expulsion. The contours of the Messianic vision became much more fully elaborated, articulated around the basic motifs of political and religious redemption.[17]

Both of these motifs, but especially the latter, were fraught with many antinomian potentialities vis-à-vis the predominant mold of the Halakhah and became the foci of many talmudic and philosophical expositions and controversies. There existed the tension between the "spiritual" religious and the more mundane, especially political dimensions of the Messianic history. The famous talmudic ruling that there is no difference between the Messianic and the contemporary reality except "Shibud Malchuta" ("The Yoke of the Nations") that is, the lack of political independence, which was frequently upheld by many sages, including Maimonides, probably was oriented against the more religious, spiritual component of the Messianic vision, with its very strong antinomian potentialities. Such components of the Messianic vision often were closely connected to the different primordial, political, and metaphysical attitudes to Eretz Israel.

Without ever denying any of these visions rabbinical orthodoxy always tried to keep them within these strict limits. It was suspicious of the potential religious innovations or antinomies inherent in the "spiritual" dimensions of the Messianic vision, as distinct from political, and their power to disrupt both the authority of the Halakhah and the precarious existence of the dispersed Jewish communities. Maimonides, who did not belittle the reformative, potentially utopian components of Messianism, did yet negate any escatological transhistorical and antinomian potentialities thereof. Despite these efforts, however, the Messianic visions and hopes did not remain merely intellectual exercises confined to limited circles of cognoscenti nor latent and unrealistic hopes. They erupted, in more or less dramatic fashion, as popular movements, led by would-be aspirants to the role of Messiah or forerunner of the Messiah; for example, David Hareubeni and Shlomo Molkho in the early sixteenth century and later, the last and most dramatic episode, Shabbetai Zevi and the Sabbatean movement, which shook the foundations of rabbinic Judaism.[18] Naturally these tendencies erupted in times of troubles: persecution, expulsion, great international upheavals that could be interpreted as the harbingers of new times, of the war between Gog and Magog. When such popular movements arose, however ephemeral they might be, they drew on the rich reservoir of images, of themes and thropes, provided by esoteric or mystical circles, who always emphasized redemptive rather than political Messianism. Whatever their foundations, these movements always threatened the predominance of the rabbinical mold—not only its specific religious injunctions, but above all its tendency to opt out of the contemporary historical-political scene, its suspension of the Jewish civilizational mission.

Another basic theme that became fully articulated during this long era, a sort of dialectical counterpart or complement to the Messianic hope, was martyrdom.[19] Kiddush Hashem, the sanctification of God's name through martyrdom, went back at least as far as Roman times. It reached full expression in the wake of persecution and pogroms, legitimized in terms of the basic religious chasm between Christianity and Judaism, in which the Jews often were called upon to choose between apostasy and death. Martyrdom developed as a reaction against the sages, who sanctified the preservation of life and tried to minimize the overt tension with the host people—though, of course, not at the cost of apostasy. It became a permanent theme of Jewish identity, emphasizing the Jews' complete commitment to their tradition.

A complementary theme was Jewish solidarity, Ahavat Israel, the necessity to close ranks in the face of external threats. This theme, which emerged at both the ideological and more popular levels during the long period of Galut, was closely related to the self-imposed segregation, to the intolerance toward other religions, to the ambivalence toward other nations. In its extreme manifestation it could easily turn into intense xenophobia.

These different themes were continuously interwoven with the different modes by which the tradition was interpreted: the philosophical, mystical, pietist, and legal-ritual. They constituted the foci of the intellectual and institutional creativity and dynamics of medieval Jewish civilization, the symbolic boundaries of Jewish life as it developed in the Diaspora.

Heterogeneity and Dynamics within the Rabbinic Mold

The proponents of these themes saw them as a natural continuation of the older ones, even though many were in fact new constructs with roots in the earlier periods.[20] But, just as in former periods, these various themes did not necessarily coexist in full harmony. There was continual tension among them, as well as among the different groups or persons that articulated them, attesting to the continuous heterogeneity within the mold of the Halakhah. Even when this mold became predominant, the older elements and orientations (eschatological, mystical, or philosophical) persisted and became transformed within it; moreover, they often reappeared as harbingers of various trends (mystical, ascetic, philosophical, and contemplative and, cutting across them, Messianic) that were extremely powerful even within this mold. There also were tensions among some of the specific attributes of the new mold: between the elitist attitudes that emphasized study and learning and the popular attitudes of prayer, piety, and ecstasy—sometimes with strong mystical components; and between those who stressed political-communal leadership and activity and those who emphasized the importance of religious-legal study.

The great heterogeneity within the rabbinic tradition was fed by both internal and external forces. Internally there were the various religious, intellectual, and social orientations mentioned earlier. True enough, they were denied symbolic and especially organizational autonomy; they usually were subsumed within the mold of the Halakhah as secondary elements; and they were not allowed to develop into heterodox sects. Nevertheless they represented important components of Jewish life, foci of cultural creativity and potential subterranean developments. The struggles among these orientations gave rise to a great variety of interpretations of the tradition—all of them promulgated by different elite sectors and groups, by the various types of leadership that developed in the Jewish communities. These struggles, and the related variety of cultural creativity, were closely connected, as we shall see later on, with "external" developments, namely, the relations between Jewish communities and their "host" societies.

This creativity first of all was intellectual, but it was more than that as well. Its focus, confirmed by frequent disputes and discussions, was the delineation of the symbolic and institutional boundaries of the collective existence of the Jewish people in exile and the attempts to maintain them.

Such dynamism was closely connected with different emphases on the interpretations of the tradition—the philosophical, mystical, pietist, and legal-ritual. The different communal orientations were linked to the basic themes of Jewish civilization being crystallized in this period. In principle these all could have become the nuclei of "heretical" trends and secessionist movements, like those that developed in the first centuries after the destruction of the Temple and persisted, at least in the Near East, on the margins of Christian and Islamic civilization. Later, however, most of them were marginal to the mainstream of halakhic Judaism, which emerged as a full-fledged orthodoxy for the first time in the history of Jewish civilization—although they certainly continued to influence the dominant mold. Perhaps the most articulate and fully developed of them were the Karaites, who emerged in Mesopotamia and the rest of the Near East in the second half of the seventh century, contemporary with the full crystallization of rabbinic orthodoxy and its attainment of hegemony in the Jewish world. They denied the validity of the Oral Law and tried to rely only on the Written Law, the Torah, attempting to create a different, nonhalachic rabbinical model.

This potential for heterodoxy existed, even if latently, within medieval Judaism, articulated by various groups of mystics, pietists, and philosophers. The later potentially heterodox dynamics developed within the mold of the Halakhah—in the institutions and networks of prayer, study, and legislation. New types of leadership developed within the framework of these institutions. Despite the far-reaching changes that occurred after the destruction of the Second Temple, these types of leadership maintained a striking continuity in their basic characteristic, especially in their heterogeneity and orientation toward the common framework. The combination of these different types of leadership, the modes of communal organization, and the basic religious and institutional orientations gave rise to an intense dynamic in both Jewish communal organization and the patterns of cultural creativity that developed within it, whence came the potential for heterodoxy and sectarianism.

On the whole, though, and until the threshold of modern times, these forces did not develop into full-fledged heterodoxies or secessionist movements, whether in the religious and cultural sphere or in communal affairs. All of them were encompassed within the relatively broad fold of rabbinic Judaism and accepted its basic premises, on one level or another. They erupted only with the Sabbatean movement and later in the manifold intellectual and social movements that started to emerge in early modern times and reached full development with the processes of emancipation in nineteenth-century Europe.

Some Concluding Observations on the Specificity of the Jewish Historical Experience: The Ancient and Medieval Periods

In the preceding three sections we analyzed some of the major aspects of Jewish civilization as it has crystallized in the periods of the First and Second Temples and as it has become transformed from late antiquity throughout the medieval period. We analyzed in some detail some of the most important differences between the premises of the Jewish and the two other monotheistic civilizations: Christianity and Islam.

We analyzed how the basic orientations, which constituted the core of the Jewish civilization, and their concrete cultural and institutional specifications have crystallized through the continuous encounter with other civilizations—first with the surrounding pagan ones in the period of the Second

Temple, some of which, especially the Hellenistic and the Roman ones already evinced strong universalistic orientations characteristic of Axial civilizations. Later on with the Christian one—and, of course, were greatly influenced by the attitudes of these civilizations to the Jewish one. This was especially true in the Medieval-exilic period when the Jews, politically and economically, were dependent on their host civilizations.

Throughout our analysis we have provided numerous illustrations for our main contention: that the best way to understand the Jewish historical experience, in civilizational terms, is to look at Jewish history as the history of a civilization in the meaning used throughout this analysis, and not only as the history of a people or a religion. Only from such a point of view is it possible to begin at least to understand the great riddle of that historical experience, its continuity.

Throughout the periods of ancient history, the periods of the First and Second Temples, many kingdoms, including the kingdom of Israel, were destroyed and many peoples were exiled. Most, probably all, of these kingdoms or states have disappeared. The same on the whole is true of most of the exiled people, although some have survived as small ethnic or linguistic enclaves. Only the remnants of the Kingdom of Judea who came back to Eretz Israel from the Babylonian Exile were able to recreate both a political, as well as a national and religious Jewish entity—the carriers of which saw themselves as continuing the ancient Israelite, or rather Judean, entity. This continuity can be understood only by realizing that the leaders of this reconstruction saw themselves, to use our terminology, as carriers of a distinct civilizational vision, even if, of course, they did not employ them then. Their conception of their collective identity and their religious experience was couched in terms of such a vision; that is, in terms of attempts to construct a specific type of social and political model in line with their conception of transcendental reality, with its strong universalistic orientation.

This vision, in their eyes, had a validity beyond the confines of their own community, potentially a universal validity. By virtue of these claims to such validity, the ancient Israelites and the Jewish community defined itself, as we have seen, in political and religious terms alike. At the same time there did not exist within this community, as among most of the nations of antiquity, a total identity between these components of collective identity. Rather, these components coexisted in continuous tension with one another as they also did, in somewhat later periods, in the Hellenistic and Roman civilizations and much later in Christianity and Islam. The continuous combination and tension between these components, defined in terms of the overarching civilizational vision, was transmitted throughout different periods of Jewish history, even if the concrete definitions of these components, as well as the concrete religious practices, beliefs, and orientations, changed continuously.

Here the comparison with some sects or with the many ethnic groups that crystallized in late antiquity, such as the Samaritans, in which these components did not exist in tension and were not connected with overarching civilizational visions or with purely religious groups or sects, is very instructive. Those among these groups that did not disappear survived as small enclaves, with little impact beyond their immediate environment.

Also by virtue of these characteristics of their collective identity, as we have seen, the designation of the Jews as a pariah people is basically inadequate and even wrong. Late antiquity and the Middle Ages have witnessed far-reaching transformations with respect to the fate of vanquished peoples and religions. Whereas, many have disappeared, of course, others have survived as ethnic or religious minorities or enclaves within the framework of broader civilizations, to a much greater extent than in earlier times. Many of them indeed have become some sort of marginal or pariah people. Others managed to maintain even some sort of marginal or collective political existence. In comparison with most such groups that developed within the framework of the Hellenistic-Roman and, above all, the Christian and Muslim civilizations, the specificity of the Jewish historical experience stands out. The Jews lost their political independence and territorial concentration; but unlike many other groups, whose fate was similar, they never gave up the political and territorial components of their collective identity. These components were transformed not only into merely historical memories or vague futuristic hopes; such memories and hopes were closely connected with the broader civilizational vision and couched in terms of this vision, a vision that was in constant competition with the host civilization and was perceived as such by these civilizations. In their attachment to this vision, the Jews differed from the many other minorities, marginal groups, pariah peoples, even from those that maintained some political independence, in late antiquity and the Middle Ages. Indeed, this attachment of theirs to this civilizational vision, as we have seen, comprised political, primordial—ethnic or national—and religious components, which existed in a state of continuous tension that enabled the Jews to maintain the continuity of their collective existence and identity. This civilizational vision provided the framework within which all these components of a collective identity were brought together but maintained in a state of continuous mutual tension in the specific ways that distinguished the Jewish from other civilizations.

The Historical Experiences of the Three Monotheistic Civilizations and the Impact of Heterodoxies: Some Comparative Observations

These basic institutional and cultural contours of the Jewish medieval civilization, like all Axial Age civilizations, were shaped by the interplay among the different constellations of cultural orientations analyzed earlier, their carriers and their respective visions of restructuring the world, and the concrete arenas and historical conditions in which such visions could be concretized. The different combinations of these two sets of conditions, the "cultural" or "civilizational" and the structural and ecological ones, have been most important in shaping the broad institutional contours and dynamics of the different post-Axial Age civilizations. It might be worthwhile now to compare the Jewish, Christian, and Muslim civilizations, which we began in the preceding chapter, concentrating now on their respective historical experiences, especially on the relations between the basic ontological conceptions prevalent in them and the institutional, especially political and cultural, dynamics that developed within them.

One central focus of such dynamics has been in all these civilizations the tendency to the development of heterodoxies and to the confrontation between orthodoxies and heterodoxies.

Such confrontations were not purely intellectual or theological—they entailed visions of the proper institutional order, and hence also very intensive political struggle focused on the attempts to institutionalize such consceptions and on the right of different groups to be the gatekeepers of this order.

Many of these struggles were focused on two closely related problems, namely the identification of the proper areana for the implementation of the basic transcendental vision of these civilizations, and of the accountability of rulers and the nature of the groups who could call, or at least attempt to call the rulers into account. But whereas such a conception and groups developed in all these civilizations, they differed greatly in the basic criteria of accountability of rulers and the specification of institutional loci and processes through which such accountability could be effected.

The different ways in which the concern with accountability of rulers developed in these civilizations was closely related first of all to the basic ontological conceptions of the nature of the chasm between the transcendental and the mundane spheres and of the ways of bridging this chasm; that is, to the different implementations of the transcendental vision, conceptions of salvation, or equivalent terms that were prevalent in these different civilizations. These civilizations, on the one hand, strongly emphasized that there is a sharp discrepancy between the ideal order, as prescribed or envisaged by their transcendental visions, by the commandments of God, by the ideals of cosmic harmony or the like, and the mundane order as constructed by the exigencies of social and political life and by the vagaries of human nature, often guided by purely utilitarian conditions or considerations of power or raison d'etat. On the other hand, however, concern developed within the reflexive traditions of these civilizations about how to overcome this chasm between the ideal and the mundane order, how to bring the two more closely together. The nature of such concern differed greatly among these civilizations, in close relation to the different ontological visions and different conceptions of the soteriological meaning of various mundane activities that developed within them.[21]

Some civilizations, especially the "otherworldly" one like the Hinduistic and Buddhist, tended to develop a certain basic skepticism with respect to the very possibility of attaining such goals, although even here extreme millenarian utopian sects always developed that attempted to create some "Kingdom of Heaven" on earth. Ancient Greece and in China, with their very strong this-worldly orientations (albeit with a much stronger emphasis in Greece on the political arena and activities as the major focus of concretization of such orientations), tended to develop much stronger emphasis on the possibilities of some concrete ways of bridging the ideal and the existing, real, mundane social order, searching for some ways to bring the two orders more closely together at least.

Thus, in the Greek and Hellenistic traditions, and with the very strong emphasis on reason (logos) as the governing principle of the universe, the discrepancy between the transcendental and the mundane orders was not emphasized so strongly as either in the otherworldly or monotheistic civilizations. Even here, however, the very development of the Platonic vision attested the recognition of such chasm, while at the same time the search for understanding the concrete ways in which different social, or rather sociopolitical, orders, including the potentially best ones, are constituted and operate, formed a large part of social and political inquiry that developed in Greece and Rome. This type of inquiry became most fully epitomized in the work of Aristotle, which has become, as is well known, an important component of the later (both Medieval and modern) Western tradition of political-social inquiry.[22]

In China the legalists viewed human nature, and the possibility of bringing it into harmony with the cosmic order, rather pessimistically, stressing the necessity of "total" regulation of behavior of the population by the rulers. At the same time the predominant Confucian schools developed a more optimistic view of human nature and the cosmos in general, and hence emphasized the importance of cultivating the moral qualities of rulers and subjects alike. Within the Confucian tradition a continuous tension indeed developed between the search for an ideal moral order in full harmony with the transcendental cosmic vision, as against the realities—often rather grim—of the existing political order.[23]

Above all the monotheistic religions or civilizations, because of interweaving within them of the worldly and otherworldly conceptions of salvation, were more complicated. They were more complicated because of the continuous tensions between an ontology that emphasized a very strong chasm between transcendental and social order with an almost unbridgeable chasm between them and, indeed as a sort of "other side" of these ontologies, intensive searches for at least some ways to bridge the gap between the transcendental and mundane orders and bring them more closely together.[24]

Whatever the basic attitude prevalent in any of these civilizations to the possibility of overcoming the chasm between the transcendental and the mundane order, some search for ways to bridge this chasm—and how to implement the transcendental visions developed in all of them. Such a search, in these civilizations, was most fully articulated and promulgated by some of the sectarian movements and heterodoxies; by different utopian movements that developed in these societies, which often challenged the existing orthodoxy. But such utopias and heterodoxies differed greatly among these different civilizations, and these differences have greatly influenced the conceptions of accountability of rulers in these civilizations. The impact of these conceptions on the political dynamism of these civilizations could be seen most clearly in the ways in which major heterodoxies became interwoven with sociopolitical movements in the different civilizations.

In the otherworldly civilizations (Hinduism and Buddhism) in which the political arena was not viewed as a major soteriological arena, the major utopias, promulgated by the major sectarian movements that developed within them, were oriented against those institutional solutions that seemed to be compromising the negation, the renunciation, of the mundane world; and they were very strongly oriented to reconstruction of the inner experience of the believer.

The mode of utopias, their eschatological visions and conceptions of accountability of rulers, and the characteristics of sectarian movements that were the bearers of these utopias developed in an opposite direction in the monotheistic civilizations in which the political arena was seen as one arena of salvation—but only one, even if in some cases or historical periods as the central arena. Jewish, Christian, and Islamic utopias and sects, in their basic orientations, have shared strong tendencies to develop some vision of a new political and, to some extent social, order based on a combination of the reconstruction of the basic ontology with that of political and social centers.

These different soteriological conceptions have greatly influenced the different conceptions of accountability of rulers and the political dynamics that have developed in these civilizations. But the political dynamics that developed in these civilizations can be understood only if we also take into account the specification of the institutional processes and arenas through which such accountability could be effected.

Such specification was closely related to two other dimensions of the respective ontological visions and visions of social order prevalent in these civilizations, dimensions that cut across different soteriological orientations. The first such dimension is the conception of membership in the community and especially the access of the members of the community, first, to the sacred, soteriological arena and, second, to the political centers of the community—the two not always being the same. The second such dimension, closely related to the first, but not identical with it, is the relative importance, to follow Rainer Baum's distinction, of an "ex-toto" as against an "ex-parte" conception of the social order.[25] The combination of these dimensions with the soteriological conceptions has greatly influenced some of the major characteristics of the centers and center-periphery relations of the different Axial Age civilizations and the conceptions of accountability of rulers that developed within them.

With respect to the first dimension, of special importance was whether the access to the sacred, or to the political center, was open directly to all members of the community (however defined) and on what terms or whether it was mediated by some group or category of people which had some sort of monopoly over such access. Both in Judaism and Islam a very strong emphasis developed on the direct access of all members of the community to the sacred, the religious centers—albeit, as we have seen, combined with different conceptions of the relations between God and man, highly contractual in Judaism and based on total submission to God in history in Islam. In close relation to these last conceptions there developed in Judaism a much stronger tendency than in Islam to direct access of all members of the community to the political center.

The fullest combined ideological and institutional manifestation of the autonomous access to the political center of all members of a community crystallized in the concept of citizenship. This concept was incipient in many tribal traditions, and it first developed fully in ancient Greece and Rome, then become transposed in a greatly transformed way in the West, in Europe.[26] The crux of this transformation was the move from the direct participation of all citizens in the central political arena to the development of representative institutions. These institutions were rooted in many tribal traditions, such as the tribal assembly depicted in the sagas; and they were transformed first in the feudal age and later in the development of modern territorial state.[27] Only in some of the Italian city-states of the Renaissance, however, were attempts undertaken to revive some of the institutional traditions of the city-states of antiquity, giving rise to one major tradition of modern political discourse: the Republican one.[28]

At the other pole, from the point of view of the institutional location of accountability of rulers, were those Axial Age civilizations in which there developed potentially—only potentially because, given the level of development of communication technology, the centers could not permeate the periphery even if they wanted to—"uninhibited" or partially inhibited centers that were conceived both as the bearers and embodiments of the transcendental vision and that controlled the access of the periphery to itself. Such a center could be like in Tsarist Russia a purely imperial center or some combination, like in China, of an imperial one combined with autonomous but relatively exclusive bureaucracy and groups of literati,[29] that has enabled autonomous access to the overall cultural community but not to the political center.

In Indian civilization a strong emphasis developed on the mediation of the access to the sacred centers by the Brahmins and to the political one by the Kshatrya. As the political center was not seen as the major soteriological arena, however, its ideological reach—insofar as it was not connected with the priestly one—was not very deep beyond the ritual arena, and the actual access to it was relatively flexible.

There exists, of course, a close elective affinity between an ex-toto conception of social order and "monopolistic" control of all access to the center. But an ex-toto conception of social order also can exist together with a conception of general, universalistic membership of the community and access to the center. This was the case in Islam and also to some extent in many contemporary Latin American countries. Such a combination often gives rise to rather very volatile political dynamics.

The pattern of political dynamics and sectarianism in Islam was closely related to Islam's basic drive to create a civilization with its own specific premises, of which one crucial aspect was the conflation of the political and religious communities (in which military conquests constitute an important element) as expressed in the ideal of the ummah. Truly enough, from relatively early periods in the formation and expansion of Islam, the possibility of attaining the ideal fusion between the political and the religious community of constructing the movement as a basic tenet of Islam actually was given up, although never fully. Instead, the mainstream of Islamic (Sunni) religious thought stressed the legitimacy of the Muslim community and any ruler who assures the peaceful existence of this community.[30]

Paradoxically enough this de facto giving up of the possibility of the idea of the ummah occurred side by side with the final crystallization of this universalistic ideology, which took place with the so-called Abbasid revolution. This revolution, which as M. Sharon has shown was connected with a shift in the legitimation of rulers from direct descent from the Prophet and consensus of the community to seniority legitimized by the fulfillment of the Prophet's will.[31] In parallel with the institutionalization of this universalistic vision, a de facto separation developed between the political and religious elite groups, only partially legitimized by the religious leadership—as shown by H. Gibb and more recently by I. Lapidus.[32] At the end of the Abbasid period the phenomenon of soldier-slaves and military rulers first became prominent. This was also connected, at least during relatively "quiet" periods, to a relatively strong segregation between this-worldly and otherworldly activities, with a generally stronger emphasis on the latter.

The historical spread of Islam also was connected with a strong dissociation between the political and the religious elite groups, as well as with a strong ideological dissociation between the universal community of Islam and the various primordial ones and between these elite sectors and the local community. The religious elite enjoyed a high degree of symbolic autonomy—but only minimal organizational autonomy.[33] The religious leadership was dependent on the rulers and did not develop into a broad independent and cohesive organization. Religious functionaries were not organized as a separate entity, nor did they constitute a tightly organized body—except when, as in the Ottoman Empire, they were organized by the state. But a strong latent orientation toward unifying state and religion always prevailed in Islam. Because of these historical processes, only under very special circumstances did imperial regimes develop in Islam.

The combination of religious elite groups and the relationship between elite groups and local ascriptive communities, which developed along with the spread and institutionalization and expansion of Islam, gave rise, in imperial and patrimonial systems alike, to a unique type of ruling group, most closely connected with the specific type of Islamic patrimonial sultanism. These military-religious rulers emerged from tribal and sectarian elements and developed the system of military-slavery that created new channels of mobility—the gulam ("Youngsters recruited to service") system in general, and the Mameluke system and Ottoman deruishime in particular—through which the ruling groups could recruit new members from alien elements.[34]

Therefore, the relative prevalence of the sultanic patrimonial regime was due not to the persistence of traditional "tribal" elements, but to the internal dynamics of the institutionalization and expansion of Islam. Hence these regimes manifested several important characteristics that distinguish them from other "traditional" patrimonial regimes in Southeast Asia or the early Near East, just as the Islamic imperial regimes also evinced some very specific characteristics. A central clue to understanding these specific characteristics is that, despite the de facto impossibility of institutionalizing the ummah, Islam continued to aspire toward the unification of the religious and political spheres and elite sectors.

The reconstruction of this unity constituted a continuous ideal with far-reaching repercussions on the political and religious development of Islam, and it was the source of some of the most far-reaching differences from other civilizations. Its repercussions on the social and political dynamics of Islamic civilization can be seen in several crucial manifestations.

First of all is the politics of ruler accountability and the patterns of political organization in most Islamic regimes. On a purely symbolic level, the rulers were supposed to uphold the ideal of the ummah and be accountable to it; but this ideal was surrendered quite early in the history of Islam and replaced by theological acceptance of any ruler as preferable to anarchy.[35] Because the religious leadership was not organized into a separate hierarchy independent of the rulers and because the broader strata had no autonomous ascriptive base of access to the center, political participation was relatively limited, confined mostly to court cliques and the bureaucracy—or to sectarian outbursts. The various religious sects and popular movements that developed in these states did not provide effective checks on political authority, as revolt was the only machinery for change. In stable Islamic societies, then, there were few effective routine checks, religious or otherwise, on the authority of rulers. At the same time, however, the religious leaders, the ulema and the sufi-sheikhs, were the keepers of the law and, through it, of the boundaries of the community. They thus were an indispensable partner in coalition with the rulers.

The fact that this vision, this ideal of the ummah was never given up and the impact of the continuity of this utopian vision of the original Islamic ideal—the fact that this ideal was both never fully implemented and never fully given up—became evident in some specific characteristics of the political dynamism of Islamic regimes and sects. These dynamics very often were imbued with a very strong religious dimension or vision, as could especially be seen in the potentially strong "semirevolutionary" sectarian activities oriented to religious-political change, as well as in Islam's initial patterns of expansion and the constitution of its international system.

True, within Islam there never developed, as Bernard Lewis has shown, a concept of revolution.[36] But at the same time, as Ernest Gellner indicated in his interpretation of Ibn Khaldoun's work, a less direct yet very forceful pattern of accountability of rulers arose, manifest in the possibility of rulers being deposed by the combination of sectarian groups with the resurgence of tribal revival against "corrupt" or weak regimes.[37] These tendencies were related to the nature of Islamic sects and potential heterodoxies, which played such an important role in its history, and to the place of such sectarianism in the expansion of Islam.

At the core of these special traits of the Islamic sects was the importance of the political dimension in their basic religious orientation. This dimension could be oriented toward active participation in the center, its destruction or transformation, or toward a conscious withdrawal from it—a withdrawal that, as in the case of Sufism and Shi'ism, often harbored potential political reactivation. Thus the political orientation was potentially inherent in any Islamic religious setting and generated some of the major movements, political divisions, and problems in Islam, starting with the Shi'a. In appropriate historical circumstances it could be activated by new and dynamic political elements.

A very important characteristic of Islamic societies was that the internal sectarian political impact often was connected with the problem of the expansion of Islam and especially with the continuous impingement on Islamic politics of tribal elements who presented themselves as the carriers of the original ideal Islamic vision and of the pristine Islamic polity. This tendency was closely related to the famous cycle depicted by Ibn Khaldoun: the cycle of tribal conquest motivated by internal solitary and religious devotion, giving rise to the conquest of cities and settlement in them, followed by the degeneration of the ruling (formerly tribal) elite sector and its possible subsequent regeneration out of new tribal elements from the vast, old or new, tribal reservoirs.

Significantly enough, many tribes (e.g., the Mongols), after being converted to Islam, transformed their own "typical" tribal structures to accord with Islamic religious-political visions, and often became the symbol of pristine Islam. Thus they, along with the seemingly dormant tribes of the Arabian peninsula, become a dynamic political force in Islamic civilization, its interstate relations in general, and its social and political formations in particular.[38]

A different situation developed in the Christian civilization or civilizations, especially in the Catholic-Medieval one. The view promulgated by St. Augustine, which stressed very much the chasm between the city of God and the city of man, for a long period, was the dominant one.[39] But Christianity, from its very beginnings, contained as we have seen a very strong this-worldly orientation that became reinforced, after it became the dominant religion of the empire. Such this-worldly orientation, to some degree, became reinforced from the later Middle Ages on, possibly as Eric Voegelin indicated, even if probably in an exaggerated way, by the growing permeation of gnostic orientations into the mainstream of Christian thought against the original Augustine vision. This permeation gave rise to continuous and intensive attempts to bridge the gap between the ideal and the existing reality, and many attempts based on belief in the possibility of infusing the existing community with the ideal vision and transforming it, to have it emerge the epitome and full realization of the ideal order.[40] Therefore, indeed a major characteristic of the various heterodoxies and sects in Christianity in general but especially in the West was the fact that the alternative vision they carried usually comprised a very strong this-worldly component, a very strong orientation to restructuring and controling the political and cognitive arenas and a strong predilection to enter into coalition with movements of social and political protest.

This was very closely related also to the characteristics of orthodoxies in the West: first to the existence of some type of organized church that attempts to monopolize at least the religious sphere and usually also the relations of this sphere to the political powers; and second, to the attempt by the Church to promulgate and regulate doctrines, according to clear, cognitive criteria and to counteract boundaries of the realm of cognitive discourse. This tendency to promulgation and regulation of doctrine was rooted in the prevalence, within the monotheistic civilizations in general and Christianity with its strong connections to the Greek philosophical heritage in particular, of a strong orientation to the cognitive elaboration of the relations between God, humankind, and the world. This tendency became closely related to the fact that, in all these monotheistic religions, with their strong interweaving of this- and otherworldly orientations that developed within the activities in the mundane world, the reconstruction of the mundane world was seen, even if in different degrees, as at least one focus of salvation or implementation of the transcendental vision. Hence the proper designation of such activities became a focus of central concern and contention between the ruling orthodoxies and the numerous heterodoxies that developed within them.

Throughout the Middle Ages, and even later on in the Catholic tradition of the Counterreformation, the heterodox anti-Augustinian tendencies were hemmed in by the basic, official, mainstream recognition of the chasm, as it were, or at least the basic discrepancy between the ideal order as envisaged by the transcendental vision and the actual, existing social and political order or orders.[41] This view was espoused by the Church and also by most political authorities, both attempted very strongly to bracket out the utopian and eschatological orientations from the political avenue.

The tensions in the basic premises and orientations were common to all parts of Christianity, as were the basic institutional arenas in which these tensions were played out: state-church relations, monastic organizations and orders, family and community. But the concrete way in which these basic tensions were played out varied greatly in the different parts of Christianity and within each of them in different historical periods. In Europe, especially in Western and Central Europe, they worked out in a rather specific way, greatly influenced by several basic historical and political-ecological aspects of the development of European civilizations.

Among the most important such historical aspects of the European historical experience was the prevalence in Europe of a multiplicity of cultural orientations that developed out of several traditions: the Judeo-Christian, the Greek, and the various tribal ones. This multiplicity greatly reinforced the tendency to the multiplicity and complexity in the ways of resolving the tensions between the transcendental and mundane orders, through either worldly (political and economic) or otherworldly activities.[42] Concomitantly these different cultural traditions were not structured in hierarchically organized segments but were in a state of continuous interaction and competition. Thus, for instance, in contradistinction to the Byzantine Empire, several orientations rooted in tribal traditions, such as equality of access to the sacred and the centers of power, were much more strongly articulated in Europe.

Among the economic, structural, and political aspects, of crucial importance is the type of structural pluralism that developed in Europe.[43] This pluralism was characterized above all by a strong combination of low (but continuously increasing) levels of structural differentiation with the continuously changing boundaries of different collectivities and frameworks. The combination of the multiplicity of the cultural traditions and the concomitant modes of resolving the tension between transcendental and mundane order, within these structural and political-ecological traditions, explains why in Western and Central Europe, perhaps even more than in other Christian civilizations, continuous tensions developed between hierarchy and equality, between the strong commitment and autonomous access of different groups and strata to the religious and political orders, on the one hand, and the emphasis on the mediation of such access by the Church or political powers, on the other. Closely related to this was the tension between quality and hierarchy as basic dimensions of participation in the political and religious arenas.

The combination of the multiplicity of symbolic models and structural conditions generated several basic institutional characteristics of "traditional" Western European civilization, that distinguish it from other Axial Age (including Christian) civilizations. This distinctiveness is epitomized in the crystallization of rather specific definitions of the political arena and the rules regulating the political arena and its dynamics, in the patterns of legitimation of authority, and in the structure of the center, center-periphery relations, and the major collectivities that developed in Western and Central Europe.

Not only was that the construction of political arenas conceived as one major possible way of bringing together the transcendental and the mundane orders, as the major arenas of implementation of the transcendental ontological vision; for this was also the case, even in a more pronounced way, in Islam. In Europe unlike in Islam, however, this arena (as well as most collectivities) was defined, very much under the combined influence of Greek philosophy and of the basic sociological conceptions of Christianity, as a distinct ontological entity.[44]

The impact of such definition could be seen in some crucial aspects of the institutional formations and dynamics of Europe. Thus the patterns of legitimation of political order that developed in Europe were characterized by a tension and continuous oscillation and separation between the sacred, primordial, and civil dimensions of legitimation in different arenas of social life and by a strong tendency for collectivities to define themselves mainly in primordial terms, the Church to define itself in purely sacred ones, and so on. On the other hand, however, each collectivity and center also attempted to arrogate all the different symbols of legitimation for itself. The combination of these two tendencies was closely connected with a continuous restructuring of the boundaries of the major collectivities—primordial, political, and religious—and the relations among them, giving rise to continual conflict.

These patterns of legitimation and structuring of collectivities also were related to the structure of centers and center-periphery relations that developed in Western and Central Europe. In common with imperial societies, China, the Byzantine Empire, Western and Central European societies were always characterized by a relatively strong commitment, by center groups and the periphery alike, to common "ideals" or goals; the center permeated the periphery to mobilize support for its policies, and the periphery impinged on the center to influence the shaping of its contours. Contrary to imperial societies, however, Europe developed multiple centers: political, religious, and regional. But the mere existence of multiple centers, and especially multiple political centers, is not unique to Europe. It can be found, as we have seen, in India as well. What distinguishes the European experience is not the multiplicity of centers, but certain characteristics of this multiplicity.

These different centers did not coexist in a sort of adaptive symbiosis, as in India and to a smaller degree in Islam, with the religious legitimizing the political, and the political providing the religious with protection and resources, while they battled with each other over the relative terms of this adaptation. In Europe these multiple centers and subcenters, as well as the different collectivities, tended to become arranged in a complicated but never unified rigid hierarchy, in which no center was clearly predominant, but in which many of them aspired not only to actual but also to ideological predominance and hegemony. Accordingly, different centers and collectivities tended to struggle over their relative standing in such hierarchy, and the centers were continuously changed and restructured.

Various movements of protest and heterodoxy have played a very important role in the reconstruction of the various centers and collectivities. This was so because many movements were oriented to the reconstruction of the political arena—or, in other words, such reconstruction constituted, in marked difference from the Indian case for instance, a very important component in their orientations.

In close relation to the place of such heterodoxies in the processes of reconstruction of the centers, many of these centers aimed at universal expansion that would encompass all the other centers and communities. Such expansion often was legitimized in religious and ideological terms, often giving rise to wars of religion or to ideological wars.

Hence European political dynamics were characterized by strong tendencies to continuous expansion and consolidation of territorially, ideologically compact units and by a continuous tension between such different centers and collectivities and their respective leaders, potentially giving rise to a very fierce struggle between them. Given the political-ecological pluralism of the European civilization, however, these also could develop into some peaceful coexistence between such centers.

Throughout the Middle Ages the relative segregation between the political centers and heterodoxies persisted. It started to crumble with the Reformation and Counterreformation and with the great revolutions of modernity. With the Great Rebellion (or Civil War) in England, with the American and French Revolutions, the political realm became imbued with a strong religious—often very strongly utopian, eschatological, and millenarian—orientation that later became transformed in a more secular direction in the Enlightenment and in the French Revolutions.

The Jewish Historical Experience in Medieval Times in a Comparative Framework: Heterodox Potentials and the Sovereignty of the Court

The Jewish historical experience, especially after the destruction of the Temple, differed greatly from that of the other monotheistic civilizations. The "external" facts of this experience are well known: loss of political independence, territorial dispersion, continuous migration and concomitant shifts in the centers of their territorial existence, and the continuous struggle for survival in alien, usually hostile, always ambivalent, environments. Already these basic facts make the Jewish historical experience unique among the different civilizations. But the full import of these seemingly external facts on the Jewish historical experience, on the possibility of implementing their civilizational vision, can be understood only if one examines the impact of these facts on the working out of the ideological and institutional implications of the basic premises of Jewish civilization. We earlier analyzed most of these implications and now bring them together only to emphasize the differences of the Jewish historical experience from that of other civilizations.

The first such implication was that these very facts of eternal existence—the dispersion, exile, the loss of political independence, the hostile relations with the environment that generated the possibilities of martyrdom—have become major ideological themes, major components of Jewish collective identity. The second such implication, as we have seen, was the narrowing of the scope of the institutional arenas in which their civilizational vision could be implemented to those of communal arrangements, to study, prayer, and ritual; and to various intellectual endeavors. The possibility of implementing this vision in the political and other mundane arenas, the possibility of actively participating in world history, was transposed into the Messianic future. At the same time, wide-ranging transnational, transcommunal networks emerged among the Jewish communities, providing continuous frameworks of solidarity and common endeavors.

In the Jewish tradition, the discrepancy between the ideal, transcendental and the given mundane order and attempts to reconstruct such order according to utopian solariological visions was quite strongly emphasized in the periods of political independence: especially in the period of the Second Commonwealth. Later on, after the destruction of the First Temple and the Babylonian Exile and especially after the destruction of the Second Temple, given the special historical circumstances of the Jewish people (their dispersion and lack of political independence), the concrete, actual political dimension of the transcendental and utopian visions became subdued among the Jews, although certainly it did not disappear, and reemerged after the expulsion from Spain.

In the long period of the Babylonian Exile the attempts to bridge the tension between the given, mundane order and the ideal one were transposed to the future, stressing the difference between the existing reality in exile, devoid in itself of any ultimate meaning and the Messianic future. But the attempts to bridge such tensions in the present would erupt from time to time in Messianic movements—above all in the greatest of them, the Sabbatean one of the seventeenth century.[45]

This did not mean that the various attempts with their heterodoxical potential to bridge over this temporal gap did not develop in Medieval Jewish civilization; rather, as we already have seen, on the whole, they were hemmed within the halakhic framework. These heterodox potentials were greatly reinforced by some components of the Jewish political tradition that crystallized in the earlier period and continued albeit in a transformed way in the Medieval period. Among the most important such components of the Jewish political tradition was that of principled political anarchism.

What is meant by *principled political anarchism*? I do not mean the tendency, which well may be found in most human societies, to attempt to avoid the demands of the law or develop an instrumental or adaptive relation to it. True, such a tendency naturally has been reinforced among the Jews by the long historical experience of being an oppressed minority under alien rule. At the same time, however, a countertendency developed among the Jews to accept and legitimize the law of the land as their only protector. The principle of Dina di-malkhuta dina (the law of the kingdom is the law) has acquired important halakhic standing. These tendencies indeed are important for our topic; but their full import can be understood only when we combine them with other, more principled attitudes to the law that developed within the Jewish civilization. One is the tendency, articulated by some groups, to deny the validity of the law of the land—particularly that of any independent state ruled by Jews—in the name of some higher, often divine law (which, obviously, is represented by these very groups).

The concrete expression of this tendency obviously depended very much on concrete historical constellations—be they internal, external, or some mixture thereof. Moreover, such principled expressions often may be only an ideological mask for concrete interests and demands. Yet these are not enough to explain the specificity and intensity of these expressions, because in other societies similar circumstances do not necessarily give rise to such extreme ideological expressions.

This tendency is rooted in central aspects of Jewish civilization that we analyzed in the preceding chapters, some of which have been seen as the Jews' distinct contribution to human civilization (see, for example, Michael Walzer's recent book, *Exodus and Revolution*).[46] To some degree this emphasis on a higher law and the concomitant tendency to principled political anarchism is not limited to Jewish civilization: it is a central component of all the monotheistic civilizations, of which the Jewish was the first one; and even of other "great civilizations," especially the so-called Axial Age civilizations analyzed previously.

In the Jewish civilization, this tendency to uphold a higher law probably arose during the First Temple period—the period of the Judges, priests, Levites, elders, and Prophets—and developed further during the Second Commonwealth—when the new element of experts in learning, study, and prayer, the precursors of the talmudic sages, as well as the various sects, appeared on the scene. This tendency toward principled political anarchism occupied center stage in Jewish public life during the Second Temple period and immediately thereafter.[47]

This tendency was reinforced by two components of the Jewish religion that distinguish it from Christianity and Islam, the other monotheistic religions and civilizations. The Jewish religion, as distinct from Catholicism and to some degree from Eastern Christianity, does not accord one group a monopoly on access to the sacred. During the Second Commonwealth, even the priests, despite their high standing, had a monopoly only on rituals, but not on legal exegesis or prayer, which spread as the major modes of religious experience and access to the realm of the sacred. In principle, all members of the "holy community" created by God's covenant with the people of Israel had access to this realm, with the partial exception of access to the Temple ritual. Hence, all could claim a basic equality. There was no Pope or Church in Israel (although under appropriate conditions of concentration of power, the representatives of each of the "elite" groups—the exilarchs, groups of rabbis, the priests, or the keepers of "holy places"—would willingly have assumed such a position). Even Maimonides, the towering figure of Medieval Jewry, was never fully accepted as the ultimate authority; indeed, he was criticized for attempting to be such an authority.

In contrast to Islam, which in principle also recognizes no mediators, the Jewish emphasis on the covenant between God and the people of Israel means that the relation to God is not one of total submission (as the very name of Islam connotes). As against such total submission, the covenant implied some sort of partnership, albeit between obviously unequal partners. Jewish folklore, from the Midrash down to Levi Yitzhak of Berditchev and then to Sholem Aleichem's Tevia, is full of stories in which God seemingly is called to account.

The combination of all these factors—the belief in a higher law, the weakness of mediating groups, and the covenantal relation between God and the people of Israel—explains the development within the Jewish political tradition of tendencies toward principled political anarchism. Indeed, some of the most prominent and revered figures in Jewish history, such as the Prophets, were among the exponents of this very strong political—and not purely intellectual—orientation, as their very apt characterization by Max Weber as political demagogue attests to.

The mention of the prophets, the priests, and the elders of the community brings us to what is probably the most crucial aspect of our analysis: the problem of the social forces or groups through which cultural orientations, intellectual dispositions, and ideologies become articulated. Cultural orientations and ideologies are important, but they are not enough to explain institutional behavior.

I mentioned earlier (in the first section this chapter) the idea of the mandate of heaven in China. It was a very important ideal, but had relatively weak institutional underpinnings as compared with other Axial civilizations. Except for the astrologers and censors, few institutional bases existed in China to counter the strong tendencies to imperial autocracy.[48] True enough, when Chinese political dynamics are compared, for instance, with those of Japan, where no conception of a higher law existed and the Emperor-God could be killed but not called to account, they do show the importance of even such weak institutional underpinnings.[49]

Some of the social and institutional characteristics of both ancient Israelite and Jewish society developed from the very beginning of Jewish history, which can explain the concretization of these strong tendencies toward principled political anarchism. Indeed we already analyzed most of these; here we recapitulate and elaborate on those most relevant for the point of view of our present analysis.

Thus, throughout Jewish history some aspects of the structure of the elite and center groups evinced an amazing continuity of "formal," yet in many ways crucial, characteristics. First, a multiplicity of autonomous elite groups developed, particularly carriers of models of cultural and social order. Second, all of them developed a strong orientation toward the mundane, especially in the political and social arenas. The distinction between religious and other functions was not sharp; even when a particular elite group specialized in one arena, it maintained strong orientations toward the other arenas. Third, although the elite groups generally had no permanent single center or organization, they maintained an identity and continuity of orientation and networks and continuously emerged anew, albeit in changed organizational constellations. Fourth, great heterogeneity developed within all these elite groups, such as the priests and the Prophets. At the same time, there were conflicts and tensions between these elite groups and subelite groups, connected not only with the representation of different specific interests but also with different interpretations of the tradition and different emphases on its major components: cultic, legal, and ethical. Fifth, they all competed for acceptance as the representatives of the higher authority to which rulers and community were accountable.

Of course the concrete characteristics of these various elite groups (political, social, or religious) varied greatly, as we have seen, in the different periods of Jewish history. But the basic structural characteristics just indicated continued throughout Jewish history, and in the long period of exile from the end of late antiquity throughout the Middle Ages.

This continuity in some aspects of the characteristics of the elites was closely related to the fact that these elites continued to transmit, develop, and elaborate the same cultural orientations and basic conceptions of the social order through their educational, cultural, and communal activities. The most important orientations included the stress on open and unmediated access to the sacred and the parallel denial of mediation, denoting the covenantal relationship between God and His chosen people, Israel, from which the tendency to principled political anarchism developed. They emphasized legal exegesis, Torah study, and communal responsibility. Given this continuity in the structure of elite sectors and cultural orientation, the tendency to principled political anarchy also continued.

Needless to say, the tendency to principled political anarchism weakened during the long period of the Babylonian Exile and Diaspora, when most political activity was limited to the "domestic" realm and took place within territorial boundaries and political and legal frameworks established by other institutions. It should be noted, however, that even in that period consensus was not complete. Many older elements that could challenge the boundaries of Jewish collective identity established by Medieval Halakhah, especially negation of the political orientation and postponement of

Judaism's claim to universalism, could be found in various movements, including Messianic, philosophical, agnostic, and Kabbalistic movements.

In principle all these could have become the nuclei of heretical trends, heterodoxies, and secessionist movements. Such nuclei did develop during the first centuries after the destruction of the Temple and persisted in parts of the Near East, in the Christian and Islamic civilizations and also in the Jewish one. Later on, however, most of them became either marginal to the mainstream of halakhic Judaism, which for the first time in the history of Jewish civilization emerged as a full-fledged orthodoxy, or had a subterranean existence within this fold.

Yet, as we have seen, the potential for heterodoxy did exist, even if latently, within the heritage of Medieval Judaism. In fact, however, only a few real heterodoxies developed within Judaism. The most articulate were the Karaites, who appeared in Eretz Israel and the Near East in the second half of the eighth century. As we have seen, they denied the validity of the Oral Law and attempted to go back only to the Written Law, the Torah. It perhaps is no accident that they appeared at the very period when the Oral Law had become fully implemented as the dominant orthodoxy; and only with the beginnings of the disintegration of the hegemony of the Oral Law in the seventeenth century did the second great heterodoxy, the Sabbatean one, appear. But, on the whole, from the emergence of Karaism to modern times, heterodoxies developed neither in the religious and cultural spheres nor in communal affairs.

A similar picture—of great creativity, heterogeneity, and tensions, yet kept within common bounds—could be found as well in the major arena of Jewish civilizational creativity, in what may be called, in a very broad sense, the continuous construction, study, and elaboration of the Halakhah. Within this realm, as we have seen above, developed different emphases on different contents or dimensions of the tradition of learning and prayer—those of pure legalistic and ritual learning, those of mystical ascetic and pietistic orientation, and those of philosophical study and contemplation—as well as different schools in each of these fields. Within all of these spheres was continuous and extensive creativity, with close contacts with the host civilizations, although the relative importance of each varied in different periods and there were frequent conflicts between them.

These tensions and controversies focused on the relative importance of the different bodies of knowledge and learning in the construction of Jewish tradition and the symbolic universe of Jewish civilization. They also focused on concrete details of halakhic legislation, above all in the sphere of learning and ritual observance. There was a constant tension between the more elitist traditions of learning and the more populist traditions of prayer with an admixture of mysticism, a tension that in the eighteenth and nineteenth centuries became explicit in the division between the Hasidim and their rabbinical opponents.

All these conflicts and controversies centered on control of the institutions of learning and their curricula, as well as on the major halakhic injunctions, that is, on the construction of the symbolic and institutional boundaries of Jewish communities. These conflicts and tensions often were connected with others more closely related to communal organization and life.

The combinations of these elements and the ensuing conflicts varied greatly in different communities and different periods of history in ways that have yet to be studied systematically. The relations between the different elite groups, their patterns of cultural creativity, and the tensions between them also varied. Until the Sabbatean movement and the Emancipation, these potentially disruptive movements for the most part remained underground and marginal.

Compared with any "merely" religious or ethnic groups, the degree of cultural and institutional creativity and heterogeneity was very great indeed—belying, as we have seen, Toynbee's allegation of the Jewish Medieval civilization constituting a "fossil." This creativity and heterogeneity were due not only to the fact of dispersion, the multiplicity of local customs and influences (important as these were), but also (and perhaps above all) to the great heterogeneity of social and cultural actors and forces that existed within this civilizational framework, like those in other civilizations. Unlike their host civilizations or other far-off Axial Age civilizations like the Indian, Confucian, or Buddhist ones, however, the possibility of the concrete institutional implementation of such heterogeneous creativity was much more limited in the framework of the Jewish civilization. It was limited, first of all, because of the basic "external" facts of their existence—their dispersion, the lack of political independence and access to the political arenas of their host civilizations, the limited institutional arenas under their control—and also, perhaps above all, because of the necessity to maintain their own solidarity in face of a hostile, potentially competitive environment.

But these various potential heterodoxies, the various tendencies to principled political anarchism, were hemmed in not only because of such of dispersion. The very possibility of such hemming in was greatly reinforced by the final crystallization of another institutional component of the Jewish political tradition, the nuclei of which already existed: that of the sovereignty of the court, not only of the Law. We do not know exactly when it became fully articulated and institutionalized, possibly only after the destruction of the Second Temple, when the experience of the former period and the exigencies of the new one reinforced it.

Of course, in the Bible, especially in Deuteronomy, one already can find a strong emphasis on upholding the law. The stress on law, as we have seen, was one of the central aspects of Jewish tradition and civilization, epitomized in the figure of the great prophet and legislator Moses. Indeed, the strong emphasis on law as a way to reconstruct social life was one of the important aspects of Jewish civilization.

But Moses was the only person who was presented in this tradition: simultaneously Prophet, legislator, and political leader. In later times these functions were separate, and this diversification reinforced the potential toward principled anarchism. This potential could clash with the idea of the sovereignty of the court—any court, any legislator—just as in earlier periods, including those of the First and Second Commonwealths (all the stories about the judicial sovereignty of Sanhedrin not withstanding). I stress the tradition of the sovereignty of the court—not of the law—because the emphasis on the law always involves the problem of who is its true interpreter.

The idea of the sovereignty of the court first of all probably was oriented against the political elite sector, as exemplified in the case of the Hasmonean king Alexander Yannai (Yannaeus), who intervened for one of his aides when the aide was brought before a court. This interference gave rise to the injunction, though I have some doubts to what degree it indeed was ever upheld (especially the first part), that a "king does not judge nor is he judged." The idea of the sovereignty of the court, however, was oriented even more against prophecy, once prophecy had been codified and the end of prophecy declared. With the weakening and ultimate loss of political independence, it was above all from prophets or sects that challenges to the sovereignty of the court might be expected to arise.

The talmudic tradition is full of stories of the courts' opposition to prophecy and against the Bat Kol (echo) that claims direct, charismatic, and authentic relation to the sacred, unregulated by the court. One such story involves the Tanna Rabbi Yehoshua, who claimed, on the basis of his examination of witnesses concerning the appearance of the new moon, that Yom Kippur should fall on a certain day. His view was overruled, and Rabban Gamaliel ordered him to appear before the court with his staff and backpack on the day that, according to his reckoning, was Yom Kippur. When he hesitated to do so, his friends and colleagues argued with him that unless he complied he would undermine the authority of all the courts of Israel, starting with the court of Moses himself. Although it is probably true that this incident can be seen as part of a struggle between the Nessiim "The Exilarchs," the more secular authorities, and the scholars, the very instance of the argument and the decision are extremely significant.[50]

Throughout the Medieval period this sovereignty of the court was extremely powerful, closely related to the initial assumption that the study

and exegesis of the law constituted the central, though not the only, arena of
Jewish cultural creativity. This tradition of the sovereignty of the court within the framework of halakhic institutions and of communal arrangements (the
network of prayer, study, and legislation) together with family and community organization, provided the major mechanisms of Jewish continuity in that
period.[51] We encounter here a rather paradoxical situation: public life
became more orderly precisely when independent political power was absent
or very weak, when no state existed and no tradition of a state could develop.

The development of Jewish public communal law in this period is of
great interest. Jewish communities, as M. Elon has shown, were even able to
develop public law. He has analyzed in detail how Jewish communities in
the Middle Ages developed communal arrangements not previously recognized by the Halakhah during the eras when the Jews had enjoyed some form
of political sovereignty, as in the Second Temple period or Babylonia of the
Gaonim.[52] It should be emphasized, however, that these arrangements were
more of a communal than a state-political nature. They lacked the political
and social framework that goes beyond family and communal solidarity and
is characteristic of political independence. They did not have to face problems related to running a state nor did they bear ultimate responsibility for
enforcement of the law.

Moreover, whereas these communal arrangements and legislation were
legitimized by Halakhah, they were not, as Jacob Katz has recently shown,[53]
a natural part of the Halakhah. Public law, in distinction to ritual-religious
prescriptions and interpersonal "civil law," whether dealing with marriage or
commercial relations, was developed only weakly in the talmudic tradition.
The purely political aspects of such communal arrangements of course were
even less well developed.

Not all the rabbis and centers of learning wanted to engage in these
communal matters; they often left decisions to the representatives and leaders of the community. In the first centuries after the destruction of the Temple the heads of the yeshivot in Babylonia and Eretz Israel already were displaying a tendency to shy away from participation in communal-political
authority to be able to pursue their studies in an independent way and not to
be dependent on the communal powers or be entangled in communal conflicts.[54] Other rabbis—especially, but not only, in modern times, when they
felt threatened by the winds of tolerance and modernity—did engage in such
public activities and conflicts, as did many communal courts. The existence
of these different tendencies on their part, rooted in the basic premises of the
Jewish tradition, added to the tensions and dynamics of communal life.

In the context of these tensions, as well as of the continuous communal
problems and conflicts, a strong tradition developed of adherence to the decisions of courts in general, and to those of public communal courts and the vari-

ous takanot kahal (community regulations) in particular.[55] Thus, this tradition added a strong element of civility and acceptance the legal frame, as against the more anarchic tendencies in the life of the Jewish communities. The authority of the communal courts and the translocal organizations on the whole was upheld, thus adding, or at least reinforcing, an important component in Jewish political tradition and building on the attitudes of Jewish solidarity.

A strong emphasis on Jewish solidarity developed in the Medieval period, cutting across these two political orientations, principled political anarchism and the sovereignty of the court. I am not referring here only to the natural solidarity of various groups, even of oppressed groups, but rather to the ideologization of such solidarity into something much more principled, based on the need for mutual protection and assistance among different members of the groups, but legitimized by the fact that the group is the upholder of a special civilizational and religious vision.

The emphasis on solidarity often could be applied to the whole people, to those in need or in situations of oppression. But given the facts of Jewish existence in that period, it also could refer to any sector or group, become focused on demands for special allocations from communal funds, and could sometimes, though not always, contravene the strength of the legal tradition and the tradition of civility.

The Social Conditions of the Tradition of Sovereignty of the Court and Civility in Medieval Jewish Communities

These communal conflicts and tensions on the whole were kept within the bounds of the Jewish communities by a combination of the basic solidarity of the communities and the legal powers vested in them and their courts. The most extreme sanction was the herem (or ban), through which individuals were threatened with ostracism and even expulsion.

The combination of solidarity and legal power was continuously articulated by the tradition of communal institutions and communal courts. It also was rather limited and circumscribed, however. it was naturally limited to internal community affairs, usually to the respective localities or to such translocal arrangements as the Council of the Four Lands, and to some degree to its relations with the authorities. It did not address itself to the political institutions of a sovereign entity. The courts never faced the problems, already prominent in the First Temple period and later crucial during the Second Commonwealth and eventually in the state of Israel, of a confrontation between the law of the Jewish state and the higher authority of the Halakhah. At most they were concerned with problems of the degree of validity of Dina di-malkhuta (the law of the land), usually stressing the obligation to accept it in all secular matters.

The ultimate sanction against potential secession, the herem, was often upheld, not by internal forces, but by the authorities. Later on, in open modern societies, when the kehillot became entirely voluntary bodies, without the full sanction of the laws of the land, secessionist tendencies often became very strong.

Several crucial factors assured the containment of all these heterodox potentials within the framework of rabbinic Judaism. One was the close internal cohesion of the Jewish communities, due to a combination of internal solidarity and the maintenance of basic cultural traditions. This solidarity was rooted in the strong cohesion of the family and was extended and reinforced through the close interweaving of all the different leadership elements. Second, as mentioned earlier, many would-be apostates actually left the fold. Third, and in a way most paradoxical, the very fact of dispersion helped (as already alluded to) to maintain the internal cohesion of the communities, preserve the boundaries of the faith, and keep many within the fold. The dispersion and lack of a unified central authority provided multiple arenas for many of the more autonomous and even semianarchic elements inherent in the basic cultural and social orientations prevalent among the Jews. The same probably was true, as we have seen, in the field of learning in its broadest sense and in the sphere of Halakhah proper.

Here, too, there was no single accepted authority; different scholars and centers of learning jealously guarded the right of collegial and even individual interpretation and legislation within the common bounds of the accepted, yet constantly changing, tradition. Some of the controversy around Maimonides, the most towering intellectual figure of Medieval Jewry, focused not on his strong philosophical predilections and the concrete details of his halakhic interpretations and mode of codification, but against the possibility that he, and later his work, would attain some sort of monopoly in all these fields and close the gates of interpretation.

The decisions of one court were not necessarily binding on others, although they could serve as references and precedents. On the whole, not only in communal matters but also, as we shall see later, in halakhic matters proper, a strong emphasis developed on the relative autonomy of different courts and scholars in matters of legal interpretation.

Thus in this sphere, too, the fact of the dispersion, the lack of any single ultimate authority, combined with the numerous contacts among these communities and centers of learning, provided flexible common frameworks that allowed for some heterogeneity and different types of creativity. These limitations on the power of the courts in many ways were the source of their strength; they allowed for considerable flexibility and provided legitimate arenas for the basically apolitical, as against communal or legislative, aspects of these frameworks. But the heterodox potential, the potential of principled political anarchy, because of the factors mentioned above, could not be fully implemented within the existing institutional framework; and it led to a kind of subterranean, even if a very intensive, existence.

However, only insofar as the respective boundaries of these civilizations as envisaged in these relations were maintained, could the potentially heterodox orientations that continuously developed within the framework of the Jewish communities—as well as the changes in their economic structure and internal composition—be maintained within the framework of the halakhic mold. The continuous maintenance of this collective existence and identity therefore was predicated mainly on the attitude of the host civilizations to the Jews: an attitude of hostility and ambivalence rooted in their common historical origins, continuous mutual reference, and latent competition. But this very attitude in turn was predicated on the view of the Jews as carriers of a broad civilizational vision and not just a religious, ethnic, or national group.

The major assumptions of the civilizational perspective we have presented here are borne out by the preceding analysis of Medieval exilic Judaism. We have seen its great heterogeneity and dynamism, the tense and ambivalent attitude with its host civilizations and the continuous interactions between them, the strong continuity of the basic problems and themes of Jewish civilization and the symbols of its collective identity, together with far-reaching changes in their content, and the same combination of the basic characteristics of the elites together with changes in the nature of their concrete composition and activities.

Only in terms of such a civilizational perspective—and not by seeing the Jews as merely a religious group, a pariah people, or a fossilized civilization—can all these characteristics of Medieval Jewish life be understood. Also, only in terms of such a civilizational perspective can we understand some of the major aspects of Jewish life in modern times—assimilation, national movements, and, last but not least, the development of Israeli society. In the following chapters we shall address ourselves to some of these patterns—above all some of the distinctive characteristics of Zionism as a national movement—as well as to some of the most important characteristics of Israeli society.

4

The Disintegration of the Medieval Jewish Civilizational Framework in the Modern Period and the Integration of Jews in European Societies

The Period of Transition: Sixteenth to Eighteenth Centuries

The basic framework of the Medieval Jewish cultural and institutional framework, of the rabbinical mold, the mold of the Halakhah, started to change, and ultimately to disintegrate, with far-reaching changes in the relations of the Jewish to the surrounding civilizations. These changes attest to the crucial importance of intercivilizational relations in shaping the Jewish historical experience. Such changes started to take place in the sixteenth and seventeenth centuries.

The economic, political, and cultural changes that took place in Europe from the sixteenth through the eighteenth century became very strongly interwoven with far-reaching change in the civilizational premises of European civilization. Hence they have changed not only the specific contours of many Jewish communities, but they also started to undermine many of the basic intercivilizational relations between the Jews and their host societies. It is the combination of these processes that has signalled the potential of a far-reaching transformation of traditional Jewish societies.[1]

The historical starting point of all these changes of course was the expulsion of the Jews from Spain and Portugal, which had a very traumatic effect on Jewish collective consciousness. It also gave rise to the most intensive processes of migration and transplantation that Jewish communities experienced, in such a relatively short time, in the history of their Exile.

The Eastern European Diaspora concentrated in Poland, where the Jewish community initially had built up one of the most prosperous and well-organized Jewish centers with extensive supracommunal organizations and centers of learning. Later, this community became threatened by the infamous pogroms led by the Ukrainian leader Chmielnicki in 1648, one of the most fearful in the history of persecutions of Jews. But the effect of these traumatic events and far-reaching processes can be understood fully only if we take into account their interweaving in very intensive processes of economic, political, and cultural changes that had been taking place in Europe and the Ottoman Empire and their close relations to the civilizational premises of European civilization in this period.

Let us comment only briefly on these rather well-known processes. In the sixteenth and seventeenth centuries far-reaching changes and transformations took place in entire European economy. These transformations were composed of several interconnected processes—the rise of mercantile economies, international trade and expansion generated by the great discoveries; shifts in location of centers of economic activities, especially the shift from the relative hegemony of Mediterranean Cape routes and the Ottoman Empire—to the rise of Atlantic economies. Closely related were the great changes in the technology of communication, the invention of printing and of new modes of transportation, which greatly intensified the possibility of continuous interaction among different societies and within them.

In parallel, of course far-reaching changes were generated by the Reformation and Counterreformation, which totally transformed the place of the religious arenas in the construction of European civilization, the religious component in the definition of the collective boundaries of European societies, and the bases of legitimation of the social and political order. At the same time, and in close connection with the impact on the religious arenas proper and the development of printing and other modes of communication, new types of schools, educational systems, and cultural activities developed; and above all science and humanistic learning developed as autonomous arenas of cultural creativity. Many of these trends came together later and culminated in a way in the Enlightenment.

Closely related to the changes in the cultural arena were those in the political arena, the most important duly connected with the rise of absolutist state with the attempts to create centralized policies already based on a new mode of legitimation. Such states attempted to reorganize social life; and in conjunction with some of their cultural processes analyzed earlier, this gave rise to what Norbert Elias has called the *Civilizing Process,*[2] a process of far-reaching transformation in all the arenas of culture, in the very conception of personality, in public and private spaces, and of the relations between high and popular culture.

All these changes in the cultural and political contours of European civilization were speeded up by two additional processes: the new and continuous confrontation between Christian and Muslim civilizations as it manifested itself in the establishment and expansion of the Ottoman Empire up to the late seventeenth century; and the so-called crisis of the seventeenth century, all of them also closely connected to the emergence of the new international economic and political systems.

The upshot of all these developments was not only a series of far-reaching economic, political, and social changes, but also the transformation in the very basic premises of the European civilization. Most important in this respect was the beginning of a shift from the traditional religious definition of membership in the civilizational community and different indirect, corporate forms of membership in the political community (as manifested, for instance, in the system of estates) to that of a secular universalistic membership in the civilizational frameworks and a direct, unmediated one in the political community. All these changes had far-reaching impact on the overall intercivilizational relations between the Christian-European and Jewish civilizations.

All these developments had a far-reaching impact on the structure of the Jewish communities. These developments, as so many other changes in the fortunes of the Jews in Medieval times, gave rise within the Jewish communities to far-reaching economic changes, as well as to changes in the composition of different elite groups, in the balance of power between different elements and groups, in the structure of communal organizations, and to new patterns of cultural creativity.[3] Thus, first of all, a continuous intensification took place in various internal potentially "heterodox" trends, mysticism and philosophy, and Messianic movements, up to the Sabbatean movement. The intensification in the development of these movements, their often close relationship to one another, and their mutual impingement probably was unparalleled in Jewish history, which in itself was an important indication of potentially far-reaching changes in the structure of Jewish society and tradition.

Second, parallel to the efflorescence of these various types of cultural creativity, and in close relation with them, were far-reaching changes in the internal structure of Jewish communities. New types of cultural and lay communal leadership emerged, new types of economic entrepreneurs, as well as changes in the relation between them and traditional scholars. Moreover, under the impact of new developments in printing and education new types of educated enlightened public and audiences developed, and new patterns of interaction emerged between them and the different sections of leadership. Aided by the dissemination of printing, interaction between what might be called popular and high culture became much closer, bearing some similarities to the "process of civilization" already mentioned.

The intensity of all these changes was greatly enhanced by the intensification of contact among different Jewish communities, facilitated especially by the continuous migrations, the impact of printing and its dissemination, and technological developments in transportation. Such intensity also was enhanced by the intensification and diversification of contact of Jewish communities with their host societies, by the concomitant growing sensitivity to interreligious (Christian-Muslim) relations, and the relatively quick dissemination of the different historical experiences of different Jewish communities throughout the entire Jewish world.

In all these developments a new social element, the Marranos, Jews who were forcefully converted into Christianity, constituted a very important factor. Those among them who came back into the fold of Judaism constituted a special agent of social change and cultural fermentation; they also constituted one of the most internationally mobile groups within the Jewish communities—thus serving as an important channel of such dissemination.[4]

But the most important aspect of this new situation was that these various changes and movements became interwoven with the beginnings of the transformation of the premises of Jewish civilization, heralding the possible undermining of the prevalent religious premises and the relations between the Jewish, Christian, and Muslim civilizations. Such possibilities were enhanced by the traumatic experiences of the expulsions and the pogroms together with the transformation of the premises of European civilization. Hence, these new developments could constitute challenges to the existing premises of Jewish Medieval civilization. This was due to not only the proliferation of all these movements, but rather to the radical tendency among many of them to look for new bases of legitimation for their own activities beyond the world of the Halakhah, very often, as was the case in many Christian sects of this era, in religiously antinomian terms that challenged the traditional bases of legitimation. Such challenge often was effected by transformation of these terms into those of natural reason and in a concomitant promulgation of Messianic themes in such terms.

Thus, in many of the Jewish communities new types of tensions started to develop between new, "secular" orientations and the established religious and communal elite sectors. These tensions gave rise to strong attempts to reestablish orthodoxy or tradition, albeit in new ways, as evident in new modes of codification, as manifest above all in the Shulhan Arukh, as well as in the growth of more popular types of didactic religious literature.

These various processes to a large degree have been common to all Jewish communities in this period, but they have worked out in different ways in each of them, according to the specific historical constellations in each, giving rise to different modes of accommodation between the traditional, halakhic framework and the new forces, with each heralding some potential transformation of the basic premises of Jewish civilization.

Several broad development can be distinguished. One, the seeming forerunner of the full "crisis of tradition,"[5] can be found in the Dutch and to a smaller degree English Diaspora. Second were the well-researched developments, yet perhaps bearing a reexamination, in Central Europe (especially France) under Absolutism, forerunners of Haskalah and the beginning of Haskalah Diaspora. Third was the development of new intellectual activities and of close relations with Christian scholars in such Jewish communities in Easter Europe as Prague and Krakow in this period.

Perhaps of special importance is the impact of these processes in the Eastern European Jewish communities on the rise of Hasidism. Although this movement, of course, remained within the fold of the Halakhah, yet in fact it constituted a far-reaching transformation of the basic premises of this mold, the social structure of its elite groups, and the bases of their legitimation. However, only with the onset of modern times, with the great revolutions, the American and especially the French one, did these variant kernels of the transformation of the basic premises and institutional framework of halakhic Jewish civilization start to bear fruit.

The Modern Period: Introduction

The Opening of the Gates of European Societies

The modern era proper of Jewish history started with the opening of the gates of European society before the Jews. This opening—often slow, intermittent and yet continuous—was connected with the rise of the modern capitalist economy, the modern state, and above all a marked shift in the basic premises of European civilization. The rise of the capitalist economy and industrialism and their expansion throughout the world, but first of all in Western and Central Europe, opened up new economic opportunities. These opportunities were seized upon by the Jews, who already had started to participate, haltingly, in the first stages of the developments in Western and Central European countries, mainly in finance and large-scale trade but also to a smaller degree in manufacture.

But the impact of these changes on the whole format of Jewish life can be understood only in conjunction with another basic change, the change in the basic ideological premises of European civilization that took place with the emergence of modernity. These premises crystallized first of all in the absolutist states and later on in the great revolutions—the English, American, and above all the French one—and in the consequent social and national movements that developed in Europe throughout the nineteenth and early twentieth centuries. The shift in these premises was a triple one, even though between the three aspects of this shift there developed some significant contradictions, especially as they affected the destiny of the Jews. First of all was the shift from the traditional religious definition of membership in the civilizational European community and indirect, corporate membership in the political community to a universalistic membership based on secular criteria in the civilizational framework, and a direct, unmediated participation in the political community. This latter conception already had been promulgated to some degree by the absolutist states, but it was epitomized most fully in the French Declaration of the Rights of Man and Citizen of 1789, which declared universal rights of citizens in purely secular terms—seemingly obliterating, certainly weakening, the strong traditional-religious Christian components in the prevalent definitions of the boundaries of membership in European political communities. Despite this change, in many European countries (Germany and Scandinavia, for example) belonging to some religious community was taken for granted and embodied in law for relation. The second shift, did not always run in tandem with the first one, although the two converged in the French Revolution and in most countries of Western and Central Europe by the end of the nineteenth century. This shift concerned the weakening of the traditional legal power of rulers and their traditional legitimation. The trend stressed the right of access of all citizens to the centers of power and the reformulation of the premises of these centers in an open, modern, universalistic way. The third shift, which sometimes developed in opposition or reaction to the first two, was the emphasis on strong religious and primordial components of the new mode nation-state.[6]

All these shifts constituted a marked change in the basic premises of European civilization. The former Christian eschatology became, as we have seen, secularized and focused, especially in connection with the great revolution, the Enlightenment, in the political and social arenas. However, not only the shift from the religious to the secular premises is of crucial importance here, but also, and with close connection, a far-reaching restructuring and reordering of several basic components of these premises. Far-reaching changes took place in the relations between universalistic and primordial components. In the Medieval European civilization the various primordial components were subordinated to the universalistic religious ones. The shift to secular-universalistic premises generated the possibility that various primordial and historical components would become secularized and "absolutized" and that the religious components, which became secondary, would reinforce such tendencies. New eschatological visions, couched in secular terms, could develop both in universalistic and in primordial directions. All these changes in the basic premises of European civilizations, as manifest in the three shifts mentioned earlier, had far-reaching repercussions on the relations between the Jews and the European civilizations.

The Transformation of Jewish Communities

The first two shifts changed the basic relations between the European civilizations and Jews, apparently opening the way for Jews to cease to be strangers in the lands of their settlement. The second shift in particular made them eligible for citizenship in the new emerging political systems, opening the various arenas of European civilization and society before the Jews. These developments could provide new avenues for the implementation of various heterodox orientations hitherto latent in the fold of rabbinical Judaism but that started to become more variable from the sixteenth century on, reinforcing the possibilities of the breakdown of the premises and frameworks of the halakhic mold.

The attainment of full citizenship, *emancipation* as it was called, was not an easy process. In most European countries it was attained only after prolonged struggles, struggles that constituted a central focus of modern Jewish history in Europe in the nineteenth century. Yet it seemed to constitute the master trend and the most facial experience of the modern Jewish European history.

But the possibility of emancipation—the opportunity of lifting the various restrictions on the participation of the Jewish population in the economic and, above all, the political and cultural life of the societies in which they lived—was connected with the development of a new type of demand toward the Jews. The crux of this demand was that Jews define themselves only as a religious and not as a national or political community. Their persistence as a distinct and separate national or political identity was seen as a challenge to the emerging civic and national (especially Western) European communities to the modern nation-state, to the ideas of universal citizenship, and basically incompatible with them.

These demands on the Jews were inherent to some degree in the politics of many absolutist rulers, like Joseph II of Austria (1780–1790), who as promulgated in his Edict on Toleration (1782) was willing to look upon Jews as legitimate domiciled subjects and not just strangers in his land; but at the same time such rulers abolished the corporate status of the Jewish communities. This demand became formulated most fully and explicitly in the French Revolution and its aftermath and was taken up later, even if in different formulations, in other countries, above all in Germany and to a smaller degree in the multinational Austro-Hungarian Empire. The articulation of these demands, when taken together with the process of economic development, heralded the beginning of the incorporation of Jews into the modern European societies, in the modern European nation-states, albeit in different modes in different European societies and of far-reaching changes in the structure of the boundaries of Jewish civilization.

The opening of the gates of Western European society, before the Jews gave rise to a very great economic, occupational, and educational mobility and to far-reaching changes in the patterns of their lives, first of all in direction of assimilation.[7] Jewish life tended to become more closely interwoven into the institutional matrices of the host societies. Jews no longer legally were segregated in distinct communities that defined, under the aegis of the Halakhah, the basic boundaries of their collective life and the arena for the implementation of their specific civilizational vision. These boundaries began to be opened to change, entailing the definition of their collective identity in relation to the surrounding society. Participation in that society was seen as a legitimate endeavor, indeed as the way to achieve their own civilizational mission, insofar as they were still interested in maintaining it.

Accordingly, far-reaching changes took place in the whole complex of Jewish institutions and associations, with their weakening. Admittedly, many of the specific institutional features of the Jewish communities—above all synagogues, organizations of mutual help, and to some degree the traditional institutions of learning—persisted, and new ones, as we shall see, did develop. But they no longer constituted the central matrix of Jewish life, nor did they alone define its boundaries. The specific Jewish institutions—the synagogues, educational and philanthropic activities, different communal organizations (many of which developed new centralized patterns like the board of Deputies in England and the Consistoire in France), and the new institutions of Jewish higher learning or journalistic activities—no longer encompassed the whole of the life of the Jews nor, except (and even among them, only partially) among the neo-orthodox, were they seen as the major arena of Jewish civilizational creativity. Similarly, on the level of daily life, although the largest parts of the Jewish population moved in mostly Jewish circles, they found the various specifically Jewish social and cultural institutions and patterns of life secondary.

Moreover, Jews started and continued to participate visibly in some central (academic, literary, journalistic) arenas of the general societies in which they lived, and their participation and visibility in these fields became very pronounced, especially in Germany and Austria to some degree in France and England and later on, as we shall see, in the United States. They also started to participate in another arena naturally barred to them in the former period: general social and political movements. As the more conservative parties of the establishment usually were closed to them, they were most active in the more radical political movements, such as the liberal and later on the socialist ones. The changes in the Jews' patterns of life, together with those in their educational and occupational structure, were strongly connected with the weakening of the hitherto institutional and symbolic boundaries of the Jewish communities, of the Jewish people. This became evident first of all in the radical changes in the official, judicial standing of Jewish communal organizations. The traditional powers and jurisdiction of the Jewish Kehillot were removed, thus also ending their status as specific, distinct estates of strangers. Instead the Jews, in principle at least, became legitimate inhabitants rather than strangers and, somewhat later on, full citizens of their respective societies.

Emancipation and Antisemitism

These trends developed in all European Jewish communities but in different modes. The first such mode of incorporation developed in Western Europe: in France in the wake of the Revolution; in Germany; in a different, less dramatic mode in England, Holland, and later on, in the Scandinavian countries. In these countries, first of all in France, Jews were promised emancipation—that is, granting of full citizenship rights—if they become a religious, but not a national or ethnic group. These trends seemingly were going to do away with some of the specific characteristics of exilic existence as the Diaspora, with its Jews being conceived as strangers and potential outcasts, as being basically different from their host societies and from other sectors thereof.

All this was, of course, tantamount to the weakening, even the total disappearance in many places, of the rabbinical Halakhic symbolic and institutional mold, its premises, and legal-ritual arrangements as the predominant institutional and specific civilizational framework of the Jewish people. As a result of these developments in Western Europe, France and Germany, and to a lesser degree in England or Holland, there developed dramatic tendencies to redefine the Jewish community as above all a religious community and semingly to give up entirely its political, national, and in principle also primordial, elements. Such redefinition could be connected, as among some of the modern neo-orthodox groups, with a very strict maintenance of the religious observances and the religious collectivity. In such cases it entailed also the retainment of some of the primordial or ethnic components of collective identity, but in a rather diluted way.

In the context of these trends arose the main problem to which we shall address ourselves in the forthcoming analyses: whether the mode of this incorporation differed, not only in details such as various customs, forms of family, and communal life, but also in some principled ways, from that of other ethnic or religious minorities in the Western nation states. If this is found to be the case we then shall inquire whether, and to what extent, some central characteristics of this mode or modes of incorporation into the host societies and the interrelation between the Jews and these societies were influenced by the specific characteristics of the Jewish civilization analyzed earlier.

Some of the distinct characteristics of the incorporation of Jews into the modern European nation-states already were visible in the demand made on them to become a "normal" religious group. Such a demand indicates a rather unusual attitude on the part of the newly emerging modern states. The very fact that this demand was made on the Jews indicated the basic assumption that till then at least they were not just such a group.

The same attitude later could be discerned to a large extent with respect to the conception of Jews as a "national" or ethnic group that developed later on, toward the end of the nineteenth century above all in Eastern Europe. Here, the Jews on the whole were not seen as a "natural" national minority. Because of the lack of a territorial basis as well as the strong religious component in their national identity and their "cosmopolitan" attitudes they were seen as rather distinctive type of minority, distinguishing them from other such groups. In all these attitudes the perception of the Jewish collectivity as some sort of an entity, with claims far beyond that of just a religious group or ethnic minority, combining primordial and religious components as well as universalistic and particularistic orientations, persisted even if in ways differing from those that were prevalent in the Medieval period.

Therefore, it came as no surprise that these trends to the incorporation of Jews into the modern political life of European nations, based on the two first shifts in the premises of European civilization, were to some degree counteracted by the third trend referred to earlier. This trend was the emphasis in the formation of the modern political community of the nation-state on the more primordial-, territorial-, historical-, linguistic-, and kinship-free components of the emerging political communities—be it French, German, or Italian—rather than the more universalistic premises. The older Christian component, as well as the various primordial ones, often continued to be of importance in the construction of these communities. Indeed the primordial components, reestablished in secular terms, could attain predominance they did not have before. The importance of these components in the construction of the collective identity of the modern nation-states, and the struggle over them, was greatest in those countries, like Germany and to a smaller degree France, as against England or the Scandinavian countries, where such national communities and identities did not crystallize and could not be taken for granted, and where no strong tradition of civility had developed. For these reasons the very construction of such national identity often constituted in these societies a focus of political and ideological struggle. In such cases, the demand on the Jews to give up their national or "ethnic," primordial and political, as against purely religious, identity not only became very strong, but also became connected with the growth of strong and principled rejection of the Jews by many sectors of these societies, with a rejection of the very possibility that the Jews indeed would become such a group. This rejection was built on the old religious bases but went beyond them. It was formulated in modern, secular, national and racist terms—as they developed in modern antisemitism—and it denied the possibility of the Jews becoming part of the new European nations.

Modern antisemitism, which arose in conjunction with the resurgence and overemphasis of such primordial elements in the constitution of modern nation-states, cannot be seen as just another, even if rather extreme, manifestation of international, interethnic, or racial conflict. Its more extreme expressions constituted, as Jacob Katz has shown, a transformation of the interreligious and intercivilizational tensions between Jews and Christians in Medieval times. Only the combination of a "usual" interethnic conflict and the transformation of the intercivilizational tensions can explain the ultimate culmination of modern antisemitism—in the fact and ideology of the Holocaust.[8]

The Major Directions of
Jewish Collective Life and Cultural Activities:
Haskala, Reform, Assimilation, and Jewish Scholarship
in Western and Central Europe

Some specific traits could be identified not only in the attitudes of the modern nation-states and modern European societies to the Jews, but in the modes of Jewish incorporation into these modern states and societies and in the patterns of activities developed by the Jews themselves. Truly enough, many of the processes of such incorporation—learning the language of their host societies; the ecological, occupational, and above all educational mobility briefly analyzed earlier—could be seen as normal trends of assimilation of minority groups into the modern nation-state. Yet, alongside these "normal" trends, some very distinct characteristics developed in the different modes of Jewish incorporation into the modern nation-states that distinguished them from other religious or ethnic minorities, and made the trends to assimilation less than the whole story of their incorporation into modern nation-states. It was not the whole story because, unlike most other ethnic groups, the decomposition of traditional Jewish society and the rabbinical mold gave rise not only to "usual" assimilation if there exists such a "usual mode," but also, often in conjunction with it, to the search for new arenas in which to articulate the specific Jewish civilizational experience, to reconstruct the Jewish tradition, its contents and premises, and to methods of reconstructing in rather distinct ways the boundaries of their collective life. These challenges of the decomposition of the traditional pattern were taken up on the level of social-communal and cultural organization as well as the more ideological level. Such a search for the reconstruction of Jewish collective life was taken up in a variety of ways by different groups within the Jewish communities, becoming a focus of continuous endeavors and conflict within them. Parallelly, the entire pattern of the organization of Jewish life developed in a rather different way from that of many other religious or ethnic groups.

The major directions of the reconstruction of collective life, cultural activities, and identity lie in the Haskala Reform, assimilation, and Jewish scholarship. The attempts to reconstruct Jewish life and tradition, its contents, premises, and the boundaries of collective life, developed in Europe from the eighteenth century on in several directions, giving rise to cultural, ideological, and social trends.[9]

One such direction was the development within the Jewish communities of special social and ideological movements aiming at the reconstruction of the institutional arenas and types of activities that could serve as foci for the implementation of some of the major themes of Jewish civilization. The second such direction, closely related to the former but not always identical with it, was the various attempts at the reconstruction of the Jewish religious practice in ways that would seemingly become attuned to the premises of the modern "secular" age, especially of the Enlightenment. Third were the attempts to imbue the very process of emancipation and assimilation with principled ideological dimensions in terms derived from the basic premises of the Jewish civilization and historical experience. Fourth, in conjunction with the two former trends, a plethora of new modern types of Jewish scholarly activities and institutions developed. Last was the development of neo-orthodoxy and the new orthodoxy.

All these developments combined in different ways the development of new types of organizations and institutions and the articulation of different themes of Jewish civilization or tradition, Jewish collective consciousness. There no longer was just one dominant mode of promulgation of these themes and these connections with institutional organization. Different civilizational themes or combinations were promulgated by different groups and in different communities and even within the same communities. Moreover, such themes were promulgated in new, "modern" ways, and such types of promulgation often were formulated in ways that in the earlier period would have been seen as heterodox—and so they were seen by the orthodox circles. Many different such heterodoxies would be developed, each entailing rather different cultural programs of Jewish modernity and their activities were not confined to the internal arenas of the Jewish communities. Each such program selected and reconstructed different combinations of the universalistic and particularistic, primordial and religious components of Jewish collective consciousness. The modern Jewish historical experience entailed not only the continuous working out of such different, yet interrelated, programs in different Jewish communities, but also growing differences in the historical experience, and the consciousness thereof, of different Jewish communities.

Let us briefly illustrate these distinctive dimensions, these distinctive trends of Jewish incorporation into European societies in the nineteenth century in somewhat greater detail, starting with the first: the development of ideological movements aiming at the reconstruction of Jewish life and civilization. The major movement—intellectual and, to some degree, social—that heralded the incorporation of different Jewish communities into various European societies was that of the Jewish Enlightenment, the Haskala.[10] Its central theme was the reconstruction of Jewish life, tradition, and civilization according to the precepts of Enlightenment, "rationalism," to make it a full participant in the emerging universal rational, civilizational mold while potentially contributing to this mold some specific Jewish ingredients. Although in itself not necessarily antireligious in the narrow sense—its first heralds, like Moses Mendelssohn (1729–1786) or Naftali Herz Weisel (1725–1805), insisted on strict observance of the halakhic laws—the movement did negate the exclusive predominance of rabbinical Judaism as the major institutional framework of the Jewish communities in the modern world. It also rejected definitions of the boundaries of Jewish collective identity in terms of radical segregation and exclusiveness from the neighboring nations. Instead, it emphasized the possibility and even the necessity of reconstructing many aspects of Jewish life, starting above all from education and encompassing to some extent economic production as well as cultural and social activities, in the direction of greater incorporation into the general European societies.

The actual orientations of the Haskala movement, and the different activities within the Jewish communities that developed in its wake—above all their implication for the reconstruction of modern Jewish life, its vision of Jewish participation in the new civilization and its possible contribution to it—differed greatly, as we shall see later on, in the Western and Eastern European Jewish communities. Somewhat later, but in close relation with the Western Haskala the second trend, mentioned earlier, developed: various quite spectacular attempts at the reconstruction of the Jewish religion, especially of religious rituals and patterns of religious observance, in the light of the more universal tenets of the Enlightenment. There was a move away from the strong emphasis of the legal-ritual dimensions of the Halakha in the direction of the more "ethical" and prophetic elements of Jewish religion.

Thus from the first half of the nineteenth century the various movements developed of 'reform' or liberal Judaism, changing the religious practices of the Jews in what seemed to those involved to be a more modern direction. These changes of course were connected with the attempts to define the Jews as a religious community, whose religion was part of a wider universal panorama of monotheistic religions, sharing with them, perhaps especially with Christianity, as with more general philosophical deistic orientations or discourse, many common assumptions, moving together into an era of common tolerance and enlightenment.

Third, even the very attempt at emancipation or at least assimilation often was couched in terms of the specific premises of the Jewish tradition, in terms of some of the basic Jewish premises of Jewish civilization. Thus, as J. Katz has put it:

> The greater part of the community, however, and especially the newly evolved elite of the enlightened, the maskilim, not only accepted naturalization and emancipation as a welcome deliverance from the dire circumstance of the Ghetto, but lent it an historical and spiritual significance. Naturalization and emancipation were hailed as traditionally reserved for the Messianic Age, to the point of identifying kings and princes, the guarantors of the new civil status, with the person of the messiah. This identification should not be dismissed as an ideological embellishment of the new political and social achievement. It was more than that. As conceived by the original initiators, naturalization and emancipation were meant to provide a new perspective and prognosis for the future of Jewry. The abolishment of alienage was to replace the expectation of a Messianic delivery from the predicament of aliens on foreign soil. According to this conception, the various segments of the nation would be granted a home in their respective environments, thus achieving for the individual, in terms of legal and political status, what the Messianic expectation held out for the nation as a whole.[11]

This attitude was evident in the way that Jews participated in the cultural and political life of these European societies. They concentrated in the more liberal and radical movements, in the more critical academic subjects like sociology (where, for instance, Emile Durkheim propagated a new secular morality and civic consciousness), and in the more critical and liberal parts of the press, and with an intensity seen by many as something specifically Jewish.

Indeed, this universal, liberal, ethical message often was seen by many Jewish intellectuals in Western and Central Europe, and in a less fully articulated way also by the wider sectors of the Jewish community, as the essence of the Jewish civilization or its possible contribution to modern life. It necessarily entailed abandoning the idea of Jewish self-segregation, stressing the ingrowing participation in general society as full citizens and participants in its civilization. At the same time it portrayed Jews as carrying a special mission to the nations—a mission no longer embodied (except among the neo-orthodox circles) in the more traditional tenets of Rabbinical Judaism, but that still retained, albeit in transformed ways, many of the basic orientations of Jewish civilization. Indeed many Jews saw in these more liberal and civic attitudes, and in the specifically Jewish intellectual activities, an articulation of that aspect of universalistic Jewish heritage which had not found a proper expression in Medieval times: the emphasis on universal ethical principles uniquely expressed in the prophetic tradition, attesting as it were to their special mission—a modern version of being a chosen people.

The fourth process connected with the incorporation of Jews into European states was the development of new, modern type of Jewish scholarship, of a great intellectual movement, that of the Wissenschaft des Judentums, a movement out of which modern Jewish historical and philological study and research emerged, represented by figures like Abraham Geiger (1810–1874) and Leopold Zunz (1794–1886), the founders of modern Jewish scholarship, and later on the great historian Heinrich Graetz (1817–1891).[12] This great intellectual creativity, especially of the first generations, was guided by a certain paradox. Their official program and vision was gradually to transform the Jews into a religious community and shed their national identity. Yet their immense scholarship and their publications enhanced the historical self-consciousness and identity of the Jewish collectivity and put the study of Judaism in the framework of modern scholarship.

Of special importance in this context were two types of activities closely related to the dominant intellectual modes in Western Europe in general and in Germany in particular: philosophy of history and history proper. One of the major intellectual activities that developed in the context of the Wissenschaft des Judentums was that of religious or historical philosophy. Scholars like Nahman Krochmal (1785–1840), Abraham Geiger, or Solomon Ludwig Steinheim (1808–1889), and later on Hermann Cohen (1842–1918), Franz Rosenzweig (1886–1929), and Martin Buber (1878–1965), building on the Jewish Medieval philosophers but going beyond them to develop a positive attitude to other religious civilizations, attempted to define the specific Jewish contribution to the religious consciousness of humankind and to the unfolding of universal history. Often they emphasized not only the religious, political, or ethical components of Jewish life, but also its collective identity.

From this point of view Heinrich Graetz provided an important turning-point in Jewish historical research. Instead of trying to explain the course of Jewish history in terms of the movement of some disembodied Hegelian spirit, he wrote his massive history of the Jews as a history of a political and national community, greatly contributing to the development of a collective consciousness among many 'modern,' educated Jews.

The last most interesting development within the Jewish communities in the modern times was that of orthodoxy or neoorthodoxy.[13] These terms connoted those sectors within the Jewish communities that did not accept the attempts at new definitions of Jewish religion and practice, the changing of the basic halakhic molds. The sectors insisted on continuing the rule of Halakhah, on observance of all the precepts and rituals, hence their definition first by themselves, then accepted by others, as orthodox or neo-orthodox, as they were later called, indicated already their own recognition that they were not just simply continuing the older patterns of the mold of the Halakhah.

The very employment of the terms *orthodox* or *neo-orthodox* entailed a rather paradoxical element. Despite these designations, the orthodox or neoorthodox sectors of the Jewish communities in fact, toward the end of the first half of the nineteenth century, already constituted a minority within the Jewish community. They certainly did not represent the orthodoxy or orthodoxies prevalent in these communities, which were mostly some version of liberal and reform practices and organizations. The newly designated orthodoxy was of a semischismatic kind, with strong utopian, and what today would be called fundamentalist, overtones and orientations. These orthodox or neo-orthodox sectors tended to organize themelves as separate groups within the official, Jewish, communities or, in some cases in the second half of the nineteenth century in Hungary, as distinct communities. The extent of their organizational separation depended on various local circumstances, their own relative strength, and the legal standing of the Jewish communities.

But whatever the specifics of their organizations, the details of which we cannot enter into here, theirs was not the regnant mode of the Jewish communities. Although they portrayed themselves as continuing the "old" halakhic tradition, in fact this was not the case. It was not the case not only because they constiuted a minority within the Jewish community, but above all because their own ways and organization already were set within the framework of the new social, economic, and political reality of the Jewish communities in Western and Central Europe in the nineteenth century. The Jews belonging to these sectors became, like all the other Jews, subjects or citizens of their respective countries; they, or most of them, sent their children to general schools or had to incorporate large parts of the general curriculum in their own schools; they participated in the economic and ideological mobility of the Jews, in some cases being among the economically most advanced. Many of them saw themselves also as participating, even if perhaps passively, in the general cultural life of their societies. Implicitly or explicitly, they accepted the designation of the Jewish communities as religious ones. The ideologically most articulate and innovative groups among them, led by Rabbi Z. Hirsch (1808–1888), coined the slogan of "Tora veDerech Eretz," Torah and (something like) civic behavior.

In Central Europe even this formulation was opposed by the more extreme (new) orthodox groups, the most important leader of which in the early and middle nineteenth century was the Hatam Sofer (Moses Sofer

1762–1833) in Hungary, who proclaimed a much more militant segregative view. But whatever the—many fascinating—differences among them, there indeed was a new, more schismatic, orthodoxy of a minority group or sect within the Jewish communities.

Common to all these directions and trends were attempts to redefine Jewish collective identity in ways that entailed a basic reformulation of the major themes and tensions inherent in the Jewish collective self-definition: above all the tension between the universalistic and particularist orientations, between the eschatological vision and the present; of the concomitant identi-fication of the proper arena for the realization of the Jewish civilizational vision, and the restructuring of the boundaries of the Jewish collectivity in relation to those of other collectivities or civilizations. With respect to these themes the most far-reaching changes took place in relation to the Medieval rabbinical vision and tradition. The concrete arena for the implementation of the Jewish civilizational vision no longer was limited to the daily reality of a segregated national-religious community nor did it point only or even mainly to a distant future. This arena was envisaged more and more as the present, contemporaneous European civilization, to which the Jews were to make their specific contribution, but not as a segregated community. Among those groups that held this view, the universalistic orientations were heavily emphasized, stressing the universal message inherent in ethical prophecy, as against what was seen as the more particularistic definition of the rabbinical mold and the concomitant almost total self-enclosure of the Jewish commu-nity. All these attempts included a radical revaluation of the temporal and spatial orientation of Jewish Medieval civilization, the proper arena for the realization of the Jewish civilizational vision, as well as radical changes in the restructuring of the boundaries of the Jewish collectivity in relation to those of other collectivities or civilizations.

These various developments had some very interesting repercussions on the attitude toward Galut, Diaspora. We already have seen that since the period of the Second Commonwealth the existence of a Diaspora, or Diaspo-ras, and since the destruction of the Second Temple also of exile has been a major and continuous characteristic of the Jewish historical experience. Indeed from about the sixth or seventh century CE, throughout the Medieval and modern periods, Jews lived mostly in the Diaspora, in exile; the Jewish Medieval civilization, concretely speaking, was an exilic civilization.Many other nations had their Diasporas, too, but only in the case of the Jews has life in the Diaspora—and exile from their own land—constituted such a con-tinuous, widespread, and central experience. Moreover, probably only, cer-tainly especially, for the Jews has the problem of exile, of Galut, as Y. Baer has shown in his classic *Galut*[14] constituted a central problem of their collective consciousness, expressed in theological and mythical terms, some of which we have discussed.

The fact of living in Galut, that the great majority of the Jewish people lived in the Diaspora, constituted a basic problem or component of their collective consciousness in modern times as well, despite the breakdown of the walls of Medieval ghettos and the opening up of the gates of European society before the Jews. Seemingly their successful assimilation within their host communities in the nineteenth century should have done away with the conception that living in the Diaspora constitutes a special problem. And yet it continued to constitute such a problem for large sectors of the Jewish communities, especially to some of their intellectuals and leaders.[15]

Truly enough the basic attitude to the existence in Galut has changed greatly. The total negation of the actual existence in Galut has disappeared. Rather the evaluation of this existence has become a continuous focus of ideological concerns, at least among Jewish intellectuals.

But whatever the attitude of the different groups to life in the Diaspora—ranging from the denial by Zionists of the legitimaty and viability of life in the Diaspora up to its positive evaluation of some of the recent ideologies in the United States—the existence in Galut combined with the fact that Jews lived in many Diasporas constituted a continuous problem in Jewish collective consciousneses. It was not simply taken for granted, on the whole, except on the level of daily life and even here not always. The exilic existence in the Diaspora remained, albeit in greatly reformulated ways, a continuous problem in the collective consciousness of the Jewish community.

The awareness of this problem was reinforced by the fact that the process of Jewish assimilation and integration into modern European societies, and lateralso into the societies beyond Europe, has evinced some very specific characteristics that distinguished it from the Diasporas of other people, be they Irish, Greek, Italian, or even American. It also was reinforced by the fact that the majority of Jewish people live in Diasporas, a rather unique fact among different Diasporas, with the possible partial exception of the Armenians.

Jews differed from other religious groups or ethnic minorities not only in the ideological aspect of Jewish incorporation into modern European societies. Some very distinct, specific characteristics, closely related to the premises of Jewish civilization and the Jewish historical civilizational experience also developed with respect to the institutional or organizational aspect of Jewish life in these societies and the patterns of Jewish social life in Western and Central Europe in the nineteenth century.[16]

First was the relatively high degree of de facto social segregation, of endogamy, although of course this was not peculiar to Jews and it did weaken in varying degrees among the more assimilated. Second was the very multiplicity and scope of activities of Jewish associations or organizations—be they religious, philanthropic, or scholarly—that on the whole went far beyond those found among other religious or ethnic groups. Many of these were concerned not only with keeping up some remnant of tradition, but in actively redefining it—often, as already indicated, in those terms that characterized it throughout Jewish history. Moreover—and this is of crucial importance—most of these Jewish organizations were "international"; they were concerned with helping Jewish communities throughout the world, often enough as "coreligionists" but nevertheless stressing the international dimension of Jewish existence.

Interestingly enough, the first such development took place in the first country of intensive semi-ideological assimilation, France. In 1860 the Alliance Israelite, was established by some professional Jewish groups from within the French periphery, designed for educational, semipolitical work in a modern vein among all Jewish communities, challenging to some degree the assimilated leaders of the Jewish community in Paris and setting a pattern for similar developments in other Jewish communities.

Even the more internal religious Jewish organizations, whether those of Reform Judaism or the institutions of Jewish learning and scholarship in different countries of Europe, were in continuous mutual contact, helping each other, reinforcing or counteracting each other, but always maintaining a range and intensity of contact among different Jewish communities that rarely was found among other religious minorities, with the exception of course of the Catholic Church or councils of Protestant groups, all of which saw themselves as bearers of the Christian civilizational vision, or among other ethnic groups.

All these processes—intensive occupational mobility, increased Jewish participation in many arenas, attempts to reconstruct Jewish tradition and collective identity, cultural, public, and economic creativity, the reactions to all these, and the continuous connection among Jewish communities in different countries—distinguished the Jews in Western Europe from other religious groups and, later on, in Eastern Europe and especially in the United States from other ethnic or religious groups.

Variations among Different Western and Central European Jewish Communities: Heterogeneity and Common Orientations

The historical experience of different Jewish communities was not identical in the different countries of Western and Central Europe. In each country—be it France, England, Germany, Austria, Hungary, the different parts of Poland—rather distinct patterns of Jewish cultural and social activities developed.[17] Such distinct patterns were influenced by the interrelations between the internal structure of the Jewish community and the general society: its rulers, its occupational and economic contours, and above all the definition of the modern national and civic community that developed within it; its principled attitudes to minorities; and its tolerance of religious, national, or ethnic minorities.

The great divide here was between Western and parts of Central Europe—especially Germany, in which the Jews constituted a relatively small part of the overall population that enjoyed a relatively high level of economic and occupational mobility—and Eastern Europe and the parts of Central Europe under the Hapsburg Empire and Russia. In these latter societies, which were economically less fully developed, Jews already constituted much larger parts of the population (up to 10 percent). They were one among many large minorities in societies in which the basic conception of the body politic was that of a multinational traditional empire in which traditional antisemitism was rampant and within which many national movements developed. Moreover the Jews in Eastern Europe continued to live to a much greater extent within their traditional framework than those of Western and Central Europe.

Within each of these broad categories of Jewish society a great variety of concrete patterns of life of organizations developed, including different types of intellectual, social, and political activities. These various patterns naturally were greatly influenced by the institutional patterns and intellectual trends prevalent in the respective countries. It would be beyond the scope of the discussion here to analyze these various patterns in detail, so some illustrations, chosen at random, will have to suffice.

The centralist mode of organization of French political life gave rise to a parallel centralist tendency in the organization of the major Jewish institutions, especially the Consistoire, and the sharp articulation of political controversies in nineteenth-century France greatly influenced the intensive participation of many Jewish persons in this field. The central place of historical and philosophical studies in the intellectual and public life of Germany was very conducive to the rise of the Wissenschaft des Judentums and studies concerned with a philosophical and theological interpretation of Jewish historical and collective experience. Also, the more decentralized state of German intellectual and political life, even to some degree after the establishment of the empire, facilitated the development of more diversified and dispersed Jewish institutions. Similarly the relatively low degree of concern in England with the philosophical or ideological dimension of political life minimized the scope for such activities among the Jews, and the more traditional civic and aristocratic organization of public life facilitated the acceptance of Jews as a quasi-ethnic community and the development of their central organization (the Board of Deputies, the Chief Rabbinate) in keeping with such a civic-oligarchic mode.

Whatever the examples, in general the specific details of Jewish life and even some modes of the expression of Jewish identity to a very large extent were shaped by the host societies. Concomitantly, through education and participation in the civic life of their societies, Jews in different countries acquired some aspects of their host societies' mentality or mentalities, above all with respect to their conception of public life and their definition of those aspects of this life—such as the relations between Church and State—most important for them.

The great heterogeneity of Jewish life that developed in this period in the Jewish communities in Europe went far beyond the heterogeneity of customs that could be found in different Jewish communities in the exilic period. In modern times, such heterogeneity entailed not only differences in customs or in the scope of communal, educational, and cultural activities, nor in the relative importance of such different activities. This heterogeneity already entailed far-reaching differences in some of the very central aspects of Jewish life: of communal organization, in the patterns of religious observance, and above all in the very definition of Jewish collectivity and collective identity; in the ideological meaning that was attributed to these different patterns of religious observance and in their relations to their host societies.

This profusion and variability constituted the great diversity of modern Jewish history, much more reminiscent of the period of the Second Temple, the Hellenistic and Babylonian Diasporas, and its immediate aftermath in the period of the Gaonim, than of the "classical" Medieval rabbinical era. And yet, despite these great differences, Jewish communities shared some common characteristics beyond a common heritage of customs and beliefs or some mentalities. With the exception of the majority of the totally assimilated, they shared a concern with problems of Jewish emancipation, a collective identity or a reference to such an identity, continuous mutual references among the different Jewish communities that cut across national boundaries and that, notwithstanding the efforts of the groups oriented to assimilation, was not purely confessional. On the ideological-political level, they shared concern with the problems of Jewish emancipation and the search for some way of reconstructing their identity and special civilizational vision.

These mutual references were rooted not only in a feeling of a common heritage, but also in continuous common concern on how to find some new ways of implementing some of the major themes of Jewish civilization, even if they differed with respect to which of these themes they emphasized as well as which arenas of Jewish or the general society constituted the most appropriate arenas for implementing this vision. But even these differences constituted foci of continuous mutual debates among different Jewish communities, attesting again to the existence of common bonds between them. On the more practical-organizational level, they shared concern about Jewish educational, philanthropic, and semiphilanthropic activities. The flow of immigration and the continuous influx of new immigrants into established Jewish communities, with all the tensions between them, also provided a continuous link among different Jewish communities.

All this does not mean, of course, that these common concerns were shared continously by all members of the Jewish communities. Quite large sectors of the Jewish communities did indeed become assimilated, disappearing at least until the Nazis reminded them of their heritage. Many others, although still keeping some attachment to the Jewish tradition, were not interested in their daily life with either these ideological or philanthropic concerns. It course very difficult to know how much these concerns affected the daily life of different Jewish communities. Certainly the challenge of the reconstituting the boundaries of Jewish collectivity was taken up above all by small groups of leaders and intellectuals, but this has always been the case in instances of articulated cultural creativity, just as, for instance, the tradition of Halakhah, in the Middle Ages, was articulated by such leaders. Be that as it may, many parts of the Jewish communities, and especially many intellectuals and leaders, accepted these various challenges to reconstruct Jewish life.

In all these ways the reality of Jewish life, even under the aegis of emancipation and incorporation into European societies, evinced some combination of social and cultural creativity, multiplicity of activities, mutual contacts and relations, that went beyond the attempts to redefine Jewish identity in purely religious or diluted ethnic terms. Thus all these processes belied, except for those who succeeded in shedding all or almost all Jewish identity, the possibility of full assimilation or defining the Jews as a purely religious, confessional community. Such possibility also to some degree was belied by the fact that the very shedding of the corporate Jewish identity, and even the weakening of attachment to the religious tradition, paradoxically enough could bring out the more primordial components of Jewish identity, often also giving rise to sharp antisemitic reactions among many sectors of the general society.

Thus, from the point of view of the economic advancement of the Jews in nineteenth-century Western and Central Europe, their social and cultural creativity, and their consequent potential integration into the framework of the general societies, a paradox emerged. The crumbling of the walls of the ghetto opened up to them many economic, professional, political, and cultural arenas for creativity—arenas that no longer in any sense were specifically Jewish. At the same time, however, the intensity and mode of participation of the Jews in these fields increased their visibility as a special, distinct, socio-cultural element, emphasizing some specific characteristics.

To some sectors of European societies these activities of the Jews were seen as a positive element in the emerging national or civic culture. But other elements—the more conservative and populistic elements, especially in periods and places when the activities of the Jews were caught up in far-reaching social upheavals, in the development of national movements, and above all when these processes, as in Germany, were combined with an autocractic regime—evaluated this participation of the Jews in negative terms. Many sectors saw in this active and visible participation, especially when connected with very rapid economic and occupational advancement, a manifestation of the pushiness of the Jews, of their rootlessness and "cosmopolitanism." These themes increasingly were promulgated by the developing modern antisemitic movements, which stressed the unique character of the Jews and their inability to assimilate themselves fully and defined them as an alien caste or race.

In these modern antisemitic movements and ideologies the older religious competition and animosity was transformed in a more radical racial direction. These movements and ideologies were strongly connected with the third shift or trend from the Medieval or early modern society to the modern period proper in European history. As mentioned at the beginning of this chapter, this third trend (the first two being the shifts in traditional religion to a universalistic secular definition of secularity in the community and from traditional legitimation to a secular legitimation of rulers) was the tendency to imbue the new national collectivities with strong primordial and religious components.[18]

These primordial components, emphasizing a common language, history, and territory, of course, were promulgated by the various national movements. Such promulgation was weaker in those European societies, like England, Sweden or Denmark, and to some extent Holland, in which the national community crystallized side by side with the consolidation of a unified state in a relatively early period.

In other European societies, like Germany, the Austro-Hungarian Empire, or many of the Eastern European societies, where no such temporal coalescence of the national community with the establishment of a state took place, the promulgation of such primordial components of national identity was much stronger. And their relative importance in the construction of the collective identity of the different societies constituted a focus of continuous discourse and political struggle.

These struggles were of crucial importance in shaping the relations between Jews and their host societies in Europe. It was this combination that made European societies especially sensitive to the primordial religious and historical components of Jewish collective identity and the continuous interweaving of universalistic and particularistic elements in the construction of this identity. Such sensitivity could provide a very fruitful ground, especially in those societies in which national identity and state formation did not coincide, for the development of modern antisemitic movements and ideologies.

Modern Jewish Historical Experience in Eastern Europe

The Jewish modern experience developed in a rather different direction, moving between somewhat different poles in Central and above all in Eastern Europe. All the processes of modernization—the economic, political, and educational ones—developed here, as we have seen, in a much slower and more convoluted way. The disintegration of the "traditional" Jewish society also was much slower; and in some parts, such as Poland, that society persisted, if in a rather truncated way, in some sectors of the Jewish community in the period between the two world wars.

Yet, from the very beginning of this period some far-reaching changes were taking place. In the wake of the failure of the Sabbatean movement, there arose in Poland and Russia the first massive semiheterodox, or at least sectarian, movement of rabbinical Judaism, that of the Hassidim, which developed successfully despite the acrimonious struggles with a large part of the orthodox rabbinate, as a part of traditional Jewish society.

Whereas this movement fully accepted the basic premises of Halakhah, it shifted the focus of Jewish religion from learning and legal-ritual observance to personal religious experience, with strong mystic elements, and vested some mediatory power, in a way previously almost entirely unknown in the fold of rabbinical Judaism, in the leaders, the Tsadikim, giving rise to whole dynasties of such leaders. The rifts between the Hassidic movement and the "orthodox" rabbinate split the traditional Jewish community in a way, with the exception of the Sabbatean movement, unknown in the whole history of "Medieval" or "exilic" Judaism, at least unknown since the period of Karaite secession in the seventh century. Later, some common front was established by these different sectors of orthodoxy against the onslaught of the Enlightenment and later on various Jewish nationalist movements, especially of Zionism. But the rift that developed between the Hassidim and the orthodox rabbinate was not only indicative of the great changes within traditional Jewish society, but also contributed to undermining the walls of this society.

These walls did indeed start to crumble from the end of the eighteenth and the beginning of the nineteenth centuries with the spread of the Enlightenment and modernization in Eastern Europe in general and among its Jewish communities in particular. But the Eastern European Haskala, although greatly influenced by that of the West, nevertheless developed in almost entirely different directions. The relative slowness of economic development, the persistence of traditional-autocratic regimes, the existence of a multinational reality, the development of multiple national revolutionary movements, and the relative ecological density to the challenges of modernity of the Jewish settlement, generated in Eastern Europe some additional dimensions that went far beyond those identified in the responses of the Jewish communities of Western Europe. These dimensions became much more predominant in the Eastern European Jewish historical experience, and they accounted for the distinctiveness of that development.

The Eastern European Haskala shared with the Western European one the stress on the negation of the old type of Jewish self-segregation, a search for a new arena for the implementation of their civilizational vision (an arena that would be part of the modern world), and full participation in this world. But beyond this it differed greatly from the Western Haskala and its consequent movements. Ben Zion Dinur, the eminent Israeli historian, has aptly defined the difference between the Western and the Eastern European Jewish Haskala: in the West, where the whole orientation of the Haskala, as we have seen, was toward incorporation into the general society, it was a bridge; in the East it was a lever for the internal institutional reconstruction of the Jewish society.[19]

Therefore, in the East, especially in Russia and Poland and to a lesser extent in the Austro-Hungarian Empire, the Haskala movement was oriented above all to internal reconstruction of the Jewish community itself, to its internal—to use a more recent expression—modernization in some type of collective institutional mold. The bearers of Haskala in Eastern Europe viewed the incorporation of the Jewish community into the general society in terms of such collective reconstruction; they defined the Jewish community in some national, political or ethnic—and not only religious—terms; they saw the Jewish community connected with intensive internal bulding of modern economic, educational, and social institutions. The various movements of religious reform, although they did develop in these Jewish communities of Eastern Europe, on the whole were rather secondary to this broad spectrum of institutional-social, economic, political, and cultural reconstruction. These processes of internal institutional reconstruction were closely related to special characteristics of the ecological and economic reshaping of the Jewish population in Eastern Europe, to their greater concentration in cities relatively heavily populated by Jews who were engaged not only in commerce and artisanship but also in industry, giving rise to a strong, even if highly diversified, working class.

This basic difference between the Western and Eastern Haskala, and the broader economic processes and social movements connected with it, manifested itself in almost all aspects of cultural activities and social life.[20] The history of the Eastern European Jewish communities in the nineteenth and twentieth centuries up to the Second World War is a history of continuous modern institution building that remained, far beyond what could be found in Western Europe, within the framework of some, even if certainly on the whole no longer traditional, Jewish communal life. The institutions included educational institutions, ranging from kindergartens to vocational schools, modern high schools, and institutes of higher learning, teaching in some combination of Hebrew, Yiddish, and the major languages of their respective societies; very widespread journalism in Hebrew and Yiddish; and later on political parties, social and nationalistic movements, trade unions and labor organizations. All these movements developed concomitantly and continuously, and they developed within this framework of an—already largely modern—Jewish collective life. Within this framework they exhibited some very specific characteristics, reminiscent of the period of the Second Commonwealth: intensive ideological conflicts, the difficulty of accepting any common authority yet working in some common organizational and political framework, a very diversified leadership often at loggerheads with one another, but coming together in periods of political upheaval or pogroms.

The political activities that developed among the Jews in Eastern Europe indeed were very varied, comprising participation in a variety of political movements and organizations. Initially, from the last decades of the nineteenth century up to the First World War, most Jews were active mainly within the Jewish communities. After the First World War, with the establishment of the various "succession states" in Eastern Europe—above all Poland, Lithuania, Czechoslovakia, Hungary, and Romania—in which Jews were on the whole granted, at least finally, full citizenship, they also participated in the general political life. They formed special Jewish parties or blocs (including those of the orthodox) or cooperated with other general political groups, participating in one way or another in parliamentary life and attempting to take care of the specific Jewish interests. It was as Peter Medding[21] has defined it, a survival of economic and political accommodation. Some Jews also participated as individuals in other parties or blocs; but, with the exception of the socialist movements, they were not very prominent within them. The most important manifestations of such collective endeavor, of course, were the various national movements that developed within the Jewish communities in Eastern and Central Europe: movements aiming at the establishment of some sort of Jewish national identity within the multinational states of Eastern Europe; territorialist movements that aimed to find some territory outside Europe to establish a Jewish state; and, of course, the Zionist movement.

Within the framework of Jewish institutions and communal life, modern

Hebrew and Yiddish literature attained a very high level of cultural, sometimes even literary, creativity in the works of people like Abraham Mapu (1835–1867), Judah Leib Gordon (1831–1886), Mendele Mokher Sepharim (1835–1917), or Chaim Nahman Bialik (1873–1934), to mention only a few. Modern Hebrew and Yiddish schools, journalism, and theatre also developed that, like the internal and extensive communal political associational life and processes of institution building, lasted up till the Holocaust.[22]

There also developed in Eastern Europe intensive Jewish scholarship, historical and philosophical, that although building on the achievement of Wissenschaft des Judentums did not necessarily share its vision of Jewish history. The work of historians like S. Dubnov (1860–1941) and M. Balaban (1877–1942), building on Graetz but going beyond him, developed a much more nationally orientated vision of Jewish history, emphasizing not only religious beliefs but also the communal organizations and even various heterodox movements, like the Frankist one. There was also greater emphasis on the study of the economic history of the Jews contributing also to statistical or demographic studies of contemporary Jewish communities.[23] Needless to say, not all modern activities of the Jews in Eastern Europe were confined within the framework of the Jewish community. Many Jews participated in the different institutional arenas of general society, becoming especially visible in the more radical and revolutionary movements. They also were involved in the various cultural arenas, although here their participation was more limited than in Western Europe. In many fields, above all in academic life, and especially in Russia until the First World War, conversion often was a condition of access and participation.

In addition in Eastern Europe significant developments took place in the traditional "orthodox" sectors, going in two directions. One direction was especially evident within the traditional camp itself, particularly in Hungary and to a much smaller extent in Austrian Galicia, and not dissimilar from the development among the neo-orthodox in Germany, although more intensive. Here, orthodox communities already organized in relatively modern ways, sent their sons to general schools, but maintained a very strong Jewish institutional and communal framework. The other such direction was more prominent in Eastern than Western Europe. Here, among the orthodox group arose a modern semipolitical organization, culminating in the establishmenmt of Agudat Israel in 1922, which developed in the successive states as parliamentary blocs or parties but also led to the establishment of many modern philanthropic and even educational associations.

In some countries, like Hungary, the orthodox groups maintained totally separate communities, barely participating with other Jewish congregations in common activities. In other countries, especially in Poland, they participated in such common institutional and even political organizations.

The restructuring of Jewish life in Eastern Europe, unlike that in Western Europe, was characterized by the continuous creation of modern institutions and participation in them. This intensive building of institutions within the framework of Jewish communities was connected with the development of specific modes of the reconstruction of Jewish collective identity and the articulation of some of the perennial themes of Jewish self-definition.

The definition of the Jews as a purely or mostly religious, confessional group was rather marginal, except, paradoxically enough, to some degree among the more orthodox. Religious reform played only a very secondary role in the entire plethora of Jewish communal life in Eastern Europe. Among the majority of the Jews, their own social density, the multinational context within which they lived, the strength of various national movements against the Russian or Austro-Hungarian Empires, and the negative attitude of the autocratic Russian regime tended to give rise to very intensive collective movements. Secular or semisecular definitions—some explicitly antireligious, others not denying the religious component of Jewish tradition but minimizing its predominance—developed within the fold of Eastern European Jewry. Their number was legion, ranging from variations on some concepts of collective, cultural, semipolitical autonomy (as developed, for instance, by the eminent historian Simon Dubnov) to the Bundists' populist-socialist ones.

Most of these definitions stressed the possibility of maintaining such collective frameworks even without a specific Jewish territorial concentration. Others, the so-called territorialists, claimed the necessity of some such territorial concentration as a prerequisite for the maintenance of such autonomy; however, in contrast to the Zionist movement, without emphasizing the uniqueness of the old historical territory in Palestine.

Common to all of these definitions was the emphasis on Jewish education in the Hebrew or Yiddish language (the upholders of each, needless to say, developing bitter and intensive controversies), but combining it with general modern European education, and the stress on some national institutions and organizations, specifically Jewish political organizations and autonomy. This last theme became perhaps the most central new orientation in the late nineteenth and early twentieth centuries.

The more universalistic components of Jewish collective self-definition were much more subdued here. They were taken for granted as distinct components of the new restructuring of this definition and collective identity. In contrast to the Jews in Western Europe, the universalistic theme usually was not defined in Eastern Europe as a cultural mission, but rather as a specific Jewish manifestation of a more general historical trend.

Only among the more radical socialist groups did this theme become combined with the reformulation of the Jewish cultural identity. Among some of the more Jewish members of extreme revolutionary socialist and later Communist movements there developed a strong denial of the specificity of the Jewish collective identity and the necessity for a solution to the Jewish question. Among them there developed the assumption that their contribution to the general revolutionary movement would illustrate the universalistic component of Jewish tradition and, by wholly integrating the Jews into the future revolutionary society, also solve the specific Jewish question.

Among most of the Jewish movements in Eastern Europe there developed a strong connection between such universalistic orientations and collective internal institution building within the framework of the Jewish communal life, however without any very strong belief in a universal religious mission to be carried out by Jews. This connection in the Eastern European Jewish context was strongly interwoven with another theme almost entirely lacking among the Jews in Western Europe (except perhaps in the very first wave of Enlightenment in the eighteenth century): that of "productivization" (in the economic sense) and concomitant "normalization" of the Jewish occupational structure, a theme closely related, of course, to the general emphasis on institution building.

Such productivization and normalization were seen as a major key to the possibility of creating a viable, creative Jewish existence in the modern world. In a paradoxical way, many of these movements, and later on the Zionist movement, developed a rather negative evaluation of the existing Jewish occupational structure in the Diaspora—not dissimilar from that of many of the antisemitic pronunciations—and urged the Jews to move from parasitic ghetto occupations into productive agriculture and industry. Accordingly they initiated a vast ideological and institutional program that took the form of educational institutions in general and vocational education in particular, establishing agricultural settlements, schools, and migrating to new areas (like the famous attempt by Baron Hirsch in Argentina) where these programs could be realized.

This emphasis on economic modernization or productivization was related very closely to two additional themes that developed in the wake of Eastern Haskala. The first such theme was that of "normality" or "normalization," making the Jews into normal people, not necessarily denying their specific cultural heritage but making the realization of this specific heritage contingent on such normalization. The second such theme was the very strong stress on the physical, demographic, and economic aspects of the Jewish question, on the necessity for the search for some proper solution to the economic plight of the Jewish masses. The Jewish question or problem here was defined above all in terms of physical survival and economic productivization, and it was hoped that productivization might provide such solution. After the late 1920s a very strong shadow was cast on all these attempts in

Eastern and Central Europe. In this period the combination of economic recession, the closing of the gates of emigration to the United States, the growth of antisemitic movements, and the instability of the political regimes of most Eastern European successor states (with the exception of Czechoslovakia), began to undermine severely the situation of the Jews in these countries. The search for new outlets of migration and settlement became very intense—especially, of course, after the rise of Hitler to power—but most of it came to naught, and with the outbreak of the Second World War the Jewish communities in continental Europe—Eastern, Central, and Western alike—were pushed into the road toward the Holocaust.

Whatever the differences of the different Jewish communities in Europe—Western, Central, and Eastern—until the Second World War, they shared a basic common framework. This framework was rooted in the decomposition of the traditional European society and civilization and the formation of new political and civilizational frameworks and new political and cultural collectivities. These processes of decomposition and recrystallization were ushered in by the combined effects of the French and the Industrial Revolutions and the construction of the modern nation-state.

Common to the encounter between the Jews, and the various modern European nations and nation-states was the very fact that the modern universalistic or civic components of collective identity were combined not only with the older religious ones, but also with very strong primordial ones. In all modern European societies the primordial components of such identity, continuously reconstructed in such modern terms as nationalism and ethnicity, were confronted continuously by the modern universalistic and civil components. The mode of interweaving these different components of collective identity greatly shaped the nature of pluralism that developed in them and their impact on the mode of incorporation of Jews into these societies. Insofar as the primordial components were subsumed relatively successfully under the civil and universalistic ones and all were "peacefully" interwoven in the construction of their respective collective identities (as was to some extent the case in England, Holland, and the Scandinavian countries) these societies could allow a relatively wide scope for Jewish integration, but at the price of negating or weakening the primordial components in the Jewish experience.

In those societies or sectors within which there developed strong tensions between the primordial and the civil universalistic components in the construction of the collective identities of the modern nation-state (as was the case in Central Europe, above all in Germany and in many social movements in Western Europe and in other countries of Central Europe), the impact on Jewish experience went in a different direction. The tension between the primordial, civil, and universalistic components in the construction of their collective identity gave rise in these societies and movements to strong and negative emphasis on the centrality of the primordial components in Jewish collective identity. This emphasis became closely connected with principled denial of the possibility of any incorporation of Jews into the modern nation-state. These tendencies, as we have seen, ultimately led to the Holocaust.

In Eastern Europe, with its multinational empires or states, these primordial components were not necessarily denied. But the acceptance of the primordial components of Jewish identity did not necessarily facilitate the incorporation of Jews into these polities. It also could lead to a denial of the possibility of incorporation of Jews into these polities; whether on traditional grounds, in traditional antisemitic terms, in terms of modern antisemitism, or in some mixture of the two.

The major challenge before the Jews in Europe was how to become incorporated into this framework, either totally assimilating or in some way reconstructing their own collective boundaries and identies. Europe moved between several poles: between the struggle for emancipation often combined with very strong tendencies, often principled, to assimilation; modern antisemitism; the various attempts at the reconstruction of the collective boundaries of Jewish communities, as a part of those social spaces in which different modes of pluralism were allowed in the context of the modern nation-state.

Common to all these tendencies was, first, the strong tendency to principled, ideological formulations of the different options, including assimilation, which were seen as open to the Jewish communities; second, the potential confrontation in all such formulations of the primordial historical and religious components of Jewish identity with such components in the construction of the different European nation-states.

Another mode of Jewish historical experience developed in the eighteenth and nineteenth centuries among the so-called Oriental Jewry. Oriental Jewry—the Jewish communities living in the various Arab and Muslim countries: North Africa, Egypt, Syria, Iraq, Iran, and Yemen—constituted numerically a very significant part of Jewish population; and their specific historical experience differed greatly from that of the European Jews.[24]

In the middle of the nineteenth century about 500,000 Jews lived in the different parts of the Ottoman Empire: in Turkey itself, in what was to be Iraq, in Egypt and North Africa, in Syria and Palestine, and in far-away Yemen. Most of them had been there since ancient times, or at the latest since the expulsion of the Jews from Spain in 1492. They identified themselves as different parts of what were later to be called *Sephardi* or *Oriental communi-*

ties, be they Maghrebian or Egyptian Jews, some emphasizing their pure Sephardi ("Spanish") origin, very often split into many subcommunities.

The days of economic and cultural glory of these communities, on the whole, ended with the decline of the Mediterranean trade and the continuous weakening of the Ottoman Empire. Since then many of them lived in relatively closed communities, maintaining their traditional ways of life in some symbiosis with their neighbors—sometimes in relatively peaceful relations, sometimes in very tense and antagonistic ones—but always as a subjugated minority. They maintained the specific Jewish institutions of prayer and learning. Some of these, as for instance those in distant Yemen or in Iraq, constituted not insignificant centers of learning; but on the whole they did not retain the relative centrality in the Jewish world that they had held from the ninth to the twelfth centuries and later, after the expulsion from Spain, in the sixteenth and seventeenth centuries.

The existence of these communities, always rather precarious, was predicated on the traditional mode of pluralism prevailing in Islamic civilization, providing minority religious communities, especially those belonging to the monotheistic religions, some segregated and highly controlled living space, closely distinguished from that of the majority. From about the end of the eighteenth century, parts of these communities were slowly incorporated into the framework of modern economic expansion and social-cultural movements, which above all came in the wake of European colonial expansion.

With the growing impingement of European colonization and imperialism and the continuous weakening of the Ottoman Empire, these Oriental communities, from about the last third of the nineteenth century, started to undergo far-reaching processes of change and modernization. Of special importance here was the French colonization of the different North African countries (Algeria, Morocco, Tunisia), the growing European penetration into Egypt, and the competition of the European powers in all parts of the Ottoman Empire.

In North Africa (Morocco, Tunisia, Algeria) there was an intensive Jewish migration from the hinterland to the coastal cities: about one-third of the Jews of Morocco moved to these cities between 1830 and 1900. New Jewish elements also emigrated to these countries: Italian Jews came to Tunisia, French Jews to Algeria, and Central European and Russian Jews to Egypt.

These processes were combined with a continuous weakening of the old traditional milieu and elite sectors, as well as their dependence on the Ottoman powers. Many Jews attempted to receive the protectorate of European powers. All the Jews in Algeria became French citizens by virtue of the famous Cremieux edict of 1870, In other places they tried to find protection from the European powers to emancipate themselves from the yoke of the Ottoman state.

All these developments undermined the traditional communities and the authority of their secular and rabbinical leaders and produced far-reaching educational and occupational changes among the Jews. On the eve of the First World War about 48,000 children in North Africa attended the Alliance schools; and there were several other such institutions. Many of the higher-class Jews in Egypt lived in a very cosmopolitan atmosphere. This trend, of course, intensified after the First World War, not only in the communities of North Africa but also in Iraq and Syria; and new, modern Jewish organizations, including different Zionist organizations and movements, developed in these countries.

The overall modern historical experience of these communities differed greatly from those of the European Jewish comunities. This difference was rooted in the fact that the Muslim countries in which they lived did not undergo the same type of process of internal change and reconstruction from traditional to modern times that took place in Europe. Modernization came to those countries from the outside, as part of European expansion and usually under the aegis of colonial or semicolonial rule. Closely connected with this can be the fact that the secular dimension of modernity, in most of these countries, with the exception of Kemalist Turkey, was relatively weak and did not become a crucial component in the construction of their modern national-political identities.

This was true first of all with respect to the older traditional regimes that existed in all these countries till the end of the First World War and the Ottoman Empire. During this period, the mutual relations between the Jewish communities and their host societies continued to be based on the old traditional premises and no new principal demandsme a crucial component in the con their modern national-political identities.

This was first of all true with respect to the older traditional regimes that existed in all these countries till the end of the First World War under the aegis of the Ottoman Empire. During this period, the relations between the Jewish communities and their host societies continued to be based on the old traditional premises, and no new principal demands were made on the Jews to change in any way their traditional collective identity. However, in some of the cosmopolitan circles such tendencies to assimilation, resembling the European pattern but without its ideological overtones, did develop.

The various processes of modernization, economic, and educational, could be connected with some social participation and even assimilation in the cosmopolitan sectors of this society, as was the case in such cosmopolitan semicolonial centers as Cairo or Alexandria. But such participation or even assimilation was never connected with principled demands for changing their collective identity.

In other countries, like Iraq, far-reaching processes of modernization in the economic, occupational, and education took place within the framework of the existing Jewish communal institutions and relations, with but little attempts at assimilation. The ideology of European Enlightenment at most was of secondary importance among them. Within the framework of the basic traditional, Islamic premises of the Ottoman Empire, as well as those of the colonial situation, there was no special stimulus for the development of such religious movements as Reform or Liberal Judaism. The traditional Sephardi rabbinate and community organizations prevailed, but losing much of their authority to the more modern or secular ways of life, without at the same time facing any new and powerful ideological challenge either in religious or in liberal or national terms.

Hence, no movements of religious reform or very strong secular or semisecular national movements developed, and concomitantly no militant modern orthodoxy, developed there. There were no attempts to reconstruct Jewish religious life in a new, modern "nonorthodox" way, and (with the partial exception of some sectors of North African society) there was no ideological attempt at incorporation into the existing colonial sector.

Later on the various Middle Eastern, mostly Arab national movements and the new semicolonial states that developed before and after the First World War and the modern states that crystallized after the Second World War developed a cultural program of modernity radically different from the European ones. This program, to no small degree, focused on the tension between seemingly secular nationalism and the Islamic components of their collective identity. Whatever different solutions to this tension crystallized in different states and in different periods, the universalistic-secular components and the historical program of the European enlightenment were almost entirely lacking there, as they were among most sectors of Jewish communities. Hence, on the whole, no demands were made on Jews to give up the collective or primordial components of their identity. The existence of such components was taken mostly for granted, except in the secular Kemalist Turkey or the assimilationist French sector of North Africa.

Therefore, although some sectors of the Jewish communities continued in their traditional ways of life, others, often members of the same communities or even families, could easily slide away from such traditional framework, into more assimilation ways, without the necessity to give up, in a principled ideological way, their attachment to Jewish collective life— although they could easily drift away from it. Yet both the traditional and the more modern sectors often could encounter the religious hostility of the traditional sectors and the political-religious one of modern national movements or semisecular regimes. Such hostility naturally would grow with the permeation of the Zionist movement into these communities and later on with the establishment of the state of Israel.

5

The Incorporation of the Jews in the United States

Introduction: The Distinctive Characteristics of the Jewish-American Experience

The pattern of incorporation of Jews into a modern society that developed in the United States was distinguished by some very specific characteristics. It differed from the modes of incorporation of Jews into different European societies, not only quantitatively (in the number of Jews in one country or in their economic and occupational advancement) but also qualitatively (in some of the very central characteristics of the mode of their incorporation into the general American society).[1]

Truly enough there were many basic similarities between the fate of the Jews in the United States and Europe until the Second World War. The Jews in the United States like those in Europe constituted a minority in a country the majority of which belonged to a different, historically hostile religion or civilization. Although the United States did not promulgate an established religion and institutionalized the separation of Church and State with very strong emphasis on freedom of religion, it often was designated as a Christian country. Such designation for a long time constituted a basic component of the identity of the large sectors of American society, even if they admitted the legitimacy of other religions. The importance of this emphasis varied in different periods in the history; and the emphasis on it naturally became greater in periods of great immigration, when the predominant "WASP" groups felt threatened by these waves of different initially alien groups. Similarly, as in all other modern Western countries, the Jews, however politically emancipated, usually were socially relatively segregated or self-enclosed. Most of their social life, and in some periods also occupational interaction, was with other Jews, as was so brilliantly described by the Zionist leader Haim Arlosoroff in his essays on American Jewry published in the 1920s and 1930s.[2]

Antisemitism constituted a constant element on the American scene, to erupting in periods of economic depression and great immigration and economic dislocation. In certain periods, especially in periods of great immigration, the first generation of children of immigrants were barred from many occupations and in the twenties a system of quotas was established in the major universities.

These "segregative" tendencies existed to some extent throughout Jewish American history, but great differences developed in their importance in different periods in this history. In the colonial period the Jews, few in number, although on the whole tolerated, were looked upon among the Puritans as objects of semimissionary attempts, to be persuaded to convert. The strong affinity of the Puritans to the Old Testament, often perhaps paradoxically, has reinforced this view of the Jews. Only the "free" urban atmosphere in New Amsterdam or New York was more tolerant, and limitations barring Jews from owning landed property and later even of holding office were gradually removed.

In the first decades of the republic, from the very beginning, Jews were granted full political rights, Even with the influx of the German Jewish immigration from about the 1830s, these segregative tendencies were weakened. Such weakening of these segregative tendencies became predominant again with much greater force and visibility, from the 1860s and on. However, the segregational tendencies with strong antisemitic overtones became most predominant after the great immigration starting in about the 1880s and, perhaps above all, as the first generation of American-born or -bred children of these immigrants started to climb up the educational and the economic ladder, resembling the pattern of incorporation of Jews in Western and Central Europe. But even in this period the similarity with the European Jewish experience was only partial, even if often overemphasized by many intellectuals and leaders for whom the European experience was paradigmatic. In reality this similarity was overshadowed by some very distinct American patterns.

Among these distinct American patterns the most important were the granting of full citizenship to the Jews and, as a result the absence of any struggle for emancipation in the European meaning of the term. A Jew could be, or at least aspire to be, accepted as part of the American collectivity without giving up some type of Jewish collective identity and activities. Jews could combine such activities with being fullfledged American citizens viewing themselves and seemingly accepted by their host society as full citizens in that society and not just, as in Eastern Europe between the wars, as one national minority group among other such groups, having to struggle for their legitimate place in the political arena.

The constant reconstruction of such Jewish identity and patterns of life took place in a new, specifically American way, one in which the development of communal, philanthropic, political, and cultural activities with specific Jewish goals and maintaining some distinct Jewish identity on the whole were taken for granted. Even if some, sometimes quite wide, sectors of the Jewish community tended to stay away from any such expression of Jewish collective identity and moved in the direction of assimilation, only a very few defined such assimilation in principled ideological terms, as was the case in Europe. Only relatively few Jews converted, under passive persuasion. Probably some of these were children of immigrants of the mass immigration who have found their ways blocked in professional or academic arenas; although the number of those who drifted away from any Jewish framework was always quite high, especially, and perhaps paradoxically, in the more "benign," "tolerant" periods.

We shall not deal at any length with some of the well-known features of American Jewish life, such as the unusual educational and occupational mobility and advancement. Rather we shall focus on what seems the most distinguishing aspect of American Jewish experience, the incorporation of Jews into almost all the arenas of American life and the effects of such incorporation on the structuring of Jewish life and self-perception.[3] The most distinctive characteristics of the mode of incorporation of Jews in the United States have been the combination of great and continuous economic and occupational advancement; the incorporation of Jews into most arenas, including public arenas, of life; and the relatively general, even if intermittent, public acceptance of collective activities of Jews and of the primordial components of Jewish identity.

This mode of incorporation of Jews in the United States, especially in the last two or three decades, and the kernels of which could be found already in the nineteenth century, has been manifest above all in the burgeoning of Jewish institutions, first of all religious and educational ones, then also broader communal and political ones; in their public visibility and acceptability; in the definition of their collective identity by American Jews with strong emphasis on elements of peoplehood, and in the mode of their participation in the general institutional, especially political and intellectual, arenas of American society.

The common denominator of these various tendencies has been the open public display and acceptance of the communal Jewish experience and activities, defined not only in religious terms, but often, especially lately, also in broader, "ethnic" national terms or in terms of "peoplehood." Jewish identity, collective consciousness, and collective endeavors were not restricted to semiprivate religious and philanthropic spheres; although they were, as we shall see, usually based in religious symbolism and institutions.

This new attitude accepted and even emphasized, in contrast to the nineteenth century European experience, the combination of the communal, "ethnic," and political components of Jewishness and of their peoplehood, even if religious organizations long served as the major bases of such communal organizations. This pattern of incorporation of Jews into American society became visible, as hinted earlier, from the late 1960s, but has its beginnings in the nineteenth century before the great immigrations of the 1880s, when for a period of two to three generations it became muted. Thus, for instance the ideology of American (Jewish) Reform, as it developed in the nineteenth century, was based on the assumption that religious reform was something common to all Americans. And, although the extreme derivatives of this ideology were not followed by many congregations, the ideal of becoming part of the American scene without losing a sense of Jewishness was quite widespread. It is not surprising perhaps that some of the most ardent Zionist leaders later emerged from within this Reform movement.

The Specific Premises of American Civilization; American Pluralism; and the Incorporation of Jews

This specific pattern of incorporation of the Jewish minority into American society developed in the context of the distinct premises of American civilization, the basic characteristics of its collective identity that distinguished it greatly from the European ones.[4] The major components of this collective identity were rooted in combination of Puritanism with Lockean political orientations and the basic orientations of the Enlightenment with nonconformist religious orientations. They became crystallized in the Declaration of Independence, the Constitution, and the Bill of Rights, giving rise to the peculiar type of what R. N. Bellah defined as "civil religion" as one of the most forceful components of its collective identity. This collective identity developed out of the fusion of religious sentiment with political values. Such fusion imbued both the social and political realms of American life and the construction of the American collectivity with a unique and often soteriological meaning in the eyes of the seventeenth, eighteenth, and nineteenth centuries American society.

This fusion entailed a strong "Messianic" and millenial nature of the early American sociopolitical endeavor, the particular combination of solidarity and individualism as central components of American collective identity, and the antistatist orientation that evolved in American society. It also explains why the American nationalism or collective identity was based neither on primordial elements nor rooted in an organic historical development, as well as the strong future orientation of American values and belief systems.[5] The fusion included, above all, the very strong emphasis on achievement and equality, republican liberties, and disestablishment of any official religion.

One of the most important aspects of the American civilization, in comparison with the European ones, rooted in the premises of metaphysical equality just mentioned and the lack of a symbolic (as against concrete) hierarchy, was the principled openness of the center to all members of the community. The most crucial difference between the basic civilizational premises of the United States, as against Europe and also Canada, has been the strong emphasis in the United States on the strong metaphysical equality of all members of the community, stressed so emphatically already by de Toqueville, on the concomitant unmediated access of all members of the community to the center, and on the almost total denial of the symbolic validity of hierarchy (as against, of course, values hierarchy) as a basic component of these premises. In the United States, given all these premises, the access to the center, in principle, was given to all citizens. It did not, in close relation to conceptions of equality mentioned earlier, constitute, as in Europe, a focus of principled struggle.

Concomitantly, the confrontation between State and Society, so central to the European experience, became weakened as society became predominant and in a way submerging the state under itself. This predominance was evident among others in the weakness in the United States of the concepts and ideologies of the state (as distinct from those of the people, the republic) or, to use R. Nettl's expression, the very small degree of "stateness" in it, as against the great importance of such conception in continental Europe and the milder one in the British conception of the "Crown" or "Crown in Parliament."[6]

This new collective identity and its political expression was not based on traditions defined in historical and primordial trends, as was the case in Europe. Although it derived from religious premises, it was transformed into what Robert Bellah[7] called "civil religion," based on the separation of Church and State, and future rather than past oriented. The definition of the American way of life was constructed in terms of a common political ideology with religious overtones and an emphasis on Christian heritage, rather than a combination of religious tradition with historical, ethnic, or national identity. In Samuel Huntington's words:

For most people national identity is the product of a long process of historical evolution involving common conceptions, common experiences, common ethnic background, common language, common culture and usually common religion. National identity is thus organic in character. Such however is not the case in the United States. American nationality has been defined in political rather than organic terms. The political ideas of the American creed have been the basis of national identity.... The United States thus had its origins in a conscious political act, in assertion of basic political principles and in adherence to the constitutional agreement based on those principles."[8]

The crucial fact here is that American collective identity is constructed in terms of political ideology, with almost no territorial or historical components. Though it shared a strong orientation to the Bible with the Zionist movements, the new territory was not sanctified in terms of primordial attachment to a land of the Fathers, or as the natural locus of a long history.

Within the framework of these premises in the United States a mode of pluralism and an attitude to minority groups developed that differed greatly from such attitudes in most European countries. Given the weakness of the primordial components in the construction of American collective identity, the potential developed here for a much greater tolerance, not only to religious diversity, but also to groups defined in terms of primordial components, predicated, of course, on the acceptance by them of the basic ideological-political premises of American civilization. Even with respect to religious tolerance, the attitude that developed in America was not a simple development to religious tolerance in the European sense, based on the limitation or disestablishment of an established church, although the expressions of such tolerance often were still couched in European terms. The separation of Church and State in the United States developed not as an outcome of struggles against a history of long tension between the two, but from the basic fact that America was formed by members of various Protestant sects. Because of these basic characteristics, America had potential to accept, even if haltingly and intermittently, religious, political, and ethnic diversity—with the crucial initial exception of the Blacks—as long as members of the different groups accepted the American political creed. Accordingly, immigrants, including the Jews, did not have to struggle to gain full citizenship rights. The question of Jewish emancipation never arose.

This attitude became first fully epitomized in George Washington's famous message to the Hebrew Congregation of Newport, Rhode Island, in 1790.

The citizens of the United States of America have a right to applaud themselves for having given to mankind examples of an enlarged and liberal policy—a policy worthy of imitation. All possess alike liberty of conscience and immunities of citizenship.

It is now no more that toleration is spoken of as if it were the indulgence of one class of people that another enjoyed the exercise of their inherent natural rights, for, happily, the Government of the United States, which gives to bigotry no factions, to persecution no assistance, requires only that they who live under its protection should demean themselves as good citizens in giving it on all occasions their effectual support.

May the children of the stock of Abraham who dwell in this land continue to merit and enjoy the good will of the other inhabitants— while every one shall sit in safety under his own vine and fig tree and there shall be none to make him afraid.[9]

The distinctive American attitude to religious and group diversity as related to Jews could also be found in a series of later legal promulgations.

In 1810, Congress passed the Sunday Mail Law, which decreed that mail should be delivered on Sundays. As Seymour Martin Lipset notes, twenty years later, in 1830, "a Senate committee report...endorsed by a priority of that House, stated...laws proclaiming that the government should not provide services on Sunday would work an injustice to irreligious people or non-Christians, and would constitute a special favor to Christians as a group." The report was written by a deeply religious active Baptist:

The Constitution regards the conscience of the Jew as sacred as that of the Christian, and gives no more authority to adopt a measure affecting the conscience of a solitary individual than that of a whole community.... If Congress shall declare the first day of the week holy, it will not satisfy the Jew nor the Sabbatarian. It will dissatisfy both and, consequently, convert neither.... It must be recollected that, in the earliest settlement of this country, the spirit of persecution, which drove the pilgrims from their native homes, was brought with them to their new habitations; and that some Christians were scourged and others put to death for no other crime than dissenting from the dogmas of their rulers.... If a solemn act of legislation shall in one point define the God or point out to the citizen one religious duty, it may with equal propriety define every part of divine revelation and enforce every religious obligation, even to the forms and ceremonies of worship; the endowment of the church, and the support of the clergy.

...It is the duty of this government to affirm to all—to the Jew or Gentile, Pagan, or Christian—the protection and advantages of our benignant institutions on Sunday.[10]

Jewish Collective Activities; Incorporation in the Mainstream of American Life; Modes of Assimilation

Truly enough, the existence of such basic premises of toleration did not mean that the acceptance of full open Jewish participation in American life always was easily attained. Continuously religious and social tension developed between the Jewish community and different sectors of American society. In the context of such tensions manifestations of antisemitism abounded in all periods, but its strength varied in different periods and in different sections of American society. In the beginning of the first half of the nineteenth century, Jews were accepted, as indicated earlier, especially beyond the Eastern seashore, in areas of territorial expansion, into general social life, and so were open Jewish group activities, which at that time were mostly religious and to some extent philanthropic. But the situation changed greatly with the mass immigration at the end of the nineteenth century. This mass immigration gave rise, among the predominant WASP circles, to the fear that the basic cultural and social ambiance, within the framework of which the original toleration developed, would be undermined. In this period, when the very influx of many new immigrant groups seemed to threaten their hitherto "natural" predominancy, or in periods of economic recession or growing competition between immigrant groups and American-born workers for limited jobs, antisemitism would erupt in the United States.

Antisemitism manifested itself in the exclusion of Jews from many economic sectors, in various popular outbursts and often in the general social ambiance. Indeed in this period, the most far-reaching restrictions on Jewish participation, and advancement—quotas in universities, restriction of access to many arenas of economic activities—abounded. Also in this period assimilationist tendencies resembling the Western ones developed in relatively wide sectors of Jewish society.

But the expression of antisemitism, not only in this period but also before it, in the United States never assumed the intensity or scope of their nineteenth and twentieth century parallels in Europe, nor have they impeded for any length of time the occupational advance of the Jews, and their growing public collective visibility.

American antisemitism, though often widespread and sometimes quite rampant and virulent, has differed in several crucial ways from European. In the United States, antisemitism was not connected with nationalism, nor has been an integral part of an historical ideology. Nor has antisemitism been a particular focal point of American hate groups. In Jonathan Sarna's words American antisemitism has "to compete with other forms of animus, Racism, anti-Quakerism, Anglophobia, anti-Catholicism, anti-Masonry, anti-Mormonism, anti-Orientalism, nativism, anti-Teutonism, primitive anti-Communism, these and other waves have periodically swept over the American landscape, scarring and battering citizens. Because hatred is so varied and diffused, no group experiences for long the full brunt of national odium. Furhtermore, most Americans retain bitter memories of days past when they or their ancestors were the objects of malevolence. At least in some cases, this leads them to exercise restraint. The American strain of antisemitism is thus less potent than its European counterpart, and it faces a larger number of natural competitors. To reach epidemic proportions, it must first crowd out a vast number of contending hatreds.... The Founding Fathers, whatever they personally thought of Jews, gave them full equality. Hence, in America, Jews have always fought antisemitism freely. Never having received their emancipation as an "award," they have had no fears of losing it. Instead, from the beginning, they made full use of thier right to freedom of speech.[11]

Whatever the ups and downs of intergroup tensions and antisemitism, from the late 1950s or early 1960s on, but above all in the 1970s and 1980s, the specific mode of Jewish incorporation into American society has crystallized. This mode was characterized by a combination of the burgeoning of Jewish organization and attributes together with a very strong emphasis on the promulgation of Jewish collective identity and a specific pattern of intensive participation of Jews, not only in occupational and economic, but also in political and cultural arenas of American life.

Also in the period of the mass immigration far-reaching attempts were promulgated at homogenization of the new immigrants. In the midst of this period the ideology of the melting pot developed among some minorities, especially the Jews. Although accepting the idea of ultimate similarity, the ideology also emphasized that each group would contribute to this "pot" some distinct ingredients. During this period, and especially during the Great Depression, the ideology of homogeneity became promulgated in schools and the media and the development of more particularistic identities for a relatively long time was seemingly possible only in the private sphere. Yet, even in the period of mass immigration the actual experience of life in America permitted some such diversity even with the influx of mass immigration in the late nineteenth and early twentieth centuries and the Jewish experience in the United States differed greatly from that in Europe.

Even in this earlier period of mass migration, the very gradual economic advance of the Jews did not on the whole necessarily lead to the abandonment of their religious and communal activities. Family solidarity and communal cohesion and help remained very strong—as did also positive religious, primordial, and even political identification with the Jewish people—even if, among the second and third generation of immigrants, these elements often became, initially at least, generally weakened, often undermined by the ideology of the melting pot, the social pressures connected with it, and various manifestations of antisemitism. But even in the third decade of this century, when many mobile Jews were experiencing these restrictive aspects of American life, some very significant new developments in the mode of Jewish organization and ideology indeed were taking place.

All these developments, which burgeoned fully later, developed within the framework of the distinct ideological premises and institutional frameworks of American civilization. Here, the distinct characteristics of the Jewish American experience briefly alluded to earlier developed. The kernels of these characteristics had already developed, as we have seen, in the first two thirds of the nineteenth century, when some of the distinct characteristics of the Jewish organizations and Jewish collective consciousness in the United States developed. Among the most important such characteristics have been the important place of the religion, the synagogue, and the concomitant proliferation of numerous Jewish organizations, related in one way or another to the synagogue, all structured in specific American ways; the almost total lack of Jewish national movements; the open participation as individuals, but also as collective organized Jews in the general political arena, but not as representing only the Jewish constitution.

Although Jewish organizations, activities, and the public promulgation of Jewish themes and identity abounded, most of them (with the exception of the ultraorthodox sectors) were set in the general framework of American society and not, as in Eastern Europe, within distinct Jewish frameworks.

Significantly enough from relatively early on Jewish communal activities have been focused in religious institutions, Rabbinical seminaries—the Reform "Hebrew Union College" in Cincinnati established in 1875, and the Conservative Jewish Theological Seminar in New York in 1886, their respective synagogues and their common assemblies. The various Orthodox *Yeshivoth* were rather weak until before the Second World War when many distinguished Orthodox Rabbis who emigrated from Europe challenged the existing situation among the orthodox circles in the United States.

The Reform and Conservative synagogues and federations resembled in their theological orientation as well as their general religious stances many of the Protestant congregations. In the first stages of its development, the Reform synagogues and the Hebrew Union College emphasized the more spiritual almost deistic conceptions of Judaism; later on, especially from ca. after the First World War, more conventional religious conceptions—and after the Second World War the primordial components of Jewish collective identity—became more prevalent among them. The Conservatives espoused from the very beginning more traditional religious and communal conceptions—moving also in the direction of growing recognition of the Jewish people.

The latter was less true—especially with respect to their interpretation of religion—of the Orthodox—but organisationally even they have greatly adjusted themselves to the American scene.

Relatively early Jews started to organize themselves in more diversified ways beyond mere religious, cultural, or philanthropic activities; first of all in a very vigorous way on the local level in a series of decentralized communities, later also in various countrywide religious and philanthropic organizations. They started to organize themselves actively against discrimination, as in the Anti-Defamation League founded in 1913 to organize help for the Jews in difficult situations and in the Joint Distribution Committee founded in 1914.

Probably even more dramatic was the development of new types of Jewish organizations, as well as of ideological definitions of Jewish life, both perhaps best epitomized in the work of Mordechai Kaplan (1881–1982), although certainly not confined to him. Kaplan first propounded, although probably building on some former attempts, the program of transforming the synagogue from a place of prayer to a base for a wide range of Jewish communal activities.[12] This organizational conception, often resisted by the older Jewish religious establishments, Reform and Conservative, was very closely connected with this ideological conception of Jewishness as it developed in connection with "Reconstructionism." Although in purely religious terms this went beyond even extreme reform, it was connected in his view with the conception of Jewish peoplehood, with Jews as carriers of a distinct civilization that could be part of the American civilization, but not necessarily only of it.

In this period the synagogue became the basis of the plethora of Jewish organizations. This was not as a place of worship but, much more in accordance with Kaplan's vision, a center of multiple communal activities and different expressions of Jewish peoplehood, without however accepting Kaplan's religious views. Thus, as Nathan Glazer has commented, Kaplan's practice was accepted, but not his ideological formulation or his religious tenets.

This development was especially important among the second generation of the East European Jewish immigrants, and the descendants of the earlier groups of immigrants. It was closely connected with the movement of Jews into mixed urban suburbs. Organizationally it followed very much the general American (especially Protestant) congregational mode of religious organizations, but in the scope of its activities and its overall conception it went far beyond most of them.

The synagogues and religious organizations that developed in the United States were not like those in the more traditional sectors of Jewish European society: a central focus, a traditional society, or a self-enclosed community with quite clearly structured boundaries. Nor, as in the case of the more diversified in patterns of Jewish life, in Eastern Europe, from about the last third of the nineteenth century, were they just one of many sectors or organizations, most of which no longer focused on religious life and organized mostly in the secular way, but oriented only to Jewish constituencies. Nor was the synagogue a purely religious organization in the modern Western European sense, which defined itself in a restricted religious sense, as distinct from ethnic or national ones, and which at most engaged in some religious education or philantropic activities.

The synagogue in the United States of course focused on religious activities, but such activities were not conceived as an all-encompassing, self-enclosed entity, but mainly as a basis for many other collective activities that no longer necessary were religous. Nor was religion or religious activity the only manifestation of Jewish collective identity.

The synagogue and community centers also became the bases for the most important Jewish institutions in the United States, the different types of Jewish education, the day schools (relatively rare except within the orthodox circles), "Sunday" school, and afternoon schools, which became one of the most important institutions in the transmission of Jewish identity.

In addition, beyond the synagogue centers but usually based on them, or at least closely related to them, multiple countrywide Jewish organizations developed, above all the United Jewish Appeal founded in 1934, but also the Committee of Jewish Federations and Welfare Funds, the American Jewish Community, and many others that developed a very wide range of activities, mobilizing financial resources and communal and political support, the likes of which could not be found in any other "ethnic" or religious groups in the United States.

Needless to say, for many Jews, even those attached to the communities, the synagogue was not so central and many other semiformal forms of interaction among the Jews developed. But on the whole, the synagogue and the closely related community center constituted the central kernel of Jewish organizational life.

The central place of the synagogue and religion in Jewish life in America was so much in tune with the general American way of life, as in a way was heralded by Will Herberg in *Protestant, Catholic and Jew* (published in 1955), stressing both the centrality of the religious component in Judaism and its full legitimation as part of the (religious) diversity of the American scene or way of life. But even at the time of the publication of this book, and certainly later on, this view of American Judaism did not tell the whole story. The view indeed was correct in stressing the full legitimacy of such diversity, as well as the central place of the religious activities. But it did not take into account the very great diversity of collective activities much beyond the purely religious field that developed from the religious congregational bases and that emphasized and articulated the collective, "ethnic," and even political components of Jewish identity, of what began to be called Jewish "peoplehood," as well as the great diversity of Jewish activities, very much in tune with these varied components.

One of the most distinct manifestations of this mode of incorporation of Jews in the United States and one that distinguishes this mode of incorporation especially from the situation in Eastern Europe, has been the absence of national movements among the Jews. Kernels of such movements, such as the Bundist or other Yiddishist movement, were brought over with the great immigration in the last decades of the nineteenth and the first decades of the twentieth century, but they petered out in the second generation. Only the Zionist movement was successful in strengthening roots in the American Jewish community; however, its basic characteristics, brought over initially from Eastern and Central Europe, were transformed very quickly. From very early on it was viewed as the search for a safe haven for those Jews who needed it and not the cultural renaissance, on the search for a new arena for the reconstruction of new modern Jewish culture. This was predominant in the attitudes of large sectors of the Zionist movement in the United States.

With the establishment of the state of Israel, whatever initial ideological orientations existed in this movement became transformed mostly into a strong sentimental identification with the state of Israel and a movement of political and economic support for it—and not on the whole with the reconstruction of the internal life of American Jews. Truly enough in the early 1950s the very establishment of the state of Israel, its becoming a member of international community, its military success, more and more legitimized the political dimension in the activities of American Jews. But with the passing of time this was taken for granted more and more and has only intensified among the Jews the feeling of being a part of American life.

The weakness, basically absence, of Jewish national movements in the United States, of course, was connected very strongly with some of the most important aspects of their incorporation in American society and the basic characteristics of American collective identity, with its being constructed around a political identity and not a historical primordial one. Accordingly, one of the most important aspects of this mode of incorporation of Jews in American society, and one closely related to the lack of national movements among them, was also the weakness of Jewish historical consciousness.

In contrast to Jewish experience in Eastern Europe, where different sectors and movements vied with one another in the continuous reconstruction of different components of historical consciousness among the Jews, Jewish collective consciousness in the United States was constructed much more around religious cummunal and cultural symbols and activities. The construction of such collective consciousness referred only tangently to the Jewish historical experience in the United States or in other countries. Lately such consciousness became focused around the Holocaust, depicting the passive fate of Jews and not their active construction of their own life. In place, as it were, of such national movements, Jews in the United States developed a plethora of activities set firmly within the general American setting.

Especially since the 1960s the specific characteristics of Jewish American experience, kernels of which developed, as we have seen, in the first two-thirds of the nineteenth century, became fully crystallized. This more general contemporary acceptance of Jewish distinctiveness was connected with the transformation, beginning in the late 1950s, of the American scene, especially with the weakening ideology of the melting pot and with the upsurge of ethnic pride in general.[13]

During this period a rapid process of educational and occupational advance took place. Major universities, which until this time had had de facto quotas for Jews, allowed open enrollment. Jews entered these universities, graduated from them, and moved on to become prominent in professional, academic, cultural, and mass media fields. Though many sectors, such as banking and top industry, remained closed to most Jews untill the late 1960s or early 1970s, from about the mid-1970s, many additional economic areas opened their doors to them.

For large sectors of the Jewish community, the progression of economic and occupational mobility gave rise to an expanding scope of collective Jewish ventures and the growth of Jewish education on both the local and national levels. Although this process became stronger after the early 1970s, the roots could be traced back twenty years.

Concomitantly from the mid-1950s, the burgeoning of collective political activities closely connected with the state of Israel provided a central focus for Jewish endeavor. The image of the state, based as it was on the myth of a pioneer conquering of the wasteland, rooted in a biblical vision, was very close to some basic components of the American myth and helped greatly to legitimize these undertakings. Later on organized action on behalf of Soviet Jewry became another central focus of Jewish political life.

There were some general reasons or causes beyond the specifically American one that contributed to the crystallization of this new mode of Jewish historical experience in this period, of course, such reasons are closely related to central aspects of post-Second World War history, especially the Holocaust and the establishment of the state of Israel. The impact of these traumatic and dramatic events could be discerned not only in the Jewish community in the United States, but also in various Jewish populations in Europe, particularly in England and France. In all these countries we find development not only of economic advancement, but also more open and widespread Jewish communal organizations, but it was on the American scene that these developments appear most far-reaching.

Truly enough, even in this period, at times strong resentment developed among certain sectors of American society at the Jew's economic advances and growing cultural, social, and political visibility. From the late 1960s on, the great upsurge of ethnicity in the United States also gave rise to growing antisemitism among some minority groups—especially the blacks—and the demands for positive discrimination, for quotas, often de facto were directed against Jews. Tensions between many sectors of the black and the Jewish communities increased and continously erupted throughout the eighties—on the local and the more central political levels alike.

Many individual Jews became active in politics, Jewish lobbies developed, and Jews became politically organized very intensively—particularly on behalf of Israel and Soviet Jewry and, as we shall see later, this heated exchange gathered momentum from the 1970s on. Yet, in direct contrast to the situation in Eastern Europe up to the Second World War, no Jewish parties developed and no specifically Jewish representatives were elected to Congress.

A very important and significant transformation also took place in this period in the status of Jewish intellectuals. The Jewish immigration to the United States was not composed of great numbers of intellectuals. The first stages of the mass immigration included only very few outstanding intellectual figures among the Jews. Among the sons of older immigrants, above all there were some great legal figures, like Brandeis and Cardoso, and later some reformist ones.

The first generation of Jewish college graduates was not greatly concerned with Jewish problems. The nature of their own Jewishness was not a center of the major writers of this period: in the first writings of American Jewish writers, like Saul Bellow and Bernard Malamud, the Jewish themes, although certainly visible, were rather muted. This was even more true of the Jewish intellectuals or academics of that generation, who found the gates of American colleges and universities closed, and who became very active in radical socialism, and seemed to be alienated from the broader American—and Jewish—communal scene.

But all this changed very quickly, giving rise in the late 1950s, to an entirely different picture. Many of the Jewish writers who became very eminent on the American literary scene—such as Saul Bellow, Bernard Malamud, Philip Roth, and many others—unlike most of their counterparts in Western and Central Europe, did not aim at assimilation. They did not deny or reject their Jewish heritage or concerns. Indeed, very often it was quite the opposite. In their works they often stressed Jewish themes and Jewish persons as part of the broader American scene: many of them closely identified themselves with Jewish activities and their connections with political or communal Jewish groups were often very close. But at the same time, unlike the Jewish writers in Eastern Europe, they did not create a specifically Jewish, Hebrew or Yiddish literature for Jewish audiences.

Among the Jews an aspect of culturalism developed, sponsored by

Jewish organizations but oriented to a large degree to the general problems of American society. The developments combined Jewish themes with open participation in the intellectual life of America, attempting to provide a specific Jewish dimension to the more general discussion of American problems. *Commentary,* the independent monthly published by the American Jewish Committee, and more recently *Tikkun,* published by more "leftist" Jewish intellectual, are indicative of this focus.

A wide spectrum of Jewish educational institutions has developed. But most of these institutions, of which the various types of Sunday schools usually connected to synagogues, were appendages or supplements to the general educational system that constituted the major educational framework for most Jewish children. Only the orthodox sectors had full-scale Jewish educational systems: encompassing kindergarten, primary school, and junior and junior high school, often in connection with traditional type yeshivoth developed already in the 1950s or 1960s. Only lately, some new trends combining general and Jewish curricula, recalling to some extent the modern Jewish educational institutions of Eastern Europe, developed to a somewhat greater extent in other sectors of the Jewish community. But these new developments still comprise a relatively small proporation of the Jewish educational scene, and on the whole remain firmly set within the framework of the general society. Recently there has been a parallel emergence of Jewish study centers in many universites and their placement in general academic departments or schools.

The unique patterns of political participation briefly alluded to earlier, gathered momentum in the late 1960s. In addition to the numerous political activities of Jewish organizations on behalf of strictly Jewish causes, Jews and Jewish leaders were active in general political movements. Indeed many of their own, specifically Jewish activities, were oriented to the general American scene. Ideals of social justice were promulgated by Jewish leaders and organizations as being "natural" to the Jews—but unlike in Western Europe they were promulgated as part of Jewish collective activities and not as justification for active Jews to leave the fold of these organizations and join the general movements. The civil rights movement is the single most important illustration. Unlike the participation of Jews in European radical movements, this often was openly presented as a Jewish contribution to American political life or rather as a seemingly natural contribution of organized Jews.

From the late 1970s, individual Jews, as mentioned, became also more mobile and visible in political life, nationally as well as locally. Even when various Black organizations turned against the Jews and when the experience of Jewish students and young radical activists in the 1960s and 1970s became problematical given the strong anti-Israel stand of these movements, the feeling of Jews that, as Jews, they are perhaps adding a special dimension to American political life, has not abated.

It is interesting to note that the Jews have begun to move away from the left or liberal sector of the American political, social, and intellectual scene toward the more center or right wing one. This is evident in the general ambience of *Commentary* and in the relative prominence of Jewish intellectuals,, many of them (such as those close to *Commentary*) members of leftist movements in their youth in the 1920s. This was not just a case of individual Jews adopting conservative tendencies or of being center or right wing idealists (as could be found in Central or Eastern Europe; for instance, Walther Rathenau). What is significant here is that a fairly large proportion of Jewish intellectuals and journalists moved to the right, signalling, as it were, that their full participation in American public policy need not only take the form of a protest from the left against the conservative or traditional center, but may also embrace the values of the (American) center.

The mode of Jewish communal organizations in the United States, as well as of the participation of Jews in the general arenas of American life, has brought out the specific themes of Jewish civilization in a rather specific way.[14] Both in their communal activities and their participation in the general arenas of American life, Jews often emphasized that they were articulating some of the specific themes of Jewish civilization, especially the more universalistic, ethical ones; and they often presented such themes as a distinct Jewish contribution to the overall panorama of American life. Yet this contribution was not promulgated, as among Jewish communities in Western Europe in the nineteenth century, as some vague almost metaphysical, specifically Jewish mission to Western civilization that at the same time may be connected with the disappearance of the Jewish collective entity.

The promulgation of these themes of Jewish civilization in the United States usually was strongly connected with the development of Jewish communal, social or cultural Jewish activities, as well as with open direct access, as a distinct group, to the central arenas of American life. Most Jewish intellectuals or leaders did not hesitate, especially since the 1970s, to promulgate the legitimacy, within the general context of American life, of the specific collective Jewish interests; although they were quite sensitive to their collective image in many sectors of American society.

Against the background of these various trends, among the Jews, and to a lesser degree also among their host nation, a new vision developed of collective Jewish existence. The major characteristic of this new vision was the definition of the major problem of Jewish experience in the modern world in terms of different ways to express Jewish identity, Jewish peoplehood, in the Diaspora. The search stressed not only the religious but also the political and civilizational dimensions of Jewish identity. At the same time, however, the Jews still saw themselves as full members of their respective societies or nationalities.

Basically, despite many misgivings and fears about an ultimate lack of viability of Jewish existence in the Diaspora, this vision took the existence of Jewish collective distinctiveness as a part of the general society for granted while searching for different ways to express that identity. The feeling became increasingly prevalent among American Jews that it was possible for them to see themselves as both Americans and Jews. Unlike in Europe, in the nineteenth century and first half of the twentieth century, American Jews did not see any contradiction between these two identities, even as they emphasized the collective, historical, and political dimensions of their Jewishness.

Closely related to this vision, the Jewish communities developed a variety of ways to articulate patterns of Jewish life. The dichotomy of living as an American or as a Jew seemingly no longer held. Many Jews were continuously changing the patterns of their life and did not lead lives that were primarily Jewish, but they did not want to lose their Jewishness—however they defined it. This led to different, continuously changing patterns of reformulation, a restructuring of their identity, and an increasing attachment to different elements of the Jewish tradition or traditions and the different interpretations of the Jewish experience.

There was a return to religious customs that had become symbols of a collective peoplehood: candle lighting on Hanuka or on the eve of sabbath, the celebration of circumcision, bar mitzvah, marriage, and funerals. Although this return to tradition did not necessarily signal the acceptance of the Halakhah as the basic framework of Jewish life, such a process took place to some extent. The upsurge of orthodoxy and neo-orthodoxy constituted a closely connected process.

The most interesting aspect of this process is that no simple relationship between attachment to Jewish customs and commitment to Jewish identity developed. Even within orthodox circles, in the last two decades there has been increasing participation in some of the "general" arenas of life, such as higher education and political activities, which would have been anathema to the older Eastern European traditionalists.

Another element that developed in the period after the Second World War was the emergence of collective Jewish political activity in the general political arena, to which we have referred earlier. Probably for the first time in modern exilic history, Jewish communities throughout the world became active and openly conscious as Jews in the political arena. Truly enough—although they perceived themselves as totally free—they imposed on themselves, as we shall see in greater detail later on (in chapter nine), and Alan Dershovitz claimed in his best-selling "Hutzpah"—rather far-reaching limitations. But these limitations notwithstanding, the scope of their communal activities in the general political arena was unprecedented in Jewish exilic history.

It is a moot question to what extent these tendencies make invalid the basic Zionist tenets about the inevitability of assimilation or demographic decline or in the extreme intensification of antisemitic movements and perhaps destruction. Indeed, visions of the Holocaust have become prevalent in the collective memory of American Jewry. In this context it is also difficult to assess the impact on the Jewish community of the growing political importance of the Black population, of the tensions between the black and the Jewish communities, or a possible rift between the U.S. and Israeli governments, although many rather problematic indications can be seen.

Despite all these possibilities, those among the Jews who are concerned with such matters apparently were able to combine their historical community with full participation in American society. Seemingly many American Jews, those who uphold their Jewishness, refuse to view antisemitism as a threat to their incorporation as Jews into the general American society. They often point out that even intermarriage could have unexpected results and that fairly often, certainly much more frequently than in Europe, assimilated Jews who marry Gentile women are brought back to some Jewish framework by their wives, who want to uphold tradition.

Thus, instead of the "classical" problem of physical and cultural survival in the modern world, the crucial question for Jews becomes how to find new ways of authenticating their Jewishness in this new setting.

The Paradox of Jewish American Life: Communal Activity and Drifting Away

Therefore, from this point of view of the comparative analysis of the incorporation of Jews into Western societies, the American Jewish experience is rather paradoxical. The relative weakness of the primordial components in the American collective identity, the specific mode of American pluralism, and the consequent difference between American and European antisemitism seemingly should have facilitated Jewish assimilation and the dissolution of many of the specifically Jewish aspects of their communal life.

Assimilation in the European sense—a conscious, often ideological crossing of collective boundaries—indeed could be found among Jews in the United States, especially in the first half of this century, when the ideology of the melting pot emerging in wake of the great immigration was predominant. Yet this was not the whole picture, not even the major component of the picture of the incorporation of Jews into American society. The weakness of the primordial elements and historical consciousness in the construction of

American collective identity and the combination of a highly religious society—in many ways the most religious modern society—with the principled separation of Church and State, as we have seen, have legitimized the articulation of the various primordial and religious components of Jewish collective identity and enabled the development of multiple Jewish collective activities as well as open Jewish participation in the central orders of American life. Tendencies to assimilation abounded. But the whole tenor of this assimilation, on the whole, was entirely different from the European one. Truly enough, pressures to convert, to deny their Jewishness, especially from the 1920s through the 1950s, were exerted on Jews and many, especially probably among the more professional, college educated Jews, acted accordingly.

But the greater part of assimilation lacked the principled ideological dimension so prevalent in Europe. As the American collectivity was not defined in primordial, historical, or territorial terms, but more in political ideological terms—in terms of the "American way of life"—the United States did not develop a very strong demand for the principled denial of the primordial components of the different minority groups. Most of the pressure was in the direction of drifting away.

Such tendencies to drifting away are reinforced by several processes. The movement to small communities and the general demographic decline of the Jews, that same decline that at least partially accounts for their economic advancement, may make the maintenance of Jewish communalities and activitites more difficult. Growing participation in general arenas of life may deplete the reservoir of leadership for specifically Jewish activities, as shown by the influx of orthodox Jews within them. The attraction of Jewish college youth in the 1970s to various religious sects, like the Moonies, may have a similar influence. As noted, the impact of Black political power, increasingly disdainful of Jews and Israel, must be taken into account. Demographic trends reinforced such possibilities. Recent studies predict a "long-term" reduction in the Diaspora Jews, from 10.7 million in 1970 to 9.7 million in 1980, to a projected 7.9 million by the year 2000, due to migration, secularization, modernization, and assimilation.[15]

Perhaps most important is the possibility of gradual, painless Jewish assimilation or drifting away, which is facilitated by the fact that it is not demanded. Paradoxically such possibility may be reinforced by the ability to maintain a minimum of collective Jewish identity within the mainstream of American Jewish life, and hence to many it may seem that no specific effort is needed in this direction. Indeed those very processes, which facilitated the continuous development of Jewish activities and organizations, helped by the demographic trends just noted, may encourage a relatively fast and smooth assimilation simply because such absorption can take place without demands for changing religion or denying the sense of Jewishness.

In rather paradoxical ways they have strengthened such possibility, while at the same time they also have changed the nature of the process of assimilation. Such assimilation has become less and less a matter of principled crossing of religious or ethnic boundaries. The ideological component of assimilation, so strong in Europe, was almost entirely lacking. It took on more the form of drifting away; a drifting away that, paradoxically enough, was facilitated by the very high visibility of Jewish communal activities that seemingly assumes that there will always be somewhere to return.[16]

Thus, for instance, a recent survey indicated that "change from just a generation ago, American Jews today are as likely to marry non-Jews as Jews. But even as this assimilation accelerates Jews are clinging to religious traditions; roughly 60 percent of Jewish-gentile households, for example, report that they either attend Passover Seders or light Hanukkah candles."[17]

These and similar findings have given rise to contradictory evaluations by different sectors of the Jewish communities. Many leaders and rabbis voiced their growing concern about the dangers of intermarriage and the closely related dilution of religious services, injunctions, and observances, while others would stress the importance of finding new ways to reach out to the children of intermarriages or others who might drift away.

These processes may lead to the development of three sectors of Jewish community in the US., as well as among other contemporary Jewish communities, as we shall see. The first would be composed of various orthodox communities that more and more would move into a narrow, sectarian direction, abandoning the more universalistic orientations of the Jewish heritage. The second sector would be a small hard core within the non-orthodox majority that, mainly through attachment to Jewish education, would attempt to maintain a strong Jewish identity while continuing to participate in the general society. This sector, however, could be threatened both by the orthodox group and by the third sector, the great majority who, after a few generations, would move into a painless, drifting assimilation.

Thus, the success of the Jews in being accepted in the United States, the development of numerous Jewish activities, and the diversified patterns of participation in various spheres of American life do not by themselves assure the continuity of Jewish collective life and creativity. Rather this success—if not changed by internal developments in the United States or continuous recombination of the relations among Jewish communities in general and within Israel in particular—together with demographic decline may lead to a fatal weakening of Jewish identity and collective cohesion.

6

Modern Jewish National Movements and the Zionist Movement

Introduction

One of the most important aspects of modern Jewish life in Europe, especially in Eastern Europe, was the development of a variety of national or nationalist movements. In our discussion of the Eastern European Jewish experience, we briefly mentioned some of the major characteristics of these movements: their plentitude and their different often competing ideologies. This plentitude went far beyond what could be found in other national movements that developed in Europe in that period. It was not just the multiplicity of different emphases—moderate or extremist, religious or secular—within basically common programs. Although all Jewish national movements, by definition, shared the aim to reconstruct Jewish national life in modern terms, they differed greatly, as we have seen, in some of the most central aspects of such reconstruction, especially in how to maintain the viability of such Jewish collective life in modern times, given the specific characteristics and anomalies of Jewish the historical experience and life, and the lack of a territorial base which was seen as the core of any modern national movement. The movements also were rooted in the fact that they aimed not at overthrowing other rulers, or those notables who collaborated with them and at finding new ways to elaborate and articulate different dimensions of the existing national heritage, language, folklore, literature, and history. Rather, the Jewish national movements entailed a rebellion against the prevailing traditional ways of life and attempts to reconstruct their national tradition and heritage and to find new ways to implement the major themes of Jewish civilization.

The different national movements promulgated different ways or programs for attaining such reconstruction. However, the greatest division among them was between movements that aimed at attaining such reconstruction in the lands of the Diaspora and the Zionist movement that denies that such reconstruction is possible in the modern Diaspora. In this sense the Zionist movement was the most radical modern Jewish national movement; it was basically a revolutionary-ideological national movement. Because of this it indeed could be seen as the epitome of the modern Jewish nationalism, as that closest to the various modern European national movements. And yet a closer look at it will reveal that in many crucial ways it differed from these movements, perhaps even more than the other Jewish national movements.

Therefore, the question before us is, To what extent does Zionism differ from other national movements, beyond the various local differences that always exist between different national movements? My thesis is that it differs in several profound ways, and that some of the peculiar characteristics of the Zionist movement can be understood only by reference to what we have called Jewish civilization and the Jewish civilizational frameworks discussed in previous chapters.

I do not mean to deny those aspects that Zionism has in common with other movements. We all know that Zionism arose in the era of nationalism in Eastern and Western Europe and that it shares many characteristics with other national movements. It also shares the vocabulary of these national movements, perhaps even more than it shares other characteristics with them. For obvious historical reasons, the formative vocabulary of the Zionist movement was derived mainly from Eastern and Central European, rather than Western European, nationalist thought and ideologies. Whatever the explanation of the common historical framework of these movements (a task that has been undertaken in many works, most recently in Ernest Gellner and Benedict Anderson's provocative analyses[1]) the formation of nationalism is a phenomenon of modern history, and specifically of the modern era in European history.

I would like to begin my analysis by stressing the rather obvious but sometimes forgotten point that modern nationalism is one very important case of the ways in which collective identities, symbols, and boundaries formed and crystallized in human history. Modern national movements share some elements with the processes of construction of collective identities in other eras of human history; but due to their historical circumstances they have also evolved specific characteristics of their own. Among the traits they share with the processes of crystallization of collective identity in other eras, above all, are the emphasis on primordial identity connected with land or language, and probably also with religious tradition and historical experience. In the nineteenth century these elements formed within the national movements in Europe in different ways than those by which such elements became components of collective identities in other periods of human history.

The Zionist movement shared its historical framework with most European national movements (especially those in Central and Eastern Europe). Yet it evinced some significant differences from them with respect to these crucial symbols of collective identity. It is my thesis that these differences can be best understood by relating them to the major aspects of Jewish history and Jewish civilization already analyzed.

Let us start with some basic facts about the Zionist movement, although we shall not attempt to present a history of the movement, as this can be found in many excellent works.[2] The first heralders of Zionism, such as Rabbi Yehudah Shlomo Alkalay (1798–1878) and Rabbi Zevi Hirsch Kalischer (1795–1874), appeared in the mid-nineteenth century among both rabbinic and secular Jewish intellectuals. Those who came from more traditional circles held Zionist beliefs that combined traditional semi-Messianic elements with modern nationalist elements, stressing either the political aspect of their aspirations or the practical necessity and possibility of reestablishing a viable Jewish settlement in Eretz Israel. Such settlement was envisaged as a preparatory stage for the coming of the Messiah, which was seen as beyond the realm of human endeavor and left entirely to the will of God.

A modern utopian socialist version of Zionism was developed by Moses Hess, the socialist leader and ideologue, in his *Rome and Jerusalem* (1862). Here the Zionist vision, based on a recognition of the universal significance of the specific type of Jewish religiosity, was couched in Hegelian terms of the dialectic of universal history.

The Zionist movement itself began to coalesce in the 1870s in the groups of Hovevei Zion (Lovers of Zion), principally in Russia, and gathered momentum following the pogroms of the early 1880s. One reaction to these events was the publication in 1882 of one of the first full-fledged Zionist tracts, *Autoemancipation,* by J. L. Pinsker (1821–1899), the title of which speaks for itself. Zionism developed into a full-blown political movement with the meteoric appearance of Theodore Herzl (1860–1905) and the convening of the First Zionist Congress in Basel in 1897, at which the World Zionist Organization was established.

The 1880s also saw the beginning of Jewish immigration to Palestine, spearheaded by the Hovevei Zion. Settlement activity continued thereafter, first with the help of the Baron Edmond de Rothschild and later under the aegis of the World Zionist Organization.

The Zionist movement entered full stride in the period between the two world wars: from the Balfour Declaration of 1917 and the establishment of the British Mandate in Palestine, and the consequent growth of the Yishuv; along with the establishment of the successor states to the Russian and Austro-Hungarian Empires in Eastern Europe (Poland, Czechoslovakia, Lithuania, Latvia, and Hungary) and the fuller affirmation of the independence of slightly older Eastern European states (Romania, Serbia—which became Yugoslavia—and Bulgaria).

Zionism as a National Movement: The Revolutionary Dimension

A large proportion of the Zionist ideology was couched in the idiom of modern nationalisms, whether that of Mazzini, Cavour, or the German Romantics. Hence it is only natural that the Zionist movement and ideology sometimes have been defined as the culmination of modern Jewish nationalism or as the Jewish counterpart of other modern nationalist movements.

Although this definition is partly true, it does not exhaust the meaning of Zionist ideology and belief and fails to do justice to several crucial elements of this ideology. It does not take into account the fact that the Zionist movement and ideology, in their full articulation, constituted the most radical response to the decomposition of the traditional Jewish halakhic civilization as it developed in the Middle Ages. Zionism was a reaction to the various attempts by European Jewry to reconstruct the boundaries and contents of Jewish civilization within the sphere of modern civilization, and particularly within the modern European nation-state—a reaction that denied the validity of those other responses, as well as that of the older halakhic mold.[3]

Zionism shared with these responses the basic assumption of the possibility, and even the necessity, of finding an arena in the modern world wherein the Jewish civilizational vision could be realized. With the other national movements that developed within Eastern Jewry it shared the assumption that the incorporation of the Jews into world history, into the family of nations, could be based only on a process of collective reconstruction that defined the Jewish community in national, and not merely religious, terms. It also adopted a theme that had been developed by the Eastern European Haskalah (Enlightenment): "productivization," the normalization of the occupational structure of the Jews, with a strong emphasis on the importance of building modern institutions.

One basic premise separated it, however, from the whole gamut of Jewish responses to modernity, however, and made it the most radical and revolutionary of all the modern Jewish movements. This premise was the insistence that implementation of the Jewish civilizational vision, the reconstruction of the Jewish collective identity in response to the challenges of modernity, was possible only by creating a Jewish collective entity in its natural, national, territorial environment. In contrast to all the other Eastern European attempts at the collective reconstruction of Jewish life, the Zionist movement and ideology stressed that such a collective reconstruction, such a national collective life, could be implemented only in Eretz Israel. It would be a renewal of the covenant between the Jewish people and Eretz Yisrael. According to Zionist ideology, Eretz Israel—the Promised Land, the historical cradle of the Jewish nation, the land in which the Jewish people and civilization originally had been constructed and that constituted a continuous component in Jewish collective consciousness—was the only place in which a Jewish collective entity and environment could be reconstructed, the only place where the Jews could reenter history and become a productive, normal community responsible for its own destiny.[4]

The Zionist rebellion or revolution thus was directed against the idea that a full and meaningful Jewish life and tradition, and even mere Jewish physical existence, could be maintained within the societal framework of the modern European nation-state. It was a fundamental tenet of Zionist ideology—in many ways going against the mainstream of modern Jewish history, of the various attempts at incorporation into Western society—that within such a framework the Jews were threatened with either physical or spiritual and cultural annihilation, because of incomplete assimilation and the inability of modern societies to digest them. Only in Eretz Israel could a new, modern, viable Jewish society be established and thrive; only there could the specific Jewish civilizational vision be implemented.

Most factions within the Zionist movement emphasized that only under such circumstances could even the simple survival of Jews in modern society be assured. In their eyes, this lay at the core of the "Jewish question," especially in Eastern Europe. They believed that the establishment of a new Jewish polity could provide a haven for the Jewish people.

Because of this last tenet, it often was claimed that Zionism was merely a response to modern antisemitism, but this is only partially true. Antisemitic occurrences like the Dreyfus Affair and the pogroms of the early 1880s indeed did trigger the Zionist response; and a crucial component of this response was the search for a secure home for the Jews. But they triggered off other responses as well, including immigration to the Americas and to South Africa, migrations that were numerically far greater than the membership of the Zionist movement or the settlement in Eretz Israel.

The Zionist insistence that a safe haven could be found only in Eretz Israel was based on a particular perception of the nature of the "Jewish problem." Another crucial component of this perception was the stress on cultural creativity or institution building, which could claim to constitute not only an adequate solution to the concrete problem of settlement in Eretz Israel or the physical aspect of the Jewish question but also to possess universal significance. Thus, many segments of the Zionist movement articulated, in a new way, the old combination between the particularly Jewish and the universal significance of Jewish tradition—of Jewish civilizational premises—and stressed the universal elements in that particular tradition.

Admittedly, it was not always entirely clear what kind of Jewish society would be established, nor what were the exact implications of this vision. Numerous answers have been given in Zionist literature, comprising various traditional, revolutionary, religious, secular, and socialist aspects and dimensions. Perhaps clearer than the positive contents of these ideologies are their common negative elements, such as the kind of society that was not wanted. None of the Zionist answers wanted to perpetuate the traditional Medieval Jewish society that still existed in many places in Eastern and Central Europe; nor did they accept the assimilated Jewish communities, defined only in religious terms, that had developed in Western and Central Europe. They all looked for a synthesis between Jewishness and Western enlightenment or modernity; most of them rejected neither Jewish tradition nor modernity as such. Extremists such as J. H. Brenner (1881–1921) and M. J. Berdyczewski (1865–1921) indeed did attempt to deny large parts of Jewish tradition. But even they tended, on the whole, to look within Jewish history in search of old elements to be revived anew. Similarly, only a handful rejected any form of modernity. Though many Zionist socialists emphasized some sort of socialist utopian society oriented against the evils of capitalist and "mass society," most of them, especially the more westernized Zionists, envisaged a modern liberal-democratic state with some degree of socialism.[5]

Thus, as Professor David Vital has pointed out in his recent book,[6] the attempt to reconstruct a new way of Jewish collective life explains why Zionism has been almost the only national movement that sought to work a sociopolitical revolution. By *sociopolitical revolution* I do not mean overthrowing a traditional sovereign or liberation from political oppression but a full-fledged attempt to create a new type of sociopolitical order, although not necessarily a socialist regime. Large parts of the Zionist movement—Labor Zionism, for instance—attempted to merge the two trends, nationalism and socialism, that the late Jacob Talmon, in his last book, stressed as the most contradictory trends of the nineteenth century; but they did it in a rather special way, and even those parts of the Zionist movement (essentially the majority of it) who did not belong to the Labor Zionist camp shared at least some components of this revolutionary vision.

Only one case is similar to the Zionist experience in this respect: the American one. Although much has been written about American nationalism, I rather doubt, as I shall show later in this chapter, whether it is an appropriate term for defining the American collective identity.[7] What took place in the United States was not the development of a national movement, but rather, as de Tocqueville clearly saw, the crystallization of a new and distinctive modern civilization, emerging from a distinctive revolutionary religious tradition.[8]

In both cases, the United States and the Zionist movement and pioneering settlements in Israel, there was a similar experience of colonization. Unlike other colonizing societies (such as Australia, Canada, or even South

Africa), here colonization was connected with an ideology of creating a new sociopolitical order. Contrary to Louis Hartz's famous analysis, the United States and the Yishuv were not merely fragments of the European societies from which they came, as could be claimed with greater validity for the White dominions.[9]

It is true that one cannot speak of a social revolution in the United States in its specific "socialist" meaning, but one can indeed speak of the creation of new civilizational mold. Later on, we shall explore the differences between Israeli society, the major offshoot of the Zionist movements, and the United States. Here it suffices to point out two basic differences between the Yishuv, on which we shall also dwell in greater detail later, the Jewish community in Palestine and later in the state of Israel, and the American case. One such difference lies in the importance within Zionism of the visions promulgated by the different Labor groups, which was totally absent in the United States. Of even greater importance is the fact that the Zionist movement, with all its revolutionary ideology, placed a heavy stress on the primordial and historical components of Jewish collective identity, elements absent in the American case.

Because it shared these components with other national movements, it indeed is appropriate to see Zionism as a national movement. At the same time it differed greatly from other national movements in ways that are closely related to the revolutionary characteristics it shared with the American case. The full impact of these differences can be understood only if we take into account the continuous relation of this revolution to the Jewish historical civilizational experience.

Specific Dimensions of Zionist Nationalism:
Territory, Language, and History

The major differences between the Zionist movement and other European and later Third-World national movements, differences closely related to the Jewish civilizational experience, can be discerned in some of the central components of national movements, namely, in the construction of symbols of national primordial identity, symbols of territory, history, and the culture of the people. Let us take the first and obvious difference, the territorial dimension. Zionism, like most other national movements, emphasized the equation of political identity with territory; but unlike other national movements, again, except for the American one which in this sense was not a national movement, it did not emphasize an existing territory in which the members of the collectivity it was trying to shape actually lived. Also unlike the American case, it emphasized a territory that was in some sense primordial, though not in the same sense as the territories of most Western national movements.

Zionism shared with the Medieval Jewish civilization the combination, analyzed in Chapter 3, of primordial and ideological attachments to a territory and the tension between them. The territory to which the Jews looked as their only natural one, during the period of the exile, became an important and almost metaphysical element in the Jewish self-conception, but it was not the territory in which they actually lived. This complicated attitude to their national territory constitutes one crucial difference between Zionism and other national movements.[10]

Such a metaphysical, ideological, and mystical attitude toward the territory can be found to some extent in the American case, and it, too, significantly enough, was combined with strong biblical symbolism and imagery.[11] Unlike the American case, however, the Zionist movement worked for the return to a territory that for a long period of Jewish history had been the Jews' natural homeland, a territory toward which they had a strong primordial attachment and that constituted a continuous element in their collective identity throughout their history.

Another important difference between the Zionist movement and other national movements may be found in its attitude toward national customs and traditions. The Czechs, Poles, and other European peoples proclaimed that the customs according to which their respective collectivities lived would become more articulated in political and even cultural terms, and that they accordingly would flourish in the new setting once their collectivity was liberated from foreign rulers and oppressors—the Czar, the Habsburg Emperor, the Ottoman Sultan. This was not the Jewish case. The Zionist movement, in fact most of the modern European Jewish national movements, did not romanticize the Jews' existing customs and ways of life. Quite the contrary, all of them, and especially Zionism, rebelled against these customs.

Still another difference from other national movements involves the revival of the national language. Unlike some other such movements, the Zionist movement did not attempt to revive a "dead" language, nor did it sanctify the existing vernacular. The Zionists, in contrast to the various Jewish autonomists and the Bundists, rebelled against the language actually spoken by a majority of the Jews in Eastern and Central Europe: Yiddish. Instead, the Zionist movement revived Hebrew, which has always been a basic component of Jewish life, the language of prayer, religious meditation, and legal and commercial discourse. Furthermore, as we shall see in greater detail, the way in which they revived it was utterly different from the similar attempts made by other national movements.

An important and interesting aspect of the revival of the Hebrew language within the Zionist movement is the conscious transition from the Ashkenazi to the Sephardi pronunciation. This transition was rooted in the

Zionist movement's rebellion against the Diaspora. The Ashkenazi pronunciation, used in prayer and to some extent in social intercourse, was seen as part of the Diaspora pattern of life. The Sephardi pronunciation was seen as more ancient and authentic, and perhaps above all as the language of the greatest period of secular Hebrew creativity in the Diaspora, the flowering of Hebrew poetry in Muslim (and to a lesser degree Christian) Spain.

The Zionist evaluation of the Jewish historical experience also displays crucial differences from other nationalist movements, differences that may constitute the crux of Zionism's distinctiveness. The national movement of every people goes back to their history and attempts to reconstitute it. This usually involves a high degree of territorial and temporal continuity, in that they attempt to reconstitute, within an independent territorial framework, their recent history in the places where they live.

Zionism's attitude toward Jewish history was different. It referred to a full political history that had existed 1800 years earlier. The Zionist movement did not go back to the relatively recent memory of the Polish or Czech or Slovak people, state, or territory, but to a remote history that had not been forgotten throughout the experience of Galut. At the same time it rejected the Jews' most recent historical experience, life in Galut. Thus the Zionists shared the basic view of the rabbinic halakhic mold that the present, the Galut, is not meaningful in terms of their ideological aspirations as a people and a civilization. They rebelled, however, against the rabbinic view that the Jews must wait for the Messiah rather than taking their history into their own hands. Thus, the historical experience that they sought to reconstitute and reinterpret was quite different from that of other national movements.

The Zionist movement intensified the radical change in Jewish historiography that had begun earlier in the nineteenth century: the return to full-fledged historical writing. Historical writing had existed to some extent among the Jews, especially the Hellenized Jews of the Second Temple period, of whom the most prominent example is Josephus. But the loss of independence and the predominance of the halakhic mold, with its conscious opting out from history, put an end to real Jewish historiography; even chronicles were relatively rare.[12]

The first signs of the renewal of historiography could be discerned among the Jews during the Renaissance, but only in the period of the Enlightenment did it truly blossom, above all in the works of the German Wissenschaft des Judentums school.[13] It gathered further momentum with the development of an active collective consciousness among the Jews of Eastern Europe and the emergence of the Zionist movement. The historians influenced by the latter stressed the Jews' active construction of collective life in all periods, even the Middle Ages, thus disassociating themselves from the halakhic mode of Jewish self-definition and self-consciousness.[14]

Specific Characteristics of Zionist Revolutionary Orientations

The Zionist movement thus reconstructed the basic primordial elements—common history, land, language, ancestors, and so on—in a different manner than other national movements, although indeed the same types of components were reconstructed. Like other national movements, Zionism endeavored to combine the reconstruction of such components with the reconstruction or creation of a nation-state. At the same time, however, the way in which these components were reconstructed and combined differed greatly from those of other European national movements.

All these distinctive characteristics of the Zionist movement bring us back to the point that Zionism was not just a national, but also a revolutionary, movement, albeit a very peculiar one. It was revolutionary because it wanted to reconstruct the Jews' own way of life, not merely to liberate them from their oppressors. It was not a movement of liberation in the narrow political sense, because there were no internal rulers to overthrow. Unlike most modern nationalisms, especially the European varieties, the Zionist movement did not rebel against a foreign ruler, not even to the extent the Americans did. Its rebellion was against the Jewish life-style of nineteenth-century Europe; it is because of this rebellion that it can be seen as a revolutionary movement.

The Zionist movement rebelled first and foremost against the basic modes of Jewish reality then existing in Europe: the assimilationists in Western Europe and the old (though in fact already transformed) traditionalists in Eastern and Central Europe, as well as rival Jewish collective movements. It refused to accept the answer of the Jewish revolutionaries that the Jewish problem awould utomatically disappear after the revolution.

This had a major impact on the definition of its enemy. All Jews, of course, knew that they were oppressed; but they had known this throughout the Middle Ages. What was new was the perception of how liberation could be achieved. This was not by overthrowing the Sultan or the Czar (some of the Bundists and other Jewish political groups may have thought so, but not the Zionists). The Zionists were not interested in overthrowing the political regime in the lands where the Jews were living. They perceived liberation as a change in their current way of life, as not accepting the major trends—assimilationism, already transformed orthodoxy, and the new secular collective movements—that had developed among the Jews during the nineteenth century.

Thus the Jewish Zionist rebellion was directed against the existing Jewish way of life, not against external oppressors; although the fact of such oppression as a basic component of Jewish life in the Diaspora was of crucial importance for the Zionist claim that no full and independent Jewish life could be attained in the Diaspora. Hence the central focus of the Zionist rebellion was the wish to reconstruct Jewish society, Jewish culture, Jewish civilization, again—I use this word advisedly—in a new, collective, modern way.

Let me sum up my thesis. The Zionist movement, with its unique character as a political national movement rooted in the nineteenth-century experience, was an attempt to reconstruct many elements of Jewish civilization in a revolutionary way; not necessarily revolutionary in the socialist sense (although socialist ideologies were of great importance within it) or by overthrow of oppressive rulers, but rather more in the American way of creating a new civilizational mold. Unlike America, however, it stressed strong historical and primordial elements and orientations. There was, as we shall see in greater detail in Chapter 8, no attempt in the United States to reconstruct and continue an old civilization; rather, a new civilization and political entity were constructed out of political, ideological, and civilizational components. Because of this, the United States in many ways constitutes the most purely ideological society in the world without strong primordial elements, which is why it is difficult to speak of American nationalism. Here, to my mind, lies the greatest difference between the American revolution and the Zionist movement. The Zionist movement also was highly ideological and highly revolutionary, but it combined these elements with the strong primordial and historical components of Jewish identity, with which its political aspirations were connected. It was not purely ideological in this nonhistorical, nonprimordial sense, as was the case in America.

Zionism, or at least large parts of the Zionist movement, saw itself as the carrier of a revolutionary reconstruction of Jewish civilization. With its adversaries—the already transformed halakhic mold, the principled assimilationists, and the various Jewish national movements in Eastern and Central Europe—it shared the emphasis on the Jewish civilizational vision; but it took issue with them on how best to realize this vision. Zionism insisted that this vision could be attained only by establishing a national, territorial, and ultimately political entity in Eretz Israel. For this reason, the Zionist movement, when compared with other national movements, has constructed the various components and themes of its tradition and civilization in a special and unique way.

The Zionist reconstruction gave rise to the full articulation and far-reaching reformulation of several cultural and ideological themes or emphases that were latent, secondary, or taken for granted in the traditional rabbinic mold and largely negated within the assimilated groups. The most important of these themes were the rebirth of the Hebrew language and the reemphasis of the Land of Israel and the biblical components of the Jewish historical tradition.

The revival of the Hebrew language was a great accomplishment, begun during the Haskalah period and later fully realized by the Zionist movement and the Jewish settlement of Eretz Israel. The modern reconstruction of the Hebrew language, building on the continuous tradition of Medieval times, made it the common national language: the language of the kindergarten, school, and daily speech; at the same time Hebrew has proven itself able to meet the demands of science, modern literature, and technology. The Hebrew language now occupies a special place among traditional languages, and its development has had important implications for the cultural structure of Israeli society, as we shall see in the next chapter.

The emphasis on Eretz Israel shifted from mainly religious or metaphysical orientations, strongly regulated by the rabbinic tradition, toward an emphasis on the physical features of the land and its landscapes, often presented in idyllic or mystic terms; on the primordial attachment to the land, on its secular-metaphysical glorification; and on a new mode of religious, semimystical sanctification of the holiness of the Land. This last mode went beyond the rabbinic orientation and was more in line with philosophical and poetic expressions, especially among the Jewish poets and philosophers of Medieval Spain, like Yehudah Halevi.

The emphasis on the Land of Israel and the revival of the Hebrew language were closely connected with the revival of the biblical component of the Jewish tradition. This was a secondary component in the rabbinic mold, subsumed under the legal and ritual orientation and its emphasis on talmudic scholarship and prayer, and was denied by the more assimilated groups (even if they stressed the ethical orientations of the Prophets). The revival of this element had begun in the literary activity of the Eastern European Haskalah, in such works as Abraham Mapu's romances *Ahavat Zion* (The Love of Zion) and *Ashmat Shomron* (The Guilt of Shomron), and became even more pronounced in connection with various nationalistic movements in general and with Zionism in particular.[15]

The Zionist Vision and the Basic Themes of Jewish Civilization: Exile, Return, and Redemption

The reconstruction of different cultural symbols gave rise to a far-reaching reformation of some of the perennial themes of Jewish civilization and the tensions among them. The Zionist vision naturally drew on some of the perennial themes of Jewish civilization and reformulated them in terms of its own basic orientations. The strong emphasis on national reconstruction and renaissance necessarily drew on the older Messianic themes of redemption, even if they were redefined in secular, political, or social terms, as David Vital puts it: "Exile, Return, Redemption."[16] This emphasis reactivated the tension bewteen the pragmatic-political and the eschatological dimensions of the Messianic vision.

This secular transposition of Messianic beliefs seemingly entailed a particular type of solution to the perennial dilemmas of Jewish civilization. Above all it stressed the Jews' capacity to re-enter the historical arena as autonomous agents. The Zionist movement also emphasized the theme of Jewish solidarity, which had become pronounced in the Medieval period, and imbued it with a strong political dimension.

In close relation to the articulation of these themes of the Jewish tradition, the Zionist movement developed a parallel reconstruction of the different elements of the Jewish collective identity: political, national, and primordial. All these themes were closely interwoven with what was perhaps the central motif of Zionism, the principled negation of Galut, a motif that existed in Medieval times as well, with the hope that the reestablishment and renaissance of the Jewish nation in Eretz Israel would abolish both the political subjugation (Shiabud Malchuyot) and the metaphysical fault implicit in Galut.

At the beginning of the Zionist movement, and later on with the settlement of Palestine, the Zionist vision of a national renaissance combining all these varied themes often was portrayed as resolving many of the perennial dilemmas and tensions of Jewish tradition. It would do this by integrating them into a new mold of civilizational creativity and imbuing this creativity with broad universal significance, making the Jewish people part of the family of nations and bringing them back into history. This was a naive and utopian vision. Its purest expression perhaps can be found in the writings of Ahad Ha'Am (the pseudonym of Asher Ginsburg, 1856–1927), Herzl's ideological opponent, as well as in Herzl's utopian romance, *Altneuland,* which was a sort of blueprint for the liberal and peaceful implementation of this vision.[17]

The attempts to implement this vision revealed the tensions and contradictions inherent in it, and that constituted a reformulation in a new mode of many of the basic tensions of Jewish civilization: between the universalistic and particularistic approach; between the pragmatic and the eschatological; between inward-looking segregation and outward-looking, more open orientations; between political solidarity and the institution building and universalistic cultural dimensions of the Zionist vision; between the aspiration to become a "normal" nation and the quest for a special Jewish state or society that would be a "light unto the nations"; and between the ambivalent attitude toward the Diaspora and the dependence of the Zionist movement on the Diaspora. The implementation of this vision also gradually brought out the entire range of problems connected with the reconstruction of the different elements of Jewish tradition and identity in the modern setting. All these polarities were connected with the basic tension between the problem of physical security and the civilizational aspect of Jewish existence, between the political and the social and cultural dimensions of Zionist activity.

Zionism was confronted by a new intercivilizational situation. The long-standing antagonism of other religions and civilizations had weakened greatly with the advance of the modern age with its more secular, and seemingly benign, premises (which yet in fact contained within themselves the seeds of the modern racial antisemitism that culminated in the Holocaust).[18] The Zionist ideology thus tended to look for specifically Jewish approaches that were yet not antagonistic to other, especially Western, civilizations toward their common civilizational aspirations.

Some of these tensions and contradictions long remained dormant and became fully visible only in the later development of the Yishuv and the state of Israel. On the other hand, those concerned with ideological orientations, and to a lesser degree with institutional reality emerged in the first stages of the Zionism movement.

The tension between political action and ideology and the establishment of economic and cultural institutions appeared at the very beginning of the movement. The stress on an autonomous political Jewish entity constituted one of the main tenets of the Zionist movement and later of the state of Israel. But the initial attempts at a quick political solution did not reap great success. Herzl's efforts to obtain a charter from the Sultan failed; this led in 1903 to the Uganda proposal, by which the British government would allow the Jews to establish an autonomous territory in East Africa. The proposal split the young Zionist movement (the Territorialists like Zangwill founded their own organization) and considerably weakened its emphasis on the political dimension. This was replaced by a strong emphasis on constructive colonization and institution building in Eretz Israel, with universalistic, sometimes eschatological, orientations. Although far from devoid of political implications, this emphasis moved away from the sanctification of political activity for its own sake and from seeing the immediate attainment of political goals as the major thrust of the Zionist movement.[19] At least during the initial phases of the development of the Zionist movement and settlement in Israel, then, neither political Messianism nor an emphasis on purely political activity was prominent. But each continued to exist, if only latently, within the Zionist movement and the process of settling Eretz Israel.

The political dimension of Zionist activities intensified in the late 1930s, due to increasing political conflict with both the Arabs and the British. Paradoxically enough, the Zionist Labor movement, whose initial emphasis was on the constructivist institutional building dimension, came to the forefront in stressing political action. Also during the 1930s the Revisionist movement, under the leadership of Vladimir Jabotinsky, strongly articulated such attitudes.[20]

The tension between these emphases, along with that between, on the one hand, the great political visions and eschatological orientations and the exigencies of practical politics and institution building on the other, continued throughout the course of the Zionist movement and the state of Israel. The conflict between the aspiration to become a "normal" society or nation and the aspiration to be a "special" nation was hardly apparent at first, chiefly because the quest for normality was itself an ideological-revolutionary reaction, articulated especially by the pioneers of the early Aliyahs, against the reality of Jewish life in Europe. But the crystallization of the social structure of the Yishuv and of the state of Israel made the contradictory nature of these two attitudes more and more apparent. Tensions surfaced on the ideological and institutional levels as well, stimulated by the political vicissitudes of the Yishuv and the state of Israel, by the growing Arab and British opposition to Zionist settlement of Eretz Israel, by the need to invest ever-greater resources in security and defense, and by the growing impact of the realities of being a small country and society.

There were further tensions between the universalistic and particularistic elements, between inward-looking solidarity and more open, outward-looking attitudes, between the great visions and pragmatic politics, which seemingly ought to have been resolved by the implementation of the Zionist vision. The implementation of that vision also revealed, in a variety of ways, many of the potential contradictions among the different components—primordial, ethnic, political, and religious—of the Jewish collective identity, emphasizing them individually or in combination, often in rather surprising directions.

The Diaspora in Zionist Ideology

All these tensions were closely connected with the Zionist attitude toward the Diaspora, another unique phenomenon not relevant to other national movements. This attitude can be explained only in terms of specific characteristics of the Jewish civilizational and historical experience.

Here, too, we can distinguish several strains. In its original and basic conception, Zionism necessarily stressed the inadequacy of the Diaspora as a viable framework for either the physical or civilizational and cultural development of the Jewish people. In point of fact, however, the Zionist movement was interwoven with the life of the Jewish communities within which it evolved. The combination of a principled negation of Galut with a strong involvement with the life of the Diaspora communities made Zionism's ideological orientations toward Galut quite ambivalent and often unclear. The Zionist movement accordingly developed a certain blindness to the ideological implication of its relationship with the Diaspora.[21]

Many great figures of Zionism, especially those who saw Zionism as the solution to the dilemma of Jewish existence, assumed that the realization of the Zionist dream would bring to the Land of Israel, to the Jewish State, every Jew who was interested in maintaining a special Jewish national identity, and the others would be able to assimilate peacefully in the lands of the Diaspora. This assumption was prominent in the public consciousness of both Jews and non-Jews and was taken up again in the 1960s by the French-Jewish sociologist Georges Friedmann, whose small book *The End of the Jewish People?*[22] elaborated the thesis that the successful establishment of Israel would bring about, through assimilation, the end of the Jewish people.

The extreme negation of the Galut, reinforced by the revolutionary nature of the Zionist movement, was long prevalent in the Yishuv and the state of Israel. But even those Zionists who did not share this position did not face up to the implications for Zionist ideology of a continued Jewish collective existence in the Diaspora. Ahad Ha-Am, the renowned publicist who wielded immense influence within the Zionist movement and opposed Herzl's political emphasis, conceived of Zionism as creating a spiritual center for the Jewish people. This concept did not negate the establishment of an independent Jewish state in Eretz Israel, but assumed the continued existence of Jewish communities in the Diaspora, who would be illuminated spiritually by the national cultural center in Palestine. Like almost all Zionist ideologies, however, it did not endow the Diaspora communities with any special civilizational meaning; neither did it provide any concrete ways for defining and constructing a meaningful Jewish existence within them. Consciously or not, this approach shared with all other Zionist orientations the negation of Galut, or at least a certain evasion of the problem posed by it. This evasion would become more pronounced with respect to that new Jewish community that crystallized at the same time as the Zionist movement, that of the United States.

The Reconstruction of Collective Identity and Traditions: Zionism and Religion

All these themes indicate the strong attachment of most Zionist ideologies to many dimensions of the Jewish tradition, and their quest for those elements or components within that tradition that could be used for the construction of a new Jewish collective identity and civilizational mold. At the same time, however, these ideologies indicated quite clearly that they went far beyond the rabbinic mold and the specific configuration of the different components of the Jewish tradition that had crystallized in the institutions and symbols of the Halakhah. The Zionist movement aimed not merely at continuing Jewish tradition, but also at reconstructing it.

The opposition to Zionism displayed by those Jewish groups who saw themselves as perpetuating the halakhic mold is of major importance for understanding some of the specific characteristics of the Zionist movement and Israeli society, particularly some of the salient aspects of its contemporary political scene. This is another facet that distinguishes Zionism from other national movements as well as from the American experience.

Many leaders and members of the Lovers of Zion, and later of the Zionist movement, were religiously observant; some were even prominent rabbis. Moreover, the religious-Zionist party (the Mizrachi) developed very early (1902–1905) in the history of the movement.[23] But the religious Zionists always were a minority within both the Zionist and the religious camps. Most Zionist activists were not religious; some, especially the socialist pioneers of the Second and Third Aliyahs, were vehemently antireligious. In any case, they all, religious and nonreligious alike, avowedly or not, worked within a framework that did not accept the symbols and the institutions of Halakhah as the only, or even the principal, framework of Jewish civilizational creativity.

This was obviously true of the nonreligious majority in the Zionist movement, who did not accept religious tenets or even rebeled against them. But even those who did adhere to these tenets did not necessarily find their major inspiration for the new symbols of collective identity and above all of institution building in the traditional halakhic mold. The reconstruction of Jewish life in an autonomous setting constituted, as we have seen, the epitome of the Zionist movement vision. Although this assumption did not necessarily go against the various halakhic injunctions, it certainly went against some of the deepest premises of the halakhic civilization with respect to the political activity of Jews in the contemporary historical arenas.

The religiously observant segments of the Zionist movement seem to have assumed that the new institutional reality, once established, would adhere to Halakhah. Some of them began to be concerned with the applicability of Halakhah to new problems and conditions. But few, if any, derived their inspiration for the new institutions to be developed in the Land of Israel from the existing halakhic mold. Some great religious figures, like Rabbi Abraham Isaac Kook, the first Ashkenazi chief rabbi of Eretz Israel, developed a new philosophical-mystical interpretation of Jewish existence in general and the reconstruction of Eretz Israel in the light of religious tenets; others stressed the roots of the Zionist ideology in the religious tradition and its symbols. Beyond stressing observance of halakhic prescriptions and the need to include the tradition in the new curricula (for instance, the study of Talmud), however, almost none could clearly define how the halakhic mold might guide the creation of new institutions and a new political and collective identity. Rather intensive religious-intellectual activity developed later in the religious kibbutz movements; but here too the original momentum for building new institutions did not necessarily develop from within the existing religious mold, although eventually their legitimacy was demonstrated in terms of this framework.[24]

The ultraorthodox were fully aware of this essential trait of Zionism. Their fierce opposition to the movement was rooted in their recognition that the Zionist vision, however strong its attachment to many traditional symbols, went beyond the basic premises of the halakhic mold and wanted to take the collective fate of the Jews in its own hands, in the here and now of history. They saw Zionism's secular usurpation of the Messianic elements, as well as the possibility of attaining "redemption" in the present, as very dangerous.

The basic confrontation between the Zionists and the bearers of the extreme halakhic mold was over more than just the cultural or religious ambience of the Jewish state. Zionism often was locked in a fierce disagreement with religious groups; many Zionists were extremely secularist and antireligious. But this was not the crux of the matter. From the very beginning a sort of modus vivendi developed between the secular and religious camps in Eretz Israel. The "status quo" has been challenged repeatedly—but there was mutual accommodation from the very beginning. It was agreed, for example, that no work would be done on Keren Kayemet lands on the Sabbath. It was the Zionist movement, not the traditionalists, that created the post of the chief rabbinate in Palestine, based on a coalition between the Zionist leaders and the religious Zionists. On this practical level, then, there was continuous accommodation.

The crucial problem, as the ultraorthodox knew very well, did not involve the level of Kashrut or sabbath observance. It lay in the fact that the Zionist movement negated the basic ideological premise of the halakhic mold concerning the nature of the Jewish people as an active factor in human history. The Zionist movement negated the demand, central to the mainstream of the Medieval Halakhah, that Jews not take their political and historical destiny in their own hands, but leave it to the Messiah. The main orthodox opposition to the Zionist movement had to do with the Zionist rebellion against the basic premises of the nature of Jewish civilization as it had developed in the mold of Halakhah. True, the halakhic mold does include the concept of Yishuv Eretz Israel, the settlement of Eretz Israel; but it does not accept that Eretz Israel should be settled as a new type of society, which takes its political destiny into its own hands.

We have already seen that Medieval Jewish life included not only elements of Messianic dreams and hopes, but also of a more active political stance. These tendencies existed in the various Messianic movements and erupted most prominently in Sabbatean movement, whose ultimate fate seemingly supported the premises of the halakhic mold.

It was around these premises—not just around the degree of religious observance, important as this may have been in itself—that the major controversy between the orthodox and the Zionist movement developed. Naturally, the controversy was also closely connected with the two camps' contradictory claims to be the legitimate interpreter of Jewish civilization, the gatekeepers of the boundaries of Jewish collectivity.

This type of confrontation is not to be found in other national movements. In every national movement of course there were more secular and more religious groups, with an ongoing rivalry between them. There was also a confrontation between national movements and the Catholic Church as a universal church. But these rivalries and confrontations were never of the type found between the Zionist movement and orthodoxy.

The nature of the controversy between the Zionists and the halakhic mold provides another illustration of our point about the specific characteristics of Zionism as a national movement, and particularly about the close relationship of these characteristics with the Jewish civilizational and historical experience. In subsequent chapters we shall analyze some dimensions of this experience in order to clarify certain aspects of Israeli society.

7

The Formation and Transformation of Israeli Society

The Formation of Israeli Society and Its Initial Institutional Mold

Introduction

In this chapter we analyze some of the characteristics of Israeli society from the point of view of our comparative concerns. We examine the distinctive characteristics of Israeli society as a revolutionary-ideological-settlers' community and inquire to what extent these can be understood within the context in terms of some of the basic Jewish civilization themes of the specific Jewish historical and civilizational experience. The analysis naturally follows that of the Zionist movement, Israeli society being the major outcome and realization of the ideals of this movement.

After the analysis of some of the major characteristics of Israeli society, in the next chapter, we concentrate on some specific characteristics of Israeli society through a comparison between Israel with the United States, comparing them as modern revolutionary-ideological societies of settlers and immigrants.

The Background and Development of Israeli Society

In the last decade, Israeli society has undergone many far-reaching changes, to the extent that doubts have been expressed as to whether it remains the same one that crystallized in the period of the Yishuv (the Jewish community in Palestine under the Ottamon Empire and during the British mandate) and during the first years of the state of Israel. The most visible manifestations of these changes have been in the political field: the political mahapach (change) of 1977, when for the first time since the mid-1930s the Labor Party sat in the opposition instead of forming the ruling coalition; the continuous political turmoil and verbal (for a while, indeed, not only verbal) violence that came to the fore especially before and after the 1981 elections; the emergence of new, often divisive, themes—ethnic, religious-secular, political; the growing tensions between the religious groups and other sectors of the society; the great divisiveness surrounding the war in Lebanon and its aftermath; the emergence of a very strong populist trend in the ambience and tone of political debate; challenges to the rules of law; and the growth of extraparliamentary and extremist movements. It probably still is too early to evaluate the full impact of these developments. Although the democratic and constitutional frameworks have so far evinced great strength and, as we shall see in more detail in the next chapter, in some respects have even been reinforced, there can be no doubt that significant changes have taken place in Israeli society and particularly in its political and cultural molds, going beyond changes in the composition of the parties and their leadership.

To understand both the continuity and the change, we must examine the forces that shaped the initial mold of Israeli political life and also, as we shall later see in more detail, unwittingly generated far-reaching dynamics and transformations within it. The analysis will proceed from two complementary points of view: first, that of the transformation of revolutionary societies, and second, that of the crystallization of a new type of Jewish society—a modern Jewish society, within which the perennial themes of Jewish civilization have been worked out in a distinctive pattern.[1]

Basic Problems and Characteristics of the Yishuv and Israeli Society. The Zionist settlement in Ottoman and Mandatory Palestine (the Yishuv) and Israeli society have shared many of the processes and problems of transformation with other postrevolutionary polities: the USSR, Mexico, many of the emrging Third World nations, and perhaps even the early nineteenth-century United States. The most important of these processes included the transformation of revolutionary groups from sociopolitical movements into the ruling elite groups of states; the concomitant institutionalization of the revolutionary vision in the framing of the modern states; economic expansion and "modernization," with a concurrent increase in social differentiation; and the absorption within the framework of such economic expansion of relatively "underdeveloped" sectors of the population.

The Yishuv and later Israeli society shared important characteristics with some nonimperial, colonizing societies, both revolutionary like the United States and nonrevolutionary like the White British dominion societies. They had in common, first, a strong emphasis on equality, at least among the initial settler groups, and the consequent lack of any strong hereditary, feudal, aristocratic landowner class; second, the development of a strong concentration of various types of economic and administrative activities within broad, unified, organizational frameworks, in common with other sectarian colonizing societies; and last, again in common with other colonizing societies, Zionist settlement emphasized the conquest of wasteland through work, as shown in the expansion of productive primary occupations and the colonizing frameworks and frontiers.

Similar combinations of cooperative endeavors and economic, colonizing enterprises could be found also, for instance, in the settlement of wasteland by the Mormons. The combination of trade unions with the industrial and financial activities of the entrepreneur could be found as well in other politically oriented labor movements, especially in Scandinavia and, to a lesser extent, in England. However, the fusion of these features as developed within the Histadrut (the General Federation of Labor) seems to be unique and is explained by the Histadrut's political character and outlook. This also explains its political power, although economically it has never been the largest sector of the country.

These characteristics became closely interwoven with other components of Israeli society, such as the sectarian or social movements, strong messianic eschatological orientation, strong totalistic outlooks of the pioneering groups and factions, with their strong internal ideological cohesion, and the institutionalism of this ideology in face of growing social differentiation. However, unlike many such groups (like the various utopian settlements in the United States), the pioneering groups from the beginning wanted to be the trailblazers of a modern society and committed themselves to many institutional frameworks and organizations that might be forerunners of such a development and through which broader groups of Jewish society could participate in the economic, ideological, and political life of the Yishuv.

Out of the sectarian and social movements of the Yishuv another crucial trend developed: the strong elitist ideological bent, aiming at the achievement of a new society through the implementation of an ideological program most fully epitomized in the image of the pioneer and in the first communal settlements, above all the kibbutzim, but also the moshavim. In this, Israel was akin to some other revolutionary societies, such as the USSR, Yugoslavia, or Mexico, which attempted to mold relatively traditional societies into specific modern patterns. However, the ideologies developed within the Zionist movement contained more variegated and heterogeneous elements than those of either closed religious sects or revolutionary political movements. This ideological diversity was greatly reinforced by the coexistence of many different groups within the federate structure of the Yishuv, creating new institutional nuclei orientated toward broader, more universalistic, cultural and social values. Moreover, the Yishuv, unlike later the state of Israel, was not faced with the problem of molding "traditional" elements to such ideological visions as a central problem.

Israeli society also shared many features and problems with other countries that had large-scale immigration. It had to deal with continuous waves of immigrants and their integration into its emerging institutional framework. But it also developed specific characteristics of its own, rooted in the basic pioneering motivations and orientations among the immigrants and in their strong emphasis on national and social goals.

The Yishuv society, especially, also contained many elements and problems similar to those of other developing countries, especially those developing a modern economic framework either in underdeveloped settings or with traditional populations. This similarity could be found in the establishment of a new political framework by the elite sector under a colonial ruler and the consequent transformation of this elite sector into a ruling class. However, several important differences stand out.

Unlike many contemporary developing societies, the initial institutional framework in Israel was established by modern elite groups and along modern lines. These elite groups had a large pool of educated persons committed, by ideology, outlook, or creed, to the creation of a modern society. The traditional elements were taken into these frameworks only much later, and the process of their modernization was quicker and more intense than in any other newly independent developing country. Furthermore, and again unlike most new states, the attainment of independence did not create a sharp break with the past, because the Yishuv and the Zionist movement already had developed manifold political, administrative, and economic organizations. The emphasis on the "political kingdom" therefore was much smaller, even if not on eschatological orientations.

Different institutional molds have emerged in each of these postrevolutionary societies. The starting point of such transformation in each was the attempt made by the postrevolutionary elite sector to direct new developments and find ideological and political support and legitimation for such new directions. In all revolutionary societies the central focus of the concomitant transformation of the revolutionary ideology had been first the restructuring of the relations between the revolutionary and postrevolutionary ruling elite groups' ideological starting points and processes of economic modernization; second was the relation of this restructuring to the revolutionary symbols; and third was the impact of these transformations on the new regime's bases of legitimation and support.

The specific characteristics of Israel as a revolutionary society and the processes of its transformation were shaped by several factors: its small size; its geopolitical location; and last, but not least, its derivation from the Zionist vision and rebellion against the Jewish community of the nineteenth-century European Diaspora. The formative characteristics of the Yishuv by now have been well studied.[2] The Yishuv and later the state of Israel developed from the activities of the Zionist groups that emerged in the late 1890s in Eastern and Central Europe. Zionist ideology assumed that only in Palestine could a new, modern, viable Jewish society and polity be established and that only in Palestine could a new synthesis of Jewishness and universal human culture of tradition and modernity be evolved.

The Yishuv was built from the different waves of immigration, of Aliyot (singular, Aliyah; literally, "ascent"). The First Aliyah (1882–1903) was initiated by the first Zionist movement, Hovevei Zion, in Russia and Romania, which had the wave of pogroms that flooded South Russia in 1881 as its main driving power. These immigrants looked on land settlement as a primary condition for the rejuvenation of the Jewish people. During this period of the first Jewish agricultural settlements such as Petah Tiqva, Rishon Lezion, Rosh Pina, Zikhron Yaakov, and Hadera were established, and the foundations of the Yishuv were laid. The Second Aliyah (1904–1914) consisted mainly of members of various Zionist labor groups in Russia, who had become disappointed with the social reform movement there (in which they had taken an active part) and that ended in pogroms with the Revolution of 1905. They came to Palestine in a period of crisis both in that country and in the Zionist movement. Although "workers" proper were in the minority during the second Aliyah, it nonetheless is considered a labor immigration, because the workers' initiative and energy changed the whole structure of the Jewish community. New methods of land settlement were adopted, and the foundation was laid for the whole structure of the labor movement in Palestine. During this period the World Zionist Organization started work in Palestine (1908), and the first mixed farming villages were established. This period also witnessed the beginning of urban development. The foundations were laid for the all-Jewish town of Tel Aviv (1909), and here and there the rudimentary beginnings of industry could be found.

The Third Aliyah (1917–1923) began while the First World War was still raging in 1917, following the Balfour Declaration, which the Jewish world interpreted as the creation of a new start toward the establishment of the Zionist ideal. It consisted mostly of young people trained through the Halutz (pioneer) organizations prior to their departure for Palestine and ready and willing to do any work the country might require of them, no matter how hard.

The Fourth Aliyah, which began in 1924 and continued until about 1931, was activated partly by improved economic conditions in Palestine, which made the absorption of further immigrants possible, and partly by the worsening economic position of the Jewish community in Poland, which was caused by the Polish government's policy of eliminating Jews from many trades. The main new element in this immigration was middle-class people with small means, most of whom settled in the towns and entered commerce or industry or became artisans. However, if account is taken of the absolute number of immigrants, the pioneer element predominated in this period, too. This Aliyah was followed by a considerable emigration from Palestine, as a result of the acute economic crisis that broke out during that period of influx.

The Fifth Aliyah began in 1929 but did not reach its peak until 1932, when a larger volume of immigration was resumed and which resulted in great economic prosperity. Up to 1935 about 150,000 Jews, many of them from Germany, came in; they brought considerable capital and helped to develop industry, trade, and agriculture on a large scale. From 1936 to 1940, a period of severe troubles in the country, immigration was limited by the government, and only about 100,000 Jews, including about 15,000 "illegal" immigrants, entered.

The first pioneers, especially those of the Second Aliyah (1904–1914) intended that the Yishuv become a modern nation in every sense of the term, and one that embodied wider values of universal and possibly transcendental significance. This represented a continuation and transformation of the legacy of traditional Jewish society, which combined an ardent yearning for universal meaning with the realities of life for an oppressed minority. As long as this minority remained closed unto itself, the tension between this yearning and reality produced, as we have seen in Chapter 3, considerable cultural, but much more limited institutional, creativity, relegating to the distant future any hope that its universal claims would be accepted. When, at the beginning of the nineteenth century, the gates of European society began to open partially before them, many members of the Jewish community were able to enter social and cultural arenas in which they could be highly creative. At the same time, however, they faced the possibility of losing their collective Jewish identity or not being fully accepted into the broader European society or both.

The Zionist movement, as we have seen (Chapter 6), aimed at providing the opportunity for cultural and social creativity of universal significance within the framework of a free, modern, self-supporting Jewish society. This combination accounts for both the tremendous emphasis it placed on sociocultural creativity and the strong elitist orientations of the leading groups of this society, at least in the initial stages of its evolution.

The vision or visions of the different groups of settlers and the Yishuv, as we have seen, were composed of several components, above all of the basic Zionist tenets and orientations, as well as, at least among the pioneering-revolutionary groups, a strong admixture of different varieties of socialist visions. The "pure" Zionist vision stressed the establishment of a modern Jewish community where Jews would live among themselves as a normal, economically and politically, modern nation and the ideology of national renaissance and the rebirth of the Hebrew language. The more specific "labor" pioneering groups combined these trends with two other themes. One such theme, to some degree shared by all Zionist groups, was a very strong revolutionary emphasis on normalization and production within the Jewish nation. This was to be achieved through the return to agriculture and industry, and above all through the crystallization of a working class, of a normal occupational structure as against the traditional Jewish concentration in small trades and the like. The second such theme was more a specifically socialist vision, even if in rather vague and utopian terms, stressing egalitarian, non-exploitative communal life and collective frameworks, often, especially after the First World War, in terms of a radical ideology of class.

These visions and orientations were borne by the first pioneers, mainly intellectual youths rebeling against their parental background in the Diaspora (especially in Eastern and Central Europe), who organized themselves into small rather sectarian-pioneering groups and went to the old homeland in Palestine to establish a new, viable, modern Jewish society. These characteristics of the first immigrants shaped some of the most prominent features of the Yishuv. Especially important was the development of an ideological focus; that is, a society in which the basic collective identity was couched in ideological terms: in terms of national renaissance, cultural creativity, and social vision.

The original ideological-revolutionary impetus of these groups crystallized around the image of the pioneer (halutz), and stressed the attempt to develop a state in which social values were closely linked with the national effort. It emphasized that these values were not conceived in purely utopian terms, but rather as inseparable elements in building the organization and institutions of a new nation.[3] It did not however necessarily negate the eschatological components of these orientations—even if these components became weakened with this continuous institution building.

The specific tendencies and orientations and the major perennial problems that the Yishuv and Israeli society have been facing from their beginnings emerged from a combination of these visions and ideologies and attempts to realize them in a small, relatively underdeveloped country, a land new both to the founders and to many generations of new immigrants, and in the framework of a strange, even hostile environment. Even though their concrete expressions changed, problems remained relatively constant throughout the development of the Yishuv and of Israeli society. They included initial immigration and absorption of new arrivals; the development of a modern economic base; the challenges of development and modernization; the effort to crystallize symbols of a collective Israeli identity, in relation to Jewish tradition and collective consciousness, on the one hand, and to the modern world and the Middle East, on the other; and the problems of sinking roots in a strange, basically hostile environment, with the concomitant emphasis on security.

The Zionist settlement in Eretz Israel has created a situation of continuous confrontation with the incipient Arab nationalism and later with the newly emerging Palestinian one. Arab nationalism gathered momentum, first after the First World War and the creation of many Arab and mandatory states on the ruins of the former Ottoman Empire and second after the Second World War. The crystallization of the Yishuv and the creation of the state of Israel, in face of a war waged against the incipient state by the Arab countries, intensified this confrontation, giving rise to Palestinian nationalism, which gathered even further momentum after the Six-Day War and the occupation of the West Bank (Judea and Samaria) and Gaza by Israel. The confrontation between the state of Israel and Palestinian nationalism became even further intensified, emphasizing the centrality of this confrontation in shaping the formation and development of Israeli society.

These problems were exacerbated by the constant tension between the social and cultural reality of a small, relatively modern society and its aspiration to be a center of social and cultural creativity, out of all proportion to its size, both for the Jewish people and humankind at large. Israel displays some of the basic problems of all modern small societies, chiefly the difficulty of maintaining a standard of economic and sociocultural life more or less on the same level as that prevailing in the international system.[4] This problem is especially acute for such a small polity, given that the internal market is not large enough to create sufficient economic momentum for development. Small countries therefore have to orient themselves toward large, highly developed states and their markets. Because small states must find outlets for their products in the highly competitive and relatively open global market, they usually have to specialize and find areas in which they can promote or create advantages stemming from either their geographic location or their social and economic structure.

To understand this special characteristic of the Yishuv and Israeli society, we must remember that one of its major "external markets" has been the Jewish communities in the Diaspora. The major changes that occurred in the relationship between the Yishuv and Israeli society and the Jewish communities in the Diaspora, as we shall soon see in greater detail, were important causes or indicators of significant transformations in the structure of the Yishuv and Israeli society.

The responses to these problems were influenced above all by the character of the institutional structure shaped in the early periods of the Yishuv. The major institutional formats of the Yishuv developed during the period of the first Aliyot. There were various settlements (the moshavot, the kvutzah, the kibbutzim, and the moshavim), their various federations, the urban centers in the three main cities (Jerusalem, Tel Aviv, and Haifa) and in many secondary centers such as Tiberias, Safed, and others; major educational institutions, political organizations and the nuclei of the self-defense forces; and the Histadrut (the Federation of Labor) established in 1920, constituting a unique combination of the various settlements, trade-union activities, the Sick Fund, many industrial concerns, and housing, trade and transport cooperatives—all under one central canopy of the Hevrat Ovdim (The Company of Workers, the economic branch of the Histadrut) and becoming one of the major, if not *the* major, center of economic and political power in the Yishuv.

The rather complex institutional structure of the Yishuv established during this period was shaped by the combination of four major forces or factors that were very closely related to the basic themes of the Zionist movement and the concrete situations in which it was active: first, the initial revolutionary vision of the different groups of pioneers, settlers, and immigrants; second, the concrete problems that arose out of the necessity to realize, implement, this vision in the concrete conditions in Ottoman Empire and British mandate in Palestine; third, the relations of the different sectors of the Yishuv with the Jewish communities in the Diaspora; and fourth, the momentum of the internal development and structure of the Yishuv itself.

The crystallization of the political economy of the Yishuv was guided, especially since the 1920s, by the decision to create, insofar as possible, an independent Jewish economy—and not together with the British, of a colonial economy like, for instance, in Kenya, Rhodesia, or South Africa. This decision promulgated, advocated, and implemented especially by the labor sector, created a competition within the newly created economic sectors of the Yishuv between the Yishuv and Arab workers. In the economic sphere this structure was characterized by the concentration of public capital in the main sectors of economic development alongside the constant growth of the private sector.[5]

Specific manifestations of Israeli socioeconomic organization as it crystallized in this period included the major types of settlements, kibbutzim and moshavim; development of cooperative enterprises in the urban sector; and, above all, the unique feature of the Israeli reality, the integration of most of these cooperative and settlement bodies within unifying frameworks, particularly the Histadrut. This integration allowed organizations to evolve beyond the boundaries of the pioneering groups' early agrarian orientations and facilitated the urban development of the Yishuv.

One of the most interesting outcomes of the crystallization of the relative hegemony of the labor pioneers and their ideology in the Yishuv from about the middle 1930s, and then in the state of Israel, was that the leaders of the labor pioneers with their socialist ideology became the dominant, later the ruling, groups. Their economic activities, undertaken in terms of their ideology and legitimized by it, erected many sectors of the economy and

shaped some of the crucial aspects of the overall mode of the political economy of the Yishuv and later the state of Israel.

The second aspect of the Yishuv's social development was the strong
ideological emphasis on egalitarianism and opposition to occupational specialization. This found its initial expression in two ways: attempts to reduce
wage differentials among occupations and minimize visible social differences, and the assumption that an easy transition from one profession to
another was possible.

The Yishuv also developed special cultural characteristics, especially
with respect to the relationship between tradition and modernization. Two
phenomena are of special importance here: the revival of Hebrew as a modern language, and the relationship between nonreligious and religious circles.
The revival of Hebrew made it the common national language of the kindergarten, school, and daily speech; at the same time Hebrew has proven itself
able to meet the demands of science, modern literature, and technology. The
fact that this "religious" and "traditional" language became the national vernacular and means of communication in a modern society reduced the possibility of a split between different linguistic identities and limited the development of cultural dependence on foreign centers as major and exclusive
sources of cultural creativity. Second, as we shall see in greater detail later
on, therealso developed a distinct pattern of relations between religious and
nonreligious sectors.

In the political arena a combination of strong sectarian orientations
developed together with growing political cooperation among the various
movements. This cooperation developed within the constitutional democratic
framework established by the Zionist movement and the Vaad Leumi
(National Council) in Palestine, characterized by strong federative-constitu-
tional arrangements among the different movements, very close to the consociational model portrayed by Dutch and other scholars.[6]

The Transition from the Yishuv to the State of Israel
and the Implementation of the Zionist Vision

The characteristics just analyzed constituted the specific background of
the initial social structure that distinguished Israeli society from other revolutionary and postrevolutionary ones. These characteristics constituted the
starting point for the processes of transformation noted earlier, and which
crystallized with the establishment of the state of Israel in 1948. The establishment of the state of Israel was not just a great historical and political
event in the development of Jewish settlement in Eretz Israel, it was also a
harbinger of far-reaching social transformation and development.

Before, however, analyzing the nature of this social transformation and
development, it is necessary to point out the profound, dramatic—sometimes

tragic—changes in the history of the Jewish people historically connected with the establishment of the state. These were the Holocaust and the near total destruction of Eastern and Central European Jewry; the growing isolation of Soviet Jewry, which became the second-largest Jewish community in the Diaspora; the emergence of American Jewry as the major single Jewish community in the Diaspora, but a community that crystallized in a distinct pattern of its own, a pattern that, as it became more and more apparent, could not be explained in terms of the historical experience of European Jewry; and the reawakening, because of the combined impact of decolonization, modernization, and the establishment of the state of Israel itself, of Oriental Jewry, that is, the Jews in the lands that had belonged to the Ottoman Empire before the First World War.

All these facts had a forceful, but also rather paradoxical and contradictory, impact on the attitudes of these Jewish communities to the Zionist movement in general and the state of Israel in particular; and they gave rise to far-reaching changes in the nature of the Zionist movement. From the first years of the state, anti-Zionism and even more an anti-Israel attitude (the two were, in principle, practically indistinguishable) disappeared almost entirely from Jewish public life, except for some groups, like the American Council for Judaism, which no longer were very influential or vocal. The Holocaust, the Jews' most terrible experience in their long history of suffering, seemingly vindicated the basic Zionist premises about the impossibility of even the sheer physical survival of Jewish life in the modern (at least European) Diaspora. The combined experiences of the Holocaust and the Soviet Jewry, which lived under circumstances of pressure to assimilate and continuous strong anti-Semitism, also undermined the viability of the various "autonomist"-federalist or territorial solutions of finding some communal national existence in the Diaspora, something that still could be seen as a possibility in pre-Second World War Poland or even in such places as the Birobijan experiment in Soviet Russia. The fact that, above all only in Palestine and later on in the state of Israel would the survivors of the Holocaust— and later on the Jews from Arab countries—be openly received, strengthened the viability of the Zionist premises and vision.

At the same time, the very acceptance within the Jewish communities of the Zionist premises, or at least the state of Israel, the fact that the establishment of the state of Israel added new symbols and institutional dimensions in the life of the Jewish people in the Diaspora potentially—and in fact very quickly—weakened the revolutionary or radical component in the Zionist movement and almost totally abolished its place in Jewish life. However, for decades this fact was never fully admitted by the Zionist and Israeli leaders. Indeed, the whole pattern of the relationship between the Jewish community in Israel, the state of Israel and the Jewish people in the Diaspora changed in many ways that greatly affected, although initially almost imperceptibly, the whole internal development of Israel.

This trend was greatly reinforced by the fact, analyzed earlier, that in the United States a new type of Jewish community developed, a community that established a pattern of reconstruction of Jewish tradition and life very different from that of the historical experience of Jews in Europe before the Second World War. This new pattern later was repeated, even if in a milder form, with many variations in those European countries, like England, in which Jewish communities survived the Second World War, or in those, like France, Belgium, or Holland, in which new Jewish communities were established.

Also important were the far-reaching changes in the orthodox camp, especially its growth after the 1960s and its adaptation to the new modern settings, which we analyze in greater detail later in this and in the concluding chapter.

At the same time, these changes in the fate of the different Jewish communities had powerful effects on the social structure of the Jewish community in Israel. First of all, it greatly influenced, as we shall see in greater detail later, the demographic composition of the Jewish population in Eretz Israel. Second, the Holocaust deprived the Jewish community in Eretz Israel of its major reservoir of leadership and continuous ideologically orientated personnel, those very elements that counteracted the potentially stagnating tendencies that developed naturally. Third, the Holocaust weakened the revolutionary anti-Galut orientations of the different Zionist movements—it was difficult to maintain such orientations toward a society annihilated in such tragic circumstances.

The most important characteristics of Israeli society developed throughout the period of the Yishuv and later underwent far-reaching changes following the establishment of the state of Israel. These were the routinization of the initial vision and organization promulgated by the pioneers, their transformation into a full-fledged constitutional democratic state and the pioneer leaders into a ruling elite group; economic expansion and modernization; the intensification of the military security problem and the growing perception, by major echelons of society, that this problem is the most important one facing Israeli society; the concomitant changes in the characteristics of Israeli society as a small society, especially in its relationship with the Jewish Diaspora.

Of particular importance was the demographic expansion and the concurrent change in the demographic composition, cultural background, and ideological orientation of the population caused by the great immigrations of the late 1940s and early 1950s. These new immigrants were mainly of so-called Oriental origin (that is, from Islamic societies that until the end of the

First World War were under at least nominal Ottoman rule) and from remnants of European communities that survived the Holocaust. Both of these groups were motivated to migrate there by the search for security, but not necessarily by the more ideological "revolutionary" components of the Zionist ideology. These arrivals tripled the population in a period of only fifteen years.

These processes formed the specific pattern of Israeli modernity. This pattern was characterized by a constitutional democratic system with initially strong restrictive overtones and consociational characteristics; by the grant of citizenship to all sectors of the population; by the center's appropriation of symbols of Zionist and labor pioneering in an attempt to gain legitimacy in their terms; by the evolution of an old nation into a new state with heavy emphasis on the construction of a new national and cultural tradition; and by continuous economic development within the framework of a mixed private and public, yet relatively controlled, economy.

The Israeli political economy has been characterized by centralization, widespread public (mostly within the labor sector) ownership of major enterprises, and strong collectivistic policies.[7]

Until the late 1980s, the Israeli political economy was characterized by three features. First was the development of a strong concentration of economic resources, and hence potentially of economic power (probably more than in any other noncommunist modern society) in the hands of the state. However, the state has not become, as in the socialist or communist countries, the owner of production and the major industrial and financial enterprises. These were distributed among the three major economic sectors: the Histadrut; the private one, which continued from the Yishuv period; and the governmental one, which was of course new, most of it developing with the establishment of the state. The third characteristic was the use to which the government put its large regulative power over the economy, policies rooted in the labor-Zionist vision of building a Jewish society in Eretz Israel, a vision that became transformed with the establishment and development of the state.

The most important consequence of this vision was the decision to open the gates of the state to as many Jewish communities as possible and to create a modern economy. The concrete policies that developed out of this vision and that, in continuous encounter with the existing economic realities and forces as well as with those generated by the policies themselves, shaped the social and political dynamics of economic development in Israel, were as follows: first, a stress on economic expansion, modernization, and development; second, the regulation of such development by the government (and to a smaller degree by the Histadrut); and third, in the direction of the development of vast, continuously expanding welfare state services.

A rather distinct pattern developed also in the cultural arena, and with respect to the incorporation of different components of the Jewish historical and religious traditions. The religious components continued to constitute an important element in the reconstitution of the national and primordial elements of Jewish experience as envisaged by most sectors of the Zionist movement. However much many of the Zionists, especially the labor leaders, have rebelled against the orthodox Jewish society and the rule of the Halakhah, most of them did not deny the importance of religion in the Jewish national and historical experience. The crux of the Zionist revolution was oriented more against the political passivity implied in the rule of Halakhah than against various specific religious components of the Jewish tradition. In the period of the Yishuv and in the first stage of the state of Israel, the religious component did not play a very important role with respect to the reconstruction of a new collective identity; the secular orientations were much stronger. Even within many of the more religious groups and parties with all their emphasis on religious observance, with the partial exception of the Hapoel Hamizrahi (the Hamizrahi, or "religious," workers) in general and the religious kibbutzim in particular, there was relatively little confidence in their own hope and aspiration that the halakhic mold could serve as a driving force for this process.[8]

Accordingly a unique cultural mold developed in the Yishuv, based on reconstruction of the major dimensions of Jewish national-religious tradition and its relation to general cultural values. This mold was characterized by relative heterogeneity but based, in principle, on the basic tenets of the Zionist vision. Within this format a special combination of tradition and modernity based on far-reaching compromises with the religious groups minimized, at least initially, the rift found later among many new nations.

Within this framework a special type of arrangement developed with respect to religious sectors. Zionist-religious groups, of course, were part of the federative-consociational framework of the Yishuv and the state of Israel. As such they took part in all the federative, consociational distribution of resources—certificates of immigration under the Mandate, land, public finances, and the like—and in the tough political bargaining accompanying such arrangements. The religious groups also took care of the various local religious institutions, especially the councils and rabbinates established in most municipal settings, except those of the kibbutzim and moshavim.

Beyond this specific arrangements developed with respect to religious matters that affected not only the religious sectors, but the entire Jewish population. During the predominance of labor in the Yishuv period, and even before the hegemony of the labor movement, and then in the first two decades of the state of Israel, institutional arrangements developed within the religious arena that came close to institutionalization of an established state religion. One such arrangement was the official observance in most localities of religious holidays, the Sabbath and the rules of Shmita (the seventh year). The second was the upholding of the Sabbath not only as an official rest day, but also the introduction of various restrictions on shopping, entertainment, and public transportation in most cities (Haifa, the bastion of the workers, was a partial exception) and granting the rabbinate the powers certifying Kashrut to butchers and restaurants, hence indirectly enabling some supervision of the production and consumption of food throughout most of the Yishuv. But the arrangement that had the most far-reaching impact on the community was vesting the laws of personal status, above all of marriage and divorce and hence of the boundaries of the membership in the community, in the hands of the rabbinical courts, which were established in 1922 and which, although not accepted by the ultrareligious, did become a basic part of the structure of the Yishuv.

The establishment of an organized rabbinate, both central and local, under two chief rabbis, one Sephardi (the so-called Rishon Letzion, a title that seems to go back to the sixteenth or seventeenth century) and the other Ashkenazi, was a great innovation, created by the Zionist leaders and opposed by the ultraorthodox sectors.

This unusual Israeli institutional pattern or mold was rooted in the Zionist vision; hence, its success could be seen as the implementation of that vision. It proved, for the first time in 2,000 years, that the Jewish people could forge an independent political unity encompassing all areas of life, enter history as an active agent, and face the civilizational challenges inherent in its basic self-definition but that had remained latent during the long period of exile.

The Jews were now more conscious of this challenge and opportunity than they had been during the Second Temple period. In many ways the Zionist movement was the epitome of this awareness; and its civilizational orientations, unlike those of the Second Temple period, were directed not only to the political and religious arenas but also to the social and institutional ones. Moreover, its relationships with other civilizations were not necessarily as antagonistic as those that prevailed among the Jews during the Second Temple period and the long period of Galut. As a result of the transformation of the premises of the Western civilization in the modern world, the relationship with others was more open, seemingly benign, although many antagonistic elements persisted.

Thus, the Yishuv and Israeli society in a sense had taken up a double task: that of finding ways of building a viable modern society in a rather hostile and underdeveloped environment, as well as under very difficult security conditions, and combining this with the reconstruction of Jewish civilizational orientations. It built up a very strong army under relatively strict, if somewhat peculiar, civilian control; it certainly did not succumb to the danger of becoming a garrison state or a militarized society. Despite the precariousness of its situation with its immediate neighbors, the international standing of the state was relatively good; and its network of foreign relations, including aid to Third-World countries, has spread over many continents and countries. Moreover, the state of Israel became the common focus of identification for most Jewish communities in the world.

This society has demonstrated impressive creativity in the cultural field, including music, theater, painting, and important academic centers of international standing. There has been a great spurt in Hebrew literature and Jewish studies. And, in general, its educational, academic, and cultural accomplishments have been quite impressive, especially in light of its special problems, particularly those related to the absorption of new immigrants. The rapid success in absorbing immigrants is very impressive indeed, all the more so when compared with any other modern country of nonselective immigration and taking into account the rather impoverished economic starting point.

This society also seemed able to cope with the problems that arose from the combination of its founders' ideological vision with the attempt to realize this vision in a small and relatively underdeveloped country, a land new both to the founders of this society and to many generations of immigrants, within an alien and even hostile, environment.

Minorities in the Jewish State

The emerging institutional mold of Israeli society was also faced with the problem of the different non-Jewish minorities, above all the Arab minority. It was, indeed, the first time since the period of the Second Temple that Jews were faced with the existence of minorities among them within a Jewish State.

The fact of Israel being a Jewish state was, of course, emphasized in several ways. First, it was emphasized—and fully received by the world—in the very wording of the UN resolutions. In principle the state was also recognized in several symbolic levels; for example, the hymn and the flag were those of the Zionist movement, and the Chief Rabbis were granted places of protocol as distinguished from the heads of other religious communities.

But within this framework, the Declaration of Independence assured full equality to all citizens of Israel, irrespective of religion or nationality, and this, of course, also applied to the Arab population. Accordingly, citizenship was also granted to the Arab population and Arabic was recognized as an official language, which could be used in the Knesset and in public discussion.

Arabs participated in the elections to the Knesset and entered it either as members of general (i.e., Jewish) parties—especially the leftist ones—or as representatives of special Arab lists.

At the same time Muslim, Christian, and Druze religious institutions and courts were given wide-ranging jurisdiction in civil matters similar to those given to the rabbinical courts.

The Arabs who remained in Israel were only a small, relatively weak part of the original Arab population that lived in what became the frontiers of the state of Israel. The more active elements—whether economically or politically—left, some on their own initiative (or rather the initiative of their leaders who were sure they would come back after the defeat of the Jewish forces), others under the impact of the war, in some cases probably also prodded by the initiative of the advancing Israeli forces.

The Arabs who remained in Israel numbered about 156,000, most of them (about 107,000) Muslims, a large number of Christian (34,000), and in addition there were also about 15,000 Druzes and Bedouins. They were ecologically concentrated around Nazareth on the Galilee and in the famous Little Triangle (from the Valley of Israel in the north to Kefar Kassem in the south), with small groups in Haifa, Jaffa, and Lydda.

Economically they were mostly composed of peasants with some urban elements—mostly small shopkeepers or workers. Those from the villages who sought employment elsewhere worked mostly as drivers, waiters, or nonskilled workers in construction.

Their leadership was mostly of the more traditional types of family head and the relatively lower levels of religious leadership, but one that became isolated from the centers of Arab and Muslim activities.

The general attitude developed by the Israeli authorities toward the Arab population was composed of official recognition and acceptance as citizens in the basic democratic framework of the state mixed with strong suspicion and ignorance, and a certain blindness to their special problems.

Their recognition and acceptance as citizens was manifest, as we have seen, in the formal granting of citizenship with the right to vote to the Knesset, the recognition of the Arab language as an official one in Israel, and an extension of basic public services (education, health service, municipal services, and the like) to the Arab population. A special department of Arab education was established in the Ministry of Education.

This principled democratic attitude in the Declaration of Independence toward the Arab population was limited by consideration of security, by the fact that the Arabs who remained in Israel were part of the Arab population (many of whom fled from Israel during the War of Independence) that denied the legitimacy of the state of Israel, and by the concomitant apprehension about the loyalty to the state of those who remained.

The combination of all these attitudes gave rise to a special type of relatively benign, but also restrictive, semicolonial paternalism. On the one hand, the Arab minority was assured a very high level of economic development, though smaller than the one in the Jewish sector, and an increase in standards of living that also led to far-reaching transformations of their social structure. But, on the other hand, these measures could not efface the Arabs' rather problematic place in Israeli society. This problematic place was apparent in their objective situation but reinforced by the attitudes of the Israeli authorities and the Jewish society and by their institutional repercussions.

The suspicion toward the Arabs was manifest first in their exemption, continuing to this day, from the army, although some other minorities such as the Druzes or Circassians or even parts of the Bedouin, were asked to serve in the army. The second, more temporary, expression of this suspicion was the imposition in most Arab areas, by the military government, of heavy limitations on Arabs' free movement throughout Israel, imposed through a system of permits, which was abolished in 1965 by Prime Minister Levi Eshkol. Closely related to such suspicion was social distance and ignorance on a daily level, but also in more official frameworks. There were also attempts to control, through various paternalistic activities, the political activities of the Arabs.

Added to these security considerations was the lack of any real preparation within most parts of the Jewish community to deal with the problems of a minority population living within a Jewish state, a certain basic blindness to its special cultural problems—a blindness that could be seen, among others, in the imposition upon it of a curriculum that did not take into account their specific cultural problems, which were only gradually recognized through the growing concern among intellectuals, Orientalists, and some left-wing and more liberal groups.

In the framework of these basic parameters, a far-reaching social dynamism developed within the Arab population of Israel, evident frist of all in the demographic and economic spheres. The high level of health and educational services (high when compared with the Arab countries yet often lagging behind standards in the Jewish sector) gave rise to a concomitant demographic increase—among the highest in the world—bringing up the Arab population of Israel in 1983 to about 645,000 Muslims and 106,000 Christians.

Second was the gradual growth of an educated intelligentsia, composed of graduates of high schools and universitites. Compulsory education was enacted among Israeli Arabs. In 1973, 90.7 percent of the Arab population in the suitable age groups were attending school, compared to 98.6 percent from the Jewish population, In 1977 the percentage rose to 92.5 percent.

All these processes brought about a weakening of the "traditionality" and self-enclosure of the Arab population, undermining many aspects of their traditional social structure and encouraging an interweaving with the Jewish economic sectors, but also giving rise to new problems and tensions.

These problems, which became intensified by the developments after the Six-Day War, were rooted in the new aspirations and frustrations with respect to finding adequate places of employment suitable from the point of view of their educational (especially academic) training and with respect to the difficulties of integration in Israeli society—even if within the latter some openings were gradually appearing.

Another area of tensions, as well as of growing political consciousness and struggle and connected with the Arabs' demographic growth, focused on the problem of land—especially on its relative scarcity in relation to their demographic growth and the amount of agricultural land at their disposal. The situation was exacerbated by the land settlement policy of the state, aimed at least in principle at the growing Jewish settlement at Galilee where the Jews were losing out demographically to the Arabs.

All these problems became, as we shall see in greater detail later on, intensified and aggravated in the seventies and eighties.

The Implementation of the Zionist Vision and the Perennial Tensions of Jewish Civilization

The implementation of the Zionist vision in the Yishuv and the state of Israel seemed able to cope with the perennial problems of Jewish life and tradition. Although this Jewish entry into history was rooted in a strong rebellion against the Jewish traditional and assimilationist molds alike, it was not dissociated from many aspects of Jewish history and tradition. On the contrary, the very rebellion against Jewish life in the traditional and modern Diaspora not only reinforced, renewed, and brought into the open the basic premises latent in earlier periods of Jewish history, but also transformed them from mostly intellectual ones into themes and orientations embedded in institutional frameworks. All the major components of Jewish tradition and civilization—the tension between universalism and particularism; between self-closure and openness to the world; between a closed, inward-looking solidarity and a more flexible one as a base for far-reaching social and ethical and cultural creativity; between populist overtones and the emphasis on standards of excellence—were related to the construction and functioning of institutional formats and the state. This was true also of the tension between the emphasis on a semi-Messianic future and that on the present, which no longer was confined within the molds of the Halakhah and communal life, as well as the different orientations to Eretz Israel and Galut. It was also true of the pressures on Jewish political culture, whether those related to the issues of solidarity or to the tensions between legal order and the strong antinomian and semianarchist tendencies inherent in this culture, which we discuss in greater detail in the next chapter.

All these tensions, as we have seen, found new literary and intellectual expression in large parts of the modern Diaspora, first in Europe up to the Second World War and then, and above all, in the United States. In Eastern Europe, and to a much smaller degree in America, they also were connected to some degree with new patterns of institution building, but only in Eretz Israel did they become closely interwoven with the working of overall institutional molds of a self-sustaining, creative society, and labor of an independent polity.

Variegated patterns of such creativity did develop not solely within Eretz Israel. It was above all the connection between different cultural and political themes, with the construction and running of a territorial, national society, of a state that constituted the epitome of the Zionist revolution—and its greatest continuous challenge.

In this context, of special importance were the dialectical relations of Israel with the Diaspora. For large sectors of the Yishuv and of Israeli society, the Jewish communities in the Diaspora served as a focus of rebellion, as a reservoir of leadership that could counteract the stagnative tendencies inherent in any postrevolutionary or small society, and as a source of support as well as seemingly another possible competitive arena for the implementation of the Jewish civilizational vision. And gradually a new type of encounter with Jewish orthodoxy developed (see in greater detail Chapter 9).

The first stage of this attempt to create a territorial, ultimately politically independent, Jewish entity that would also be an arena for the implementation of the Jewish civilizational vision, the process of settlement of the Yishuv and the first phases of the state of Israel, as we have seen, was a relative success. During this stage a viable, institutional, modern, even if initially restricted, constitutional democratic society was set up, a framework that combined the construction of a national society with some of the themes of Jewish tradition and civilization and that developed a distinct, specific pattern or mode of modern society, the major characteristics of which we briefly analyzed.

This new institutional mold or pattern went far beyond what the Jews could have developed in the period of dispersion in the countries of settlement, in the networks of traditional kehillot (communities) and centers of learning or the more dispersed and diversified organizations of modern times. It was not only just development of additional institutional arenas—the political, the military, or the economic—but, above all, that these were brought together under the canopy of a new autonomous collectivity or an overall institutional framework was of crucial importance. This constituted the epitome of the entry of Jews into modern society.

Within this framework the perennial foci of Jewish civilization were closely connected with the basic themes and tensions of Jewish political culture, those related to the issues of solidarity as well as the tensions between legal order and the strong antinomian and semianarchist tendencies inherent in this culture. The emphasis on solidarity no longer was confined to communal arrangements or intellectual and literary expression, but became closely related to the functioning of political institutions and the acceptance of the rule of law, including civilian control of the military. Similarly, the emphasis on civility and the rule of law and its tensions with populist as well as antinomian and semianarchic political tendencies, with its own emphasis on a higher law, departed from the narrow intellectual confines to which it was limited in the Medieval period and became closely interwoven with the functioning of a fully fledged society and polity with institutional formats and political forces. The strong future orientation inherent in the Zionist vision also became connected with building concrete institutions and hence with the exigencies of the present, giving rise to confrontations between present and future.

The same was true, of course, of the Zionist themes, closely connected with the general Jewish ones enumerated earlier, especially the tension between being a normal nation and being a light unto the nations or a Jewish nation; between the emphasis on territorial political dimensions and institution building; between the conception of the state of Israel as a place of refuge and security as against an arena of national renaissance.

The achievement of the initial institutional and cultural mold, framework, or pattern that developed in Israel was not the obliteration of these different orientations and the tensions between them. On the contrary, they all continued to exist within it and their impact on social and political life was that much greater, given that they have become interwoven in concrete institutional settings. Rather, this achievement was manifested in the fact that the institutional mold that developed in Israel seemingly was able to regulate these tensions. At the same time, the more anarchic potentials were regulated and held in check both by the development and continuity of the central institutional frameworks of this mold and by the strong internal cohesion of the elite groups and their solidarity with the broader sections of the population.

The Distintegration of the Initial Institutional Mold of Israeli Society

The Emergence of New Problems and Conflicts

But this institutional mold, which crystallized in the first twenty-five years of the state, spawned many new problems and challenges. As in many relatively successful revolutionary societies, such as the United States in its early phase, Mexico, or in an entirely different mode in Soviet Russia, the very institutionalization of their initial vision has generated new problems and tensions and posed far-reaching challenges. These problems and tensions were generated by the very success of this institutional mold: the combination of continuous economic development; the absorption of new groups, both of new immigrants and new generations from the older sectors into the economic and social frameworks; the transformation of the older leaders of pioneering groups into members of a ruling elite sector; and the far-reaching changes in the structure of the hegemonic institutions and their relations to the broader sectors of the society.

As in many other successful revolutionary societies, the crux of these problems was the extent to which the existing elite sector could absorb new groups; whether it would be sufficiently cohesive, resilient, and capable to respond in a constructive way to new pressures and demands to maintain its unity and its ability to deal with new problems, while at the same time allow the development of a more pluralistic structure.

The initial success in absorbing a broad social strata and groups into existing structures and the continuous economic development increased the acuteness of social divisions and conflict and the salience of the problem of egalitarianism. The proximity of the various groups to one another and to the centers of the society led to continual comparison and an examination of their respective positions in the light of the egalitarian ideology. Conflicts developed among the various sectors: between manual workers and salaried and self-employed professionals; within each of these sectors, between the highest-paid, middle, and the lower-paid groups; between those occupying key economic positions who could enforce high wage demands and influence the government and those without access to such positions.

Many of these problems, and the conflicts engendered by them, were similar to those that emerged in many developing and "postindustrial" societies; they could be seen as the Israeli version of such general problems, shaped by the rather special amalgam of semi-industrial and postindustrial society that developed in Israel. But these problems became interwoven in the processes attendant on the institutionalization of the revolutionary ideological society and the specific transitions that took place in Israel.

One such specific characteristic of this transition was that a highly ideological society was transformed into a more routinized, diversified, and open pluralistic one, with a strong tendency to deideologize many areas of life.

Still, among wide sectors of the population the search persisted for some overall ideological vision, perhaps best seen in the continuous reference to the image of the pioneer and to the Zionist symbols of collective identity. Second, all these developments took place in Israel within the framework of a relatively small society, constructed within a fragile international situation, and overburdened by security problems. Third, beyond these problems loomed a more central dilemma—the growing contradiction between the older pioneering vision, which stressed the conversion of the

Jewish people to productive occupations in modern agriculture and industry, thus reversing what was seen as the inverted occupational pyramid characteristic of the Jews of Eastern Europe, and the development of a modern, diversified economy, which in many ways reinstated that pyramid—albeit giving agriculture and sophisticated industries pride of place. The Achilles' heel of this development was the relatively low status of the middle and lower echelons of industrial workers and the burgeoning in the more traditional undertones not based on sophisticated and technology, as in many developing societies of service activities, particularly in the public sector. This problem was to become much more acute after the Six-Day War, when the influx of Arab labor from the West Bank and Gaza provided the Israeli economy with relatively cheap labor to fill up the lower occupational rungs, enabling many sectors of the Jewish population to move into the higher echelons, some in the more skilled jobs in industry and others to services.

In all arenas the problem of the "Oriental communities" became central in this period. There developed great gaps between the "Oriental" and the "Western" groups in the relative standing of those of Asian and African origin in terms of education, economy, and also, to some degree, in the political sphere, as well as the disproportionate percentage of the former in the more deprived sectors of the population. This gap was more and more visible in the different sectors of Israeli society. For instance, in 1977 there was a 10.5 percent differential between the percentage of Asians-Africans in the population and their percentage among secondary-school pupils. This gap increased according to grade level, from 0.8 percent in the first year to 25 percent in the last year of high school, to 34 percent among recipients of matriculation certificates, and 40 percent at the college and university level. The only type of educational institution where the percentage of Oriental Jews is equal to and even higher than their share in the population is in vocational schools, and this in itself was often seen as discriminatory, denying the Oriental group easy access to the more prestigious occupations for which academic degrees are deemed necessary.

Similarly, when it comes to net per capita income, Israelis born in Africa and Asia constitue 55–56 percent of the lowest deciles, 53–65 percent of the seventh and eighth deciles, and 65–76 percent of the ninth and tenth deciles. This gap developed out of and in conjunction with the continuous economic expansion that took place in Israeli society, so that many of these new tensions were most visible in arenas in which a relatively high level of success was attained, attesting to the fact that this very success generated and highlighted many of the contradictions inherent in the initial institutional mold of the state of Israel.

As a result of all these developments, in the first two and a half decades of the state of Israel many cracks appeared in the social and political framework, manifest in "ethnic" demonstrations or "outbursts," in the growing number of strikes and numerous manifestations of dissociation of a young generation from the existing ideological and political framework, widely observed and commented on. Such cracks were seen, especially by the establishment, as marginal, destined to pass away. And in this period the state leaders were successful in coping with these problems within the framework of the dominant institutional mold. They might have remained as such if they had not been concurrent with far-reaching changes in Israeli society; especially with the reconstruction of major ethos and ideology, the transformation of the structure of major elite groups and their relation to the major strata, and the weakening of internal frameworks and solidarity networks.

Changes in Ethos

The reconstruction of the basic social ethos was first evident in the shift of national ideology from a strong sectarian and pioneering orientation to a strong statist one, which attempted to appropriate for itself the older pioneering symbols and orientation. A second aspect of this change was the transformation of the egalitarian component of the pioneering ethos from the elitism of the pioneering groups and sects with the strong commitment to obligations and duties to more distributive and paternalistic orientations, with a strong emphasis on economic development and a rising standard of living.

These changes in ideology were connected to several very important structural changes: first of all, to the transformation of the leadership elements of the different movements and sectors of the Yishuv into a ruling elite sector. This metamorphosis, common to all postrevolutionary societies, caused a growing segregation among the different elite groups, and between them and the broader strata of society.

Contrary to the basic ideological premises and institutional model that prevailed earlier, and to some degree to the concrete situation as well, since the late 1950s Israel witnessed a continuous process of differentiation and segregation among "specialized" elite groups—economic, military, and academic—and the political elite. Each elite group was able to develop a broad autonomous space within its special institutional framework and attain higher standards of living, but at the same time most of them were progressively distanced from the centers of power and political decision making. The political elite sector itself, especially that of the dominant labor sector, split between the upholders of "statehood" ("Mamlachtiut"), as promoted by Ben-Gurion, and those that emphasized the older movement orientations, but often in fact became closely related to the party or Histadrut bureaucracy; however, both combined in excluding other sectors from the centers of power.

One overall result of this process was the atrophy of the political process. Within the general framework of the constitutional democracy, a strong clientelistic pattern of politics developed. This characteristic pattern was most clearly visible in relations between the political establishment and the new immigrants, but a rather similar though more subtle pattern developed with respect to other sectors, with respect to many of the elite, the "older movement," sectors and, above all, with respect to the younger generations.

At the same time, all these elite groups became interwoven in the emerging upper strata whose life-styles in many ways were contrary to the pioneering and socialist ethos in which the elite sector rooted its legitimacy. This development naturally weakened their solidarity with the broader strata, especially, but not only, with many of the new immigrants. In parallel, the strong economic growth led to intensive mobility and the weakening of the networks and channels of solidarity among large sectors of the society, perhaps above all among the elite groups.

One of the most important manifestations of this changing ethos of Israeli society manifested itself in the development by the ruling elite sector of a plethora of policies with respect to the major problems that developed in Israeli society, especially to the problem of the gaps between the "Oriental" and the "Western" sectors already mentioned. The feedback between these policies and the processes of change taking place in Israeli society was crucial in shaping the direction in which the initial institutional mold of Israeli society was first transformed and then, to a large extent, disintegrated.

As in many postrevolutionary societies, the general mode of these policies was dynamic conservatism. This type of conservatism is not characterized by adherence to the narrow interests of existing groups and organizations. Instead it is quite dynamic, ready to give up narrow vested interests, confront new problems, and coopt new groups into its organizational frameworks. At the same time, however, attempts to solve new problems are made within existing cognitive, conceptual, and institutional frameworks, thus preserving the existing centers of power and the effective control of the existing elite groups of access to these centers. This resulted in a drastic alteration of the relations between these centers and the various new social groups for whom the (new) organizations were established and to whose problems the major policies were oriented.

Thus, for instance, many of the new migrants were settled into new moshavim initially patterned after the old mold. Similarly some of the basic frameworks such as the Histadrut, with its plethora of industrial concerns, cooperatives, and trade unions, and with its Health Service in which the largest part of the population was insured, opened its gates to the immigrants. But within these frameworks few opportunities developed for the new sectors to participate in the centers of power or to attempt to create new institutional patterns. The older sectors were in the positions of power in these organizations, and very often they developed fraternalistic-clientelistic relations between them and the new ones.

New common social frameworks, sharing similar cultural and social orientations and stressing qualitative standards, duties, and obligations were few and far between. Some developed later on some of the moshavim, in some army units, and in some private sectors of the economy, but not in the central institutional domains where the major organizational expansion took place.

Most indicative were the policies that developed with respect to some emerging social problems, especially those of the so-called Oriental immigrants to which we referred. The crucial fact was that these policies were mostly distributive, providing for the allocations of resources to these groups. These policies, on the whole, did not aim to create, as would be called on from the pioneering ethos, conditions for full participation in the existing settings or the creation of new ones. Most of the policies developed in these frameworks have been oriented toward distributive allocations on an ethnic or social basis, stressing more rights and entitlement and many fewer duties and obligations.

In many fields, such as education, there was also a redefinition, basically a lowering, of the standards of achievement to make them easily attainable by these groups, generating a strong populist ambience, and rather strong tendencies to at least de facto affirmative action policies developed. Implicitly or explicitly, these policies were based on the premise that the ethnic problem was rooted in the combination of certain objective facts, especially the cultural and initial educational gap between the "Oriental" and the "Western" groups, with the concomitant de facto, though certainly not de jure, discrimination against the "Oriental" groups, generated by the misunderstanding inherent in such cultural gaps.

These policies directly or indirectly accepted the ethnic and other social problems as given, not as historically and socially constituted. They neglected the fact that, in those institutional arenas where major qualitative expansion took place, few social settings developed in which new and old immigrants were bound together on equal terms with the older sectors. Thus, these policies reinforced the bureaucratic and paternalistic tutelary, closely related to the clientelistic policies that developed in Israel during this period.

As a result of these policies, all the frameworks established in response to the problems of immigrant absorption and economic development, although anchored in revolutionary Zionist-socialist ideologies, in fact went against some of the central premises of such ideologies. Although accepting, indeed emphasizing, the premises of common national solidarity and citizenship, they went against the innovative revolutionary orientations of these ideologies, as well as against the emphasis on common equal access of all sectors to the centers of power, on participation in these centers, and against the emphasis on obligations and duties. As a result a far-reaching change took place in the perception, among different sectors of the population, of the nature of the connection between the elite groups, the power structure, and the resources available to them, on the one hand, and the ideology from which they had derived their legitimacy, on the other.

Different sectors of the population perceived the connection between ideology and power structure in different ways. Whereas the ruling elite sector viewed the existing arrangements and frameworks, including their own hegemonic role within them, as natural and given, the more peripheral sectors, new immigrants but also wider sectors among the younger generations and some disaffected professional and other intellectual groups, tended to see this connection as directed toward safeguarding the power nodes of the existing frameworks. They perceived the new policies as guided by these considerations, by internal dynamism of the various power groups, and by their power considerations, more than by the impulse to realize the initial ideology in the name of which the ruling groups claimed to work and whose basic premises were accepted by these new sectors of the population.[9]

The combined changes in the predominant societal ethos, the structure of elite groups, the development of the new policies and their repercussions gave rise to far-reaching changes in the modes of institutional and cultural creativity in Israeli society. Unlike in former periods, there were no great social, institutional, or cultural innovations, like the kibbutz, the Histadrut, or the renaissance of the Hebrew language. Instead, this period was characterized by the combination of great organizational expansion with the relative exhaustion of institutional imagination and innovative creativity. In the first period of the state, such creativity was manifest to some extent in the military, industrial, academic, and economic arenas. Somewhat later, within the educational and some industrial arenas a strong impetus to innovation and creativity developed.

All these innovative tendencies, however, were of a different order from those that developed during the formative period of the Yishuv and were at least implied by its regnant ideology. They were not guided by an overarching vision or visions, combining national, social, and cultural components; above all, the bearers of such creativity did not participate in the articulation of the policies formulated in the center, and only weak connections developed among the different arenas of creativity and between them and the center. Creativity ceased within many of the central arenas, and there was a lack of response to the creative attempts of various sectors of the population. Those sectors that in the preceding periods were seen as epitomes of such creativity, such as the kibbutzim or leaders of the Histadrut, became perceived more and more as part of the establishment, the vast array of vested interests, and, in their relations to the new sectors, not living up to their own ideals of equality.

The Exhaustion of the Regnant Ideology and Its Repercussions

Thus, growing contradictions emerged between the evolving social reality and the basic ideological premises of the existent institutional mold. The most important such contradictions developed with respect to participation, creativity, and access to the center. Large sectors of the population increasingly felt excluded from the centers of society; they perceived these centers as having ossified along with the ideology on which they, and the major elites within them, rested their legitimacy. At the same time, however, the ruling elite groups continued to legitimize themselves in terms of the vision underlying their ideology and their ability to solve new problems as they emerged.

The dominant elite groups were unable to forge viable symbolic and institutional answers to these new problems out of the regnant ideology. This ideology and its promulgators and bearers, the political elite groups, especially those of the labor sector, proved unable to provide guidance for the regulation of the numerous conflicts, problems, and contradictions that developed within the major institutional arenas of Israeli society or guidelines for continuing creativity.

This situation had a significant impact on the normative ambience of the society. The clientelistic relationship between the center and the periphery perpetuated many of the more particularistic "consociational" norms that had prevailed during the former period. Now, however, these norms no longer were connected with a strong elitist commitment nor with the solidarity of the various movements. Rather, they reflected the interplay between the ruling groups' attempts to buy off the periphery and the pressures of that periphery. This contravened the universalistic premises of the state and led to a growing weakening of norms, frequently catalyzed by the behavior of the norm setters themlves, above all the political elite sector.

The new sector's acceptance of some elements of this ideology, and their skeptical view of the consonance between the ruling groups' fidelity to it and their policies and actual behavior, and the elite sectors' attempts to legitimize and maintain its positions gave rise to a growth of populist tendencies, which already were influential in the shift to the distributive policies analyzed earlier, and to a growing demand for rights and entitlements. Such tendencies were to become a central component of the Israeli scene.

The processes analyzed earlier and the continuous feedback among them, rooted in the institutionalization of the original pioneering vision and the policies undertaken by the center, attested to the fact that the elite sectors' Zionist-labor ideology, which had guided Israeli society for the first twenty-five years of its existence, had become a "spent" ideology, to use Johan Galtung's term.

All these developments, especially the growing dissociation among different elite groups, and the exhaustion of many of the creative impeta also highlighted the crucial fact that the achievements of the Yishuv and state of Israel had been attained at a certain, perhaps inevitable, cost, when viewed from the perspective of the major themes of Jewish history and the Zionist vision. First, from the point of view of Jewish historical experience, an important shift occurred in the loci of cultural and institutional creativity. The necessity to develop the infrastructure of a total society and care for the needs of that society naturally redirected much of the energy that in the Diaspora in modern times was directed to economic activities in selected fields and intellectual and academic endeavors toward institution building, particularly in the realms of security, agriculture, economic infrastructure, and public service.

Only by exceptional effort could the cultural institutions created in such circumstances compete with the great centers of learning in the United States or Europe, where more and more Jews were attaining positions of excellence and leadership and which naturally became points of orientation and reference for the Israeli institutions. Another problem developed—one inherent to the nature of a small society, and particularly in one that aspired to be a center of social, cultural, and institutional creativity and significance. Many of these cultural and academic institutions and economic enterprises, although successful, displayed an increasing external orientation, weakening some of their original patterns. This development emphasized the difficulty of maintaining high standards and international orientations while preserving distinct national patterns of creativity, and it gave rise, as we shall see in greater detail later, to a deep tension between openness and provincialism. These problems also are connected with the limited economic capacity of a small country to absorb, through its general ethos and various educational institutions, all the "products" of such institutions.

The problem of maintaining both high standards and distinct patterns of creativity in various cultural and institutional arenas (legal, military, and economic) was connected with the tension between the emphasis on innovation and excellence and the growing tendency to lower standards, which went together with the growing populist tendencies and demands. These tensions have become more accute with the growing predominance, in all these spheres, of generations born or educated in Israel and with the reduced immigration from Western countries, which created a near-balance between immigration and emigration and later a new outflow of population.

The Six-Day and Yom Kippur Wars and the Problems of Israeli Society

The processes attendant on the exhaustion of the regnant labor Zionist ideology became closely interwoven with the problems generated by the volatile internal and security situations, and by the consequent centrality of the security dimension in Israeli society. The continuous external security problems did not give rise, as was often predicted, to the emergence of a garrison state, but rather to a distinctly Israeli phenomenon of the open civilian fortress.[10] The organization of the Israel Defense Forces was modeled on the Swiss pattern of a civilian army that underwent national service for 3, 3-1/2 years, and remained on continuous reserve duty until at least age 55, together with a highly specialized and prestigious core of standing army, composed mostly of officers. These characteristics gave rise to a situation in which service in the army was part of the life of most Israelis (only some parts of the religious sectors were exempted, and this exemption constituted a focus of constant public controversy). Because of the practice of releasing career officers at the age of 45–55, the core of the army maintained a continuous orientation to the civilian economic and political sectors and did not develop into a closed corporate entity or an autonomous political force, although there naturally developed quite strong social relations among them. In the political arena, although many generals (such as Dayan, Rabin, Barlev, Weizmann, Amit, and others) entered into the political arena, mostly in the 1960s and 1970s, they belonged to all major parties.

The army from the very beginning was put under civil control, coupled with a fairly high degree of autonomy of the also civilian-controlled security establishment presided over by the Prime Minister or Minister of Defense. For many years there was little effective control by other political institutions, like the Parliament or the State Comptroller. The mechanisms of such control existed, but, at least until lately, were quite weak and generally limited to reporting by the Prime Minister, the Minister of Defense, and the Chief of Staff with regard to some of the ultimate decisions about war. Of course, there were tensions between the General Staff and civilian elements of the Ministry of Defense. But on the whole the two parts of the security establishment were very closely interconnected.

If Israel has developed as an open fortress rather than a garrison state, however, this open fortress was heavily influenced by the importance of security in Israeli life: the development of a very strong military and security ethos and the marked emphasis on being in a society under stress. The image of a beleaguered state became a basic component of the society, channeling the creativity and commitment of large sectors of the population. The consciousness and emphasis on this situation also often served as an excuse for lack of creativity in other directions. Moshe Dayan's famous saying that it is impossible to carry two flags, that of security and that of the solution of social problems, was indicative of this trend, as have been the frequent statements by public figures about the necessity to open the eyes of those living in the security and relative affluence of the cities to the hardships of service in the army and the settlement outposts.

But it was not only its importance in Israel's collective consciousness that attests to the prominence of the security dimension in the society. Of no less significance is the impact of this dimension on the actual modes of life in Israel. First, there was the continuous burden of the security situation, especially of serving in the reserves (usually until the age of 50–55); the need to be continually alert; the routine of stress and insecurity; the economic strain of wars and mobilization; the constant encounter with the possibility of death. The reality of death began with that of about 6,000 young people, many of the potential elements of the elite sector, in the War of Independence. All this is a part of the daily existence, consciousness, and awareness of the Israelis and exerts a continuous pressure, creating some fatigue and possible flight from the calls for creativity in many areas of life, although it also provides new challenges. Second, there was the growing specialization of the military elite and the development, natural in itself, of specialized avenues of career advancement were almost entirely confined within the framework of the military.

Service in the army, especially in the combat units, became the natural repository of commitment and solidarity, of sacrifice, of the combination of these orientations with various instrumental activities and with the upholding of standards, at the same time weakening these tendencies and orientations in other areas of life. This trend crystallized into what Baruch Kimmerling has called the "interrupted society": the ongoing oscillation between the high degree of solidarity and commitment manifested in times of war and the much more individualistic, somewhat disorderly, and even sometimes anarchic problem in the structure of Israeli life.[11]

The burden of security and the situation of war or hostilities strengthens the feelings of solidarity in Israeli society on two levels: that of the primary group, family, and close personal networks, and (at least until the Lebanon War) that of the overall solidarity, identification with the society as such, with its central symbols. At the same time, they often inadvertently weakened, though the very pressure of the situation, the various networks of solidarity and the connections between these two levels.

The central place of the security dimension in Israel society has been manifest, perhaps above all, in the fact that the Six-Day and Yom Kippur

Wars and their aftermaths were watersheds both for the external political history of Israel and its internal development. The Six-Day War raised the problem of the format, premises, and collective identity of Israeli society. It called into question the bases of the territorial compromise that permitted the establishment of the state and required re-examination of Israeli society's perception of its place in the Middle East, its relations with the Arab world, its relations with Israeli Arabs, and the relationship of Israeli society to its national and Zionist pioneering heritage, to the Jewish communities in the Diaspora. In other words, it reopened the problems of the overall structure of its collective boundaries and symbols and of the major institutional formats of Israeli society.

Some of these basic problems, particularly those relating to Israeli collective identity and consciousness, perhaps are best highlighted by developments in the relationship to other Jewish communities and to the Jewish and Zionist traditions. The Six-Day War and its aftermath refuted many of the current assumptions prevalent in the Yishuv and in Israeli society regarding the nature of these links and the extent and force of the Jewish element in Israeli identity. Arguments stressing its weakness were disproven. The context and strength of this component, and the nature of the relationship between Israel and the Jewish communities abroad were shown to transcend conventional Zionist formulas. Their reactions to the war revealed the deep attachment Israelis felt toward the Jewish heritage and demonstrated the solidarity of Jewish communities abroad with the state of Israel, a solidarity rooted in a common past and common destiny and in common components of identity. Even if these are interpreted in different ways by different Jewish communities, the very variety of interpretations often strengthened the common bond.[12]

The new contacts between Israel and the Diaspora contradicted the prevalent view of the nature of the link between the Yishuv and the Jewish communities, which had been derived from the original assumptions of Zionist ideology. In particular, they deviated from the belief that immigration to Israel and implementation of the pioneering ideology were the only authentic expressions of this link and that Israel constituted the only possible—and legitimate—arena of Jewish modern collective creativity.

Israel's standing among the Jewish communities of the world changed, as we shall see in somewhat greater detail in the concluding chapter, imperceptibly but forcefully. On the one hand, it became the symbol and center of Jewish history: a focus of solidarity and primordial sentiments, of hopes and dreams, a potential haven from oppression, a symbol of pride because of its achievements—or because of criticism of its failures. On the other hand, it was no longer perceived as the sole center of Jewish creativity, as in the classical Zionist ideology, as the only place where modern Jewish social, educational, and cultural innovation could develop. The creative impulse of many Jewish communities found new expression in the lands of the Diaspora; the Israeli renaissance was seen as merely one, albeit central, pattern of this creativity.

These developments minimized the "revolutionary" aspect of immigration to Israel. Such immigration usually did not evince a strong revolutionary ideological dimension and, unlike the pioneering immigrants of the Yishuv period, its ability to break through the established frameworks and the selection processes of elite groups and leaders was rather limited. With strong encouragement from both the Israeli and Diaspora leadership, they reinforced the atrophying of the process of selection of elite groups in Israel and contributed to the lack of institutional creativity, which had in the past been revitalized by new semirevolutionary waves of immigration.

In all these arenas, and in many of the internal ones, tensions and problems emerged after the Six-Day and Yom Kippur Wars, and later the Lebanon War, and their aftermaths. All the problems analyzed in the preceding section have become much more visible and central after the Six-Day and Yom Kippur Wars. Moreover, the developments after the Six-Day and Yom Kippur Wars also opened anew the problem of the relations between Israel and its neighbors in the Middle East and the implications of these issues for the internal structure of Israeli society.

Thus, the aftermath first of the Six-Day War and later the Yom Kippur War opened up the whole problem of the nature of the political settlement with the Arab countries, the basic problems of Israel's acceptance and standing in the region. The great military victory of the Six-Day War and the later, ultimate victory in the Yom Kippur War attested to Israel's basic military strength, to the impossibility of casting her into the sea, as many Arabs dreamed; but at the same time these very successes shattered the political bases of premises of what may be called the Ben-Gurion era.

On the one hand, Israel showed its military might and reached beyond the territorial settlements of the armistice agreements that were accepted by the international community; but on the other hand, this very success sharpened the general awareness, in the international community and slowly also within Israel itself, of the necessity to find a more stable political solution, some ultimate political arrangements leading to peace beyond the armistice agreements. The belief in the necessity of such arrangements, the search for different political solutions, started in the wake of the Six-Day War and gathered momentum after the Yom Kippur War and, paradoxically perhaps, even after the peace treaty with Egypt.

The very momentum of all these developments, the reopening of all these problems, gave rise to and in turn was continuously reinforced by the intensification and transformation of the Palestinian problem, by the transformation of the problems of refugees into that of the political problem of the collective fate of Palestinians. Here, of course, the most crucial process was the development of the PLO and its growing international standing and the concomitant very quick crystallization of a Palestinian national collective consciousness.

Closely connected with all these developments was the growth of internal (especially in the West Bank) and above all international terrorism against Israel, and the at least partial legitimation by such people as various intellectual and political groups; for instance, the Austrian chancellor Bruno Kreisky, of such terrorism as part of the Palestinian national movement.

The continuous Israeli military occupation of the West Bank and the concomitant policy of extending Jewish settlement into these areas gave rise to growing criticism, both internal and international, and to an initially slow but, especially after the Yom Kippur War, intensified change in the international reaction. Under the Likud government in 1977, the West Bank would come to be officially called Judea and Samaria. Israel had become an occupying power ruling over between 1 and 1.3 million Arabs, including those in the Gaza District.

The Six-Day War and later, in a changing atmosphere, the Yom Kippur War and their aftermaths also and perhaps above all reopened the problem of relations between Jews and Arabs—to a certain extent for the first time—in relatively concrete terms. The resulting situation increased the political tension between the two populations or nations, but this political tension differed greatly from the conflict between the Arab states and Israel before the wars. The principal difference, at least for the Arab population of the West Bank, but not only for it, was that Israel ceased to be a myth, merely a symbol of a foreign group injected into the Middle East, and became part of a reality of daily and stable contacts with a Jewish population. Given the nature of these relations—the continuous military rule of the Israelis over the Arabs—they did not necessarily increase the Arab population's love for Israel. In many ways these contacts, especially those related to the military government, as we shall see in greater detail later, naturally were liable to increase tensions. But at the same time they added to the mutual relations between the two peoples, in particular through the open-door policy—the relatively open bridges between postwar Jordan and the West Bank and Israel and a certain amount of traffic between the West Bank and Israel itself—an element of concrete reality that had not existed previously.

The same combination of a more realistic attitude to Israel, even a reluctant de facto acceptance of its existence, with a growing tension around possible terms of settlement with it, developed in many Arab countries. This occurred first of all, but probably not only, in Egypt, which led to the Peace with Egypt in 1979. On the other hand, the potentiality of much more fierce Arab-Islamic confrontations with Israel developed as well.

The continuous Israeli rule over the territories had also far-reaching impact on the internal structure of Israeli society. In the economic arena it gave rise to a semicolonial situation in which, contrary to the original pressures of the political economy of the Yishuv and the state of Israel, on the whole, economiclly unprotected Arab labor, coming from the West Bank and Gaza (which were not given many opportunities of internal economic development) became a basic component of Israeli economy, subversing the older Zionist vision of economic independence and self-support. This situation gave rise to many stresses between Arabs and Jews. It subverted the working ethos of large sectors of the Jewish population and became a basic component of the continuous intensification of the Israeli-Palestinian confrontation.

Naturally, these developments also affected the state of the Israeli Arab population. For the first time since the establishment of the state of Israel, the Arab minority, which enjoyed great economic prosperity and educational advancement but also social dislocation, disability, discrimination, and great difficulties in integrating into the urban sectors of Israeli society, was released from its almost heretic isolation from other parts of the Arab world and contacts were established with that world. The first stages of this meeting sharpened the problems of the Israeli-Arab identity within the Israeli framework.

The various problems and tensions that started to develop in the sixties—the search for adequate employment opportunities, and the problems of land—became intensified; and all these concrete problems set within the institutional framework of Israeli society have become greatly transformed into more principled ones.

Thus, for instance, the problem of land in fact signalled a much more basic problem or tension: the one between the settlement and territorial orientation of the Zionist movement and the legitimate right of the Arabs as Israeli citizens. This was a far-reaching transformation of the Arab-Jewish confrontation in the period of the mandate, and in principle it also differed greatly from the problems on the West Bank, where the Arabs were not granted Israeli citizenship.

These developments among the Israeli Arabs were connected with the continued opening up of the attitudes to the Arab minority on behalf of the government agencies (a continuation of the Eshkol policy) and a growing sensitivity to the problems of the Arab population among at least parts of the Jewish population, as evidenced in continuously growing public discussions in the newspapers, the media, and in many meetings.

All these developments posed more and more far-reaching principled problems about the nature of the relations between the Jewish majority and the Arab minority or, to use the title of a symposium on this subject, with every sixth Israeli.

From the point of view of the Arab population, the problem—the possibility of being a minority in a non-Arab country—was a new experience for Arab history which showed a lot of experience with foreign conquerors but no experience being a minority. The Israeli Arabs started to grope with the implications of such a situation, looking both into Israel and outside—to the other Arab countries, to the 'Arab nation'—in the context of which the Jews were seen as an alien conquering minority.

Among many of the Israeli-Arab intellectuals, and certainly even more among the broader groups of the Arab sector, there was a strong search for some possibility of becoming incorporated in Israeli public life; a testing of such possibilities, often connected with ambivalent attitudes to the Zionist component of Israeli identity; a search for the chance to construct a collective identity within the Israeli framework yet in a strong relation to their Arab identity, and demanding more autonomy in this sphere. Many of them were torn, especially in the late eighties, with the uprising (Intifada) in the territories, between their wish to find their place within the Israeli framework and their solidarity with the Arabs in the territories.

All these developments signalled that Israeli society and Israel as a Jewish state was faced here with the rather basic problem of the nature of its democracy, not only of tolerance toward non-Jews, not only of its acceptance, in the biblical terms, of 'the stranger within your gates,' but also of allowing them a full, autonomous collective cultural and political participation according to modern democratic universalistic premises.

The mere facts of the situation—above all the close interrelation between this problem and Isreal's geopolitical and internationa status—did not, of course, provide for an easy solution, but the very awareness and the growing understanding of this problem were an indicator of the changing format, from the 1970s on, of Israeli society, a change which took place under the impact of the Six-Day and Yom Kippur Wars.

They also strengthened their feeling of solidarity with Arab nationalism and the ambivalence in their relations with Israel. A trend developed toward a weakening of differences between the Israeli-Arab minority and residents of the West Bank and a growing intensification of Arab nationalism and of its questioning of the very premises of Israel, with tendencies to a growing radicalization in a direction of possible separation from Israel and greater identification with the Arab and the Palestininan national movements. Yet, at the same time, it also was connected with an increasing search among Israeli Arabs for ways to become more fully incorporated, but in a more autonomous collective way, into the Israeli political system. Thus we see that the Six-Day and Yom Kippur wars had far-reaching impacts in all the major arenas of life in Israel.

But these wars had different impacts on the institutional format of Israeli society, its evaluation of its own problems, and its self-perception. The aftermath of the Six-Day War opened up many problems that previously were dormant. At the same time, the great military victory, the massive economic expansion, and the rising standard of living seemed to justify fully the institutional formats that developed under the aegis of dynamic conservative policies. Indeed, the continuous organizational expansion reached its apogee during this period.[13]

Yet all these developments were connected with the increasing atrophy of institutional creativity, as evidenced for instance in the appearance of a political line that tended to freeze the external security situation and define it in purely static terms of "waiting." The concomitant influx of cheap Arab labor from the West Bank and Gaza created, as we have seen, a threat to old pioneering visions of establishment of a "natural" national economy. Nevertheless, a general if perhaps somewhat uneasy feeling of "we've never had it so good" came to dominate Israeli society.

This feeling of self-satisfaction was shattered by the Yom Kippur War. The course of the war and its aftermath produced an intense and widespread feeling that the existing institutional frameworks were inadequate to cope not only with the international and security problems, but perhaps above all with the intensifying economic and social problems.

After the Yom Kippur War, many portents of change intensified within Israeli society. The various signals of dissatisfaction that developed earlier, gathered momentum: ethnic protest promulgated both by the more voluble groups among the new immigrants, as well as by those caught in the vicious circle of poverty; together with strong dissociation of wide sectors of professional, academic, and cultural elite groups from the ruling elite sector. Moreover, the security and international problems opened up by the Six-Day War became the center of the political agenda, whereas internal problems, with the exception of ethnic and religious-security issues and tensions, moved more and more into the background.

All these processes were closely interwoven with great changes in the entire tenor of life in Israel, especially in the differing styles of life that developed among various sectors of the society, particularly among the second generation of Oriental immigrants, but also among new generations in general. These new patterns of life, which superseded older ones rooted in some combination of the original pioneering arenas with their strong European roots, gave rise to a great variety of new patterns with a strong Mediterranean and populist flavor.

Israeli Society in Transition

The Accumulation of Changes in the 1970s:
The Change in Government (Mahapakh)

Israel in the 1970s thus was faced with numerous problems: internal

problems stemming from exhaustion of the labor program, changing relations with the Jewish communities in the Diaspora, and the heavy burden of
security exacerbated by the outcome of the Yom Kippur War. All these led
to the labor Party's loss of political hegemony in 1977 when, after the elections, the Likud formed a new government, and all these processes gathered
momentum with the change of government in 1977.[14]

The inability of the Labor Party to form the government in 1977 was
due not only to the upsurge of the Oriental groups and their voting for Likud,
as has often been asserted, but also to the defection of large sectors of professional, academic, and business groups from the labor camp. Under the leadership of former Chief of Staff and noted archeologist Yigael Yadin, these
groups formed a new party, the Democratic Party for Change, which won fifteen seats in the Knesset (Parliament). (Large sectors of the party led by
Yadin joined Begin's government, with one small sector, Shinui, going over
to the opposition. By the 1981 election the party had disintegrated, with most
of its supporters "returning" to the fold of the Labor Party.) At the same
time, the more mobile and successful Oriental groups (the poverty sector
always asked for the Herut Party, the precursor to Likud) changed their elec-
toral allegiance from labor to Likud. Thus, the combination of the weakening
internal cohesion of the labor sector, the dissociation of many elite groups
from the centers of power, and the growing demands of new groups for
access to these centers and incorporation in them, together with the exhaustion of the Labor Party's vision and program, help to explain the momentous
change of government, "the Turnover," (Mahapakh) of 1977.

To no small degree this was because the disintegration of many of the
founding institutions, the growing democratization and intergenerational
changes, and the incorporation of new sectors of population that had been
blocked or coopted by the "older" elite groups, brought many new groups
into the political arena, competing for positions of leadership. But these
changes in the composition of elite groups were connected with the weakening of the internal coherence and solidarity of the "political class"—no leaders of stature with clear visions and executive abilities developed. The necessity to create and maintain the infrastructure of a small beleaguered society,
the heavy burden of the security situation, and the loss of the great reservoir
of potential leadership groups in Eastern and Central Europe exerted their
toll on the selection of leaders and the formation of elite groups and on their
internal cohesion and solidarity.

The change in government and the developments since then ushered in
a period, the end of which we cannot see as yet, of far-reaching changes in
many of the basic countours of Israeli society and a continuous search for a
new ideological and institutional mold or molds. Thus, the institutional mold
presided over by the Labor Party disintegrated, without the development of

any clear new program. This process of disintegration and search for new directions in many ways has sapped the energy of large sectors of Israeli society in the 1970s and 1980s. All these changes were interwoven with political struggle, internal divisions, strife, and confrontations impinging on all sectors of Israeli society and public life. Such changes, transformation and search, took place simultaneously on several fronts, all touching on the central nerves of Israeli society.[15]

The changes and struggles that took place in the central arenas of Israeli society went together with a very great creativity in many cultural areas, literature, theatre, crafts and arts. But, although sometimes this creativity was connected with the struggles, on the whole it was dissociated from the central institutional arenas. Within these arenas, within central official framework, there was but little response to the varied manifestations of such creativity.

The first arena of such struggle and contention was in the symbols of collective identity, collective consciousness. Here the search and the concomitant struggles developed first with respect to some of the basic components of the Zionist vision. Second, a struggle developed with respect to the reconstruction and incorporation of Jewish tradition. Third, such search and struggle developed also with respect to the place of Israel in the Middle East, closely connected with the impact of the security situations; and fourth, with respect to the position of Israeli-Arabs within Israel. Fifth, a whole gamut of problems arose in connection with the continuous Israeli occupation of the territories in the West Bank (Judea and Samaria) and Gaza. The second major arena of change and struggle concerned the format of the major institutions of Israeli society, above all Israeli politics and political economy.[16]

The Major Approaches to the Problems of Israeli Society

Inward and Outward Looking.   All the processes leading to the disintegration of the original institutional mold of Israeli society—changes in the ethos and the relative importance of the original ideological visions, the transformation of elite groups into the ruling class, the growing dissociation among elite groups, the weakening of solidary frameworks, as well as their repercussions—evinced several characteristics common to other postrevolutionary and other small modern societies. Israeli society shared with these the tendencies to routinize and demystify the original revolutionary vision and showed a similar stagnation in its postrevolutionary ethos. The processes leading to this disintegration highlighted, in Israel perhaps even more than in other such societies, some of the conflicting and the cross-cutting choices inherent in the very institutionalization and dynamic development of such a mold. Above it all was a choice between commitment to a monolithic ideology as against pluralism; between elitism as against populism; between the stress on duty and obligations as against rights and entitlements; between active participation in societal and cultural creativity as against the more passive or privatized ones. Finally, there was the great challenge of finding new ways to combine these various orientations without entirely giving up any of them. The ways in which these processes and their repercussions crystallized in Israeli society evinced some specific characteristics, closely related to its being a small state with aspirations exceeding its actual scope.

Two distinct approaches developed within Israeli society to cope with the dilemmas arising out of this situation. One approach assumed that these aspirations would be realized through the existing social structure and its attachment to Jewish or socialist traditions. This approach often was combined with strong extremist religious and nationalist movements and slogans, characterized by a growing intolerance. An opposing approach stressed that Israel's aspirations could not be realized through its mere existence or upholding the symbols of its identity; direct participation in social and cultural frameworks beyond its borders, close relations with various Jewish and international communities, and with other civilizations was required to forge its own identity. Such orientations tended to strengthen the pluralism of Israeli society against the monolithic tendencies of the former approach. Although these different approaches cut to some extent across the different political camps, the first was (and became even more so in the last two decades) characteristic of the right, and the second was more prevalent at the center and to the left of it.

These different approaches were manifested in the contradictory attitudes toward all the preceding problems. They became especially visible after the Six-Day War and continued to be so throughout the following periods: punctuated by the Yom Kippur War, the Lebanon War, and the Intifada. From then on the door was opened toward the Arab world and toward various movements in both Jewish and non-Jewish communities. These developments, on the one hand, strengthened the reshaping of Israeli identity toward broader and more flexible contacts. On the other hand, however, currents of sometimes extreme chauvinism appeared, combining religious and secular nationalism nourished by feelings of superiority and isolation from the outside world, extreme xenophobia toward Arabs, cultural provincialism, and increased rigidity in the construction of the Israeli collective identity.

The Resurgence of Major Themes of Jewish Political Traditions.   The appearance of these tendencies was due largely to the fact that the institutionalization of the initial Zionist labor mold and its disintegration were closely connected with, and intensified by, the problems of implementing the Jewish civilizational vision in the setting of a small, beleaguered society. And in these ways, it also highlighted the problems and dilemmas of the Jewish re-entry into history.

Therefore, the growing dissociation among different elite groups and the weakening framework of solidarity gave rise to the resurgence of different themes of Jewish civilization and the Zionist vision: the Messianic, territorial, solidary, primordial components of the collective identity. These emerged, each claiming its autonomy from the others, challenging the validity of the opposition, and claiming total predominance in the institutional formation of the society.

The resurgence of these themes was facilitated by the weakening institutional framework and ideological symbols that brought together in the initial institutional mold of Israeli society the various themes of Jewish political culture. It was easy for tendencies to develop combining the anarchic politics of the higher law and the solidarity of small sectors. Paradoxically, because of the existence of the Jewish state, such a combination could become connected with relinquishing the responsibility (quite strong in Medieval times) for the entire community and for the maintenance of some order within its framework.

Indeed, many indications suggested that these political tendencies, when transposed into the setting of a territorial state, and a modern democratic one in particular, might undermine the very viability of its institutional framework, as they probably did in the period of the Second Commonwealth.

The Struggles about the Basic Contours of Israeli Society

Collective Identity. The major efforts at reconstruction of the Zionist ethos of Israeli collective identity moved toward strengthening the political-territorial components, in tandem with the weakening of the revolutionary components of Zionist ideology and intensive promulgation of ethnic themes and symbols, as well as of the anti-Zionist or at least a-Zionist religious ones.

The most important change in the Zionist themes, one inherent in the old Revisionist vision, was the emphasis on and partial sanctification of military might and struggle. Closely related to this was the new emphasis on the territorial dimension of Zionism. Many attempts were made at the sanctification or semisanctification of this component in historical and religious terms, a sanctification that was not a very strong component of the original Revisionist vision.

The conception of territoriality changed from the perception of territory as a means for realizing the national reconstruction, as an expression of the special relationship of the nation to its land, or as a basis for national security to the almost total secular or religous sanctification of territory and settlement as an end in itself, as the very epitome of the Zionist vision.[17] The secular version of this sanctification was found among many of the supporters of "Eretz Israel Hashlema," in the labor sector, in many kibbutzim and moshavim, as well as among broad urban sectors. It combined a secular primordial orientation with a strong emphasis on settlement and security. The religious-nationalist version, which developed among Gush Emunim and those close to them, stressed the religious, historical, and sometimes almost mystical dimensions of territory, often conflating the territorial dimension with political-mystical Messianism.

Among the general Jewish and Zionist themes, those of Jewish solidarity and the religious dimension of the Jewish tradition and historical experience were stressed. This often was related to a strong emphasis on particularism, on closing oneself off from the outside world, on the inherent superiority and morality of the Jewish or Israeli collectivity, and on the weakening of the civilizational and hence also universalistic—as opposed to national and particularistic—dimensions of the Zionist or Israeli identity, as well as of the "revolutionary" institution building dimensions.

The second major change with respect to Zionist symbols, connected with the exhaustion of the older labor-Zionist ethos, was the dilution of the elitist components of this vision. Such dilution was manifest first of all in a weakening of the elitist emphasis on duty and obligation, as against the more distributive emphasis on rights and entitlements—and best illustrated in the saying "Leheitiv Im Haam" (doing right by the people)—often used by the Prime Minister Begin, but inherent in the earlier distributive policies. This tendency became a part of a much wider one: the dilution of the revolutionary, reconstructive components of Zionist ideology, those components which emphasized the recontruction of the major dimension of Jewish life.

One of the most important manifestations of this dilution was in the attitude to the exilic history, traditions, and life in the Diaspora. The original negative attitude gave way to a much more tolerant, even affirmative one. One reason for this was connected with one of the major impacts of the Holocaust, the difficulty of continuing rebellion against communities and ways of life that were wiped away in such catastrophic circumstances. As against the earlier negating, a rebellious attitude to the ways of life embodied by these communities, a more positive, commemorative one developed.

An even more positive attitude developed to the religious tradition and Diaspora in the wake of the "ethnic" tensions and revival in Israel, and with the process that probably was among the most constructive aspects of this era; namely with the incorporation of new sectors into the center. Such incorporation was closely connected with the growing inclusion of ethnic and religious themes in the central symbols of collective identity. These themes were initially promulgated in a rather divisive way. Only later did some of them, especially the ethnic and "milder" religious ones, become less divisive, forming part of a wider pluralistic spectrum of themes of collective identity.

Moreover, within some of the older sectors of Israeli society, including some kibbutzim, there developed a greater interest in various aspects of Jewish tradition: history and religion. The development of this interest was to no small degree rooted in the disintegration of the labor-Zionist ideological and institutional mold and the feeling that this mold did not do justice to the richness of Jewish tradition.

In extreme, highly publicized cases, this feeling gave rise to the phenomenon of "Hozrim Biteshuva" (those who "return to the fold"), who became as it were converted to extreme orthodoxy. Beyond these cases such growing interest did not signal any such "return," but rather a quest to find ways of incorporating some aspects of these traditions into the "nonreligious" ways of life of these sectors. Such quest could take the form of study groups, inclusion of some religious rituals such as lighting of candles on Sabbath-eve, and the like. It could also find expression in exploration of Reform and Conservative branches of Judaism brought over from the United States, thus providing yet another signal of changing attitudes to the traditions of the Diaspora.

This changing attitude toward the traditions of the Diaspora and Jewish existence within it was reinforced by new developments in the different communities of the Jewish Diaspora and by changing relations between Israel and the Diaspora. After the Second World War, the Jewish community in the United States became the leading Diaspora community. The majority of its members, or their parents, came from Eastern Europe, as did the pioneers of the Yishuv. The incorporation of Jews in the United States took place (see Chapter 5) in a different mode from that in Europe, the background against which the Zionist movement developed. This new mold entailed, as we have seen, a different reconstitution of Jewish collective life from the one envisaged by the Zionist vision. Accordingly, as we have seen among American Jews, the strong identification with the state of Israel that developed was based on feelings of solidarity, collective pride, but not on the denial of its own way of life, thus seemingly going against the basic Zionist attitude to Jewish existence in the Diaspora.

At the same time, the internal changes in Israeli society, the great surge to modernization and economic development, the intensification of the problems of a small society, especially of maintaining high economic, professional, and cultural standards, have de facto greatly changed the attitude of large sectors of Israeli society to the Diaspora. That many Jews in the Diaspora, especially but not only in the United States, were very successful in these arenas, intensified this orientation to the Diaspora. Growing contacts with different sectors of America, both academic and economic institutions, to use T. Friedman's phrase, made "America very central in the mind of Israel"; and the growing emigration from Israel, called *descent* or yeridah (as against ascent or aliyah), also seemed to threaten many of the classical Zionist premises. All these have considerably weakened and eroded the "negation of the Diaspora" attitude.

There was yet another, rather paradoxical, side to this development. The growing orientation of large parts of the "older" sectors of Israeli society toward the United States, and later also toward Europe, intensified the feelings among large sectors of the Oriental groups that what they confronted among the older sectors of Israeli society was not the pioneering spirit but rather Western patterns of life. Many Oriental sectors began to orient themselves to the Diaspora where, especially in France and North America, many members of their own communities from Iraq and North Africa have settled, often attracting many of the relatives from Israel. But this only increased their feelings of dissociation from the older mold of Israeli society and its westernizeed Ashkenazi sector.

Zionist and Religious Themes.   The emphasis on the reconstruction of various Zionist themes, the incorporation of symbols of ethnic identity, came from within the mainstream of Israeli society. However much they changed the symbolic repertoire of Israeli society, deemphasizing its universalistic components, the changes all took place within its basic, Zionist, symbolic framework. The situation differed with respect to the various anti-Zionist, or at least non-Zionist, religious orientations, as articulated by Agudat Israel and other extreme Orthodox groups. At best these groups accepted the state of Israel as a de facto given, or stressed "settlement of the Land of Israel" as against the Zionist vision of reconstructing Jewish society. Paradoxically, during this period in which the nationalist Zionist themes predominated, their stance gained at least partial legitimacy.

The importance of the religious groups generally was facilitated by their key positions as potential partners in the government coalition; but this was not the whole story. Sensing the ideological vacuum or turbulence that developed within the major sectors of Israeli society with the disintegration of the labor-Zionist mold, the religious groups launched a continuous series of attacks on the Zionist premises and symbols and presented themselves as the bearers of the true Jewish tradition and heritage distorted by the Zionist quest for the reconstruction of this tradition in a modern vein.

Here, a very interesting transformation of the original negative attitude of the ultraorthodox groups to the Zionist movement took place, which we discussed in the preceding chapter. The basic negative attitude to the "revolutionary" dimensions of Zionist ideology, those dimensions concerned with the reconstruction of Jewish tradition, continued and even intensified in some of the more extreme groups among the ultraorthodox. But at the same time most sectors of the ultraorthodox accepted de facto the state of Israel, legitimizing it as indicated, in terms of settlement in Eretz Israel or as a viable existing Jewish community that has to be guarded. They participated more and more in the political life of Israel, making more demands not only for allocations for their institutions but also, as we have seen, for imposing their own conceptions of public life in Israel.

At the same time, as indicated earlier, the tensions between these extreme Orthodox groups and the other sectors of Israeli society became intensified. Such tensions grew, paradoxically, but naturally enough, with many of those in these sectors who joined Reform or Conservative congregations and evinced strong interest in Jewish historical and religious traditions.

This continuous struggle around the construction of the symbolic, as well as territorial, boundaries of the community was related not only to the problems of the place of Jewish tradition or traditions in the construction of Israeli society. Relations to the Middle-Eastern environment constituted another focus of ideological and political struggle around the construction of such boundaries, far beyond the direct or even indirect security problems. The return to the new-old land in the Middle East was seen as an act of great historical significance—as was the attempt at integration into the Middle East. The nature of this integration constituted a focus of potential ideological and political struggle, which was to erupt in periods of intensive confrontation with the neighboring states and the Arabs on the West Bank.

The continuous Israeli occupation of the West Bank and Gaza, the seeming unwillingness of the Israeli governments since 1977 (with the partial exception of the Governments of National Unity in 1984 and in 1988 when the Labor Party tried, unsuccessfully, to push the government in such direction) to enter into serious far-reaching negotiations with the Palestinians), the policies of settlement on the West Bank, the Palestinian uprising (the Intifada) from 1988 on have not only exacerbated the tensions between Israel and the Palestinians but also fueled wider Arab and Islamic resentment against Israel and facilitated the growing importance of Islamic fundamentalism, especially in Gaza as well as among the Israeli-Arabs.

If the peace between Israel and Egypt and the de facto truce long-standing with Jordan indicated the possibility that the confrontation between Jews and Arabs, which started as a confrontation between national movements, might develop in the more pragmatic direction of interstate relations, these latter developments seem to indicate a regression to the former situation, with an intensification and possible widening of the confrontation. Ongoing struggles and confrontations around the collective boundaries and symbols of Israeli society were intensified by the volatility of the international security situation, which emphasized the problems of the place of Israel in the Middle East and by the demands of the Israeli-Arabs for attention not only to their growing aspirations for civil equality, but also to some of their cultural and political aspirations. All these developments intensified with the Intifada, the Arab uprising in the territories in 1987.

Thus, indeed, one of the most important repercussions of this combination of the political-ecological condition of a small society and the primordial-national and historical revolutionary-ideologic orientations of Zionism was that the problems related to the construction of symbols and boundaries of the emerging collectivity have constituted a focus of potential ideological and political contention. The potential for such struggle existed, as we have seen, from the very beginning of the Zionist movement, especially in its relationship to the Jewish historical and religious heritage and the relative importance of the different historical religious, territorial components of that heritage.

The same was true, in varying degrees in different historical periods, in the relations between the universalistic and particularistic orientations of the collectivity. The problems related to the place of these components in the construction of Israeli collective identity surfaced anew, as we have seen, after the Six-Day War and have continued to be in the forefront of political struggles in Israel.[18] All these developments and struggles very sharply posed the basic questions of the major components of the Israeli political-social format, especially with respect to upholding civil rights, civility and the rule of law.[19]

New Policy Directions: The Shift to the Right

The increased promulgation of these themes was connected with the development of new policies under the Likud government and, less sharply, under the Governments of National Unity which were formed in 1984 and 1988. The general political trend was continuously to the right, in the specific sense this term acquired in Israel: a hawkish attitude on security problems, especially with respect to the West Bank; strong emphasis on nationalistic and to some extent religious themes; and weakening of the major Zionist vision of the more universalistic or "liberal" emphases or orientations.

The shift to the right also was manifest in the fact that, throughout this period, the Likud led most of the political agenda, emphasizing security and nationalistic themes, with the Labor Party usually responding to it. But this agenda was not just political in the specific narrow sense of the word. It extended to all the major institutional arenas of Israeli society. The new orientations and their institutional implications were visible most fully in the realms of security, defense, and foreign policy, as well as in the religious arena and in more general cultural ambience.

With respect to security-military-foreign policy, the first new development, and one of great historical significance, was the conclusion of a peace treaty with Egypt in 1979 and the subsequent withdrawal from the Sinai in spring 1982. Whereas this achievement was not necessarily connected with the Revisionist or Likud ideology, it could be—and was—portrayed as demonstrating the basic correctness of this ideology, leading, after a show of strength, to peace with the Arabs.

The second development was the expansion of settlement in Judea, Samaria, and the Golan Heights. Although there was no alteration of the legal status of the West Bank—of Judea and Samaria (a term taken from Mandatory times and officially adopted to replace *West Bank* or *the territories*)—despite vocal demands by extreme right-wing groups for the imposition of Israeli law in those areas or their outright annexation, settlement in Judea and Samaria took new directions after the Likud came to power and became a focus of national controversy. This was an outcome of the Likud government's ideological and political legitimation of settling all parts of Eretz Israel, abolishing the Green Line (the armistice lines established at the end of the War of Independence), and allowing—in fact, encouraging by far-reaching subsidies—a large number of Jews to live in these areas, thus diminishing the chances of withdrawal from Judea and Samaria and the Gaza district.

This policy of settlement was closely connected with a new and more active stance in security matters, an ideology of active struggle against terrorism in general and the PLO in particular. The implementation of this conception culminated in "Operation Peace for Galilee," in June 1982, which developed within a few days into the Lebanon War. This adventure had far-reaching repercussions on the structure of Israeli society, as well as on its foreign relations and international standing. It was the first war not based on a wide national consensus—in fact it tore apart the hitherto strong consensus on security matters.

One of the most important watersheds on the international and domestic fronts was the Intifada, the Arab uprising in the West Bank and Gaza that started in late 1987 and has continued since. It caught the Israeli intelligence and security forces by surprise, and it drastically changed the entire situation in the relations between Israel and the Palestinians. The period of "benign" conquest of the West Bank ended and the West Bank was plunged, along with the Israeli security forces, into a situation of a combined civil uprising and war. In many ways the uprising was a continuation of the Arab-Israeli confict that developed from the beginning of the Zionist settlement. But it was also a civil uprising against Israel as an occupying power, and it was waged by the Arabs in rather unconventional ways. Almost no weapons were used: demonstrations, stone throwing (to a very large extent by children and women), tire burning, insults at Israeli soldiers—these were the most common means of protest. This combination of war and civil uprising undertaken in these rather unconventional ways was extremely serious for Israel on many fronts. The media, especially the international media, continuously reported the seeming brutality of Israeli soldiers who, although abstaining from use of armed weapons, used sticks or plastic bullets against women and children. The portrayal of such brutality made "hot" news, of course, and the media on the whole refrained from emphasizing the overt political use of women and children in these demonstrations, the endurance by Israeli soldiers of insults, their great restraint, on the whole, and the punishment by the courts of many of the instances of brutality—even if not always adequate in the view of wide sectors of Israeli society—often after outrage from the Israeli public.

The continuous military rule that had to face growing resistance on the part of the Palestinians gave rise, especially with the outbreak of the Intifada, to growing repressive measures by the army, generating far-reaching potentialities of brutalization in many aspects of Israei life, as well as a situation in which rule of law was not applied equally in Israel and in the West Bank and Gaza. The Intifada had other far-reaching impacts on Israeli society, intensifying the division between "hawks" and "doves," many of the latter concerned with the inevitable brutalization of large parts of the Israeli public and those soldiers assigned to maintain peace and order in the territories, as well as with the erosion of full rule of law, adherence to proper "normal" legal procedure, and the upholding of civil rights in the territories.

Far-reaching changes also occurred with respect to policies in the religious arena, specifically with respect to the place of religious groups and symbols in Israeli society and the regulation of many aspects of life by religious authorities. First of all, in accordance with their traditional strategy, the religious parties made effective use of their crucial position in the coalition to extend their influence beyond anything previously imaginable. These parties received much larger allocations for their institutions, frequently arranged in ways that contravened standard budgetary procedures, even during periods of drastic budgetary cutbacks in education, security and social services. They also became very influential in setting the general tone concerning the place of religious observance in public life, extending its scope, in fact, to change the constellation of state-religion relations and the role of religion in Israeli society. New religious-inspired legislation included, for instance, the "pathology law," which placed severe restrictions on the performance of autopsies; revocation of the relatively liberal abortion law; broader exemptions for military service by women; and the cessation of flights by El Al on the Sabbath and Jewish holidays. Attempts also were made to limit archaeological excavations (as regards digs in ancient Jewish cemeteries) and to pass the so-called "Who Is a Jew" law that would recognize the validity of conversion to Judaism only if performed in accordance with the Halakhah; that is, only by those recognized by the orthodox rabbinate.

In late 1990, when Agudat Israel joined the right-wing government headed by the Likud and Mr. Shamir, on the condition that the government would promulgate several religious laws: such as prohibition against raising pigs and selling pork, except in Christian sectors; further limitations on public transport on the Sabbath, as well as against what was defined by them as "pornographic" advertising. At the same time the amount of financial allocation to the religious sectors grew, in a period of budgetary restraints, giving rise to strong outcries by many, on the whole helpless "secular" or nontraditional sectors.

In many of the cases the rabbinate has claimed to be the arbiter of conduct, at least in the public sector, for the whole population, implicitly setting itself up as higher than the secular authorities. As a result the level of tensions between religious and nonreligious "secular" sectors was rising continuously, even if intermittently. Religious and ethnic emphases have had an increasing impact on education. An ever-larger segment of the curriculum is devoted to these themes, which tend to sanctify the past, in contrast to the largely future orientations of pioneering Zionists.

A very interesting development combining religious and ethnic elements in a new distinct way crystallized before the 1984 elections in the form of a new religious party, Shas. This party split from the Agudat Israel and was led mostly by rabbis and political entrepreneurs from various Oriental groups who rebelled against the Ashkenazi domination of the Agudat Israel. Its spiritual leader is Rabbi Ovadia Yosef, the former Sephardic chief rabbi, who worked in cooperation with the Ashkenazi rabbi E. Schach, the leader of one of the orthodox groups related to the Agudat Israel and who became the head of its Supreme Religious (and Political) Council.

The new party proved very successful in the 1984 elections and even more so in those of 1988, both on the municipal and countrywide levels. Its success was due both to the combination of ethnic and religious themes and symbols in its appeals and to its very high organizational capacity, which in many ways resembled those of the various labor groups in the Yishuv in the early stages of the state of Israel. The organizational bases were synagogues, religious schools and yeshivoth, and strong family networks.

In the religious area its leadership exhibited a militant tendency that differed greatly from the previous relative toleration predominant among the Oriental communities. This militancy, which probably was not shared, at least in its extreme forms, by the party's broad supporters, developed from within the schools and yeshivoth of the Agudat Israel, in which many of the Shas leaders were educated, as well as through encounters with the "secular Ashkenazi" sectors and centers of Israeli society.

Unlike most of the Agudat Israel, Shas was not isolated from the mainstream of Israeli life, at least initially; rather, it developed from within it. And its general orientation to Israeli society tended to be more open. Although it certainly could not be called a Zionist party in the sense of accepting the revolutionary premises of Zionism—indeed, many of its leaders often expressed ideological opposition to those premises and even declared their bankruptcy—its overall attitude to the state and its institutions was more open and positive than that of the Agudat Israel. Shas was strongly oriented to active participation in the central framework, not only of the state, but also of Israeli society. In matters of security and relations with the Arabs, at least, its leadership seemed to be ready to exhibit rather dovish attitudes.

The Shas leadership lost some of its influence in the second quarter of 1990, when its leaders first joined the Labor Party in toppling the Government of National Unity. Then, under the pressure of the leadership of one sector of the Ashkenazi ultraorthodox group, in June Shas joined Likud in the formation of the right-wing Likud government. From 1990 on, the leadership of Shas became entangled in a series of accusations by the state Comptroller and of police investigations about improper use of public funds. And in 1991 the Shas parliamentary faction was fined twice by the State Controller for disorder in its finances. But whatever the vicissitudes of its political fate, all in all it seemed to constitute one of the most original, even if possibly transient, Israeli developments attendant on the disintegration of the original labor-Zionist mold.

Changes in Political Economy and Strata Formation

At the same time, the entire format of Israel's political economy started to change slowly and painfully from a relatively controlled economy, with strong collectivist orientation, to a more open one—but one with continuous collectivist populist overtones. It is rather more difficult to pinpoint the ideological underpinnings of the Likud's economic policies when, after an initial attempt at liberalization followed by a short period of restrictive policies, Yoram Aridor was appointed Minister of Finance in 1981. Under Aridor, the new Likud or Herut policy, the so-called correct economics, was instituted, with the declared objective of curbing inflation and renewing economic growth. Food subsidies were sharply increased, taxes on consumer durables reduced, and budgetary constraints relaxed. As a result, private consumption and real wages soared during the months following the 1981 elections. This "populist" economic policy in some ways resembled that of Peronist Argentina.

These policies ultimately led to the runaway deterioration of the economic situation and an economic crisis that, starting in fall 1983, probably was the most serious one that has ever beset the Israeli economy and included a very serious crisis in the banking world. Since then, the changes in the Israeli economy have been very painful, with periodic crises, moving between growing inflation under the second Likud government, the very successful suppression of this inflation by the first National Unity Government under Mr. Peres (1984–1986), and economic stabilization tending toward stagnation and unemployment since then.

Closely related to the changes in political economy were far-reaching changes in the structure of status, in strata formation, and stratification in Israeli society. The combination of relatively strong egalitarian orientations with a strong emphasis on service in public sectors gave way to a much stronger emphasis on professional, entrepreneurial, and economic activities. A variety of status groups and patterns of life developed; income inequalities grew together with a focus on conspicuous consumption. All these tendencies had developed earlier, but until about the mid-1970s, they were hemmed in, so to speak, to a degree by the dominant ethos. This started to change in the middle and late 1970s and gathered momentum in the 1980s. Some of the bearers of the older ethos like the kibbutzim and to a smaller extent the moshavim, who had gotten into a difficult economic situation (in no small degree due to imprudent financial policies and expansion of consumption) lost their symbolic elite status. The same happened to some extent to army service and service in other public sectors. At the same time in large sectors of society many manifestations of rampant conspicuous consumption developed. But above all a rather general feeling of lack developed of no clear norms according to which economics and status were allocated and rewards attained, leading to widespread feelings of anomie. The many cases of failed financial entrepreneurs, some of whom have ended in jail and which often were seen as symptomatic of the disintegration of the older ethos, have only added to these feelings.

Concurrently, one of the most important constructive developments in this period as already indicated, was the growing incorporation of many, especially the "Oriental," sectors of the population into the central framework of society. The quest of many "Oriental" groups for access to the center and participation, among other things, took the form of demands for the incorporation of symbols of ethnic traditions into the mainstream of Israeli life. This quest found a partial response with the change of government, which was accompanied by a "changing of the guard" and, even more significant, the incorporation of new sectors of the population into the center. With this increasing mobility toward the center (although not necessarily in the occupational sector), a new leadership arose, or became more prominent in many of the development towns, as well as in other sectors, aspiring to and feeling the possibility of participation, of not being dispossessed or remote from the center. Paradoxically, attendant on the disintegration labor mold of Israeli society, these processes were manifestations of a growing democratization of Israeli society.

Contradictory Tendencies in the Political Arena

Continuity of Constitutional Democracy and Erosion of Political Process. All these developments naturally have affected the political arena also, the general political ambience as well as the working of political institutions. Throughout these formidable changes and turbulences, Israel remained a constitutional democracy with the rule of law. Indeed, at the root of many of the changes was the growing democratization of Israeli society: the opening up of the older frameworks constructed by the various policies of dynamic conservatives and the incorporation of many new sectors of the population into the central political arena. But all these changes generated developments that tended to erode some very important components of the political process.

One central development in the political arena was the emergence and continuation of a split btween two relatively equal groups: the labor camp, composed of the Labor Party (the Maarach) and several left of center groups; and the right-wing camp composed of the Likud and more right-wing groups, with the religious groups in the middle but leaning more and more to the Likud. The overt split between these camps into the "dovish" left and the "hawkish" right developed first of all around the international and security problems of Israel, and its attitudes to the Arab world, especially the occupation of the West Bank territories. This split constituted more or less the central focus of the political debate and division, being very strong from about 1980 to about 1984, subsiding to some extent under the Government of National Unity, until the Intifada, and culminating in the distintegration of the Government of National Unity in March 1990.

This split, however, was much more than just a division over problems of security and foreign policy. It also was connected, as alluded to, with growing differences between various sectors of Israeli society with respect to styles of life and modes of discourse and with some of the approaches of how to deal with the major problems of Israeli society.[20]

The great dissociation among elite groups noted earlier seemed to grow and intensify—to the point where it seemed as if Israeli society developed what may be called different communities of discourse without, as it were, a common text. This was most evident with respect to the relations between the various orthodox groups and large sectors of Israeli society. But it was also in no small degree true among many groups of intellectuals more on the left and some of the older sectors, many of the more mobile "Oriental," as well as the new Israeli-born generations. Indeed, many of the intellectuals and academics connected with the labor sector, and especially to the left wing of it, seemed to have become rather disassociated from many of these sectors of Israeli society, from these very sectors that had become much more visible in setting up the new patterns and styles of life.

Many of these intellectuals concentrated their public activities on the intellectual and security situation, on the problems of the upholding of civil rights in the territories. In many cases, as for instance in the one of the League for Civil Rights, they have done very important and constructive activities in upholding the rule of law. Yet possibly at the same time they might have given the impression that they do not share the gut feelings of large sectors of Israeli society that the Intifada is not only a civil rebellion that Israel faces in the territories, but also a war many Arabs would in principle like to wage with Israel "to throw Israel into the sea." The dissociation of many of these intellectuals from large sectors of Israeli society was reinforced by the point they often made that they felt as if they have been deposed from their position of influence, whether in government circles or in wider sectors of Israei society, as dispossessed elite groups. They did not find many arenas of common discourse with large sectors of the society, and they did not attempt to tap the widespread potential leadership and intellectual reservoirs of these sectors. Their discourse often was oriented more to the Jewish communities abroad, or to the international media. In some extreme and exceptional cases, the more leftist among them sounded as if they were not only opposing the policies of the government but also questioning the legitimacy of the state. At the same time the intellectuals or journalists more in the center, and especially on the right, who were not on the whole as visible and prominent as those on the left, did not address themselves to many of the problems of civil rights. Almost none of these groups address themselves, except with respect to the secular-religious tensions, to most internal problems of Israeli society—be they the economy or education, environmental problems, or the many problems and discourses connected with the reconstruction of the place in Jewish history and tradition in the reconstruction of Israeli collective consciousness.

On the more concrete institutional level was the development of a new relationship between opposition and government. For the first time in the history of Israel, the parliamentary opposition was numerically almost on a par with the government; in fact, after 1981 the Maarach (Labor) had three more seats than the Likud, and constituted the largest party in the Knesset. In addition, the opposition did not see itself as merely a counterweight to the government, as was the case with respect to the various rightist opposition groups during the period of predominance of the Labor Party, but as a principal opposition that did not accept many of the basic premises of the government or most of its policies. The lines of this opposition more and more were drawn around international political and security questions: the policy of territorial expansion and continuous Israeli presence in Judea and Samaria, ruling over more than a million Arabs, as contrasted with some sort of territorial compromise that would assure the democratic and Jewish nature of the state.

This emergence of a potentially principled opposition created an entirely new situation on the Israeli political scene, especially with respect to criticism of the government. The tendency to equate the government with the state had been strong throughout Israeli history, given the at least de facto acceptance of the basic premises of the government by large segments of the opposition. However, the problematic nature of such an equation became very acute with the development of the new government-opposition relations. Very often when the opposition tended to express more principled criticism of the government, such criticism was portrayed by the government as going beyond the national consensus, sometimes as touching almost on treason. Thus, this change in government opposition relations was very closely interwoven with the basic question of the contours of Israeli polity: the strength of its constitutional democracy, of civility, of rule of law.

The later developments, especially the establishment of the Government of National Unity, although temporarily weakening the repercussions of the emergence of such opposition, did not do away with them. Yet at the same time, especially during the periods of the governments of national unity, paradoxically enough the boundaries between the two major blocs blurred—at least between the two major parties, if not between the more extreme groups in each bloc. This was due to no small degree to the fact that, as we have seen, the Likud and the religious groups with their emphasis on national, security, and religious issues set the political agenda; and the Labor Party, and even the more leftist groups, mostly reacted to it. Sometimes they accepted some initiatives coming from the right; for instance, the proposal to impose Israeli law on the Golan Heights or to proclaim Jerusalem the capital of Israel (a move that resulted in the transfer of some embassies from Jerusalem to Tel-Aviv). Although many of these moves were mostly tactical, basically they attested to the exhaustion of the Labor Party's original program. This exhaustion was also evident in the fact that the Labor Party did not initiate any discourse on social or economic problems beyond concrete daily policies related to its various interests, thus reinforcing the importance of the nation's security problems, most of which were set by Likud, on the national agenda.

The more leftist groups promulgated very strongly the more dovish attitudes as well as concern with civil rights and the rule of law, but as pointed out they barely touched on any other problems of Israeli society (except the religious-secular), be they those of education, the restructuring of the economy, or the like.

This paradoxical combination—on the one hand, blurring of some of the lines between the two major political camps or at least between the two major parties, with, on the other, a growing more general split between them—was closely connected to the second major institutional development in the political arena in this period, the resurgence, in a new form, of very "consociational" politics with open division of the spoils between the major party blocs with the religious parties often leading the way. This resurgence was closely connected with a weakening of various more universalistic criteria of civility in the public services and the general importance of the society, with agrowing disregard of relevant norms, which had been gathering strength from the mid-1960s up to the time of the "Mahapakh" in 1977. This resurgence could be seen, for instance, in the growing number of party political appointments to many public bodies such as government economic corporations and, above all, to radio and television authority and the like, eroding many independent public arenas. This resurgence has greatly contributed to the erosion of the normative ambiance of public life.

In many ways, a rather strong consensus, that of a very low, if not the lowest, common denominator, developed between the labor and Likud camps, in which the religious participated actively, especially during the Shamir government from 1990 on, with a petrifying effect on any significant political discourse. But perhaps the most important negative aspect of the internal developments during the period of the National Unity Government and after its dismemberment in 1990 has been the growing immobility on the internal front: the lack of any evidence that the Likud—whose major ideological tenets, such as the emphasis on territoriality and defense, were incorporated into the basic symbols and ambience of society, and who set most of the political agenda—was able to show any new creativity in the major institutional arenas; and the failure of the labor camp to formulate either a new ideology or a new creative and innovative direction for institution building. The Labor Party then became the upholder of the vested interests of its larger concerns, such as the Solel Boneh construction firm, the Kupat Holim health fund, and the kibbutzim.

Rule of Law.   Thus, contradictory developments developed in the central political arena, above all in the continuity of the democratic regime, together with the erosion of many aspects of the constitutional political process. Indeed, in this period several contradictory trends which were always inherent in Israeli politics became much more visible. Many of these contradictions connected with the eruption of many tensions among the different orientations of the Jewish political tradition were attendant on the disintegration of the initial mold of Israeli society.

One such trend was the continuous oscillation between, on the one hand, the special Israeli type of horse trading, or "pork-barrel politics"—more appropriately, kosher-beef-barrel politics—and solidarity, a readiness for self-sacrifice revealed in time of stress.

Another oscillatory movement typical of Israeli political life, although also found in other societies, here follows a unique path. The pendulum swings from pragmatism and "horse trading" at one extreme to ideological debate and an unwillingness to meet on ideological grounds at the other. The same people alternately occupy each extreme—and in earnest. Though occasionally mere lip service, ideological disputes frequently are much more. They can be bitter and merciless, characterized by an unwillingness to acknowledge the legitimacy of one's opponent, who is to be placed beyond the pale. Although part of this delegitimation is tactical, it often is more than that. This sort of oscillation becomes more prominent in times of deep cleavage and division—for instance, between the 1981 and 1984 elections—when the acrimonious ideological disputes that could also endanger the pragmatic arrangements become most evident.

All these phenomena denote a certain weakness of civility, an unwillingness to accept the law of the land, whether in the name of some higher law (religious, national, or social), or through claims of solidarity that also may be taken to represent a higher law. But perhaps above all it was the tension between the rule of law and the tendency to principled political anarchism that we identified as a basic component of the Jewish political tradition.

In Chapter 3 we analyzed the roots of this tendency and its "fate" in Jewish life in the period of the Second Temple and the Medieval period. The potential for principled political anarchism reawakened with greater vigor in the aftermath of the crisis that beset Judaism after the Sabbatean debacle and the opening of the gates of Emancipation. Since then, various movements have arisen within Judaism and remolded many of the elements and orientations that had been dormant during the Middle Ages; and they also have revived the tendencies to principled political anarchism.

From the point of view of our discussion, the most important such development after the start of the Emancipation related to the national movement and the establishment of the state of Israel. However, some developments took place within autonomous Jewish organizations in the Diaspora, under conditions of partial or complete equality within an open society. Thus, for instance, Professor Salo Baron has shown how difficult it was, even impossible, for the orthodox communities of nineteenth-century New York to impose any uniformity of action. Disputes arose not only between different religious movements, but within the orthodox movement itself as soon as external conditions changed.[21] Such characteristics come quickly to the fore when Diaspora countries become less restrictive. They developed with greater intensity, however, when the movement for the establishment of the state of Israel began. The debate over the shape of society and state in Israel sprang up afresh: the doors were reopened for an autonomous search by various groups and movements for a solution to these problems. The cultural and social energies inherent within Jewish tradition and Jewish civilization were released, with all the problems and tensions that had once marked this tradition. The Halakhah became only one of many feasible paths; its adherents formed one of several diverse groups that could compete with other groups, and later with the various institutions, including the legal ones, of the state of Israel.

The various contradictory orientations in the Jewish political tradition naturally erupted with greater force with the establishment of the state of Israel, especially because it was created out of revolutionary visions implemented by highly ideological groups with rather totalitarian claims orientations, or tendencies, and given the special conditions in which this society developed. The establishment of the state of Israel, as at least the first step in the implementation of Zionist vision, heralded the entry of Jews into history. Although rooted in a strong rebellion against the Jewish traditional and assimilationist molds, this entry was not dissociated from many aspects or dimensions of Jewish histroy and tradition.

On the contrary, as we have seen, this rebellion against the reality of Jewish life in the traditional modern Diaspora not only reinforced, renewed, or brought into the open the basic themes and orientations latent in earlier periods of Jewish history, but also transformed most of them from purely intellectual ones into themes embedded in institutional areas and frameworks. The specific achievement of the institutional mold that developed in Israel was manifested in the fact that the institutional mold that developed in Israel seemingly was able to regulate these tensions, especially the more anarchic potentials. But this achievement could not be taken for granted: the very establishment of a sovereign state created the potential for these tendencies to erupt anew, to break through the existing institutional mold, thus generating continual challenges for Israeli society and the political system. A brief look at the development of the legal institutions and of the attitude toward them in the Yishuv and the state of Israel would be helpful here.

The Mandatory period had a strong influence on the development of Israeli legal institutions and attitudes toward them and the law. The rule of law, upheld by the political limitations set by the British Mandatory government and by British police, on the whole was accepted (in the realm of civil and public as distinct from political matters), reinforcing the strong belief in the rule of law that many of the immigrants had brought from Europe.

At the same time, these attitudes were weakened by the growing political tensions between the Zionist movement and the Mandatory government; the emergence of independent defense organizations (the Hagana and the Irgun); and the open violation of British restrictions on immigration and acquisition of land. All of these sanctified the contravention of the law of the land (in this case that of the Mandate) in the name of higher collective aims; they often gave rise to far-reaching evasions and contraventions of the law of the land in daily life as well.

With the establishment of the state of Israel, the basic institutional framework had changed, but often in rather paradoxical directions. The paradox is rooted in the relationship between the older injunction of *Dina dimalkhuta dina* versus the potential for nonacceptance of the law of the state as rooted in the different tendencies of the Jewish tradition in general and in that of political anarchism in particular.

An independent court system following the Mandatory pattern was established at the same time as the new legislature, the Knesset. As the court system of an independent state, it seemingly should have been fully accepted without reservation. But as we have already seen, this was not the whole story. Precisely because the executive, legislature, and judiciary were all part of a new and sovereign state, they could become the foci of strong tendencies toward various principled political orientations.

Acceptance of the law of the land as laid down by foreign rulers, and for which the Jews did not have full responsibility, could not be automatically transferred to the institutions of the state when the state authority became Jewish. A Jewish state ought to be responsible for the implementation of Jewish civilizational vision. Different groups and sectors of the population might interpret this vision in different ways, leading to intense political controversy that could not develop with respect to the laws of a non-Jewish state.

Nevertheless, the legal system, especially the Supreme Court and the office of the Attorney General, experienced a continuous growth of influence. The court is secular and purely judicial, not legislative. Legislation remains in the hands of the Knesset, which in principle can invalidate any verdict of the High Court, though in fact this has happened only rarely. In fact, the authority of the Supreme Court has always been respected, and its de facto initiation of many legislative principles has expanded, as have its injunctions against public authorities and the government. At the same time, however, possibly in relation to the consociational dimension of politics in the Yishuv and in the state of Israel, only a rather weak tradition has grown up of a conception of "state" or "raison d'etat," as distinct from considerations of security and general public interest.

Even within this framework, however, some inherent tensions have arisen with respect to the rule of law. One involved the relationship between the secular court and the religious circles and courts. The extreme orthodox circles did not acknowledge the legitimacy of the secular legal system and particularly of the Supreme Court. They had little recourse to them, almost exclusively in civil (commercial) matters; and on the whole tended to use their own internal courts or quasi-legal institutions. Thus a situation developed that in a sense, paradoxically enough, was rather similar to that of Medieval times, the relative segregation of the different courts, but already within the framework of a unified territorial state.

Much more paradoxical was the situation with respect to the official rabbinical courts of the state of Israel. These courts perpetuate the situation of the Mandate, with antecedents in the Ottoman period, when a system of rabbinical courts and (Sephardi and Ashkenazi) chief rabbis was established. In the state of Israel this system has become fully institutional; in accordance with Knesset enactment, it is part—but a distinct and separate part—of the state court system.

The jurisdiction of the rabbinical courts extended, as we have seen, to all matters of personal status (marriage and divorce) for the Jewish population (parallel powers are vested in the religious authorities of the Muslim, Christian, and Druze communities) and to supervision of kashrut. Thus the basic criterion of membership in the community, as applied in controlling marriage, remains in the hands of religious groups.

The rabbinical courts are in some ways subject to the jurisdiction of the (secular) Supreme Court. Although there is no direct appeal from the rabbinical to the "secular" courts, the Supreme Court, when sitting as the High Court of Justice, can reverse judgment of the rabbinical courts on grounds of their subverting basic "natural" principles of justice. This creates the possibility of continuous tension between them. Especially in recent years, religious groups have frequently denied the legitimacy of this subordination of the rabbinical to the secular court—or of any judicial review of political and administrative actions taken by religious ministers acting in accordance with their view of Halakhah.

But such tendency to principled political anarchism developed not only in the seemingly marginal religious sectors, which were, however, continuously moving into the center. In contemporary Israeli politics this tendency has become much more visible in the central political arena.

The tendencies to principled political anarchism—to engagement in the politics of a higher law, on the one hand, and those emphasizing distributive allocation, often in the name of Jewish solidarity or of the solidarity of different sectors of Jewish community, on the other—during the Medieval period and the first twenty-five years of the state of Israel were hemmed in by their respective institutional frameworks, became more and more visible after 1977, with the disintegration of the Labor Party mold, and continue, as we have seen.

In contemporary Israeli politics, this phenomenon is quite conspicuous on the right end of the political spectrum: first of all among Gush Emunim (The Front of the Faithful), the extreme front of nationalist religious groups that emerged and became a prominent element on the Israeli political scene since 1967, but also among many of the secular adherents of the ideology of Eretz Israel Hashelema (The Whole Eretz Israel), and more recently among the so-called "Jewish underground," a group of extreme religious-nationalists who perpetrated and planned to perpetrate in the early 1980s a series of criminal attacks against the Arab population and institutions in the West Bank.

Not always have the right wing of the political spectrum, or the extreme religious groups, taken this line. In the first period of the state, through the early 1950s, this tendency was much more evident on the left, as in the intense controversies about the Palmach and the structure of the army, and the nature of civilian control of the military; in the controversies about the nature of relations with Soviet Russia, a controversy connected with one of the most traumatic events in the early history of Israel society, the split in the kibbutz movement. Even today some relics of this attitude may be found on the left, for example in some of the more extreme groups, like "Yesh Gevul" (There Is a Limit) that opposed the Lebanon War, and were criticized for their call not to serve in the army even by the major opponents of the war among the leftist parties, as well as in some outbursts of the more leftist groups.

At the same time the increase in the distributive consociational (?) policies has intensified many aspects of illegalism that developed, as we have seen, under the British Mandate.[22] Some rulings of the Attorney General and the High Court became foci of public controversy, disputed by some sectors of the public and sometimes even by members of the government. At the same time, extraparliamentary extremism increased in scope. There was a deterioration in the quality of public life and growing intolerance, brutality, and violence. Many aspects of civility and the rule of law were weakened. One manifestation of this was the growing and unprecedented involvement of military leaders (especially the then Chief of Staff, Rafael Eitan) in political matters. Another manifestation involved the application of the law in Israel, especially in the relations between Arabs and Jews in Judea and Samaria. The combination of all these developments—the weakening of civic virtue—divisions among social groups and between the major political blocs and their supporters, the breakdown of many of the normative restraints on public behavior, and the weakening of feelings of shame—led to an intensification of violence and to growing intolerance.

Nevertheless, other tendencies also have been at work. Above all, the basic democratic framework and most of the rules of the democratic game have been upheld—despite the many threats to them, despite the polls indicating doubts about democracy among large sectors of the population. At the same time, even at the height of the Lebanon War, a war not based on consensus, the openness of society and the lines of communication between the people and the authorities was maintained. Despite some initial efforts to hamper journalists, the Lebanon War was reported fully in the media, some-times even beyond the legitimate limits of military censorship, in sharp con-trast with, for instance, the Falklands War. Moreover, within this general context, the tendency to uphold the law, the modern secular equivalent of the sovereignty of the court, and of the rule of law of the land have also been strengthened.

The continuous extension of the authority of the legal system, and par-ticularly of the High Court and the Attorney General, was due to several rea-sons. First, it was probably due to the growth and development of the country itself, opening up of many new problems and potentials for conflict, as well as with the initial institutonal mold of Israeli society, with economic growth and growing social complexity. Second, it was closely connected to the weaken-ing of the other branches of the government, especially the executive, and the growth of political dissent. Such periods saw increased recourse to the High Court or the Attorney General, sometimes by the government itself.

The rule of law has indeed been strengthened in many ways, even if it was not always fully accepted and sometimes even became a focus of public controversy. Such an extension of the rule of law could be seen during the Lebanon War, in the establishment of the Kahan Commission (named after the then-President of the Supreme Court), which investigated the conduct of some aspects of the war, censured many political and military figures, and recommended that the then Minister of Defense, Mr. Sharon, and several high officers be relieved of their positions, and in the perhaps only partial and yet unprecedented acceptance of its far-reaching verdict, the like of which could not be found in any other democratic society.

To give only a few additional illustrations, the High Court ruled against the Television Authority when it banned the broadcast of interviews with PLO or antigovernment Arab leaders. Similarly, the Court, against the wishes of the police, permitted a demonstration in memory of the murdered peace activist Emil Grinzweig. Later, after negotiations with the Inspector General of Police, the Attorney General issued a directive that it is the duty of the police to assure the security of legitimate opposition demonstrations, even if large parts of the public are against them and the demonstrations thus seemingly threaten public order. Similarly, the Attorney General's office provided the initiative for the establishment of the Karp Committee to inves-tigate the application and implementation of law, especially toward Jews in conflict with Arabs in Judea and Samaria. One of the latest manifestations of this independent stance of the Supreme Court was its injunction to the army in January 1991, on the eve of the Persian Gulf War, to distribute antigas masks to the Arab population of the West Bank. Many more illustrations could be given. Indeed, recourse to the High Court in controversial political and public matters has become a basic part of the Israeli political scene.

Needless to say, these were not the only trends. Many signs of weakening civility, divisiveness, and intolerance continued and even intensified. Some rulings of the Attorney General and the High Court became the foci of public controversy, disputed by the public and sometimes even by members of the government.

The tensions surrounding the rule of law and the standing of the Supreme Court in Israel emerged quite forcefully in the General Security Service case in July 1986. From the point of view of our discussion, perhaps the most interesting aspect of this case is that, despite many efforts to deal with it outside the usual legal institutions, the case was more or less closed only after the Supreme Court upheld the presidential pardon granted to the former head of the service and several of his aides, a pardon that gave rise to intensive public controversy, and after the juridical inquiry headed by the Attorney General had absolved the Prime Minister (Mr. Shamir) of connivance in the misdeeds (the murder of captured Arab terrorists and lying to a government commission of inquiry) attributed to the members of the Security Service. Throughout this period, the media were of crucial importance in supporting the upholding of the rule of law, often bringing on themselves the ire of many, especially, but not only, right-wing politicians.

A rather similar picture emerged with respect to another agency of great importance in the upholding of appropriate norms in the public sector—the State Controller. The State Controller's reports, with the nomination of Mrs. M. Ben-Porath, former Deputy President of the Supreme Court, became much more aggressive with respect to the breaches of such norms by governmental, public, and political bodies, and gave rise in an unprecedented way to intensive public outcries, discussions in the Knesset and the media.

Thus, contradictory tendencies developed both with respect, first, to the continuity of the basic constitutional-democratic framework, between the tendencies to democratization and the continuity of the constitutional process, especially given more ambivalent attitudes toward these frameworks evinced by large sectors of the public, including many political leaders. Second, such contradictory tendencies developed with respect to the tensions between the rule of law and the different anarchic tendencies, whether those rooted in principled political anarchism or in different conceptions of solidarity. With respect both to the latter and the rule of law, tension developed between the maintenance and reinforcement of the basic constitutional framework.

Israeli Society in Transition: Conclusions

The period from 1977 on has been very turbulent, and the story continues to be full of contradictory tendencies. Throughout the 1980s, the situation continued to move in the same direction of continuous turmoil, without crystallization of any clear institutional mold or molds and with contradictory developments.

Many of the tensions so prominent in the earlier period, between the Orthodox and secular sectors and between the Jewish and Arab sectors, continued to simmer and often erupted anew. In addition, Arab-Israeli relations continued to deteriorate, both on the West Bank and in Jerusalem, with the growth of resentment among the Arabs against the continuing Israeli occupation, the constant eruption of terrorist activities, the outbreak of the Intifada that has radically changed the terms of the Arab-Israeli conflict, and the concomitant intensification of anti-Arab feelings among large sectors of the Jewish population, including violent outbursts against Arabs in reaction to Arab killings of Jews. More and more signs of the development of a vicious circle of mutual hatred emerged, with all the potentially destructive tendencies on many aspects of life in Israeli society and on the prospects of some political settlement.

At the same time this period continued to be characterized by cultural and even institutional creativity in various sectors of Israeli society, combined with erosion of many aspects of the political process and atrophy of many central institutions of the society. There developed a huge discrepancy between the great potential of creativity manifest in many arenas of life and the strong tendencies to ossification in the central institutional arenas. The challenge of Israeli society to reconstruct its institutional formations, of its capacity to break through the strong tendency to institutional stagnation that became very strong in the 1980s is still before it.

One of the most dramatic developments since 1989 was the great influx of Jewish immigrants from Russia, the number of which by the end of 1990 reached about two hundred thousand. Whatever the vicissitudes of the integration of this immigration, which posed one of the greatest challenges before Israeli society, there can be no doubt that like all the other immigrations, the various Aliyot, this one also will greatly transform the Israeli society. It naturally is too early to indicate in which direction it will take place.

The very continuation of these tendencies attests yet again to the fact that Israeli society is in a state of transformation. This transformation is still going on, and it would be beyond the scope of our discussion to go into all its details or analyze all its aspects. It is important from the point of view of our discussion, however, to point out that it is impossible to understand the story without taking into account some central aspects of Jewish civilizational or spiritual traditions. Thus, the weakening of the sense of civility highlighted certain themes of Jewish political culture—intransigence, the emphasis on points of a higher law, the stress on distributive allocations in the name of solidarity—that had been evinced but were to some extent dominant during both the Medieval period and the first twenty-five years of the state of Israel.

As in times gone by, these tendencies have been activated not by the mere existence of various ideological orientations in the Jewish political tradition, but by the activation of those themes connected with strong social forces; namely, various social groups, elite groups, and movements that saw themselves as the carriers of these visions. These orientations were intensified by the processes of change in Israeli society.

The tensions among the basic themes of the Jewish political tradition play an important role in this process; the resolution of these tensions, in terms of confrontation of accommodation, or the development of a new institutional mold or molds that will be able to regulate these tensions will influence the outcome of this process and provide an important indication of the directions in which Israeli society will develop.

8

The United States and Israel:
An Essay in Comparative Analysis

Some Common Characteristics of the United States and Israel: Constitutional, Modernizing, Revolutionary, Ideological Societies

It might seem rather curious, even inappropriate, to attempt a comparison of the United States and Israel. The differences between these two countries are obvious and staggering: one is a superpower, the largest industrialized nation, stretching over a huge territory, with a population of over 220 million; the other is a small besieged country of about 4.5 million, in a hostile environment, its economy shaky, and its political system turbulent and potentially unstable.

Yet despite these obvious differences there are some very interesting affinities and similarities between these two countries. On the simplest, but a very important level, is the close "special" relationship between the United States and Israel since the establishment of the latter.[1] The de facto recognition of the state of Israel by the United States, granted a few hours after the proclamation of Israeli independence on May 14, 1948, heralded the beginnings of its acceptance in the world community. Since then the United States has been, as is well known, the most important ally of Israel. However great the differences of opinion on detailed policy matters, such as the problem of the territories on the West Bank and in Gaza ruled by Israel after the Six-Day War, the support of the United States in the face of wide ranging criticism and even military attack has sustained Israel in the international arena.

Indeed the economic and military aid of the United States has been of crucial importance for Israel's economy and security—perhaps too crucial, making Israel in many ways very dependent on the United States. But even in policy disputes the amount of pressure put on Israel by the United States seems relatively light compared to the amount of aid and support.

Of course, there have been disagreements and misunderstandings on governmental levels and in relations between public groups and some sectors of the media which arose during the Lebanon War and escalated from the end of 1988 with the Arab uprising in the territories. Yet all these disagreements notwithstanding, there can be little doubt that a very strong bond between the two countries developed early on, and the importance of this bond manifested itself again very forcefully during early 1991 with the eruption of the Gulf War.

To no small degree this affinity can be explained by the strength, acceptance, and visibility of the Jewish community in the United States, the special history of that community, and its great influence on American political life. But this is not the whole story. The specific characteristics of Jewish historical experience in the United States can be explained only in connection with the unique history of America itself and the American way of life, which in some ways bear comparison with the experience of Israeli society. Such comparison may bring out some rather paradoxical similarities that perhaps may help account for the strong affinity as well as special relationship between the two societies, and also explain some rather critical differences between these two countries—beyond the obvious ones of size, numbers, wealth, and economic and international standing—which may become sources of tension and misunderstanding not only between the two nations, but also between Israelis and American Jews. The seeds of both parity and disparity can be found in the early history of settlement in America, long before the establishment of the state of Israel, which provides an important background for the later developments.

One such seed is the very special place of the Bible, especially the Old Testament, and its imagery and symbolism in the history of Puritan settlement in America. For instance, many of the Pilgrim Fathers conceived of America as the Promised Land, and the image of desert wilderness and its conquest and government—that of the Covenant—constituted crucial components of the collective identity and political culture of the colonies.

Various affinities between the Protestant, especially sectarian, American and the Jewish American experience also arose. Sometimes it was but an extension of the general principle of tolerance, with respect to the Jews in particular, as exemplified by George Washington's famous letter, referred to in Chapter 6, to the members of the synagogue in Newport, Rhode Island. Sometimes it went beyond this, as for instance in the suggestion made in the early 1920s by the eminent sociologist Robert Park, that given the great affinity between the mentalities of Jewish and Puritan Americans, Jewish history should be made part of the curriculum in American schools. There arose in the United States, as in England, in the nineteenth century, many harbingers of the vision of a Jewish state. But the implication of these varied remarks cannot be understood fully except in the framework of some of the basic characteristics of the American society, which may be compared with some of those of the Jewish community in Palestine, in the Yishuv and the state of Israel.

The most important characteristics shared by both polities are their constituting

1. Revolutionary ideological societies;

2. Pioneering colonizing societies;

3. Constitutional democratic societies, with rather distinctive constitutional regimes and one common characteristic;

4. Societies that have generated modern, industrial economies out of the original impetus of colonization;

5. Societies in which the development of those economies was facilitated by waves of immigration that differed greatly from those of the earlier settlers or pioneers.

Accordingly the problem of incorporating these immigrant groups into the institutional framework established by the pioneers and their impact on the framework constituted one of the central problems in the development of both countries. We next enlarge on these cross-national similarities, some of which already have been touched on in Chapter 6, in the analysis of the Zionist movement.

Both the United States and the Yishuv and Israeli society developed out of conscious efforts to create a new society that rebelled against the old ones from which the pioneer immigrants came. In both cases these efforts were founded upon strong utopian, even eschatological, religious or social visions. The Puritan settlement in the United States was in rebellion against Anglican England (and to some extent also against some sectors among the Puritans) and aimed to establish a new society uncontaminated by High Church ideology and corruption.[2] In the case of Yishuv and Israeli society, the rebellion was against the Jewish historical experience, especially in the modern Diaspora, and aimed at the establishment of a society that would provide collective security for the Jews and also prove to be constitutionally and culturally creative.[3]

In both cases the rebellion or revolution did not aim initially at the overthrow of the existing political regime. Rather, it opted out of the original society by emigration from it. Initially, both emigrant societies accepted "external" rule, the American colonies by Britain, and the Jewish settlements in Eretz-Israel by both Turkey and Britain. The rebellion against this rule, the American Revolution and the Israeli War of Independence, came at a later stage of development, after the major revolutionary ideological orientations and many of their institutional derivatives had crystallized. In this respect, of course, both rebellions (or revolutions) differed from the Great European ones, the French and the Russian, and the later Chinese one in which the overthrow of the existing regime was the harbinger of instituting a totally different ideology. In both the United States and Israel the very attainment of political independence constituted a crucial step in the institutionalization of the revolutionary ideology, but it was not the starting point of such crystallization and institutionalization, although the American Revolution was seen as constructing a radically new political order.

In both the United States and Israel, these ideologies constituted a crucial component of their collective identities and fundamental premises and in the crystallization of their basic institutions. In the American colonies, this ideology was rooted in the Puritan religious orientation and symbolism, as well as in the English political and legal tradition. In Israel the Zionist orientations were of crucial importance in shaping the society's identity and institutional formation.

Because of the weakness of strong historical and primordial components in the American identity, to which we shall return in greater detail, the United States in some ways is a much more ideological society than Israel, possibly, and paradoxically, the most purely ideological of all modern societies. Some of the central ideological and colonizatory components in both the United States and Israel have crystallized around a series of rather similar images, some of which were referenced earlier. The most important of these were of pioneering; the reconstruction of wasteland, the transformation of desert into the Promised Land. Many of these images derived from the Old Testament, and all have become part of the collective identity of both societies—although, as we shall see, with some far-reaching differences between them.

In both countries the bearers of revolutionary ideological vision were called pioneers, but they were not the only important molders of their respective societies. Equally important were less ideological elements, such as the large sectors of the so-called private sector in Israel and many of the Southern semiaristocratic settlers in the American colonies.

These societies shared the colonizatory push with such countries as Canada, Australia, New Zealand, South Africa, and, in a different vein, the first waves of the Spanish and Portuguese conquest of Latin America.[4] But there were crucial differences between the immigrants in all these countries and those in the United States and Israel. Beyond the great variations in local economic and ecological conditions and in the scope and intensity of the encounter with the native populations, the crucial difference lies in the absence or at least weakness in all these societies, with the exception of the United States and Israel (and perhaps, but only partially, South Africa), of a revolutionary ideological component. In all the other colonisatory, immigrant countries, the major push to immigration and settlement usually was economic: the search for a new, better economic environment or, as in the case in Latin America, a combination of such considerations with a strong urge for political conquest and expansion. Ideological elements such as the expansion of Christianity of course played a role especially in the latter case, but they did not constitute the moving force that shaped the central institutions in these societies, even if some components of the Christian missionary ideology played an important part in this process. As against this, in the United States and in Israel the ideological revolutionary visions constituted the most important component, or at least one of such components, in the formation and development of the basic institutional framework and in shaping the symbols of collective identity. True enough, many aspects of their institutional structure, such as the importance of the representative and legal institutions in both societies, can be explained in terms of their European origins. Yet unlike the former dominions they cannot be seen, to use Louis Hartz's designation, as fragments of their European mother countries.[5] Their collective identities and premises developed in very distinct ways, far beyond their European heritage. Many of the institutions they inherited or brought over from Europe were greatly transformed in accordance with the new premises that developed.

Thus, the basic premises of the American civilization entailed a farreaching transformation of the European ones, above all in the crystallization of a new mode of collective identity and in the very strong emphasis on equality. The most important premises of American civilization, as already indicated in Chapter 6, have been the transformation of the "Messianic" and millennial orientations of the early American sociopolitical endeavor, the particular combination of solidarity and individualism in the American collective identity, the antistatist orientation of American society, and the strong future orientation of American values and belief systems.

A crucial aspect of the new American civilization focused on the construction of a civilizational mold based on a political ideology strongly rooted in the Puritan religious conceptions and in the special covenant between God and the chosen people, a covenant oriented to the creation of a deeply religious polity, yet based on the separation of Church and state.[6]

Out of these orientations, rooted in Puritan and Lockean political orientations, the Enlightenment and nonconformist Protestant religion, a new peculiar "civil" religion developed. This ideological fusion of religious sentiment and political values, with its stress on achievement and equality, republican liberties, and the disestablishment of official religion, imbued both the social and political realms of American life and the construction of the American collectivity. Because of these factors American nationalism—if this term with its European connotation is at all appropriate to the American scene—or collective identity has been based neither on primordial elements nor has it been rooted in an organic historical development of the European type.[7] Another crucial difference between the basic civilizational premises of the United States and those of Europe and Canada (or Australia) has been the former's strong emphasis on the metaphysical equality of all members of the community (brilliantly analyzed by de Toqueville), on the emphasis on egalitarian individualism, and on the almost total denial of the symbolic validity of hierarchy.[8]

Given all these premises, access to the center in the United States in principle has been available to all citizens. It did not constitute, as in Europe, a focus of principled and continuous struggle. Consequently, protest or class consciousness oriented to the abolition or transformation of hierarchy and reconstruction of the center were very weak. Instead, in the United States the unique combination of highly moralistic and pork-barrel politics developed, with constant oscillation between them and, in S. P. Huntington's words, the continuous "promise of disharmony," but a disharmony based on full acceptance of the premises of the center. The reconstruction of the center, undertaken in the Jacksonian and New Deal periods, was effected through attempts to reestablish such harmony by reconstructuring the polities of the center, not its basic premises.

These specific premises also have greatly transformed in far-reaching ways many institutions that were brought over from Europe and that distinguished the American scene, not only from the European, but also, as S. M. Lipset has lately shown in great detail, from the Canadian one.[9] Therefore, to give only a few illustrations, the principle of separation of powers; of checks and balances between the executive, legislative, and judiciary; the separation of Church and State; and above all the assumption of popular sovereignty went far beyond what can be found in England or Canada. Parallely the crucial difference in the place of law and legal institutions in the political arena in the United States and in Britain, even though in both cases it was common law as against the civil law, which was predominant on the continent, can be seen in the principle of judicial review as developed since Marbury *vs*. Madison.

The distinctiveness of the basic premises of Israeli institutional structure, as distinguished from that of the different countries of origins of the various groups of immigrants or from their communal arrangements in the countries of their origin is almost self-evident, even if the latter have greatly influenced many concrete aspects of the former. Although many of the political institutions of Israel have derived from different European models, continental and English alike, and are influenced by the Jewish communal traditions, the basic premises and dynamics of Israeli political life differ from those of the European, or Middle Eastern, countries from which the population of Israel originated. Israeli political culture cannot be understood without taking into account the specific revolutionary-ideological orientations of the Zionist movement and the distinct ways in which the basic themes of Jewish civilization were transformed through the crystallization of this revolutionary orientation.

Both societies originated as constitutional democracies. In this they were unique among revolutionary or postrevolutionary societies, not only those like the USSR, China, or Vietnam in which totalitarian regimes were established by the revolution, but also from authoritarian regimes as developed in, for example, Mexico. They also differed greatly from those earlier revolutionary societies, like England and France, in which the full development and institutionalization of a constitutional democratic regime were much slower and, at least in the case of France, much more turbulent.

In both the United States and Israel the constitutional-democratic regimes were installed from their very beginning; and, unlike in many other "new nations" (it is important to recall here Lipset's description of the United States as the First New Nation), they have continued as such regimes against many odds.[10] The establishment and continuity of constitutional democracies in both these countries was to no small degree facilitated first by the fact that their respective revolutions or rebellions took the form of immigration to new countries and not the overthrow of and existing regime and social structure; and second by the decentralized, dispersed character of their colonization, so different from the colonization of Latin America, and to some extent also from that, for instance, of Australia.[11]

In both cases the democratic constitutional regimes developed some very specific and distinct characteristics. Most of these—like the separation of powers and the separation of Church and state in the United States and the consociational characteristic of the Israeli system, as well as the rather special place of the religious establishment in Israel—are specific to each country. But in both of them also one common or parallel characteristic developed, even if with different details—the special place of the rule of law or the courts—the Israeli aspect of which we analyzed in the preceding chapter.

Many of the reasons for such relative predominance of the High Court, especially in the last ten years or so, in Israel have been to some extent accidental, such as the weakening of the executive and the legislative branches, whereas in the United States the very structure of the separation of powers has enabled the continuous growth of the power of the Supreme Court. But to some extent the supremacy of the Supreme Court in Israel, as we saw in the preceding chapter, has deep historical roots in the Jewish political tradition, with some very interesting (though possibily paradoxical) parallels to the American case.

This parallelism is rooted first of all in that cultural orientation common to Jewish civilization and American Protestantism: the emphasis on the direct relationship of the individual with God and direct access to the center, without a strong mediator, priest or church. This orientation may easily give rise, as we have seen, to principled political, anarchic tendencies manifest in prophetic or sectarian activities. These tendencies also were reinforced by some parallel characteristics of the initial historical experience of the two societies: the decentralized, semisectarian aspect of their early settlement and the challenge to orderly government that this decentralization posed.

Like most other modern postrevolutionary societies, both countries have developed (i.e., in the direction of economic development) industrialization and growth as very crucial components of the national agenda. The general character of such development, the transition from farming, manufacture, and trade to industrialization, was common to both countries, although the differences in the concrete contours, tempo and scope of these developments were enormous, of course.

The United States and Israel also shared with most of the other colonizatory countries the fact that they started not from a "traditional" social and economic structure, but from relatively (relative to their time and space) modern ones, unencumbered by the weight of all traditional peasantry. Here they differed greatly from other revolutionary societies, as well as from most of the Third World and Latin America. Most important they shared the fact that the greater push to industrialization and economic development has taken place through processes of large-scale immigration, which brought into them populations whose social and cultural background, as well as whose orientation to a new country, differed greatly from those of the earlier pioneers.

In the United States of crucial importance in the development of the country was the great immigration of the late nineteenth century, mostly from Eastern Europe, of which the nucleus of the present day Jewish community, with its unique historical experience, was a part. In Israel the waves of immigrations that took place immediately after the establishment of the state of Israel, composed partially of survivors of the Holocaust and of the so-called "Oriental" groups (i.e., those coming from countries of the New and Middle East and of North Africa), constituted the crux of its immigration. In both cases the composition and above all the orientation of these new waves of immigrants was radically different from those of the Founding Fathers and, significantly enough, in both countries they were no longer called *pioneers* but *immigrants*—or *olim* but not *halutzim* in Israel.

The crux of the difference between these new arrivals and the pioneers was the weakness or absence of revolutionary ideological motivation and orientation characteristic of the earlier "pioneers." Instead most came in search for some mixture of economic improvement and security from political persecution and oppression this was the most important motive among large sectors of these new groups. In the immigration to Israel this motivation was also mixed, especially among the so-called Oriental groups, with strong traditional semi-Messianic aspirations.

In both countries the influx of these groups of immigrants greatly changed the whole composition of the population. This change challenged the basic institutional and symbolic framework of the society and its ability to incorporate those groups into the existing institutional framework, above all within the constitutional-demcratic framework. In both countries the initial response to this challenge was a very strong emphasis on "homogeneization," manifest in the ideology of the "Melting Pot" in the United States and on the "Ingathering of Exiles" in Israel, later giving rise to ethnic revolts and the gradual, but volatile, crystallization of different types of pluralism.[12]

Ideological Differences between the United States and Israel: Individualistic versus Collectivistic Orientation

In this section we analyze some of the crucial differences between the two societies. Such differences are basically of two kinds. First are the differences with respect to the similar characteristics analyzed above. Second are the major differences in size, geopolitical conditions, and historical experience.

The crucial differences between the United States, the Yishuv, and Israel with respect to their similar characteristics just analyzed lie in the content or orientation of their respective revolutionary pioneering ideologies, especially in the respective emphasis on individualism versus collectivitism and in different types of symbols of collective identity. One such crucial difference was that, whereas one of the strongest components of the American ethos, as it crystallized from the Puritan and other components of the English tradition and as it became transformed especially in the eighteenth century, was a strong emphasis on individualism. The major ideological orientation of the more active parts of the Zionist movement, was strongly collectivistic, to no small extent influenced by the revolutionary movements in Eastern and Central Europe at the end of the nineteenth century up to, and inclusive, the October Revolution. This latter orientation was most fully epitomized in the ideology of the labor sectors, in the Kibbutz, Moshav and the various enterprises of the Histadrut. Even in the so-called private sectors of the Yishuv the emphasis on private enterprise was not connected with strong principled individualistic orientations of the kind that developed in the colonies and in the United States.

The major difference between the United States and Israel, with respect to some basic components of their collective identities, lies in the relative importance of different basic components or symbols in the construction of their respective identities. In Israel there was, as we have seen, a very strong emphasis on common collective background and on the primordial elements, common territory, common history, common renewed language, and there developed only a minimal distinct political ideology as a basic component of this identity.

In the United States these primordial components were very weak and it was above all religious political ideology, transformed into what has been called the American civil religion, later epitomized in the "American way of life" that has become, as we have noted above, a predominant ideology, the core of its collective consciousness.

The primordial components of various ethnic groups could be accomodated much more easily within this framework, even if initially often encountering the opposition of the older established groups, especially the WASPs who saw themselves as the best suited to represent and promulgate the specific republican virtues appropriate for the specific American collective consciousness.

These basic differences in the content of their revolutionary ideological orientation had far-reaching implications for many aspects of institutional life, formations, and dynamics in the United States and in Israel. Pervasive in all arenas of American life is a basic individualistic political and social ideology, rooted in the English legal and political traditions and even more in the Protestant Puritan emphasis on the individual's direct access to God, strongly reinforced by the predominance of sectarian Protestant groups.[13] It has been manifest in the strong emphasis on economic achievement and success and in the sanctification of the rights of property. In the political field this individualistic component is present in the full acceptance of the pursuit of individual interests as a legitimate mode of social and political activity. The strength of this tendency is exhibited in some predominant social criticism, among others, prevalent in the United States today. Thus, for instance, such recent works as *Habits of the Heart,* and in a different mode in the work of such critics as Michael Walzer (both with strong relations to David Riesman's *Lonely Crowd*),[14] focus on the spiritual and social poverty of individualism caused by the weakening of the tradition of community inherent in the emphasis on the Convenant and in the various religious sects.

The starting point of Zionist ideology, especially but not only the Zionist labor one, in many ways has been the opposite of the American ideology; it was strongly collectivistic. This collectivism had several roots: such as some of the components of the Jewish Medieval public life, especially the strong emphasis on solidarity; the collective ideologies of many Eastern European revolutionary socialist movements that greatly influenced the Jewish ones; and also, in the strong sectarian characteristics of these groups. Traditionally, the emphasis on rights of the individual were weaker than in the American case; the collectivity, however defined, and its interests in different arenas had higher priority, even if in principle all individuals had autonomous access to the centers of the collectivity. The overall concept of social order or common good in most sectors of Israeli society, to use Rainer Baum's terms, was an ex-toto one, as against the ex-parte one prevalent in the United States.[15]

An interesting aspect of these differences between the United States and Israel can be found with respect to the fate of "liberal" parties and ideologies in both countries, as well as with respect to the conception of "individual" or "basic" rights. In both countries specific "liberal" parties and ideologies were very weak compared with Europe, but for different, in a way opposing, reasons.

In the United States no specific liberal parties or ideologies developed because, as Hartz has shown,[16] there was no conservative tradition with strong hierarchical and collectivistic orientations against which full-fledged liberal ideologies could develop, as was the case in Europe. From the very beginning, a liberal orientation was a major component of the political ethos of the United States, basically leaving no natural space for the development of a specifically liberal, or for that matter conservative, ideology or party.

In Israel throughout its history several political parties developed, like the various groups of General Zionists in the period of the Yishuv (who later became transformed, in Israel, into the Liberal Party), composed mostly of affluent private landowners and some smaller groups, and the Progressives, composed mostly of small professional groups and some intellectuals who portrayed themselves as liberals. Although these groups usually were members of the dominant coalitions led by the Labor Party they were of secondary importance in these coalitions, as well as later on in the Likkud Party that was created in the 1970s by partial amalgamation of Herut, the party created by Menahem Beigin in the beginning of the state, mainly from former members of Irgun Zvai Leumi and that constituted the major opposition to Labor Party dominated governments, the Liberals, and some other small groups.[17]

The reason for the weakness of the liberal parties or groups in Israel in a way is opposite to that which explains their absence in the United States. This reason was rooted in the predominance of the collectivistic orientations of the hegemonic ideology and in its institutional implications. True enough this ideological hegemony of the Labor Party and its stronghold over large sectors of the economy and the political arena has given rise to attempts by the different groups, such as the "private" sectors of the Yishuv and the "General Zionists," to forge their own space in the economic as well as the political arena. But the larger of these groups on the whole have stressed their varied economic interests and only to a much smaller extent liberal principles such as civic rights. Such principles of rights were secondary and became almost extinct in these groups, except for the smaller, liberal groups when the Liberal party joined Herut in creating the Likkud in the early 1970s.

Closely related to the fate of the liberal parties in the two countries, the relative importance of individualistic and collectivistic orientations is manifest in the conception of individual civil rights in their respective regimes. Whereas this concept of course is of central importance in the basic premises of the American political system, it is much weaker in Israel. Israeli constitutional-consociational democracy developed out of a certain modus vivendi among different sectors, most of them with strong collectivistic orientations, and was not based on strong individualistic assumptions. The ideological emphasis on individual rights has been limited to the "marginal" smaller parties composed of professional and intellectual groups, such as the "Progressive" Party in the earlier stage of the state, transformed later into Independent Liberals, or in the more recent period such groups as Shinui (Change) or Ratz (the List for the Rights of People).[18]

The impact of these small groups and their emphasis on individual rights on the overall prevalent ideology and institutional practice, at least until lately, was quite limited. Significantly, so was the support of the Labor Party for such movements, especially whenever such claims went against the Histadrut health insurance or other interests of the Histadrut sector, as well as against the more general totalistic "ex-toto" conception of the social order. Only with the disintegration of the institutional and ideological mold of Labor Zionism since the 1970s has the potential importance of these groups and the emphasis on individual and citizens' rights increased and become much more central in the public agenda, often promulgated by decisions of the Supreme Court.

These contrasting ideological emphases on individualistic or collectivistic orientations in Israel and in the United States have not been purely "ideological" or "academic." They have very important institutional implications, only some of which can be mentioned here.

One such institutional implication of the strong impact of strong collectivistic-egalitarian orientations and the ex-toto conception of the social order could be seen in the tendency of many sectors—labor, religious, and to some extent the private one—to arrange their internal affairs, including disciplinary ones, internally without recourse to outside, state, agencies. Only lately, with the growing emphasis on civil rights just mentioned, were these tendencies overruled by the courts. Right of access to the courts was assured to members of all cooperatives and collectives, leaving the courts to decide the scope of jurisdiction of the internal bodies of these various collectivities. On the national level this attitude was manifest particularly in matters of security. For a long time the claims of various state agencies (ministers, high officials, and above all the army and the security agencies) were simply accepted in the courts. Again only lately has this situation, to some extent at least, started to change.[19]

Closely related to the collectivistic orientations of major sectors of Israeli society has been the very strong consociational component in the structure of Israeli democracy, and the concomitant strong organizational and ideological boundaries of the major parties and sectors in the period of the Yishuv and the early period of the state. This was true of labor and the religious and the private sectors, in the period of the Yishuv and in the first two decades of the state of Israel, and labor, different religious sectors, and the Likkud in the contemporary period—in sharp contrast to the very loose organization and dispersed federal character of such parties in the United States.

Yet another crucial implication is to be found in the differences between the basic formats of political economy of the two countries. In contrast to the United States's highly competitive, aggressive, and individualistic economy, emphasizing private property and market competition, the Israeli political economy has been characterized, as we have seen, by a high degree of centralization, regulation by the state, widespread public (mostly within the labor sector) ownership of major enterprises, and by generally strong collectivistic policies.[20] These differences between the individualistic orientations predominant in the United States and the collectivistic predominant in Israel also, as we shall see in somewhat greater detail later, had an impact on the development of policies of affirmative action in these two societies.

Ideological Differentiation between the United States and Israel: Primordial, Historical, and Religious Components in the Construction of Collective Identity

The second major set of differences in the respective ideological orientations of the United States and Israel can be identified with the construction of the major components of collective identity and its institutional derivatives in these two societies; especially in the place of primordiality, territory, history, language, peoplehood, and religion. These various components, as we have seen, were very weak in the United States, where its political ideology is derived from religious roots and crystallized in what has been designated civil religion. Not only has the United States had a relatively short history, the historical dimension was very weak in its collective consciousness, as was any attachment to territory. This had a profound influence on the incorporation of different ethnic groups, and perhaps especially the Jews into American society.[21]

The case in the Yishuv and Israel was almost the opposite; the religious, the primordial, historical, and territorial components were very closely interwoven from the very beginning. Most sectors of the Zionist movement did not deny these components and their interrelation; rather they aimed at their reinterpretation and reconstruction.

Accordingly, as we have seen, a unique cultural mold developed in the Yishuv, based on continuous reconstruction of the major dimensions of Jewish national-religious tradition and its relation to general cultural values. This mold was characterized by relatively great heterogeneity but based, in principle, on the basic tenets of the Zionist vision. Within this format a special combination of tradition and modernity minimized, at least initially, the rift found later among many new nations, based on far-reaching compromises with the religious groups. Within this framework a very special arrangement developed, as we have seen, with respect to religious question, the place of religious symbols, traditions, and the specifically religious sectors in the overall framework of the Yishuv and the Israeli society.

The differences in the place of religion in the collective symbolism and institutional structure of the two societies are of special importance for understanding some of the major tensions and turbulences that lately have been taking place in Israel as well as in the United States with respect to their respective "fundamentalist" movements. Protestant fundamentalism, an important force in the United States history in the late nineteenth and early twentieth centuries, has burgeoned again and again in the United States. Though it is oriented against many of the accepted precepts and premises of the American ethos, it usually presents itself as set entirely within the framework of the basic symbols and institutions of the American republic and Constitution. With respect to some aspects of the relations between state and Religion, especially school prayer and school curricula, these groups claimed to provide the proper interpretation of the Constitution, appealing to courts and on the whole seeming to accept, if not the verdicts of the courts, at least their legitimacy. Moreover, none of the American Protestant fundamentalists have attempted to infuse any special primordial orientations into their activities and ideologies. Their activity and orientation was set within the framework of the basic political-religious-ideological symbols of American collective identity.[22] The situation has been entirely different in Israel. Here two main religious fundamentalist trends, with many subtrends, have become very forceful with the disintegration of the Labor Party mold. The first are the ultranationalist Zionist groups epitomized in the Gush Emunim. The second, which seems to be gaining the upper hand among the Orthodox, is the anti- or non-Zionist ultraorthodox. Common to both are challenges to the basic symbolic premises of the state of Israel.[23] Both have aimed at the reconstruction of relations between the primordial, historical, and religious components of Jewish collective identity, beyond the Zionist mold. Common to both of these movements was the doubtful acceptance of legitimacy of the major organs and institutions of the state—but for opposite reasons, in the case of Gush Emunim (the "Block of the Faithful") such partial acceptance was rooted in the full acceptance of the Zionist vision, and through imbuing the Zionist vision with a full Messianic legitimacy. This was evident in the emphasis on the supremacy of a higher law, in this case a law they proclaimed that stressed the sanctity of Eretz Israel, as against the law of land; that is, against any political compromise with respect to the West Bank, Judea, and Samaria, which would deny as it were the sanctity of the contemporary era. Second, among them is an emphasis, in many ways a weaker one, on the sanctity of the Halakhah. In the case of the non-Zionist orthodox, the nonacceptance of the legitimacy of the state and its institutions, including the chief rabbinate, is based on the anti-Zionist or a-Zionist premises, by seeing their existence in Eretz Israel as existence in the "spiritual Galuth, Exile." Most of them have accepted the existence of the state at most in a de facto manner. Their attitude to the state is purely instrumental, attempting to receive as many resources from state agencies as possible without however granting them any basic legitimacy. In many, especially the more extreme, sectors of the non-Zionist or a-Zionist religious groups, as we have seen, there also is a strong tendency not to have recourse to the courts of the state, although recently some of these groups have used these courts in their internal quarrels; however this has lately changed a bit.

The combination of strong primordial components in the symbols of collective identity, together with the strong collectivistic orientations prevalent in Israeli society, also had very interesting repercussions on some aspects of the development of the "ethnic" problem in the two societies. In both societies the ethnic problem erupted in about the same period, from about the early or mid-1960s. In both societies it was connected with the decomposition of the earlier "homogeneizing" mold, although in the United States the original ideological mold itself had changed greatly by the Jacksonian era. But the ethnic problem became central in the United States about a century after the Civil War and about seven to eight decades after the beginning of mass immigration.

Some reasons for this eruption, such as protest against the economic and educational "gaps," against discrimination—protests promulgated especially by the socially and economically more mobile sectors of the ethnic groups, sometimes in coalition with more social leaders of the poverty stricken sectors—to some extent were similar, although never as extensive in Israel as in the United States. In both societies also far-reaching affirmative action policies developed; significantly enough, as we shall see shortly, such policies were initiated in Israel before the periods of ethnic upheaval and there was much less controversy around them than in the United States. Yet beyond all these common features some very important differences developed in the general orientation of the ethnic movements in the two countries.

The crux of these differences in the orientations of the ethnic groups in the two countries was the way in which the demands for inclusion, above all the symbolic inclusion of their ethnicity, developed. There were many similarities, but also some very important differences in their overall orientations.

In the United States most ethnic groups, including the Jews, aimed at the carving out broader living spaces, within the broad American framework, for their ethnic traditions and symbols, and for the legitimation or the affirmation of their ethnic activities and organizations in the public arena. Many of the struggles of these groups, especially of the Blacks, focused on the full legal equality within the American framework, and they were greatly supported, as in the civil rights movements in the 1960s, by many sectors of "White" majority population. These struggles, as those of the Jews against antisemitism, were undertaken in the name of general American values, of the basic premises of the American civilization. Significantly enough, when Martin Luther King was "canonized" by having a special day devoted to his memory, such canonization was made in the basic framework of the American civil religion. Moreover, such canonization was legitimized in terms of his contribution to the promulgation of, and struggle for, the general premises of civil equality of the United States.

Most of these groups did not challenge the basic symbols and institutional framework of the United States; although, needless to say, their very success changed the general ambience of this framework. Only the more extreme elements, for instance the Black Panthers, wanted to subvert that framework.

More recently a separatist movement developed among some sectors of the Blacks and to a smaller extent among the Hispanics. One markedly separatist tendency is to create an Afro-American, or to a lesser extent a Hispanic, culture, which could be distinct from the Western culture predominant in the United States. Colleges and universities, and the entertainment media, have become the major arenas in which these tendencies were promulgated and in which attempts at their institutionalization developed. Among some of the Hispanic groups growing demands also developed both for the extension of the use of the Spanish language as a medium in schools and public offices—demands often accepted by the authorities—up to, until now unsuccessful, attempts to declare Spanish an official language of several states.

At the same time, especially during the 1980s, far-reaching alienation developed in wide sectors of the underclass, composed mostly of Blacks and to some extent Hispanics (the latter being of much more recent origin) from the mainstream of life in the United States, reinforcing separatist tendencies among these groups. However, most of the other ethnic groups accepted the given framework, the basic components of the American way of life, with its de-emphasis of primordial components, which therefore could allow wide spaces for the primordial symbols of the different ethnic groups.[24]

In Israel the different "ethnic" especially "Oriental" groups also wanted to obtain for themselves wider living space. But beyond this the crux of the demands of the ethnic groups aimed at the inclusion into the center of themselves, their representatives, and the primordial or historical symbols of their distinct collectivities, their distinct traditions that were continuously reconstructed in Israel under the impact of the processes of absorption and incorporation into Israeli society. In Israel the quest developed for participation, "real" and symbolic, in the center, for incorporation of some of their distinct collective symbols into the overall ones of Israel, this was crucial here: a quest rooted in the strong national ethos and in the successful socialization of the various ethnic groups in this ethos. Thus, for instance, one of the central demands of the small groups of Black Panthers, that developed in Israel in the early 1970s was for being recruited, taken into the Army. Exclusion from the Army, due to their relatively low educational achievement or delinquent or semicriminal records, was seen not as a relief from an onerous and illegitimate demand, as in some groups in the United States during the Vietnam War, but as exclusion from the society.

One of the most interesting aspects of this demand for inclusion in the center were the quite successful attempts to make national some of the ethnic festivals, for instance the "Mimuna" of the Moroccans, which initially developed, in a highly reconstructed form as separatist festivals; as national festivals, they weould include participation by the President, Prime Minister, and various notables. A parallel development took place with respect to some of the cults of the Saints brought over, especially from North Africa, and reconstructed in Israel. The days of some of these festivals became official elective vacation days. Such symbolic inclusion denoted, however, far-reaching reconstruction of the basic national symbols, above all far-reaching weakening of the older revolutionary-ideological pioneering orientation but not of the overall national ones.[25] In the United States, the only case until now in which an "ethnic" or minority symbol became incorporated into the general collective pantheon, was Martin Luther King Day, which denoted not some distinct ethnic element—from among all the ethnic groups the Blacks were in many ways the "least ethnic" group in the United States—but the reaffirmation of the general American values that were subverted by the exclusion of the blame from the major sector of the American society.

It is only lately that the emphasis on multiculturalism, the derogation of Western culture, the promulgation of 'pollitically correct' stances that spread in many academic and some educational sectors in the United States seem to signal not only attempts to carve out new spaces for different cultural traditions but also potential deligitimation of many of the basic premises of American collective identity. These tendencies may perhaps be reinforced by the continuously growing proportions of non-white—black, Hispanic, Asian—groups in the population of the United States.

Some interesting differences developed, as we have mentioned briefly, also between the United States and Israel in the development of affirmative action policies. These policies were in much greater consonance with the more collectivistic orientation, with a concomitant emphasis on equality of outcome, than with the American individualist orientations and emphasis on equality of opportunity.

In the Yishuv and in the early years of development of the state, the assumption of equality of outcome to some extent was realized by the sectorial consociational characteristics of the political system. The influx of new, especially the so-called "Oriental" immigrants, generated the problem of the educational and occupational gaps between them and the, mostly Ashekenazi, inhabitants. The various strong affirmative action policies that aimed at equalization of outcome, developed with relatively less public controversy than in the United States.

The different place of religion in the symbolic and institutional structure of the two societies highlight some interesting differences with respect to the place of the legal institutions in the political arena. As Israel has no constitution (or bill of rights) and the Knesset exercises full sovereignty, the Israeli Supreme Court has no right of constitutional revision; any of its decisions, in principle, can be overturned by the Knesset. In a rather paradoxical way, this may increase the power of the High Court: there is no constitution limiting what may seem a far-reaching constitutional interpretation by the Court. Thus, for instance, when the U. S. Supreme Court lately upheld rights such as freedom of expression, as derived from the Declaration of Independence.

But perhaps the most important difference between the United States and Israel has been the attitude of the orthodox sectors to the High Court, and the relations between the different rabbinical courts and the Supreme Court. The crux of this difference, as mentioned briefly in the preceding chapter, is that for large parts of the orthodox sector, the Israeli Supreme Court lacks that ultimate legitimacy which is the very epitome of the unique standing of the Supreme Court in the United States.

It is not only that, for large and probably continuously increasing religious sectors, the Supreme Court, being part of the secular institutional Jewish state, lacks any legitimacy beyond technical legitimacy or that some of the most extreme orthodox groups would not take recourse to the state courts. Concomitantly some problems developed in the relations between the High Supreme Court and the rabbinical courts. Probably of greater importance is that, for many religious groups, the Supreme Court does not uphold that law which in the Halakhah they would like to see as the basic framework of public life in Israel—and without which the state cannot be regarded by them as a truly Jewish state.

In principle rabbinical courts, including the high rabbinical court, are to some extent under the Supreme Court. True enough, in the more formal sense, decisions of the rabbinical court cannot be appealed and revised by the Supreme Court. But the Supreme Court can decide the limits of competency for rabbinical courts, and it also can intervene in the decisions of the rabbinical courts if those seem to contravene principles of "natural justice." Whereas in some matters, such as marriage or divorce, this may not bother large sectors of the religious groups; the picture may become much more complicated when the Supreme Court declares—as its President, Justice Shamgar, has done in 1988—that it may even declare that the true boundaries of validity of the Halakhah are to be defined by the Supreme Court.

Thus, contrary to the situation in the United States, the basic cultural or civilizational premises that are related to the supremacy of the Supreme Court in the political arena may generate in Israel a potential focus of tensions between different interpretations of the higher law. This may lead even to attempts to delegitimize at least some decisions of the High Court by different religious sectors, sometimes, even if in a muted way, by the chief rabbinate. Although such active attempts were weak, on the whole, they increased recently and the potential for their eruption is always there.

Differences between the United States and Israel: Size, Political Ecology, and International Relations

Some very important differences between the United States and Israel can be identified not only with respect to their basic revolutionary ideological orientations, however. Of no small importance are the basic differences in historical and geopolitical experiences, as well as, of course, in the relative size of the countries, the populations, and the economic structure already mentioned.

The differences in size and population and some of their "natural" implication for the relative strength and wealth of these two countries are obvious. But some other implications of these differences need an explication. The most important of these are related to some of the basic characteristics of modern small societies: especially their dependence on external markets and arenas of activity, their strong outside orientation, and the impact of this dependence and orientation on patterns of institutional and cultural creativity.[26]

It above all is with respect to this outside orientation that some of the major differences between the United States and Israel stand out. However strong its exposure to outside influence, especially to academic or cultural ones among some elite groups, the United States usually has been characterized by a very strong inner centeredness, in which the orientation to the outside did not constitute a basic ideological reference point. The American way of life was often perceived as the natural one, in principle suitable for the entire world. The scope of economic dependence on external markets was even smaller, closely related also to the relative isolation of the United States.

In Israel the orientation to outside markets was a continuous component of its basic orientation, even if in constant tension with the more inward ones, and its dependence on various external markets—economic and cultural, be they the various Jewish communities abroad or the international academic and professional communities—was a continuous one.

Yet another crucial difference between the two societies lies in their different political-ecological situations. The United States, from the colonial period until at least the First World War, developed in relative isolation from the main currents and settings of international politics of its time—and also tried, as evident in the Monroe doctrine, to isolate itself from these currents. Such isolation, as well as the relative underdevelopment in that period of the media of communication, enabled the colonists and later the United States government to pursue policies of expansion in their immediate enviornment in relative peace, without drawing too much attention from the international community.[27]

The situation of the Yishuv and the state of Israel, of course, was totally different. From the very beginning the Yishuv and Israel developed in a very volatile internal and international environment, reminiscent in many ways of the situation in the period of the First and Second Temples.[28]

The internal setting, both early and contemporary, was that of Eretz Israel, of repeated encounters with other settled and migratory peoples. The macro setting was that of Eretz Israel or Palestine at the crossroads of great empires of antiquity. The net results of this volatility were the continuous fluidity and openness of political boundaries, and continuous struggles around them; the constant flow and mobility of people; and difficulties in the maintenance of a stable, compact political identity and a distinct cultural identity. The most important single effect of different political ecological settings of the United States and the Yishuv and Israeli society could be seen in their relation with the indigenous population the settlers found in the new or old-new land: the American Indians in America and the Arabs in Palestine.

First of all was the great numerical differences: the much smaller number of the Indians and their relative territorial dispersion, as against the much greater, absolute and especially relative, number of the Arabs, concentrated in a much smaller territory and part of a much larger population of the various Arab provinces (of the Ottoman Empire and later Arab states). These numerical differences were reinforced by the differences in the international geopolitical situation of the two societies. The relative isolation of the United States and the absence of an international communication media made the dealings of the settlers with the Indians in a sense invisible: a purely internal, seemingly marginal affair. The location of Palestine and Israel were at the crossroads of empires in a period of modern newspapers, radio, and television made the Jewish-Arab conflict a continuous international concern.

These basic geopolitical facts had crucial repercussions on the institutional dynamics of Israeli society. One such repercussion, in marked contrast to the American case, was the centrality of security in Israeli life already discussed. Another important repercussion of the combination of the political-ecological condition of a small society and of the primordial-national and historical revolutionary-ideologic orientations of the Zionist movement was that the problems related to the construction of symbols and boundaries of the new emerging collectivity constituted a continuous focus of potential ideological and political struggle and contention. The potential for such struggle existed, as we have seen, from the very beginning of the Zionist movement, especially in its relation to the Jewish historical and religious heritage and the relative importance of different historical religious, territorial components of that heritage. The continuous ambivalent relations between the Zionist movement and various religious groups already have been discussed. Unlike in the United States, where the construction of a civil religion together with the separation of Church and State created relatively firm symbols and boundaries of collective identity and a basic institutional framework of state-church relations, no such firm symbolic and institutional framework developed in Israel.

But such a situation developed not only with respect to the religious components of collective identity. In varying degrees in different historical periods, the same was true in the relations between the universalistic and particularistic orientations of the collectivity. The problems related to the place of these components in the construction of Israeli collective identity surfaced anew, as we have seen, after the Six-Day War and continue to be in the very forefront of political struggles in Israel.

This continuous struggle around the construction of the symbolical, as well as territorial, boundaries of the community is related to more than the central place of tradition in the construction of Israeli society. The relations to the Middle Eastern environment constitute another focus of ideological and political struggle around the construction of such boundaries, far beyond the direct or even indirect security problems. The return to the new-old land in the Middle East was seen as an act of great historical significance, as was integration into the Middle East. The nature of this integration constituted a focus of potential ideological and political struggle, which was to erupt in periods of intensive confrontation with the neighboring Arab national movement or movements within the Arab states and with the Arabs in the Western Bank.

Closely related to the different political-ecological conditions of the two societies has been the different historical timing of their development and of respective historical experiences. One such difference is seemingly purely chronological: that the American colonies started to develop from the sixteenth century on whereas Zionist settlement in Eretz Israel began in the late nineteenth century and its full development took place in the twentieth century. However, this chronological difference, when closely connected with differences in the respective historical experience of the two societies, had many crucial implications for the nature of the respective historical experience of the two societies.

The settlement in Eretz Israel and the state of Israel developed in a period of much more intensive technological and economic development and the expansion and competition among various ideological-socialist, nationalist ideologies and movements than was the case in the American colonies and the United States. Closely connected with these differences were those in communication technology already alluded to; and these put the occurrences in Israel in continuous full view of the international media.

The American and the Israeli experiences are distinguished not only by differences in the chronological timing of their respective development. Of no smaller importance is the difference in the span of time in which such development took place. All the various processes common to both societies—such as economic development and industrialization, the disintegration of the initial revolutionary mold, influx of new immigrants, and the emergence of the ethic problem—developed in Israel in at most about 60 or 70 years, as opposed to 200 or 300 years in the United States.

These differences in the geopolitical dimension of the respective historical experience of the United States and Israel can be summarized in a short, and necesarily simplified, way: by saying that the Israeli historical experience has been consdensed in a much smaller space, but one burdened by very strong historical memories and consciousness—and in a much shorter period of time.

The major implication of this is that all these processes were much more intensive in Israel than in the United States. This intensity, which could be discerned easily in all the waves of life in Israel in the mentality of Israelis, of course, was greatly magnified by the smallness of the society and by its geopolitical situation and its derivatives, discussed earlier. The major impact of these differences was that, although the two societies shared many similar processes and problems, in Israel these processes have become compressed not only in space, thus always having much greater impact on the center than in the United States, but also in time, giving rise to a generally much greater intensity of expression of concern with public affairs in Israel, just as the larger space of purely private concerns and interests in the United States than in Israel gives rise to a higher level of volatility in political life and institutional dynamics in Israel.

9

Concluding Observations: The Jewish Experience in the Modern and Contemporary Eras

The Two Poles: The Holocaust and the Heterogeneity of Jewish Experience

In the preceding chapters which constituted the second part of this book, we explored several aspects of the modern Jewish historical experience: the different modes of incorporation of Jewish communities into modern societies, the major aspects of Jewish national movements, especially of the Zionist one; and some of the most salient characteristics of Israeli society. In all these explorations we addressed ourselves first to the question to what extent these modes of historical experience differed from those of similar communities or societies: from other religious or national communities or minorities, other national movements, and other ideological-revolutionary or settlers' societies. Second, we addressed ourselves to the problem to what extent such differences, if they indeed can be identified, can be attributed to the specific Jewish civilizational and historical experience, the major features of which we analyzed in the first part of the book.

Beyond these questions looms an additional basic one, about the possible fate or fortunes of the Jewish civilization. This civilization was one of the first Axial Age civilizations, the basic premises of which were couched primarily in religious terms in the post-Axial, or "postmodern," Age, an age in which civilizational premises no longer are coterminous with religious formulations, or visions, and in which also the primordial and historical components of collective identities have become transformed in far-reaching ways.

Two specific, seemingly contradictory, features of the modern Jewish experience stand out immediately. The first is the terrible and tragic experience of the Holocaust. However much some of the concrete aspects of the Holocaust can be compared to other atrocities, all such comparisons, the claims of the various (especially German) revisionist historians notwith-standing, not only are limited but basically misleading. They are misleading because the basic premise of the Holocaust was unique in the annals of humanity. It was not "only" a massacre of one people by another in war, as a result of religious persecution or even, as in the case of Armenians or Gyp-sies, an attempt at genocide of an alien minority; it was the conscious, planned attempt, based on an ideological, fully articulated premises at the extermination of one single national-religious group. The Holocaust was the only attempt to exterminate a whole nation, an entire people on the basis of a fully articulated ideology that has put this collectivity beyond the boundaries of humanity.[1]

Although the crystallization and implementation of this ideology is a basically modern phenomenon, the roots are to be found in the interciviliza-tional aspect of the Jewish historical experience, in the earlier interciviliza-tional relations between Jews and their hosts, especially Christian civiliza-tion, and their transformation in the modern period. The Holocaust thus can be seen as the tragic culmination of the components of hostility in the inter-civilizational relations between the Jews and their host civilizations, espe-cially the Christian one.

Also only in terms of this historical experience, albeit of its different aspects, can the other, constructive specific feature of the modern Jewish experience be understood; namely, the great profusion and heterogeneity of the concrete modes of the forms of collective life that developed among them in this period, a multiplicity and heterogeneity which went far beyond what could be found in the Medieval period.

This heterogeneity and profusion went far beyond what could have been found in the Medieval period of Jewish history. In that period such het-erogeneity was manifest in different customs, different modes of communal organization and different patterns of cultural identity; but most of them were set within the common framework of the halakhic mold. In the Medieval period this heterogeneity also developed within the framework of the specific intercivilizational setting shaped by the historical-religious rela-tions among the Jewish, Christian, and Muslim civilizations.

All these conditions have changed greatly in the modern and in the contemporary eras. The halakhic mold lost its hegemonic standing among the Jews, and no single hegemonic mold developed. The various components and themes of Jewish civilization were continuously reconstructed in differ-ent ways in different Jewish communities; and in none of them were they connected unequivocally with clear prescriptions of behavior and communal organizations.

At the same time the relations of the various Jewish communities with their host civilizations greatly changed in line with the changes in the basic premises of the Western civilizations. These changes opened the gates of Western civilization before the Jews, creating two possibilities that did not exist in the Medieval period: the first was that of entirely new modes of incorporation of Jews into the host societies, and the second was their total rejection by these societies, a rejection that culminated in the Holocaust.

Insofar as the possibilities of incorporation of Jews in modern societies became actualized, they necessarily increased the heterogeneity of Jewish life far beyond not only what existed in the Medieval period but also in the period of the Second Commonwealth. This heterogeneity was reinforced by the fact that different Jewish communities were undergoing different historical experiences. These experiences to a very large extent were shaped by those of their host societies. Given the changing relations between the Jews and these societies, these different historical experiences influenced not only the physical fate of Jews but also their specifically Jewish social and cultural activities and the modes of reconstruction of Jewish life that developed within them. The weakening on the contemporary scene of the classic European nation-state with its strong emphasis on the historical and primordial components of collective consciousness and identity necessarily added new dimensions to the heterogeneity of contemporary Jewish life. The weakening of these historical primordial components in the connection of the collective consciousness of many in Western society, both in the United States and lately also in Europe, also has posed new challenges for the reconstruction of Jewish life. It opened up the possibility both of the reaffirmation of Jewish collective consciousness and cultural and social activities and the continuous weakening of such consciousness.

Through the examination of this profusion and heterogeneity, with the tragic experience of the Holocaust looming prominently in the background, the questions about the distinctiveness of the Jewish modern experience and the fate of the Jewish civilization in the modern and so-called postmodern age can be approached.

The analyses presented in the preceding chapters have painted a rather complicated picture of the relations between the different Jewish communities and the modern societies into which they were incorporated. These analyses have emphasized the very strong impact of the host societies on the different modes of incorporation of the Jewish communities into these societies, with all the attendant tensions between them, and on the patterns of Jewish life and activities within these societies.

Yet at the same time within almost all the Jewish communities some distinct features developed that distinguished them from other similar, religious or ethnic, minorities or collectivities and that were common to most, probably all, the different Jewish communities. One such distinctive feature was the attempts, promulgated above all by various intellectuals and influentials, to imbue at least some of their ways of life, some of the cultural or institutional activities that developed in all these communities, with some of the broader themes of Jewish civilization; to reconstruct anew some of the components of Jewish identity and some of the themes that crystallized and became continuously reconstructed throughout the Ancient and Medieval periods.

The second distinctive feature of the modern Jewish experience was indeed the continuity of mutual relations, mutual reference, and foci of common interest that developed among the various Jewish communities of the different Diasporas and later on between them and the state of Israel. These relations focused on problems of collective Jewish existence, of mutual help among Jewish communities, as well as the different ways of reconstructing, in the modern and postmodern eras, the various Jewish civilization themes.

The third, perhaps the most new, specific feature of the modern Jewish historical experience, in contrast to the situation in the Middle Ages, was that different sectors of Jewish communities seemingly could choose which components of Jewish identity and themes of Jewish civilization to emphasize and which to shed; thus, in a sense posing the question as to what, if anything, may be seen as the minimal core of Jewish collective identity, culture, and civilizational vision, and how would these fare in the modern or in the so-called postmodern era.

The Major Modes of Jewish Experience in the Modern Diaspora

These characteristics of the modern Jewish historical experience have developed from the beginning of the modern era with the processes of incorporation of Jews into modern Western societies, but their concrete manifestation have differed greatly in different periods and in different countries. Beyond the manifold local variations, to some, but only some, of which we have briefly alluded, more general periods and types of the incorporation of Jews into modern societies can be distinguished in very broad, necessarily simplified terms.

The first type developed in Western and later in Central and Eastern Europe from the eighteenth century on. It focused around the possibility of incorporation of Jewish communities within the newly emerging European nation-states. These nation-states were constructed, as we have seen, with a very strong emphasis on universal citizenship set in the framework of relatively homogeneous national communities within which strong primordial national components of their collective identity were important, but often in tension with the civil and universalistic components of such identity.

Within this framework the Jews, in Western and Central Europe, were first called upon to transform themselves into a purely religious community.

The direction of their subsequent development was assumed to move between some type of assimilation or survival and adaptation as a religious community, whether as a new type of liberal or "reformed" one, or as an orthodox, or neo-orthodox, community living already within a basically modern, hence in principle nonreligious (in the traditional sense), environment.

We have seen that the process of incorporation of Jews into Western and Central European societies belied, in fact, these assumptions, but these assumptions constituted for a long time the major poles ideological discourse about Jewish fate in Western European societies. Even those movements, especially the "older" orthodox camp in Eastern Europe, as well as various nationalist Jewish movements, especially the Zionist one, that opposed these assumptions and that denied the possibility of assimilation, or of the Jews becoming a purely religious community, were greatly influenced by them. Their very opposition was often couched in terms of these basic assumptions.

In Eastern Europe above all orthodoxy of the "older" type fought for the possibility of continuing to exist within modern settings without seemingly giving up the mold of the Halakhah; and the various types of Jewish national movements developed. But even here the orthodox sectors did change radically, and one of the most interesting developments within Jewish communities in Eastern and Central Europe in the nineteenth century was the restructuring and transformation of orthodoxy.

In principle these orthodox groups upheld not only the importance of observing all the halakhic injunctions, as was the case with the Western neo-orthodoxy, but also the overall "Medieval" halakhic mold with its basic conception of Jewish history and civilization. Yet in fact they already had gone beyond the assumption of the Medieval mold in at least two ways. First, in common with the Western European neo-orthodoxy, they accepted the existence in the Galut, and not only as a given "temporary" fact to which one had to adjust. They had started to participate in it, especially through the distinct political organizations and parties.

Second, as the orthodox sectors lost their hegemony in the Jewish communities, they consequently became more and more militant, "conservative," semifundamentalist, loosing many of the broader civilizational orientations of Medieval Judaism and moving more and more in a sectarian direction. They entered into continuous ideological confrontation with the other camps in Jewish communities: first of all with liberal and reform Judaism, with the various secular assimilationist tendencies, and later on with various national movements.

The various national movements that developed among the Jewish communities, especially in Eastern Europe, also were greatly influenced by the premises of assimilation. Above all they shared with the assimilationists the orientation to the present, to the reconstruction of Jewish life in the present, as well as many secular orientations. At the same time these movements also, as we have seen, evinced some specific characteristics that distinguished them from other nationalities or national minorities or movements in Central and Eastern Europe, the most important of the characteristics, as was also the case with the more assimilated Jews, were the strong relations with other Jewish communities, the common concerns about the reconstruction of Jewish life and Jewish civilizational themes, and the fact of constituting continuous mutual reference groups.

In Eastern and Central Europe the question of ultimate viability of all these different modes of Jewish existence in Diaspora was nullified by the Holocaust, but some of these directions of development, as well as the problems raised by them, were transformed later on, after the Second World War. All the same, the experience of the Holocaust constituted a reminder of yet another terrible possibility.

The second major type of incorporation of Jews into modern societies developed in the United States, which has been constructed, not as a European-type nation-state but as an ideological political community. The distinct characteristics of American civilization, as we have seen, greatly influenced the mode of incorporation of Jews within it, giving rise to an entirely new pattern of Jewish modern historical experience, and to distinct ways of reconstructing some of the major themes of Jewish civilization.

Both in Europe and the United States, the incorporation of the Jewish minorities in the host societies hinged on the extent or scope of what has been the usually designated as the type of pluralism that developed within them, but the nature of such pluralism differed greatly in different modern societies. It differed above all according to the relative importance of primordial elements in the construction of their collective identities.

In all modern European societies the primordial components of such identity, continuously reconstructed in such modern terms as nationalism and ethnicity, were continuously confronted with modern universalistic and civil components. The mode of interweaving these different components of collective identity greatly shaped the nature of pluralism that developed in the societies and their impact on the mode of incorporation of Jews.

Insofar as the primordial components were subsumed relatively successfully under the civil and universalistic ones and all were "peacefully" interwoven in the construction of their respective collective identities, as was the case at least to some extent in England, Holland, and the Scandinavian countries, these societies could allow a relatively wide scope for Jewish integration, but at the price of negating or weakening the primordial components in the Jewish experience.

In those societies or sectors within which strong tensions developed between the primordial and the civil universalistic components in the construction of the collective identities of the modern nation-state, as above all in Germany and in many social movements in Western Europe and other countries of Central Europe, the impact on Jewish experience went in a different direction. The tension between the primordial, civil, and universalistic components in the construction of their collective identity gave rise in these societies and movements to strong and negative emphasis on the centrality of the primordial components in Jewish collective identity. This emphasis became closely connected with principled denial of the possibility of any incorporation of Jews into the modern nation-state. These tendencies, as we have seen, ultimately led to the Holocaust.

In Eastern Europe, with its multinational empires or states, these primordial components were not necessarily denied; but the acceptance of the primordial components of Jewish identity did not necessarily facilitate the incorporation of Jews into these polities. Such acceptance also could lead to a denial of the possibility of incorporation of Jews into these polities, whether on traditional grounds, in traditional antisemitic terms, in terms of modern antisemitism, or in some mixture of the two.

The pluralism that developed in the United States from the very beginning was based on the minimization of the primordial components in the construction of American collective identity. Hence, as we have seen in most periods of Jewish American history, the primordial component of the Jewish collective identity was never fully denied. True enough, for a very long period, although chronologically its beginnings antedated the European one, the American Jewish experience was perceived by most Jewish communities, including many sectors of the American Jewish community, as basically secondary and derivative to the modern European one. Only after the Second World War, after the Holocaust and with the continuous weakening, but certainly not obliteration, of the premise of the European nation-state, did the American Jewish experience become more paradigmatic among Jewish communities in the Diaspora.

Also after the Second World War another type of Jewish historical experience became very central. Hitherto it had seemed rather dormant on the scene of modern Jewish history, although very active within its own framework. This was the so-called Oriental Jewry.[2] We have analyzed, in Chapter 3, some of the distinct characteristics of this Jewry from about the end of the eighteenth century.

We emphasized that modernization came to these Jews from the outside, as part of European expansion and usually under the aegis of colonial or semicolonial rule. Closely connected with this can be that the secular dimension of modernity was rather weak in most of these countries, with the exception of Kemalist Turkey, and did not become a crucial component in the construction of their modern national-political identities.

The ideology of European Enlightenment at most was of secondary importance among them. Within the framework of the basic traditional, Islamic premises of the Ottoman Empire, as well as those of the colonial situation, there was no special stimulus for the development of such religious movements as the reform or liberal ones. The traditional Sephardi rabbinate and community organizations prevailed, but lost much of their authority to the more modern or secular ways of life, without at the same time facing any new and powerful ideological challenge either in religious, liberal, or national terms.

Hence, as we have seen, no movement of religious reform or very strong secular or semisecular national movements developed there and concomitantly no militant modern orthodoxy developed there. No attempts were made to reconstruct Jewish religious life in a new, modern "nonorthodox" way; and, with the partial exception of some sectors of North African society, no ideological attempt was made at incorporation into the existing colonial sector.

We have seen that, on the whole, here also no demands were made on Jews to give up the collective or primordial components of their identity. The existence of such components mostly was taken for granted, except in the secular Kemalist Turkey or in the assimilationist French sectors of North Africa. Hence, although some sectors of the Jewish communities continued in their traditional ways of life, others, often members of the same communities or even families, could easily slide away from such traditional framework, into more assimilation ways, without the necessity to give up, in a principled ideological way, their attachment to Jewish collective life, although they easily could drift away from it.

Yet both the traditional and the more modern sectors often could encounter the religious hostility of the traditional sectors and the political-religious one of modern national movements or semisecular regimes. Such hostility would grow with the permeation of the Zionist movement into these communities, and later on with the establishment of the state of Israel.

After the Second World War large parts of these communities immigrated to Israel, France, and America, especially North America (the United States and Canada). In Israel, as we have seen, they had a very strong impact on the processes of transformation of Israeli society.

Those who immigrated to Europe, especially to France, and America, especially North America, developed new and very variegated patterns of Jewish life. Some became closely related, especially in France, with various sectors of French intelligentsia. Others, perhaps most of them, developed patterns of life that combined participation in economic and professional arenas with development of active Jewish communal and political activities.

These latter patterns in many ways were similar to those that developed in large sectors of American Jewry; but they lacked the specific "civilizational" dimension of the latter and the strong emphasis on interweaving these activities into the public arenas of their host societies. The quest to participate actively as Jews in the public life and cultural areas of their respective societies and to imbue these with some specific, usually universalistic, civilizational dimensions yet closely related to Jewish communal life, was relatively weak, confined to rather restricted intellectual groups. Most sectors of these Jewish communities as it were moved almost directly from the more traditional setting into a postmodern one, at a time when the original historical program of the Enlightenment and the formation of the European nation-states started to become greatly transformed.

The specific Jewish historical experience that developed in Soviet Russia came to the fore with the great changes in Soviet Russia initiated by Gorbachev. It is much more difficult to interpret the Jewish experience in Soviet Russia, although some of the basic trends are easily discernible. One trend, in rather close parallel to the Jewish-American experience, was great ecological and economic mobility and growing urbanization, moving into tertiary occupations, a trend recognized in the 1930s, with its parallel to the United States, by the Jewish demographer, J. Leschinski.[3]

The second aspect of the Jewish Soviet experience was the mixture of official and semiofficial antisemitism, manifest in the development of many de facto restrictive policies concerning admittance to academic institutions and various occupations, although more populist expressions of antisemitism, together with other spontaneous political expressions, were usually suppressed by the authorities.

The third aspect of Jewish Soviet experience was that, unlike in the American case, there was a very strong pressure on Jews to assimilate. Hebrew-Jewish cultural institutions were suppressed from the beginning as manifestations of bourgeois-Zionist reactions; attempts were made to maintain some Yiddish ones, but these were destroyed almost totally; the experiment to establish a special Jewish republic in Birobidjan, with Yiddish as its official language, was relatively short lived; and any communal or cultural Jewish life or maintenance of any Jewish tradition was suppressed.

Thus indeed the Jews were the only religious group in the USSR not allowed any far-reaching religious organization, and the only ethnic group whose cultural activities were truncated and whose cultural tradition was not incorporated in some general or specific framework.

Within the framework of these trends some very surprising developments occurred. Not only was there a continuous persistence of some, even if highly diluted, traditional patterns of life, special family patterns and connections of de facto social segregation. Beyond this it seems that the combined effect of restrictive policies and antisemitic orientations, attitudes, and policies that intensified continuously, the establishment of the state of Israel, and to some degree of the growing contacts with world Jewry through many visits of American and European Jews to Russia activated rather strong elements of Jewish identity, at least among parts of Soviet Jewry . This gave rise to movements to leave the USSR (with—by 1987—almost 4,000, out of 2–3 million applying for permits to go to Israel, almost the only official way to trying to get out). Some of these emigrants remained in Israel, but a larger number ultimately went to the United States. The Refusenik movement grew until the late 1980s and was persecuted by the authorities, and antisemitism and anti-Zionist policies and propaganda continued.

However, as yet it is very difficult to analyze the extent and strength of these tendencies and whether the Russian Jews will go in some sort of nationalist direction or in stronger assimilatory directions. There certainly are very strong indications not only of assimilation but also of the strong development of Jewish identity among parts at least of the Jewish population, to no small degree helped by the growing antisemitic and anti-Zionist attitudes of the authorities.

At the end of the 1980s, with the opening up of the Soviet system under Gorbachev and the breakdown of Communist regimes in Eastern Europe, a resurgence of "traditional" primordial antisemitism took place, seemingly vindicating the classical Zionist tenets, but giving also rise to a great variety of different trends. The most dramatic of these trends was the great exodus to Israel from 1989 on.

The exodus of Jews gathered unprecedented force. About 250,000 of them left—about 200,000 of them to Israel, the only country which naturally, given its basic ethos, did not put any restrictions on the numbers of immigrants allowed to enter.

Obviously they left because they felt themselves insecure as Jews, even if they were not pushed out. It was not clear what being Jewish meant to them beyond a vague, even if potentially strong, sense of belonging to the Jewish collective, to the Jewish people; how much they identified themselves with the Jewish people or the Jewish tradition, of which they had but minimal knowledge. However, the very fact of their emigration has greatly enhanced the centrality and salience of Jewish collective consciousness throughout Jewish communities and beyond.

At the same time many Jewish organizations—religious, national, and secular—developed intensive programs of Jewish educational and cultural activities within Soviet Russia. It is, of course, difficult to predict how enduring their impact will be and what kind of new Jewish collective life will develop there.

Parallel (but much more intensive and more firmly rooted) Jewish activities developed in those Eastern European countries, especially in Hungary and to a smaller extent in Chekoslovakia, bringing these countries back into the fold of active Jewish communal life and cultural activities.

Also after the Second World War yet another entirely new mode of incorporation of Jews into the modern world came into full fruition: the creation of an independent Jewish society with the establishment of the Yishuv and the state of Israel. This mode of incorporation of the Jews into the world developed out of the most radical criticism of possibility of Jewish existence in the Diaspora, which developed in the Zionist movement. At the same time, the Zionist movement, which often has been seen as the epitome of modern Jewish national movements, differed in some crucial aspects from most European national movements. Parallelly and in close relation to the distinct characteristics of the Zionist movement, many of these specific characteristics, both of the Zionist movement and the state of Israel, were closely related to the Jewish civilizational framework, evident in specific ways in which Zionism has attempted to reconstruct the different components as themes of this civilization.

The Jewish Experience in the Contemporary Era

New Modes of Heterogeneity in the Continuation of Jewish Life and Collective Consciousness

Thus after the Second World War the full impact of the challenge of reconstruction of Jewish civilization in the new, modern or postmodern, era became visible; on the one hand, moving between the different modes of incorporation of Jewish communities in modern and in "post-modern" societies including the continuous reconstruction of orthodoxy, and on the other hand, establishing the state of Israel and developing Israeli society. The full impact of this challenge could be seen in the development of an entirely new mode or modes of heterogeneity in Jewish life, to which we have referred at the beginning of this chapter, the kernels of which started to develop earlier but came into full friction only in this period. This heterogeneity was manifest in the numerous ways of articulating patterns of Jewish life and identity.

First, a situation developed in which the simple correlation assumed as natural, especially in the nineteenth century in Western Europe, between shedding traditional ways of life and giving up elements of Jewish identity, no longer held. Many Jews were continuously changing their ways of life, and most of them in the Diaspora did not lead lives primarily or fully Jewish, but they might not want to lose their Jewish identity. They attempted to reformulate this identity, even if it was no longer the only exclusive and perhaps not even the predominant one, and to find social space for what seemed to them distinctly Jewish activities.

Second, and closely related to this, was the continuous restructuring of the components and symbols of this identity. Here two processes were continuously taking place. The first process was that, in addition to shedding certain of these components and symbols, continuous attempts were made to reconstruct and recombine them in different ways. The second process entailed, in most cases, both the reformulation and recombination of most of the attachments to a religious tradition, together with more primordial ones, with some elements of "peoplehood," and a reemphasis on the political component in this tradition; that is, those components seen earlier, through the nineteenth century, as antiethical to the incorporation of Jews in the modern societies.

As indicated, a new element developed in its fullest way in the period after the Second World War. This was the emergence of legitimate collective Jewish political activity within the political framework of the respective societies. For the first time in exilic history, Jewish communities throughout the world became politically active and conscious as Jews. The pinnacle of this development, of course, was the establishment of the state of Israel and the continuous relations between it and all the Jewish communities in the Diaspora.

This process of reformulation and reconstruction of different elements of Jewish identity naturally, in most Jewish communities, was very closely related to a parallel process in the selection of different elements of Jewish tradition. Here, too, was continuous search and exploration, about which we know systematically relative little. The most interesting aspect of this process is that, contrary to the previous conception, no simple relation could be found between attachment to different Jewish customs and traditions, commitment to Jewish identity, and participation in the more general arenas of life their host societies. Even within the orthodox circles, seemingly the ones in which the older components should always go together, the picture is very complex. Thus, as we have seen, the upsurge of orthodoxy and neo-orthodoxy was connected to a growing participation in the arenas of life of the general society, such as higher education and other occupational spheres, which would have been an anathema or at least alien to the older, Eastern European traditionalists. It also was connected to a growing participation in some political Jewish activities of the new kind.

The picture is even more complex among the nonorthodox. Among them sometimes a tendency developed to return to certain tradition or customs that had religious origins, but had become symbols of collective identity, such as candle lighting on Hannuka and the Sabbath, or celebration of those aspects of the tradition related to the most primordial facts of life; circumcision (which is obviously the choice of the parents), bar mitzvah, marriage, funerals. These different patterns of reconstruction of religious symbols were not necessarily related to a return to orthodoxy, to the acceptance of the Halakhah as the basic framework of Jewish life, although such a process was taking place to some extent among sectors of Jewish communities. Therefore, no simple relation between such 'contents' and the nature of Jewish identity and commitment developed among various Jewish communities.

Yet another new element, connected with Jewish civilizational activities or aspirations, became predominant. In many cases, Jews who were searching for the expression of their Jewish identity tended to combine this search with those themes and problems that, as it were, were "repressed" in the Medieval patterns and that, in the early assimilationist period, were taken beyond the scope of Jewish communal activity: the search for some sort of resolution of the tension between the universalistic and particularistic element in Jewish collective identity. In some cases the older semiassimilationist, "ethical" (liberal, socialist, or nationalist) attitudes persisted. In most cases, however, these attitudes more and more were connected with a more positive Jewish collective identity and commitment. In many cases the emphasis on these themes became closely related to activities in Jewish communal activities, institutions, and organizations. These themes were seen as a constructive, positive components of the general setting of contemporary societies, and often they were promulgated in connection with the state of Israel.

Moreover, these activities take place not only in the private space of the Jews, but also in the more central public and political arenas. Such activities are conducted mostly in the languages of their respective countries of residence (English, French, Spanish, and the like) and in the terms of the intellectual discourse of these societies. At the same time, however, they often are presented both as expressing the different dimensions of Jewish identity and as a legitimate part of the general society.

Different Jewish communities or sectors differ today as to how they go about this task. There are different emphases of various components of collective Jewish identity, collective Jewish consciousness, and nowhere is there a full distinctive crystallization of some new combination of the elements. Rather in every Jewish community or sector there is a continuous process of experimentation with the different elements of Jewish identity; no community has settled for a "solution" or end point; and all communities are in a constant state of flux. One very central and crucial aspect of this flux of course is the continuous drifting away of large sectors of the Jewish communities from any Jewish organizational framework and attachment to any Jewish traditions or symbols. The connecting elements, however, are the very acts of experimentation, the continuous search, and the mutual awareness within these different Jewish communities that they share common heritage and this common search, the details of which are greatly influenced in each community by the specific circumstances in which their members live.

Thus, today, one can be, and feel, Jewish without having a fixed and set notion of what this actually means in terms of actual contents. Because flux is difficult to capture organizationally, Jewish institutions, and education, lag considerably behind these developments and tendencies, although certain issues, such as those connected with the state of Israel or the problem of Soviet Jewry, serve as major themes for focusing of such activities.

Even more significant than the great heterogeneity in customs, in the selection of different components of Jewish identity and tradition, although closely connected to this heterogeneity, are the different modes of their modern historical experience, especially of their encounter with the modernity of their host civilization, that developed in the different Jewish communities. This growing heterogeneity of Jewish ways of life, perhaps in a somewhat paradoxical way, seems to fit well with what often is designated as trends to a postmodern society. In these which many of the clear boundaries of collectivities, national and ethnic entities of social classes and sectors, and their relatively homogeneous styles of life that characterized early modernity seemed to have been somewhat blurred, giving rise to a more variegated pluralism. At the same time, the very blurring of many of these boundaries, poses new challenges before the Jews.[4]

On the one hand, the challenges open up the possibility of growing creativity in the construction of different modes of Jewish experience. On the other hand, they enhance the possibility of large sectors of Jewish population drifting away from the Jewish fold. At the same time, these developments also could enhance the possibility of exposure of many sectors of Jewish society to a seemingly unexpected outburst of primordial components of the identity in many sectors of their host societies.

Above all, the challenges have sharpened the problem of whether it would be possible in the contemporary period to crystallize some new patterns not only of Jewish communal life and activities but also of Jewish civilization. This problem has become very acute given the great heterogeneity in patterns of Jewish life, the growing dissociation between different components of Jewish collective life: customs, different forms of Jewish communal organization, components of Jewish identity, and the promulgation of different themes of Jewish civilization, the changing patterns of the Western civilizations, and the multiple modes of interaction of Jewish communities with the societies in which they live.

These far-reaching transformations in the organization and activities of the Jewish people in the various communities of the Diaspora, especially in the United States and to a smaller degree in Western Europe, were connected to a no less far-reaching change in the formulation by large sectors of Jewish communities of the problematic of Jewish collective existence. This change went beyond the premises of the European nineteenth- and twentieth-century experience in general and classical Zionist ideology in particular, the very ideology that shaped the revolutionary and ideological premises of Israel and guided and shaped much of the Israeli perception of and attitude to the Diaspora.

This problematic was formulated, even if intermittently and not always in a fully articulated way, not in terms of the dilemma between assimilation and the maintenance of a collective Jewish life in a purely Jewish environment, whether the closed one of orthodoxy, the in principle open one of the Zionist variety, or as one minority nation in a state composed of many such nations, with one nation being the majority. Instead, among most contemporary Jewish communities in the Diaspora, of course only among those who cared about this at all, a continuous search developed to find different ways of expressing Jewish collective identity and Jewish peoplehood, stressing the political and the civilizational dimensions of this identity, while being full and equal members of their respective national or political collectivities.

Truly enough, part of these Jewish communal and cultural activities, like those of the Anti-Defamation League and different types of vigilantes, on the whole were defensive. Parts of these activities were philanthropic, seemingly in the tradition of such activities in the nineteenth century. But most of them became crystallized in more dynamic and variegated patterns, sharing the implicit assumption of the possibility of developing such activities and frameworks within the communities of the Diaspora, even if in close relation with Israel.

This problematic developed in different modes in different Jewish communities, according to their different historical experience, but the basic assumption that Jews, in different modern or postmodern societies, can search for different ways of expressing their collective identity and for incorporation into these societies seemed to be common to most of them. Basically, despite many misgivings and fears about the ultimate lack of viability of Jewish life in the Diaspora and even though existence in the Diaspora continued to constitute a problem in Jewish collective consciousness, the formulation of such problematic, within most sectors of Jewish society in the Diaspora, took the possibility of such free collective existence more or less for granted, and concentrated on finding different ways of expressing Jewish identity.

Despite all contrary trends, to be shortly analyzed, those among the Jews concerned with such matters seemingly were able to find in the new setting and the countries in which they lived not only possibilities of maintaining communal identity and activities based on primordial, political, and civilizational orientations and combining these with full participation in their societies. It indeed does seem that the majority of American, and more and more also among European, Jews, and especially those who actively upheld their Jewishness, refused to see any basic contradiction between their American (or English, French, and so on) identity and their Jewishness and refused to see in antisemitism (some even tried to deny its very existence) a basic threat to their incorporation as Jews in that society. But in fact the picture is much more complicated.

The developments in the last two decades, in various Jewish communities, especially in the United States but also in Europe, highlighted the different contradictory and yet often mutually reinforcing possibilities inherent in this new modern and "postmodern" Jewish historical experience. Thus first of all the development of specific Jewish organizations continued, with new ventures in Jewish education and communal activities and a growing political activity of such international Jewish organizations as the World Jewish Congress. Second, participation in general arenas of American (and to a smaller extent European) life was continuously growing, with many Jews moving into various occupations and economic sectors that hitherto on the whole had been closed to them, to become more and more active in political life, on the local, state, and national level.

Yet some of these developments indeed may bear within them the seed of future developments in the direction of assimilation. The ecological movement to small communities and the general demographic decline of Jews, that same decline which at least partially accounts for their strong economic advancement, as we have already observed with respect to the Jews in the United States, may make the maintenance of Jewish communal life and activities more difficult. Moreover, as the events around the Gulf crisis from August 1990 and around the Gulf War from January 1991 showed, the collective Jewish activities often were restricted or muted by the perception of their leaders of various constraints in their respective societies, the constraints of the free Diaspora.

Among many of the Jewish leaders and intellectuals a growing concern developed about the possible assimilation of Jews through ecological dispersion and intermarriage and a growing interest in strengthening Jewish educational institutions as a way to strengthen their attachment to the Jewish inheritance. But this concern is firmly set within the framework of the Jewish existence in the Diaspora, even if many of their activities and attachments to a very high degree are oriented also to Israel. For others, perhaps ultimately a majority, this concern may go together with a de facto acceptance of growing assimilation or rather drifting away from the Jewish fold.

Thus, a rather paradoxical situation indeed has developed, as we already observed with respect to the Jews in the United States; namely, those very processes that enabled the intensification of Jewish activities and organizations also could move for a relatively fast and smooth assimilation or drifting away. This could happen just because such assimilation could take place without demands for changing religion or even denying one's Jewishness. Such drifting away also may be reinforced by the fact that the various Jewish communities were traveling on different historical roads, they did not necessarily have the same types of historical experience.

It is a moot question to what extent all these tendencies make invalid the basic Zionist tenets about the inevitability in such circumstances of assimilation, demographic decline, or in more extreme cases, of antisemitic persecution and perhaps destruction. It is of great interest that this is the period when the vision of the Holocaust has become continuously more central in the collective memory of contemporary Jewry.

The New Orthodoxy

One of the most interesting aspects of the transformation of Jewish life after the Second World War took place within the orthodox sectors, again going against the basic premises of almost all the hitherto predominant modern Jewish ideologies, the assimilationist, Zionist, or orthodox alike. According to the premises of most of these "classical" approaches, rooted as they were in the experience of the nineteenth century, orthodoxy as such, in the wake of the presumed general trend to secularization, was destined to be weakened, perhaps to disappear, or at most to remain in closed ghettos completely secluded from modern life, finding some niche in various "traditional' Jewish occupations like small trade, artisanship, and the like.

These predictions indeed were true of some small extreme orthodox groups. But even the ultraorthodox groups in the United States, England, or Belgium became much more diversified and "modernized," at least economically. Moreover, these developments were part of a much broader trend of far-reaching changes as a result of which large parts of these sectors went beyond the classical ghetto experience. They became much more interwoven in the occupational, and even ecological, matrix of modern societies, and they share several aspects of the secular life style, such as work, reading habits, media watching, and the like. True enough, there is a great difference between the relatively more open new orthodoxy and the ultraorthodox, the latter trying to dissociate themselves ideologically and to some extent also socially and culturally but not economically, from the wider society. Even these sectors take part in political elections in their respective countries, especially in the United States.

Although no exact data are available, it is easy to see that the orthodox Jews abound in the centers of many cities and their numbers seem to be increasing not only in their traditional but also in new professional or academic occupations. They, or rather some of them, the more open part of them as against the ultratraditional orthodox, are very visible in universities in subjects such as chemistry, physics, and computer sciences, which earlier on seemed to them, unlike pure mathematics, to be beyond the Pale for orthodox Jews. Special general academic institutions, oriented primarily to the "new" modern orthodox public, such as Yeshiva University in New York and to a smaller degree Bar Ilan University in Israel, emerged in the orthodox sector. Many of these modern institutions and somewhat more modern ways of life were not accepted by the ultraorthodox; indeed, they were an anathema to them.

In general, since the 1930s and especially after the Holocaust, some leading orthodox scholars came to the United States and established strong Yeshivot and centers, which became powerful and dynamic. Their own specific educational institutions were extended and diversified, sometimes combining some secular subjects or allowing their students to combine the study in the Yeshiva with education in general schools. Many of the more extreme groups still were strongly opposed to such ventures, even when they had to obey the laws of the land and send their children to schools or provide them with an education in which such secular subjects had to be studied.

In their private life, many of them lead a very affluent style of life and to some degree also an intensive cultural life of their own, with a very ambivalent, often hostile attitude to the secularized Jews, sometimes attempting to proselytize among them. They also developed a special relationship with the state of Israel and their central organizations.

Contrary to the experience of former generations they do not seem—here again there are no exact data—to lose out to the secular world. On the contrary, it seems that there is a quite visible movement of younger Jews coming from more secular backgrounds turning to some variant of orthodoxy, even though it is probably less prevalent than claimed by the orthodox circles and the older pattern of many leaving the orthodox fold still continues.

Accordingly, these orthodox groups do not see themselves on the defensive, and they do not "hide" their orthodoxy in their public activities. On the contrary, they are very open about it. The older saying of the European Haskalah implicitly endorsed by at least the German neo-orthodoxy, "be a Jew in your home and a man in public life," certainly does not apply to them. Most of them, except for the ultraorthodox ones, do not hesitate to appear openly as do secular Jews, but because of their distinct patterns of dress with much greater visibility. Thus in a way they articulate yet another variant of the possibility of development of collective Jewish life, both in America where they are becoming an accepted part of the American scene and to a smaller extent also in Europe.

Among the various sectors of Jewish population they are probably the most divided among themselves, into different "Hassidic" and "non-Hassidic" communities, into different sectors often at loggerheads with one another. Yet there can be no doubt that in the mid-1980s they provide the most internally compact sectors within the panorama of Jewish life, developing educational and communal institutions and providing, as we have seen, a large part of the Jewish day schools.

Their central organizations have been very vocal in internal and general Jewish affairs, as have many individual rabbis, at the same time exhibiting their usual great internal divisiveness. Many of the orthodox Jewish, even if not the ultraorthodox, leaders have become more central in general Jewish institutions, which may be connected to the growing movement of the younger generation of university-educated Jews into more general arenas of American or European societies, including the political ones. They seem to provide a certain reservoir of Jewish leadership, thus also potentially changing the basis of support for Israel and of relations with it. Whatever the future may hold for them, these various orthodox groups, as of now, have developed as one of the new variants—a very forceful one—of modern Jewish life, in which the combination of themes of religious community and peoplehood and even political activity, both within their countries of residence as well as in relation to the state of Israel, have become crystallized in a new pattern that goes far beyond that of the European "traditional" orthodoxy or nineteenth century neo-orthodoxy. At the same time, the influence of some leaders of the various ultraorthodox, especially Hassidic, communities (among others the Lubavitch or the Satmer Rabbis) became quite great figures, with their influence expanding to many sectors of the Jewish society, sometimes beyond it.

Within this pattern two sometimes overlapping tendencies started to develop: the growing active participation in the general life of the societies in the Diaspora, and a growing tendency to sectarianism. And these have become very important, indeed predominant.

The State of Israel and the Problem of Its Centrality in Jewish Life: The Complexity of Israel-Diaspora Relations

A radically different mode of incorporation of a Jewish community into the modern world took place in the state of Israel. The specific internal development of Israeli society, the specific pattern of its development as an ideological, postrevolutionary, colonizatory, immigrant society, entailed a rather distinct mode of Jewish historical experience and recrystallization of the major themes of Jewish tradition and civilization.

Israel constituted the only Jewish community in the modern world that has attained independence as a territorial political unit. This political community was constructed, as we have seen, through the continuous interaction between its historical and ideological roots in the Zionist movement and the exigencies of creating such a political community in the specific conditions of Eretz Israel. In contrast to all other modern and contemporary Jewish communities, the construction of symbols, both of the major Jewish collective identity and the promulgation of different continuously reconstructed themes of Jewish civilization, in Israel were continuously interwoven with the overall institutional framework of a territorial political collectivity, in ways distinct from the developments in other Jewish communities. Yet, throughout its existence, the Yishuv and Israeli society were continuously interacting with the various Jewish communities throughout the world; these communities constituted part of its broader, but highly, relevant environment of Israeli society.

At the same time the distinct mode of crystallization of Jewish collective life in Israel played a very special role in the crystallization of new patterns of Jewish collective activity and identity, not only in Israel but also beyond it. First of all, it was instrumental in the revival of the political dimension of Jewish existence and the orientation to the state of Israel, which could be found in almost all Jewish communities and their sectors and constituted a central pivot of this dimension. Thus, for instance, in a country like France, with its relatively long tradition of assimilation and of the emphasis of Jewish identity as a religious community, this attitude has found its expression in such events as Raymond Aron's polemic against de Gaulle during the Six-Day War, the chief rabbi's sermon during the Yom Kippur War, and later on in the 1970s the growing political engagement of large parts of the Jewish community in connection with French policies toward Israel, an engagement intensified by the influence in the French community of younger generations, as well as of North African Jews, who became very active in Jewish activities and organizations.

The articulation of this political dimension in relation to the state of Israel was no less far-reaching in other Jewish communities. The English community has a much longer tradition of such activity, especially through the Board of Deputies and the fact that for many years London was the headquarters of the World Zionist Organization. Such activity was particularly visible in the United States, in the activities of such bodies as the Board of Presidents of the major Jewish organization; the United Jewish Appeal; the various Jewish political lobbies, and the like, and lately in the intensified worldwide activities of the World Jewish Congress. Activities related to Soviet Jewry became a major focus of such activities, in addition to those related to the state of Israel.

The state of Israel also provided a geographic center, a symbol of common heritage and common solidarity that large parts of the Jewish people accepted, indeed the only or major pivot common to all or most of the Jewish people. It also provided a central—not always easy, simple, indeed often a very ambivalent—focus of collective Jewish identity. In many Jewish communities, especially in the United States in the 1950s and 1960s, Israel constituted a central, in the beginning a very new and potent, component of their

Jewish "civic religion." It became the natural meeting place for most Jewish organizations; a sort of natural place for family gatherings and events, and by now but very few organizations of Jewish communal life are not connected in some way or another with Israel.

Many Jews search in Israel for the manifestation of those dimensions of Jewish existence and themes of Jewish civilization for which they longed; not only those of political and military strength and collective identity, but also those of social justice, full religious fulfillment, or for some great civilizationary vision, as well as those of "simple" communal-familial Jewish solidarity. The demands made on Israel from such points of view were often utopian, exaggerated, unrealistic—very diverse and often contradictory—but all of them attested to the fact that the state of Israel constituted a continuous, central focus of such orientations. Even the ambivalence and of criticism against Israel that became more and more vocal from the mid-1970s attested to the relatively central place of Israel in the construction of contemporary collective Jewish identity.

Significantly enough, the old controversies around Zionism, around the viability of the Zionist vision, which abounded within the Jewish communities in Europe and also in the United States, from the very beginning of Zionist and Jewish settlement in Eretz Israel, have almost entirely abated. The tragic experience of the Holocaust, the fact that Palestine, and later Israel, was initially at least the only place which readily accepted the Jewish refugees from Europe and Asia, the very fact of the successful establishment of the state of Israel, have made most of these controversies meaningless. When some groups, as for instance the American Council for Judaism in the United States attempted, in the late 1940s or early 1950s, to continue in this vein, they found but little resonance within the Jewish communities. In so far as controversies developed, as they did especially from the early 1970s, they became focused on questions pertaining to the degree to which Israel did indeed live up to the various ideals which were expected from it; on the degree of support to be given to it and lately around the right of Jews to dissent publicly from the policies of the Israeli government.

Only among sectors of the orthodox, especially among the ultraorthodox, has there developed a growing distance from the state of Israel, especially in its Zionist dimension but in its central focus of Jewish existence in general. But even from these circles, although they never accepted the Zionist tenets, there was a de facto recognition of the state with growing demands on it in terms of their own premisses; many settled in Israel and even more developed very close relations with those in Israel.

Many of the orthodox groups have developed very numerous activities and organizations in Israel, and have engaged in continuous attempts to influence the policies of the state of Israel in matters concerning central problems of Jewish identity, as for instance with respect to the "Who is a Jew" controversy.

Similarly the distinction between Jewish nationhood and Zionism, which constituted a central focus of ideological debate among the different Jewish national movements, in Eastern Europe, until the Second World War, abated almost entirely, aided by the fact that the antisemitic outbursts in the 1970s continuously identified the state of Israel and Jewish nationhood. But now such antisemitism did not only reinforce Zionist orientations, as was, of course, one of the original Zionist assumptions, but could also give rise to more ambivalent attitudes to Israel.

All these variegated developments went far beyond the tenets of Zionist ideology and to some degree of practice, up to the end of the Second World War, of the Zionist movement in general and of the pioneering groups in the Yishuv in particular. These developments have also changed the nature of the relations between Israel and the Diaspora, especially as perceived in Israel up to the Six-Day War. Unwittingly but very forcefully, the "terms of trade" between Israel and the Jewish communities in the Diaspora became transformed in a far-reaching way, in many ways undermining most of the Zionist tenets. Israel had been receiving from the Jewish communities of the Diaspora economic resources, political support, visits, and the like. At the same time Israel gave them the symbols of political sovereignty, the political dimension of a collective existence, the pride in Jewish statehood, a community of their own that could be compared to the home communities of many other immigrant groups, independence and, at least until the Yom Kippur War, military strength.[5]

Activities on behalf or in connection with the state of Israel often opened up for large parts of Jewish leadership channels of participation in the political activities of their own countries, even if with the passing of time many of these leaders began to take these activities and those connected with Israel for granted. Yet these activities continued to be symbols of Jewish solidarity and attachment.

For many within the Jewish communities the participation in activities connected with Israel and visits to Israel on semiofficial missions (such as the various UJA missions) provided them with the excitement of participation in creative works and access to central political figures they could rarely attain in their own countries.

As indicated, Israel indeed became a major symbol and center of Jewish identity, a focus of solidarity and primordial sentiments, hopes, and dreams, a potential haven from oppression, even to some extent a symbol of the civilizational potentialities of Jewish life, a symbol of pride because of its achievements or a focus of criticism because of its failures. Thus, Israel tended to become a central component of Jewish life throughout the world. But this very centrality, not unlike that of Eretz Israel in the period of the Second Temple and later on the period of the great mishnaic and talmudic centers, greatly weakened its potentially revolutionary impact on these communities. Israel no longer was seen according to a pristine Zionist vision, as the only place in which it is possible to reconstruct their life as modern Jews.

Nor was it not seen, as presumed in classical Zionist ideology, as the sole center of Jewish creativity, the only place in which new types of social, educational, and cultural activities and creativity of the Jewish people could develop. The creative impulse of many Jewish communities did not necessarily focus on life in Israel, and the pattern of Jewish renaissance developed in Israel was but one pattern of such creativity, even if a central one, at least until the early 1980s.

Moreover, Israel was not seen, even by those Jews strongly committed to Israel, as the only repository of true Jewishness, of the Jewish historical experience in modern time. Seth L. Wolitz, a professor of Jewish Studies at University of Texas, promulgated—if possibly in a somewhat exaggerated way succinctly—this view in an article in the *Jerusalem Post,* written during the Gulf War.

It is time for Israelis to face some unpleasant facts about Jewish Americans.

He does not feel himself in a "Diaspora" and his "Jewish" identity is basically religious with nostalgic "roots" to a "Jewishness" which is historical and closer to the fantasized *shtetl* of Chagall and *Fiddler on the roof* than to any yearnings for Beit Shemesh or Kfar Sava.

His ties to Israel are basically residual and not living. His identity to Israel is tinged with idealism and expectations of unrealistic performance.

In his heart, he believes that all Israel really wants is to be in a position to copy the benefits that America has brought him and which his monetary contributions may help bring. He does not yearn for "Israeli culture" as an Ahad Ha'am might have hoped; he is pleased with his own Nobel Prize figures that are homegrown. He believes himself not one whit less Jewish than any Israeli—but his "Jewishness" is not of a political-national expression, because his ancestors took a different tack to Zionism and *chose* the "Golden Land" of America.[6]

But the attraction of Israel seems to have abated and changed its nature in respect to more than the "revolutionary" dimension or aspects of Aliya, or as the main repository of Jewishness in the modern world. No less important, and in many ways quite shocking to many Israelis, was the fact that for many

Jews in search of security, Israel was not even the natural first place of refuge.

Israel's place in the map of Jewish immigration, even of immigration from countries in which Jews felt threatened or were persecuted, became rather secondary so long as other countries were ready to accept them. Thus, significantly enough, in the 1970s and 1980s, more Jews from South America, South Africa, Iran, and even Russia emigrated to North America or Western Europe than to Israel.

Its symbolic place notwithstanding, Israel became an ultimate, but for many years only an ultimate, place of refuge, even if paradoxically its very existence as a place of such refuge may have helped these other migratory processes. Only in the late 1980s and beginning of the 1990s, when the United States started to impose quite restrictive quotas on Jews from the USSR, have more of them have started to come to Israel, possibly signaling, as we already mentioned, a new stage in the development of Israeli society, as well as in the entire gamut of relations between Israel and the Jewish communities in the Diaspora.

The centrality of the state of Israel in the contemporary Jewish experience did not mean that the concrete relations between the Jewish communities in the Diaspora and the state of Israel always have been harmonious or stable. It indeed is a part of the relative fluidity of this experience that such relations also have been changing continuously. These relations began to change in the 1950s and 1960s, when the very establishment of the state of Israel became a source of pride to the Diaspora communities and probably greatly helped the integration of these communities in their respective countries to a great anxiety about the security of the state at the outbreak of the Six-Day War and great pride in its victory. The relations have been changing since then, giving rise to many potential and actual points of tension, and conflicts, which became intensified from about mid-1970, and especially since the mid-1980s. To no small degree the changes are in connection with the disintegration of the initial institutional mold of Israeli society and the growing awareness of the problems inherent in attempts to carry the burden of the implementation of the Jewish civilizational vision in a small society struggling to survive in a hostile environment.

The growing criticism of Israel and the policies of Israeli governments have been increasing lately, as highlighted by a very basic dilemma or problem in the relations between Israel and the Jewish communities in the Diaspora. This dilemma or problem is rooted in their basically different historical experiences. The dilemma is between a Jewish community that constitutes not only a majority in its own land but also is responsible for running a state and the Jewish communities in the Diaspora, which constitute minorities, even if seemingly fully participating minorities in their respective countries.

In the first three or four decades after the establishment of the state of Israel, when the internal assurance of Jewish communities in the Diaspora was greatly strengthened by the very existence of Israel, this difference in the basic historical conditions of existence, in their basic respective historical experiences, and hence in their respective agendas, was glossed over. Since the late 1970s, for the reasons already mentioned, the picture changed, highlighting more and more some awareness of these differences and their consequences for the relation between the Jewish communities of the Diaspora and Israel.

In the early 1970s Simone Weil, then French Minister of Education, pointed out to some of these in her speech of acceptance of honorary doctorate from the Hebrew University.

Today Judaism's values are integrated in a state; they are integrated in a society, a society which has not existed for more than 2,000 years. And we, of the Diaspora, hope that Israel will remain the defender of these values, of this Humanism. We must clearly say that this is certainly more difficult situated in the position of a state, no longer in that obligatory minoritarian position, to continue to carry a flame like this.

And I hope as a French woman, but as a French Jewish woman, and a Jewish French woman, that our countries will help each other to continue carrying this flame and that they will ceaselessly defend these values, whatever happens. And I know that for every state this is sometimes difficult, that for every state there is a need to mobilize, that states find themselves confronted with situations which could be "raison d'etat"; but that precisely we have always been proud in a certain way of being above that, of having something more, which has been possibly forced, and today, what I hope is, that the miracle of Israel, the miracle of Jerusalem will reproduce itself, and I am sure that this challenge (I am sure of it and do not just hope it) that this challenge will be your victory and ours.

It was often not easy for many Jews in the Diaspora to accept the fact that Israel has become a "normal" state or at least that in many circumstances it had to behave like any normal state in defense of its interests, and not according to some utopian criteria. With all their seeming self-assurance with respect to their standing in the countries of their residence, many, although certainly not all, Jews in the Diaspora tended to follow the tendencies of large sectors of the media to judge Israel by different higher moral standards than other nations. Such tendencies often became intensified in the

1980s, with the Lebanon War, and wih the Arab uprising in the West bank. The fact that the double standard used by many media in reporting the different sides or aspects of these events and disputes often fed on latent anti-semitic tendencies and focused them on Israel often gave rise to ambivalent reactions on part of the Jews themselves. Some would react strongly against the application of such double standards; others, possibly out of some feeling of insecurity in their own identity or standing in their countries, seemingly would accept such applications. Some of the pronouncements of Jewish leaders in the Diaspora seemed to indicate that Israel should not engage in activities which could embarrass them; which could go counter to the way in which they wanted to portray themselves in their societies. Controversies around Israel shifted from the older views about the viability of the Zionist vision to those about Israel, but not necessarily other Jewish communities in its life and policies, living up to the tenets of this vision. Indeed against the background of this paradoxical change of the place of Israel in the life of Jewish communities various trends also developed of denial of its centrality in Jewish life and ambivalence to it.

In a more extreme way this new attitude found expression in public declarations, made by many Jewish leaders, of a strong emphasis on the equality of the Diaspora and Israel in Jewish life and in criticism of Israel for its seeming failure to live up to those ideals or themes perceived by the Jewish communities in the Diaspora as constitutive of their viability as minorities in free societies or for the loss of Jewish creativity in Israel.

Since the early 1980s, if not earlier, one could hear quite often the accusation or claim that many patterns of creativity, in which Jews in the Diaspora excel—be it high academic achievement, manifest in the winning of Nobel Prizes, in economic entrepreneurship, and the like—find no counterpart in Israel, above all in that Israel which underwent all the processes of change attendant on the disintegration of the initial mold of Israeli society. True enough those making these claims seem to forget or to be unaware of the fact that all these successes of the Jews in the—above all free—Diasporas have been contingent on the Jews being a minority. Members of this minority were able to find their ways into, lately quite central, arenas or niches without having to take care, as a collectivity, of the basic infrastructure of their respective societies. In Israel, of course, the construction of this infrastructure has made major claims on the creative impulses of the leading sectors of Israeli society. It is only a few of them, for instance, Stuart Eizenstadt (in a speech before the American Jewish Israeli Relations Institute in Jerusalem) who would admit that however good and even secure the position of the Jewish communities in the Diaspora is, they do not and cannot (in constrast to the situation in Israel) control thier own collective destiny. But the very fact that such criticism is voiced continuously signals a marked change in the Israel-Diaspora relations, the development of different collective agendas in Israel and in the Jewish communities in the Diaspora.

As indicated, these changes in the relations between Israel and the Jewish communities in the Diaspora intensified in the 1980s. They intensified by the temporal coalescence of, first, the disintegration, since the late 1970s, of the initial mold of Israel society; second, the growing criticism of Israel's policies with the marked change in its international standing, above all in the media but also in international politics, and third, the growth of internal strength of the Jewish communities in the Diaspora and the intensification of their communal and international Jewish activities. All these intensified the change in the relations between Israel and the Jewish communities in the Diaspora. First of all, the self-assurance of the leaders of Jewish communities in the Diaspora vis-à-vis Israel has increased and the mode of their intervention in Israeli affairs, for instance, in the organization of the Jewish Agency or in various economic enterprises in Israel, has shifted from an acceptance of the arrangements decided by Israeli authorities to an independent stance; and such a development has also started to take place with respect to support of the policies of Israel's government.

Second, among large sectors of Jewish communities a continuous drifting away or dissociation from Israel took place. Such drifting away seems to have taken place both in sectors taking active part in Jewish affairs and those dissociating themselves from such activities. Insofar as such drifting away tended to be justified at all, it often was in terms of the disappointment with Israel, in terms of some of the basic above all universalistic Jewish civilizational themes, and with the success of Israeli society in terms of Jewish creativity.

And yet, at the same time, the central place of Israel in the construction of the boundaries of Jewish collective identity did not abate. It came very forcefully to the fore after the 1988 election in Israel when several religious parties were making strong demands, as a condition for joining the coalition, to shape the "Who Is a Jew" clause in the Law of Return (the law that opens Israel to every Jew) in a strictly halakhic direction. Such a change would delegitimize conversions and marriages performed by Conservative and Reform rabbis. It was natural that this proposal would arouse the ire of large parts of American Jewish organizations, who put great pressure on the prime-minister elect, Yitzhak Shamir, not to accede to this demand. This was the only time that the official American Jewish Organizations *directly* interceded in Israeli politics, claiming that in this case not only Israeli problems were at stake.

The centrality of Israel in Jewish collective consciousness and sensitivity of Jewish communities to the fate of Israel—and at the same time their tendency to express such sensitivity in terms of their perception of their own standing in their respective societies—also became evident in the late 1990 and January 1991, during the Gulf crisis and Gulf War. With the approachment of hostilities and the obvious threat to Israel, the concern about Israel grew throughout Jewish communities, but also the concern about the possible repercussion of Israeli behavior and policy on the reaction of the societies in which they lived and their respective governments. The reaction of the more official Jewish organizations were rather muted.

Relatively few Jews came on missions of solidarity to Israel in the pre-hostilities period, although certainly several came. Jewish tourism was smaller even than that of non-Jews. When the hostilities started and Iraqi missiles started to hit Israel, their concern grew as did the great admiration in the media and the major partners of the anti-Iraqi coalition for Israel's policy of self-restraint. The Jews also gave vent freely to their feelings of solidarity; missions of solidarity and help to Israel increased.

Even these various missions of solidarity were rather restricted, only very few came to stay for longer periods of time and some of the expressions of solidarity, like the numbers of volunteers who came to Israel, was much smaller than during the Six-Day or Yom Kippur Wars for instance.

Even during this period the activities of at least the more official Jewish organizations and media were influenced, to no small degree, by the policies of their respective governments. The long hesitancy of the French government seemed to have muted to some degree at least the behavior of the more official organs of French Jews. The missions of solidarity that came around the end of January were more predominantly from the less official sector of the Jewish community.

Thus, although Israel continues to be a central component in Jewish identity, the nature and strength of this component seem to have been continuously changing the differences in their respective historical experiences and collective agendas. And ambivalence to Israel seem to have been increasing. The years 1990 and 1991 might yet prove to be a turning point in Israel-Diaspora relations. The great influx of Jews from Russia, which continued, even if in small numbers, during the Gulf War, seemed to vindicate the basic Zionist premise that only in Israel can Jews be sure to find a place of refuge. This point was further underlined by the admittance by some leaders of American Jewry that their communities did not have the financial resources to absorb vast numbers of Jewish immigrants from Russia.

At the same time, the relatively limited expressions of solidarity with Israel (even if not of their concern with it) during the Gulf crisis, the relatively limited financial aid to Israel, with respect to the absorption of the immigrants from Russia, indicated some of the limits of the free Jewish collective expression in the "Free Diaspora." The same is true of the apprehensions of many sectors of United States Jewish communities when, in September–

October 1991, tensions arose between the U.S. Government and Israel with respect to the peace process in the Middle East

Concluding Remarks:
The Challenges before Jewish Civilization in the Contemporary Era

We have come to the end of our story—although the story itself is continuously unfolding, never ending. In the preceding chapters of the book we attempted to illustrate our major thesis: the best way to approach the analysis of the Jewish historical experience is through the civilizational approach. The major argument of this book, as pointed out in the beginning, has been that the best way to understand this experience is to look on Jews not just as a religious or ethnic group, nation, or "people," although they have been all of these, but as bearers of a civilization; that is, an overall vision that entails the attempts to construct or reconstruct social life according to an ontological vision. We have indicated that the very fact that all these terms can be applied to the analysis of the Jewish historical experience indicates that none of them is sufficient and that only if one looks at this experience in civilizational terms may one begin to cope with the greatest riddle of that experience: its continuity despite destruction, exile, loss of political independence, and no territorial continuity.

Accordingly, we examined selected aspects of the Jewish historical experience from such civilizational perspective. In the first part, the first three chapters of the book, we examined some of the basic characteristics of the Jewish civilization as they have crystallized in its formative periods, those of the First and Second Temples, and in the long exilic Medieval period, and analyzed in what way they differed from "people," nations, or religious sects or groups that were not bearers of a distinct civilizational vision but usually parts thereof. We also pointed out some of the major differences, both in terms of their respective premises and historical experiences, between the Jewish and the other civilizations: the pagan civilizations, in the framework of which the ancient Israeli civilization arose, the Hellenistic and Roman civilizations of antiquity, and above all the two other monotheistic civilizations, Christianity and Islam, the encounter with which constituted a basic component of the Jewish historical experience.

As is true with respect to civilizations, especially perhaps with respect to Axial Age civilizations, the concrete contours of Jewish civilization developed out of the combination of its basic civilizational vision. The concrete circumstances of its historical experience, especially the political and economic settings in which it developed and its encounters with other, especially but not only, Axial civilizations.

The old Israelite and Jewish civilization was, as we have seen, among the very first of the so-called Great Civilizations, certainly the first in the realm of the Mediterranean and among the monotheistic religions. Within this civilization there developed a very complex vision with very strong universalistic orientations and very distinct institutional premises and frameworks. The implementation of this vision became closely interwoven with one people, giving rise to a very complex construction of collective identity, comprising, as we have seen, primordial, political, religious and ethical components. The implementation of this vision, took place also in very specific geopolitical conditions, creating a new society at the crossroads of many nations and of great empires, a situation which repeated itself with the Zionist settlement in Eretz Israel.

The conjunction of these geopolitical conditions together with the specific combination of civilizational and national collectivity gave rise to the very turbulent history of the Jewish people and to a very peculiar pattern of national continuity and civilizational changes, of shifts in the modes of implementation of its specific civilizational vision.

This turbulent history stretched from the early settlement in Eretz Israel through the period of the Judges and of the kingdoms of Judah and Israel; the destruction and disappearance of the latter; the later destruction of the Davidic monarchy in Judah and the Babylonian exile; the return from Babylon and the turbulent history of the Second Commonwealth period, up to the destruction of the Second Temple; the loss of political independence and the dwindling of the center of Eretz Israel; and the dispersion of the Jewish people. These political changes comprised far-reaching changes in the nature of the implementation of the Jewish civilizational vision. The first such major shift took place as we have seen, in the period of return from Babylon and during the period of the Second Commonwealth. The second major shift occurred after the destruction of the Second Temple and the gradual crystallization and predominance of the rabbinical mold, the mold of Halakhah. This mold was certainly not predominant during this period, nor was it a homogeneous one. Even when this mold became fully crystallized and the predominant one in the life of the Jewish people, it was not homogeneous; it comprised many heterogeneous orientations derived from other, earlier molds, as well as a great heterogeneity in its own components.

The historical circumstances in which this mold became predominant and institutionalized—the loss of political independence and of dispersal—however, did imply a far-reaching shift and change with respect to the institutional arena in which this civilizational vision and the institutional mold generated by it could be implemented. The Jewish civilizational vision no longer could be implemented in the political arena nor in an overall societal-institutional complex of a territorial society. Such implementation became confined to the daily life of Jews in their private, communal, and cultural-religious settings, in the centers of prayer and study, and in the internal arrangements of their communal life; although within this framework it was very creative and innovative. At the same time the Jews lived as a dispersed minority, in a situation of political subjugation, on the institutional margins of other societies and civilizations. In these circumstances, the more universalistic, as well as political and Messianic, orientations became relegated to a distant future, not related to any of the concrete institutional settings in which they lived, while the host civilizations treated the Jews as a pariah people as well as potential competitors.

It is a moot question whether there was any "necessary," logical relation or connection between the full crystallization and predominance of this mold and the loss of political independence and dispersion; or whether the conjunction was accidental or at most implied, as in the talmudic portrayal of Rabbi Yohanan Ben-Zakai's move to Yavneh, the attempt to save whatever could be saved from the possibility of implementing this vision in an extremely adverse political situation. Whatever the answer to this question— if indeed there is one such answer—there can be no doubt that a conjunction developed between the two, the loss of political independence and dispersal and the growing predominance of the rabbinical mold, a conjunction that necessarily also narrowed the scope of the applications of the Hellenistic mold and its basic orientations.

This turbulent history attests to a basic aspect of the Jewish civilizational experience: that the encounter of the Jewish people and the Jewish civilization with other was rather unique, since the destruction of the First Temple, but especially after the destruction of the Second Temple with the period of Babylonian Exile and dispersion. The Jewish civilization was the only Axial Age civilization the continuity of which was not interwoven with some type of territorial continuity and relatively distinctive political boundaries. This basic characteristic continued in the modern period, with the one significant difference, reminiscent of the period of the Second Temple: one part of the Jewish people was able to establish such a territorial entity. This characteristic however intensified another problem in the construction of this civilization, the relations between the territorial center and various dispersed communities in many parts of the world, a problem that crystallized also in the period of the Second Temple. This problem was very closely interwoven with many of the tensions between some of the major civilizational themes and predominant in the Jewish civilizations; such as the tension between the universalistic and particularistic orientations, or between the legal, ritualistic, or philosophical ones, and their varied institutional implications.

These themes and the problems of implementing the Jewish civilizational vision changed greatly in the modern period, which was discussed in the second and largest part of the book. In this part we continued our analysis into the modern period, into the period in which the basic relations between the Jews and their host societies or civilizations have drastically changed. We analyzed the different patterns of incorporation of Jewish communities in some of their host societies in Western and Eastern Europe and the United States; the national movements that developed among the Jews from the end of the nineteenth century, especially the Zionist movement; and some of the specific characteristics of Israeli society.

Throughout our analysis, in all these chapters, we asked ourselves to what extent some of the crucial aspects of Jewish experience in each of these cases were similar to that of comparable groups, such as the incorporation of other ethnic and religious minorities in the modern nation-state, other modern national movements, and other revolutionary ideological settler societies, such as the United States, and to what extent such experiences have exhibited distinct, and common, characteristics that can be attributed to some of the specifically Jewish civilizational characteristics analyzed in the preceding chapters; to what extent did the Jews become dissolved into "simple" religious, ethnic, or even national groups. The analyses presented in the preceding chapters have shown that however great the basic similarities in the fate of Jewish civilization, and its relations to other civilizations, which in fact have become the host nations for the Jewish people in the Medieval and the modern periods, great differences developed in these two periods. In the Medieval period there was a sort of symmetry or homology between the basic components and basic premises of the three monotheistic civilizations. All were constructed around the attempt to implement a transcendental vision defined in and legitimated by religious terms. These visions contained several basic components, among others universalistic and particularistic primordial ones; historical and semimythical ones, ritualistic, legal, and philosophical ones. The concrete constellation of these components varied greatly among the three monotheistic civilizations, but they all were concerned with these problems. A common framework of discourse and mutual historical references developed between them.

Throughout this period the very ambivalent and often hostile relations between them helped reinforce their respective distinctive collective boundaries and concrete institutional formation. This perhaps was especially true of the Jewish civilization, the boundaries of which (of the halakhic mold) were reinforced by hostile and ambivalent relations with their host societies, as well as by the very fact of dispersion.

This situation has changed greatly with the onset of modern times, of modernity. The basic premises of Western modernity: the "secularization" and the later "postmodern" seeming weakening of the transcendental vision, the weakening of historical consciousness, the reconstruction of the boundaries of most collectivities in largely secular terms, as well as the growing distance between the transcendental vision and concrete institutional arenas. All these differed from those predominant in the hitherto Jewish historical experience and according to which the collective boundaries were constructed. The encounter with modernity changed, for better and for worse, the interrelationship between the Jewish and other civilizations.

It changed for the better because it opened up the possibility to form many new constructive ways of implementing the Jewish civilizational vision in a intercivilizational setting. The relationship to other civilizations was not necessarily as antagonistic as in the period of the Second Temple and in the long period of the (especially Medieval) Galut. The civilizational competition, as against the national or "racial" encounters with their tragic culmination in the Holocaust, given the transformation of the civilizational visions in the modern world, was more open and seemingly benign; although, of course, many antagonistic elements existed on many different levels. The attempts to implement the Jewish civilizational vision became much more heterogeneous and varied.

These attempts aimed at the reconstruction of Jewish life in the modern world could be understood best in terms of the combination of concrete practical experiences to further, with attempting a continuous reinterpretation of, selected themes of the Jewish civilization. Such interpretation and the closely related attempts at their institutionalization has varied greatly among different Jewish communities in different periods of modern history.

These differences were not only local variations on a set of common themes, as was usually the case in the Medieval period. In the modern period these variations entailed different historical experiences and types of consciousness. We analyzed the development of such different historical experiences in different parts of Europe in the nineteenth and early twentieth century; among the "Oriental" Jewish communities; in the two entirely new modes of these experiences in the United States and in the state of Israel. The differences in the historical experiences of the state of Israel, the new territorially compact and politically independent center, and those of the various Jewish communities of the Diaspora has become the central focus of the interrelations among different Jewish communities in the modern, contemporary era.

We have seen that even the development of Israeli society as a "total" society cannot be understood without reference to the ways in which some of the basic Jewish civilizational themes and the tensions between them became institutionalized within it. In Israel these themes no longer were confined to communal arrangements or intellectual and literary expression; they became closely related to the working of overall political institutions and the acceptance of the rule of law, in particular to the army and the civilian control of that army.

The specific achievement of the institutional mold that developed in Israel was not, as we have seen, that it obliterated these different orientations and tensions. On the contrary, all of them continued to exist within it and their impact on social life, given that they became interwoven in concrete institutional settings, was much greater.

The processes leading to the disintegration of the initial mold of Israeli society highlighted, perhaps even more than in other such societies, some of the choices inherent in the very institutionalization and dynamic development of a revolutionary mold. Above all, a choice had to be made between commitment to a single vision, with its monolithic potentialities and potential power orientation, and openness and pluralism; between elitist and populist orientations; between the stress on obligations and rights and entitlements; between active participation in the central framework of societal and cultural creativity and the more passive or privatized ones. And the great challenge was continuously finding new ways to combine these various orientations without entirely giving up any of them.

The sharp articulation of these choices or dilemmas in Israeli society was largely due to the close connection, an intensification, between the institutionalization of this mold, and its later disintegration, and the problems of implementing the Jewish civilizational vision in the specific setting of a small, beleaguered society. So it also highlighted the problems and dilemmas of the Jewish re-entry into history.

These developments gave rise to the emergence of different themes of Jewish civilization and the Zionist vision. The Messianic, territorial, solidarity, or primordial components of the collective identity all emerged, each claiming its autonomy from the other themes, challenging the validity of the other themes and in tension with them and claiming total predominance in the direction of the institutional formation of the society. Such developments, attendant on the disintegration of the initial institutional mold of Israeli society, posed in a very sharp way the problem inherent in building a small society in a hostile environment to carry the burden of some implementation of the Jewish civilizational vision.

Similarly many of the modes of construction of Jewish life in the various communities of the Diaspora were closely interwoven with the selection, in these communities, of different Jewish civilizational themes and their institutionalization. With respect to such selection and institutionalization these developed, as we have seen, far-reaching differences among different Jewish communities.

But the Jewish encounter with modernity and with so-called postmodern times also entailed possibilities for the worse, in two contradictory directions. The first such direction was the possibility, fully epitomized in the

Holocaust, of total destruction legitimized by a combination of older religious and modern secular forms. The second such direction was rooted in the possibility of the disintegration of some common Jewish civilizational framework because of the continued confrontation of diverse modes of its development, different historical experiences among different Jewish communities. This entailed the concomitant possibility of the loss of meaningful contact among them, the disintegration of a common framework of discourse—beyond that of survival and some attachment and mutual help. The possibility of the disintegration of any common Jewish framework in the modern times also was rooted in the tendencies to assimilation and drifting away that developed in the different communities of the Diaspora. These possibilities of loss of contact among Jewish communities as well as drifting away of Jews became even more pronounced in the contemporary era with the development of the so-called postmodern tendencies, above all with the weakening of the relatively clear national and communal boundaries that characterized the first steps of modernity in the nineteenth and first half of the twentieth century.

All these varied developments that gave rise to the great heterogeneity of Jewish life in general—the different modes of incorporation of Jewish communities in their host societies in the Diaspora, the resurgence of orthodoxy, the various developments attendant on the transformation of Israeli society, the continuous contacts and tensions among these developments—indeed have highlighted the problem of viability and nature of Jewish civilization in the modern and perhaps above all, in the so-called postmodern era. Although these developments do not in themselves provide direct answers to this problem, they do set out its parameters.

Some basic parameters could be set out in the following questions. Would it be best, from the point of view of the survival of Jewish civilization, that Israel become just a "normal" nation? Would the attempt to develop some distinct spaces of Jewish activities and the implementation of the Jewish civilizational vision in the free communities of the Diaspora be viable? Would orthodoxy be the best assurance of the survival of the Jewish people? Contrariwise, would simple drifting away and assimilation be possible? The success of these tendencies would mean the transformation of Jewish collective existence in the direction of becoming "just" religious sects; some weakly organized ethnic, religious, or intellectual groups; and in Israel, a distinct national political community.

The development of Israel into a normal small society, dissociated from the Jewish civilizational orientations reinforce many of its stagnative tendencies, to a weakening of motivation and an unwillingness to carry its apparent burden. It also might become very closely connected with the development or combination of politics of a higher law and religious fundamentalism, with the concomitant weakening of its institutional fabric.

The story of the nonorthodox Diaspora, especially but not only in the United States, indeed is a story of great success in terms of the different modes of participation of Jews in many areas of activity in their host societies and in developing special Jewish activities, especially when combined with the weakening of historical consciousness. Yet the loss of creative tension in their relations to Israel indeed may slowly erode their Jewish identity. And it is not clear to what extent the confrontation with orthodox groups in the Diaspora or the internal impetus of this sector can generate such creative tension.

With respect to the new type or types of orthodoxy, as far as one can see now, this sector of the Jewish people indeed may be able, demographically as well as culturally, to survive almost by itself in the conditions of modern society. But this type of survival is predicated on an entirely different premise from those predominant in Medieval times, in the periods of the predominance of the Halakhah. In a modern, open society, such survival involves giving up the civilizational vision, turning into a rather closed religious group or groups, with very strong sectarian tendencies.

The realization of each or all these possibilities would entail the loss of the civilizational components of Jewish life and tradition and the concomitant transformation of Jewish collectivities, in the framework of modern and postmodern civilization, into new social entities, each with different chances for survival and seemingly with a growing chance for assimilation through drifting away. It is still too difficult to estimate the chances of such development, the realization of such possibilities. On the one hand, the differences in the historical experiences of different Jewish communities may increase the dissociation among them and the possibility of actualizing each of these tendencies. On the other hand, it seems that the chances of realizing such possibilities are mitigated, but not necessarily made impossible, both by the continuous interrelations among the various Jewish communities, as we analyzed them, and by their continuous and variegated encounters with the broader environment, whether with their "host" societies or with the Muslim world and Arab states in the Middle East. These encounters indeed have changed greatly since Medieval times and the beginnings of incorporation of Jews into the modern civilizations from the late eighteenth century up to the Second World War. The major change lies in the fact seeming abatement of the older hostile relations between the Jewish civilization and people and their host civilizations and societies, with the development of the so-called postmodern era, the decline of the nation-state, and the growing tolerance in Western societies, of cultural and social heterogeneity, and with the widespread, at least official delegitimation of antisemitism after the Holocaust.

This growing tolerance can be found not only in the wider acceptance of Jews as citizens of full standing but also in many attempts at interfaith-meetings between different Christian churches and organizations and Jewish groups. But there is another side to these developments. Such occurrences as the dispute about the convent in Auschwitz; the renegation of the Archbishop of Krakow on the agreement with Jewish representatives to remove it, and the sharp words with strong antisemitic overtones of the Cardinal Primate of Poland with respect to this debate as well as the Vatican's continous refusal to recognize the State of Israel indicate that such growing tolerance may be only skin deep. Such indications are reinforced by the resurgence of strong, "traditional" antisemitism in Russia and many Eastern European countries after the downfall or reform of the communist regimes within them, and the growth of many manifestations of antisemitism in Western countries in the late 1980s, as well as the very strong propensity of many sectors of European societies, as well as of the more official organs of the European community to react very strongly to Israel's stance with respect to the Palestinian problem, a reaction far beyond that to similar activities by other states or communities.

The hostile relations between Israel and most of its neighboring states seemingly are of a different, new nature: mostly between national states and movements. But these encounters, as well as the multiple reactions to the Israeli-Arab conflict throughout the Western and Muslim world, still bear many of the seeds of the historical ambivalent, hostile relations between the Jewish people, their civilization, and their host civilizations.

The combination of such "seasonal" increases in antisemitism through-out the Diaspora,[7] and the importance of ideological components, reminiscent of the older intercivilizational and interreligious relations in the Israeli-Arab conflict and the reaction to it, may cast some doubt whether indeed the older hostile components in the relations between Jews and the civilizations and societies to which they interact, have entirely disappeared, only forty years after the Holocaust. The resurgence, or even the latent existence of these tendencies, naturally tends to reinforce the continuous connections among different Jewish communities.

The combination of all these developments, within the various Jewish communities and in their relations with other societies, will provide the answer or answers about the fate of Jewish civilization in the modern era: Which of the various tendencies pointed out here, or their combinations, will become predominant? Only the future can tell.

Notes

1. Jewish History as the History of Jewish Civilizations

1. For the way in which the term *civilization* is used here, see S. N. Eisenstadt, *A Sociological Approach to Comparative Civilizations* (Jerusalem: Hebrew University, Department of Sociology and the Truman Research Institute, 1986).

2. See, for example, H. H. Ben-Sasson, ed., *A History of the Jewish People* (Cambridge, Mass.: Harvard University Press, 1976).

3. See A. J. Toynbee, *A Study of History* (New York: Oxford University Press, 1947), especially chapter 5.

4. See Max Weber, *Ancient Judaism*, trans. and ed. by H. H. Geerth and O. Martindale (Glencoe, Ill.: The Free Press, 1952).

5. See Toynbee, *A Study of History*.

6. See Weber, *Ancient Judaism*; idem, *The Religion of China* (Glencoe, Ill.: The Free Press, 1951). Idem, *The Religion of India* (Glencoe, Ill.: The Free Press, 1958).

7. See Toynbee, *A Study of History*. See also Y. Flerzop, *A People that Dwells Alone* (London: Weidenfeld & Nicholson, 1975), pp. 21–42.

8. See Weber, *Ancient Judaism*; *The Religion of China*. W. Schluchter, *Max Webers Studie über das antike Judentum, Interpretation und Kritik* (Frankfurt on Main: Suhrkamp, 1981). Idem, *Max Webers Sicht des antiken Christentums* (Frankfurt on Main: Suhrkamp, 1981). C. Schaefer-Lichtenberg, *Stadt und Eidgenossenschaft im Alten Testament* (Berlin: Water de Gruyter, 1983).

9. References to all these figures can be found in Ben-Sasson, *A History of the Jewish People*, and in R. M. Seltzer, *Jewish People, Jewish Thought* (New York: Macmillan, 1980).

10. Thus, for instance much of medieval and early model Christian biblical exegesis was closely influenced by Jewish biblical commentaries. See, for instance, H. Hailperin, *Rashi and the Christian Scholars* (Pittsburgh: University of Pittsburgh Press, 1965). Prof. Lazarus Yaffe of the Hebrew University recently has shown that early modern Christian biblical scholarship was greatly influenced by the attempts of Muslim scholars, in confrontation with Jewish tradition, to interpret several aspects of biblical history that were seen as relevant to Islam.

11. See I. F. Baer, *Galut* (Berlin: Schocken Verlag, 1936; New York: Schocken Books, 1947). A. Momigliano, "Some Remarks on Max Weber's Definition of

Judaism as a Pariah-Religion," in *History and Theory* 19, no. 3 (1980): pp. 313–18. I. F. Baer, "Principles in the Study of Jewish History," Inaugural Lecture [in Hebrew] (The Hebrew University, 1931). For one of the most original analyses of the Jewish historical and sociopolitical experience see Y. Kaufman, "Gola Venechar" [Exile and Alienation] [in Hebrew] (Tel Aviv: Dvir, 1929–1932). For a critical evaluation thereof, Laurence J. Silberstein, "Exile and Alienhood: Yehezkel Kaufmann on the Jewish Nation," in M. A. Fishbane and P. R. Flohr, eds. *Texts and Responses, Studies Presented to N. Glezer* (Leiden: B. Porill, 1975), pp. 239–257.

12. S. N. Eisenstadt, "The Expansion of Religions: Some Comparative Observations on Different Modes of Expansion of Religions," in Craig Calhoun, ed. *Comparative Social Research, vol. 13. The Religious Field* (Greenwich, Conn.: JAI Press, 1981), or *Comparative Social Research* 13 (1991).

13. See Eisenstadt, *A Sociological Approach to Comparative Civilizations.* Idem, "The Axial Age: The Emergence of Transcendental Visions and the Rise of Clerics," *European Journal of Sociology* 23 (1982): pp. 294–314; and idem, *The Origin and Diversity of Axial Age Civilizations* (Albany: State University of New York Press, 1986).

14. Ibid.

15. S. N. Eisenstadt, "The Order Maintaining and Order Transforming Dimensions of Culture," presented to the German-American Sociological Theory Conference, 1988, to be published in J. N. Smelser and R. Munch, eds. (Los Angeles: University of California Press, 1991).

16. See Eisenstadt, "The Axial Age"; *The Origin and Diversity;* "Heterodoxies and the Dynamics of Civilizations," *Proceedings of the American Philosophical Society* 128, no. 2 (June 1984); pp. 104–113.

17. See S. N. Eisenstadt, "Cultural Traditions and Political Dynamics," *British Journal of Sociology* 32, no. 2 (June 1981): pp. 155–181.

2. The Distinctive Characteristics of Jewish Civilization in a Historical and Comparative Perspective

1. On some aspects of the emergence of these kingdoms in relation to the story portrayed in the Old Testament, see N. N'aman and Finkelstein, eds., *From Nomadism to Modernity* (Jerusalem: Yad Yitzhak Ben Zvi, and The Israel Exploration Society, 1990).

2. G. W. Ahlstroem, *Studies in the Religion of Ancient Israel* (Leiden: E. J. Brill, 1972). S. Talmon, *King, Cult and Calendar in Ancient Israel,* Collected Studies (Jerusalem: Magnes Press, Hebrew University, 1986). M. Haran, *Temples and Temple Service in Ancient Israel* (Oxford: Oxford Clarendon Press, 1978). Y. Kaufman, *The Religion of Israel—From Its Beginning to the Babylonian Exile,* trans. and

abridged by Moshe Greenberg (Chicago: University of Chicago Press, 1960), chapters 2, 4, and 6.

3. Peter Machinist, "The Question of Distinctiveness in Ancient Israel: An Essay," in Mordechai Cogan and Israel Eph'al, eds., *Ah, Assyria...*, *Studies in Assyrian History and Ancient Near Eastern Historiography, Presented to Hayim Tadmor* (Jerusalem: Magnes Press, Hebrew University, 1991), pp. 196–212.

4. See D. Weiss-Halivni, *Midrash, Mishnah, and Gemara* (Cambridge, Mass.: Harvard University Press, 1986).

5. A. D. Crown, ed., *The Samaritans* (Tübingen: Mohr, 1989), especially chapter 1. M. Mor, "Samaritan History: The Persian, Hellenistic and Hasmonean Periods." On the origins of the sect conceptions of these forms of distinctiveness among the Israelites, see P. Machinist, *The Question and Distinctiveness.*

6. Ben-Sasson, *History of the Jewish People,* part 1. S. N. Eisenstadt, "The Format of Jewish History: Some Reflections on Weber's Ancient Judaism," *Modern Judaism I* (1981): pp. 54–73, 217, 734.

7. Ibid.

8. W. D. Davies, *The Gospel and the Land: Early Christianity and Jewish Territorial Doctrine* (Berkeley: University of California Press, 1979). Idem, *The Territorial Dimension of Judaism* (Berkeley: University of California Press, 1982). For later, especially medieval attitudes toward Eretz Israel, see Moshe Halamish and A. Rawitzki, eds., *Eretz Israel in Jewish Medieval Thought* [Hebrew] (Jerusalem: Yad Yitzhak Ben Zvi, 1991).

9. Stuart A. Cohen, *The Three Crowns: Structures of Communal Politics in Early Rabbinic Jewry* (Cambridge: Cambridge University Press, 1990). D. J. Elazar and S. A. Cohen, *The Jewish Polity: Jewish Political Organization from Biblical Times to Present* (Bloomington: Indiana University Press, 1985).

10. See S. N. Eisenstadt, *The Transformation of Israeli Society* (London: Weidenfeld and Nicolson, 1986), part 1.

11. For general historical analysis of the period of the Second Commonwealth, see E. Bickerman, *From Ezra to the Last of the Maccabbees, Foundations of Post Biblical Judaism* (New York: Schoken Books, 1962). Ben-Sasson, *History of the Jewish People,* especial Part 1, the chapters by H. Tadmor, M. Stern, and S. Safrai. G. Alon, *History of the Jews in the Land of Israel during the Period of the Mishnah and the Talmud* (Tel Aviv: Hakibbutz Hame'uchad Publishing House, 1977) [Hebrew]. S. Safrai, ed., *The Jewish People in the First Century,* 2 vols. (Assen: Van Gorcum, 1974–1976). J. Neusner, *The Rabbinic Tradition about the Phaarisees before 70* (Leiden: E. J. Brill, 1973).

12. O. S. Rankin, *Israel's Wisdom Literature* (New York: Schocken Books, 1969).

13. V. Tcherikover, *Hellenistic Civilization and the Jews* (Philadelphia: Jewish Publication Society of America, 1959). M. Hengel, *Judaism and Hellenism: Studies in Their Encounter in Palestine during the Early Hellenistic Period,* 2 vols. (Philadelphia: Fortress Press, 1974).

14. See for example H. D. Mantel, "The High Priesthood and the Sanhedrin in the Second Temple," in Avi-Yonah, ed., *The World History of the Jewish People* (Jerusalem: Massada Press, 1975), vol. 7, pp. 264–281. H. Albeck, "Semikhah and Minnui and Beth Din," *Zion* 8 (1943): pp. 85–93 [Hebrew].

15. P. Frederiksen, *From Jesus to Christ: The Origins of the New Testament Images of Jesus* (New Haven: Yale University Press, 1988), p. 82.

16. See the bibliography in note 11 as well as: F. M. Cross, *The Ancient Library of Qumran* (New York: Doubleday, 1961). T. H. Gaster, *The Dead Sea Scriptures in English* (New York: Doubleday, 1964). J. S. Licht, "The Dead Sea Scrolls," in *Encyclopaedia Biblica* (Jerusalem: Bialik Institute, 1962), vol. 4, columns 639–671 [Hebrew]. A. Momigliano, *Alien Wisdom* (Cambridge: Cambridge University Press, 1975). J. M. O'Connor, "The Essenes and Their History," *Revue Biblique* 11 (1974): pp. 215–244. S. Talmon, "The New Covenants of Qumran," *Scientific American* 225, no. 5 (1971): pp. 73–81. Idem, "Judische Sektenbildung in der Fruhzeit der Periode des Zweiten Tempels, Ein Nachtrag zu Max Webers Studie über das antike Judentum," in D. Schluchter, *Max Webers Studie über das Antike Judentum,* pp. 233–281. Y. Sussmann, "The History of Halakha and the Dead Sea Scroll, Preliminary Observations on Miqsat Ma'ase Ha-Torah," *Tarbiz* 59, nos. 1–2 (1989–90): pp. 11–77 [Hebrew].

17. S. Talmon, "Exil und Ruckkehr in der Ideenwelt des Alten Testaments," in R. Moses, ed., *Exil, Diaspora, Rückkehr* (Düsseldorf: Patnos Verlag, 1978), pp. 43–47.

18. I. F. Baer, "Mekhkarim ve-Massot be-Toledot 'Am Yisrael" [Studies in the History of the Jewish People] (Jerusalem: Israel Historical Society, 1985), part 2. Idem, "Social Ideals of the Second Commonwealth," *Journal of World History* 11 (1968): pp. 69–91.

19. J. Neusner, *First Century Judaism in Crisis* (Nashville: Abington Press, 1975). Idem, "The History of the Earlier Rabbinic Judaism: Some New Approaches," *History of Religion* 16 (1976–77): pp. 216–236. E. E. Urbach, *Hazal: Pirkei Emunah ve-De'ot* [The Sages: Their Concepts and Beliefs] (Jerusalem: Magnes Press, 1969).

20. See A. F. Segal, *Rebecca's Children: Judaism and Christianity in the Roman World* (Cambridge, Mass.: Harvard University Press, 1986).

21. See Schluchter, *Max Webers Sicht des Antiken Christentums.* Momigliano, "Some Remarks on Max Weber's Definition."

22. See Weber, *Ancient Judaism.* Momigliano, ibid. Baer, "Principles in the Study of Jewish History." E. Shmueli, "The Pariah People and Its Charismatic Leadership: A Reevaluation of Max Weber's *Ancient Judaism,*" *Proceedings of the American Academy for Jewish Studies* 36 (1968): pp. 167–247.

23. Momigliano, *Alien Wisdom;* idem, "Religion in Athens, Rome and Jerusalem in the first Century B.C. and What Josephus Did Not See," in *On Pagans, Jews and Christians* (Middletown, Conn.: Wesley University Press, 1987), especially chapters 5 and 7. Y. Zussmann, *The History of Halakha.* See also S. Handelman, *The Slayers of Moses* (Albany: SUNY Press, 1982). Interesting analyses of different aspects of Jewish religious experience in a comparative perspective can be found in J. Neusner, ed., *Take Judaism, for Example* (Chicago: University of Chicago Press, 1983).

24. See Segal, *Rebecca's Children,* H. Maccoby, ed., *Judaism on Trial* (Rutherford, N.J.: Fairleigh Dickinson University Press, 1982). S. N. Eisenstadt, "Max Webers Sicht des Frühen Christentums und die Entstehung der Westlichen Zivilisation: Einige Vergleichende Uberlegungen," in Schluchter, *Max Webers des Frühen Christentums.* Idem, "The Format of Jewish History," in T. F. O'Dea, J. O'Dea, and C. Adams, *Religion and Man: Judaism, Christianity, and Islam* (New York: Harper and Row, 1972). Momigliano, *Alien Wisdom.* Idem, "Religion in Athens, Rome and Jerusalem."

25. Handelman, *The Slayers of Moses.*

26. P. Frederiksen, *From Jesus to Christ,* pp. 171–173. E. P. Sanders, *Paul and Palestinian Judaism: A Comparison of Patterns of Religion* (Philadelphia: Fortress Press, 1972). Idem, *Jesus and Judaism* (London: SCM Press, 1985). Idem, *Paul, The Law and the Jewish People* (London: SCM Press, 1983). And see also J. Neusner, W. Scott Green and G. S. Frerichs eds. Judaisms and their Messiahs at the Turn of the Christian Era (Cambridge: Cambridge University Prtess, 1987).

27. L. Dumont, "A Modified View of Our Origins: The Christian Origins of Modern Individualism," *Religion,* no. 12 (1982): pp. 1–13. S. N. Eisenstadt, "Transcendental Visions: Otherworldliness and Its Transformation. Some More Comments on L. Dumont," *Religion,* no. 13 (1983): pp. 1–17. R. N. Bellah, K. Burridge, and R. Robertson, "Responses to Louis Dumont," *Religion,* no. 12 (1982): pp. 13–27. Schluchter, *Max Webers Sicht des Antiken Christentum.* Idem, *Max Webers Studie über das Antike Judentum.*

28. Ibid.

29. See G. G. Stroumsa, "Ascese et Gnose: aux Origines de la Spiritualite Monastique," *Revue Thomiste,* no. 81 (1981): pp. 557–573.

30. See G. Bowersock, *Architects of Competing Transcendental Visions in Late Antiquity,* S. N. Eisenstadt, ed., *The Origin and Diversity of Axial Age Civlizations,* pp. 280–89.

31. See P. Rousseau, *Ascentics, Authority and the Church in the Age of Jerome and Cassio* (Oxford: Oxford University Press, 1978).

32. S. N. Eisenstadt, "Transcendental Visions."

33. See H. A. R. Gibb, *Studies on the Civilization of Islam* (Boston: Beacon

Press, 1968). G. E. von Grunebaum, *Medieval Islam: A Study in Cultural Orientation* (Chicago: University of Chicago Press, 1949). B. Lewis, *The Arabs in History* (London: Hutchinson, 1937). Idem, *Islam in History: Ideas, Men and Events in the Middle East* (London: Alcove Press, 1973). M. G. S. Hodgson, *The Venture of Islam,* 3 vols. (Chicago: University of Chicago Press, 1974).

34. I. M. Lapidus, ed., *Middle Eastern Cities* (Berkeley: University of California Press, 1969). Idem, *Muslim Cities in the Later Middle Ages* (Cambridge, Mass.: Harvard University Press, 1967). B. Lewis, "The Concept of an Islamic Republic," *Die Welt des Islams* 4, no. 1 (1955): pp. 1–10.

35. E. I. J. Rosenthal, *Political Thought in Medieval Islam: An Introductory Outline* (Cambridge: Cambridge University Press, 1962).

36. See Lewis, *Islam in History,* pp. 217–266; idem, *Race and Color in Islam* (New York: Harper and Row, 1971).

37. See M. Sharon, *Black Banners from the East: The Establishment of the Abbasid State* (Jerusalem: Magnes Press, 1983).

3. Basic Themes and Institutional Formations of Exilic Jewish Civilization: The Intercivilizational Perspective

1.. This analysis follows Eisenstadt, *The Transformation of Israeli Society,* chapter 3. For details of the history of the periods, see Ben-Sasson, *History of the Jewish People,* part 5.

2. See S. Baron, *A Social and Religious History of the Jews,* 17 vols. (New York: Columbia University Press, 1952–1983). Ben-Sasson, *History of the Jewish People,* part 5.

3. See Baer, *Galut.* Y. Kaufmann, *Golah ve-Nekhar* [Exile and Alienation] (Tel-Aviv: Dvir, 1929–1933).

4. See the analysis in Eisenstadt, *The Transformation of Israeli Society,* chapter 3. J. Neusner, *Israel's Politics in Sassanian Islam* (New York: Lanham, 1986). J. H. Gafni, *Yehudei Bavel Bitkufat Hatalmud* [The Jews of Babylonia in the Talmudic Era] (Jerusalem: Zalman Schazar Center, 1990). For later developments of transcommunal Jewish organizations, see I. Heilperin, *Pinkas Vaad Arba Aratzot* [The Records of the Council of the Four Lands], vol. 1, rev. ed., I. Bartal (Jerusalem: Bialik Institute, 1990). The full text was originally published in 1945.

5. See E. E. Urbach, *Ha-Halakhah, Mekoroteha ve-Hitpathuta* [The Halakhah, Its Origins and Development], (Giv'atayyim: Yad la-Talmud [Massada], 1984). Idem, *The Sages* (Jerusalem: Hebrew University, The Magnes Press, 1982). Neusner, "The History of Earlier Rabbinic Judaism."

6. On the different Jewish sects in the first century, see Cross, *The Ancient*

Library of Qumran. Gaster, *The Dead Sea Scriptures in English.* Talmon, *The World of Qumran from Within,* Collected Studies (Jerusalem: The Magnes Press, Hebrew University; Leiden: E. J. Brill, 1982). O'Connor, "The Essenes and Their History."

7. On the Karaites, see Baron, *A Social and Religious History of the Jews,* vol. 6. Z. Cohen, *The Halakhah of the Karaites,* New York, 1936, unpublished thesis. "Karaites," in *Encyclopaedia Judaica* (Jerusalem: Keter Publishing House, 1971), vol. 10, pp. 775–785. Z. Ankori, *Karaites in Byzantium* (New York: Columbia University Press, 1959). R. Nemoy, ed., *Karaite Anthology—Excerpts from the Early Anthology* (New Haven: Yale University Press, 1952).

8. See Cohen, *The Three Crowns.*

9. See Ben-Sasson, *History of the Jewish People,* part 5; I. Twersky, *Rashi* [Hebrew] (Merhavia: Ha-Po'alim Press, 1946). E. E. Urbach, *The Sages: Their Concepts and Beliefs* (Jerusalem: Magnes Press, Hebrew University, 1975). J. Dan and F. Talmage, eds., *Studies in Jewish Mysticism* (Cambridge, Mass.: Association for Jewish Studies, 1982). J. Dan, *Jewish Mysticism and Jewish Ethics* (Seattle: University of Washington Press, 1985).

10. In contrast to Arabic in the Islamic heartland, within medieval Hebrew there did not develop a profound difference between the written language of the high culture and the language spoken in daily life.

11. On the basic relations between Jewish and host societies, see for instance J. Katz, *Exclusiveness and Tolerance: Studies in Jewish-Gentile Relations in Medieval and Modern Times* (Oxford: Oxford University Press, 1961). I. F. Baer, *A History of the Jews in Christian Spain,* 2 vols. (Philadelphia: Jewish Publication Society of America, 1961–66). H. Beinart, "Hispano-Jewish Society," *Journal of World History* 11 (1968): pp. 22–238.

12. See Maccoby, *Judaism on Trial.*

13. See J. Katz, *Tradition and Crisis* (New York: Free Press of Glencoe, 1961); idem, *Exclusiveness and Tolerance.* Y. H. Yerushalmi, *Zakhor* (Seattle: University of Washington Press, 1975). S. D. Goitein, *Jews and Arabs* (New York: Schocken Books, 1964). B. Lewis, *The Jews of Islam* (Princeton, N.J.: Princeton University Press, 1984).

14. See G. Scholem, *The Messianic Idea in Judaism* (New York: Schocken Books, 1971); idem, *Major Trends in Jewish Mysticism* (New York: Schocken Books, 1961). R. J. Z. Werblowsky, *Joseph Karo, Mystic and Lawyer* (London: Oxford University Press, 1962). Dan and Talmage, *Studies in Jewish Mysticism.*

15. See Baer, *Galut.* H. H. Ben-Sasson, "Galut be-Yisrael" [Diaspora in Israel], in Joseph R. Hacker, ed., *Rezef u-Temurah* [Continuity and Variety] (Tel-Aviv: 'Am 'Oved, 1984), pp. 113–156; Kaufmann, *Gola ve-Nekhar.*

16. H. H. Ben-Sasson, *On Jewish History in the Middle Ages* [Hebrew] (Tel-Aviv: 'Am 'Oved, 1969). Idem, *Galut be-Israel.* Yerushalmi, *Zakhor.* M. Hallamish

and A. Ravitzky, eds., *Eretz Israel Behagut ha-Yehudit Beimei ha-Beinaim* [The Land of Israel in Medieval Jewish Thought] (Jerusalem: Yad Izhak Ven-Zvi, 1991). L. A. Hoffman, ed., *The Land of Israel: Jewish Perspectives* (Notre Dame, Ind.: Notre Dame University Press, 1986).

17. See Scholem, *Major Trends.* Idem, *The Messianic Idea.* and P. Frederiks, *From Jesus to Christ.*

18. On Maimonides' interpretation of Messianism see A. Ravitzky, *To the Utmost Human Capacity—Maimonides on the Days of the Messiah* in J. L. Kraemer, ed., *Perspectives on Maimonides* (Oxford: Oxford University Press, 1991), pp. 221–256. See A. Z. Aescoly, *Ha-Tenu'ah ha-Meshihit be-Yisrael* [The Jewish Messianic Movement] (Jerusalem: Bialik Institute, 1956). G. Scholem, *Sabbatai Sevi, The Mystical Messiah, 1626–1676* (Princeton, N.J.: Princeton University Press, 1973).

19. See, for example, Ben-Sasson, *History of the Jewish People,* part 5. Idem, *Rezef u-Temurah.* Urbach, *The Sages.*

20. See Katz, *Tradition and Crisis.* Eisenstadt, *Transformation of Israeli Society,* part 1. Scholem, "The Crisis of Tradition in Jewish Messianism," in *The Messianic Idea,* pp. 49–77.

21. See Eisenstadt, *The Origins and Diversity of Axial-Age Civilizations,* and idem, "Heterodoxies and Dynamics of Civilizations," *Proceedings of the American Philosophical Society* 128, no. 2 (1984): pp. 104–113.

22. Aristotle, *The Politics* (Cambridge: Cambridge University Press, 1988). Carnes Lord, "Aristotle," in Leo Strauss and Joseph Cropsey, eds., *History of Political Philosophy,* 3d ed. (Chicago: University of Chicago Press, 1953), pp. 118–154.

23. See, for instance, A. F. Wright, *The Confucian Persuasion* (Stanford, Calif.: Stanford University Press, 1960). D. S. Nivison and A. F. Wright, eds., *Confucianism in Action* (Stanford, Calif.: Stanford University Press, 1959).

24. S. N. Eisenstadt, "Utopias and Dynamics of Civilizations: Some Concluding Comparative Observations," in Adam Seligman, ed., *Order and Transcendence: The Role of Utopias and the Dynamics of Civilization* (Leiden: E. J. Brill, 1989), pp. 139–149. Idem, "The Comparative Study of Utopias," in ibid. pp. 1–12. Idem, "Christian Utopias and Christian Salvation: A General Introduction," in ibid., pp. 13–29.

25. Rainer Baum, "Authority and Identity: The Case for Evolutionary Invariance," in Roland Robertson and Burkhard Holzner, eds., *Identity and Authority* (New York: St. Martin's Press, 1979), pp. 61–118.

26. Carl Brinkmann, *Recent Theories of Citizenship in Its Relation to Government* (New Haven, Conn.: Yale University Press, 1927). Reinhard Bendix, *Nation-Building and Citizenship* (New York: John Wiley and Sons, 1964). T. H. Marshall, *Citizenship and Social Class, and Other Essays* (Cambridge: Cambridge University Press, 1950).

27. Helen Cam, *The Hundred and the Hundred Rolls: An Outline of Local Government in Medieval England* (London: Methuen, 1930). C. McIlwain, *Constitutionalism*, rev. ed. (Ithaca, N.Y.: Cornell University Press, 1947). Idem, *The Growth of Political Thought in the West* (New York: Macmillan, 1932).

28. Judith Shklar, *Montesquieu* (Oxford: Oxford University Press, 1987). Q. Skinner, *Machiavelli* (New York: Hill and Wang, 1981). J. G. A. Pocock, *The Machiavellian Moment* (Princeton, N.J.: Princeton University Press, 1975). Idem, *The Ancient Constitution and the Feudal Law* (Cambridge: Cambridge University Press, 1957). Idem, *Virtue, Commerce, and History* (Cambridge: Cambridge University Press, 1985). L. Strauss, *Thoughts on Machiavelli* (New York: The Free Press, 1958). Idem, *The Rebirth of Classical Political Rationalism* (Chicago: University of Chicago Press, 1989). Q. Skinner, *The Foundations of Modern Political Thought* (Cambridge: Cambridge University Press, 1978). Q. Skinnner et al., eds., *History of Renaissance Philosophy* (Cambridge: Cambridge University Press, 1988). *The Portable Machiavelli*, trans. and ed. P. Bondanella and Mark Musa (New York: Penguin Books, 1979). C. Montesquieu, *The Spirit of the Laws* (Cambridge: Cambridge University Press, 1989).

29. On Czarist Russia, see Richard Pipes, *Russia under the Old Regime* (New York: Charles Scribner's Sons, 1974). On the Chinese center, see E. Balazs, *Chinese Civilization and Bureaucracy* (New Haven, Conn.: Yale University Press, 1966); E. D. Reischauer and J. K. Fairbank, *A History of East Asian Civilization*, vol. 1, *East Asia: The Great Tradition* (Boston: Houghton Mifflin, 1960); M. Weber, *The Religion of China: Confucianism and Taoism*, trans. H. Gerth (New York: Free Press, 1964); Nivison and Wright, *Confucianism in Action;* and A. F. Wright, ed., *Studies in Chinese Thought* (Chicago: University of Chicago Press, 1953). See also J. Gernet, "Introduction," in S. Schram, ed., *Foundations and Limits of State Power in China* (London: University of London, School of Oriental and African Studies, 1987). D. McMullen, "View of the State in Du You and Liu Zongyuan," in ibid., pp. 59–86. B. L. Schwartz, "The Primacy of the Political Order in East Asian Societies: Some Preliminary Generalizations," in ibid., pp. 1–10. A. Hulsewe, "Law as One of the Foundations of State Power in Early Imperial China," in ibid., pp. 11–32. M. Lowe, "Imperial Sovereignty: Dong Zhongshu's Contribution and His Predecessors," in ibid., pp. 33–58; and H. Franke, "The Role of the State as a Structural Element in Polyethnic Societies," in ibid., pp. 87–112.

30. See P. Crone and M. Cook, *Hagarism* (Cambridge: Cambridge University Press, 1977). M. Cook, *Mohammad* (Oxford: Oxford University Press, 1983). M. Hodgson, *The Venture of Islam* (Chicago: University of Chicago Press, 1974). H. A. R. Gibb, *Studies on the Civilization of Islam* (Boston: Beacon Press). See also S. N. Eisenstadt, "Convergence and Divergence of Modern and Modernizing Societies," *International Journal of Middle Eastern Studies*, 8 (1977): pp. 1–27; M. Rodinson, *Mohammed,* London: Hutchinson, 1971). Lewis, *Islam in History*.

31. M. Sharon, *Black Banners from the East* (Jerusalem: Magnes Press, 1983).

32. H. A. R. Gibb, *Studies on the Civilization of Islam.* I. M. Lapidus, "The

Separation of State and Religion in the Development of Early Islamic Society," *International Journal of Middle Eastern Studies* 6, no. 4 (1975): pp. 363–85.

33. I. Lapidus, "Muslim Cities and Islamic Societies," in I. Lapidus, ed., *Middle Eastern Cities* (Berkeley: University of California Press, 1969), pp. 47–49. S. Goitein, *Studies in the Islamic History and Institutions* (Leiden: E. J. Brill, 1966).

34. See Crone and Cook, *Hagarism*. D. Ayalon, *L'esclavage du Mamelouk,* (Jerusalem: Israel Oriental Society, 1951). D. Pipes, *Slave Soldiers and Islam* (New Haven, Conn.: Yale University Press, 1981). Eisenstadt, "Convergence and Divergence."

35. H. A. R. Gibb, *Studies on the Civilisation of Islam* (Boston: Beacon Press, 1962), especially chapters 1, 2. E. I. J. Rosenthal, *Political Thought in Medieval Islam* (Cambridge: Cambridge University Press, 1962).

36. B. Lewis, "Islamic Concepts of Revolution," in Lewis, *Islam in History,* pp. 253–266.

37. E. Gellner, *Muslim Society* (Cambridge: Cambridge University Press, 1981), especially pp. 1–185. A. S. Ahmed, *Millennium and Charisma among the Pathans* (London: Routledge and Kegan Paul, 1979).

38. Ahmed, ibid.; E. Gellner, ibid. N. Levzion, ed., *Conversion to Islam* (New York: Holmes and Meier, 1979).

39. St. Augustine, *The City of God,* trans. Marcus Dods (New York: Modern Library, 1950).

40. E. Voegelin, *The New Science of Politics* (Chicago: University of Chicago Press, 1974).

41. Friedrich Heer, *The Medieval World* (New York: New American Library, 1962). Idem, *The Intellectual History of Europe* (Cleveland: World Publishing Company, 1966).

42. See S. N. Eisenstadt, *European Civilization in a Comparative Perspective* (Oslo: Norwegian University Press, 1987). K. Pomian, *Europa und Seine Nationen* (Berlin: Klaus Wagenbach, 1990).

43. Eisenstadt, *European Civilization,* chapters 1 and 2. Max Weber, *General Economic History* (New York: Collier Macmillan, 1967). M. Mann, *Sources of Social Power* (Cambridge: Cambridge University Press, 1987). J. A. Hall, *Powers and Liberties—The Causes and Consequences of the Rise of the West* (Berkeley, University of California Press, 1985).

44. See A. Passerin d'Entréves, *The Notion of the State—An Introduction to Political Theory* (Oxford: Clarendon Press, 1967).

45. See the bibliography in notes 16–18.

46. See M. Walzer, *Exodus and Revolution* (New York: Basic Books, 1985).

47. See, for example, Ben-Sasson, *A History of the Jewish People*. Mantel, "The High Priesthood and the Sanhedrin" in M. Avi-Yonah, ed., *The World History of the Jewish People*, vol. 3 The Herodian Period (Jerusalem: Massada Publishers) pp. 264–274.

48. See C. O. Hucker, "The Traditional Chinese Censorate and the New Peking Regime," *American Political Science Review* 15 (1951): pp. 1040–1053. Idem, "Confucianism and the Chinese Censorial System," in Nivison and Wright eds., *Confucianism in Action*, pp. 182–208.

49. See Eisenstadt, "Cultural Traditions and Political Dynamics."

50. Mishnah Rosh Hashana, 4: 8–9.

51. See H. Ben-Sasson, *A History of the Jewish People*. Katz, *Tradition and Crisis*.

52. See M. Elon, *Jewish Law: History, Sources, Principles* [Hebrew] (Jerusalem: Magnes Press, 1973).

53. See J. Katz, "The Rule of Traditional Halakhah de Facto and de Jure," in *Halakhah ve-kabbalah* [Hebrew] (Jerusalem: Magnes Press, 1984), pp. 237–255.

54. See Neusner, *Israel's Politics in Sassanian Islam*. Gafni, *Yehudei Bavel*.

55. Elon, *Jewish Law*. Katz, "The Rule of Traditional Halakhah."

4. The Disintegration of the
Medieval Jewish Civilizational Framework in the Modern Period
and the Integration of Jews in European Societies

1. See *The New Cambridge Modern History*, vols. 1–4 (Cambridge: Cambridge University Press, 1955–58).

2. N. Elias, *The Civilising Process, Sociogenetic and Psychogenetic Investigations*, 2 vols. (Oxford: Basil Blackwell, 1982).

3. H. H. Ben-Sasson, "The Medieval Period," in *A History of the Jewish People*. Robert M. Seltzer, *The Jewish Experience in History* (New York: Macmillan, 1980), chapter 10.

4. On the Marranos, see C. Roth, *A History of the Marranos* (Philadelphia: The Jewish Publication Society of America, 1932); Baer, *Galut*, especially chapters 7–11. B. Netanyahu, *The Marranos of Spain* (New York: American Academy for Jewish Reserach, 1967). J. Kaplan, *From Christianity to Judaism—The Life and Work of Isaac Orobio de Castro* [Hebrew] (Jerusalem: Magnes Press, Hebrew Uni-

versity, 1982). D. S. Katz and J. I. Israel, eds., *Sceptics Millenarians and Jews* (Leiden: E. J. Brill, 1990).

5. See Katz, *Tradition and Crisis.* Eisenstadt, *Transformation of Israeli Society,* part 1. G. G. Scholem, "The Crisis of Tradition in Jewish Messianism," *The Messaniac Idea in Judaism* (New York: Schocken Books, 1971), pp. 49–77.

6. On some of the basic trends in the development of European civilization, see Eisenstadt, *European Civilization in a Comparative Perspective,* 1987.

7. See J. Katz, *Out of the Ghetto* (Cambridge, Mass.: Harvard University Press, 1973). Idem, *Jewish Emancipation and Self-Emancipation* (Philadelphia: Jewish Publication Society, 1986). S. Ettinger, "The Modern Period," in Ben-Sasson, ed., *A History of the Jewish People,* pp. 727–775.

8. J. Katz, *From Prejudice to Destruction* (Cambridge, Mass.: Harvard University Press, 1980).

9. Katz, *Out of the Ghetto.* S. Ettinger, "The Modern Period." A. Hertzberg, *The French Enlightenment and the Jews* (New York: Columbia University Press, 1968).

10. See Ettinger, "The Modern Period," pp. 777–834. P. Mendes-Flohr and J. Reinharz, eds., *The Jew in the Modern World* (New York: Oxford University Press, 1980).

11. J. Katz, "The Jewish Diaspora: 'Minority Positions and Majority Aspirations,'" *Jerusalem Quarterly* 25 (Fall 1982): pp. 68–78.

12. In Ettinger, "The Modern Period," pp. 834–847. N. Rotenstreich, *Jewish Philosophy in Modern Times: from Mendelsohn to Rosenzweig* (New York: Holt, Rinehart and Winston, 1968).

13. M. Breuer, *Jüdische Orthodoxie im Deutschen Reich, 1871–1918* (Frankfurt on Main: Atheneaum, 1986). Idem, *The Torah-im-Derekh-Eretz of Samson Raphael Hirsch* (Jerusalem and New York: Feldheim, 1970).

14. Baer, *Galut.*

15. See, for instance, an analysis of modern Jewish thought on this problem in A. Eisen, *Galut—Modern Jewish Reflections on Homelessness and Homecoming* (Bloomington and Indianapolis: Indiana University Press, 1986).

16. Katz, *Out of the Ghetto.*

17. H. Kieval, *The Making of Czech Jewry: National Conflict and Jewish Society in Bohemia, 1870–1918* (New York: Oxford University Press, 1988). M. Meyer, *Response to Modernity: A History of the Reform Movement in Judaism* (New York: Oxford University Press, 1988).

18. See Eisenstadt, "European Civilization in a Comparative Perspective." Katz, "From Prejudice to Destruction."

19. B. Dinur, *Historical Writings,* vol. 1, *Bemifneh Hadorot* [On the Cross-roads of Generation] [In Hebrew] (Jerusalem: Bialik Institute, 1955).

20. See Ettinger, "The Modern Period," pp. 881–900; M. Stanislawski, *For Whom Do I Toil? Judah Leib Gordon and the Crisis of Russian Jewry* (New York: Oxford University Press, 1988).

21. P. Medding, "Toward a General Theory of Jewish Political Interests and Behavior in the Contemporary World" in D. Elazar, ed., *Kinship and Consent* (Ramat-Gan and Philadelphia: Turtledove Publications, 1981).

22. M. Stanislawski, *For Whom Do I Toil?* S. Halkin, *Modern Hebrew Literature, Trends and Values* (New York: Schocken Books, 1950).

23. S. M. Dubnow, *History of the Jews* 4 vols. (New York: Thomas Yoseloff, 1967). M. Balaban, *Dzieje Zydow w Krakowie na Kazimierzu (1304–1868)* (Krakow: Nakladem Izraelickied Gminy Wyznaniowej, 1912); idem, *Die Krakauer Judenge-meinde—Ordnung von 1595 und Ihre Nachtraege* (Frankfurt on Main: J. Kauffmann, 1913); idem, *Skizzen und Studien zur Geschichte der Juden in Polen* (Berlin: L. Lamm, 1911); idem, *Letoldot Hatnua Hafrankistit* [The History of the Frankist Movement] [Hebrew] (Tel-Aviv: Dvir 1935). I. Shiffer *The Economic History of the Jews* [in Hebrew] (Tel-Aviv: Stibel, 1935–36).

24. See Y. Tobi, J. Barnai, and S. Bar-Asher, *History of the Jews in Islamic Countries* (Jerusalem: Shazar Center, 1981).

5. The Incorporation of the Jews in the United States

1. See, for instance, Jonathan D. Sarna, ed., *The American Jewish Experience* (New York: Holmes and Meier, 1990). A. Hertzber, *The Jews in America, Four Centuries of an Uneasy Encounter* (New York: Simon and Schuster, 1989). N. Glazer, *American Judaism,* rev. ed. (Chicago: University of Chicago Press, 1972). Ben Halpern, *The American Jew: A Zionist Analysis* (New York: Theodor Herzl Foundation, 1956). Irving Howe, *World of Our Fathers: The Journey of East European Jews to America and the Life They Found and Made* (New York: Simon and Schuster, 1976). Charles S. Liebman, *The Ambivalent American Jew* (Philadelphia: Jewish Publication Society of America, 1973).

2. H. Arlosoroff, "New York Veyerushalaim" ["New York and Jerusalem"] and "Hatzionut Haamerikait" ["The American Zionism"], *Collected Works* [Hebrew] (Tel-Aviv: E. J. Stiebel, 1934), pp. 75–113 and 147–178. See also, for a similar view-point, Simon Halkin, *Yehadut ve-Yehudei Amerika* [American Jewishness and Jewry] (Tel-Aviv and Jerusalem: Schocken, 1946).

3. See N. Glazer, "Social Characteristics of American Jews, 1654–1954," *American Jewish Yearbook,* 1955. S. M. Lipset, ed., *American Pluralism and the Jewish Community* (New Brunswick, N.J.: Transaction Books, 1990). M. Sklare, ed., *Understanding American Jewry* (New Brunswick, N.J.: Transaction Books, 1982).

4. A. de Tocqueville, *Democracy in America* (Oxford: Oxford University Press, 1952). R. N. Bellah, "Civil Religion in America," in *Beyond Belief* (New York: Harper and Row, 1970), pp. 168–193. A. Heimart and A. Delbanco, eds., *The Puritans in America: A Narrative Anthology* (Cambridge, Mass.: Harvard University Press, 1985). S. M. Lipset, *The Continental Divide* (New York: Routledge, 1989). See S. N. Eisenstadt, L. Roniger, and A. Seligman, *Centre Formation Protest Movements and Class Structure in Europe and the United States* (London: Frances Pinter, 1987), especially chapters 1, 5, and 8.

5. S. P. Huntington, *American Politics—The Promise of Disharmony* (Cambridge, Mass.: Harvard University Press, 1981).

6. J. P. Nettl, "The State as a Conceptual Variable," *World Politics* 20, no. 4 (1968).

7. Bellah, "Civil Religion in America."

8. Y. Arieli, *Individualism and Nationalism in American Ideology,* (Cambridge, Mass.: Harvard University Press, 1964). M. Walzer, "What Does It Mean to Be American?" *Social Research* 57, no. 3, (Fall 1990): pp. 59–65. S. P. Huntington, *American Politics,* p. 23.

9. From *Publications of the American Jewish Historical Society,* no. 3 (2d ed. 1915), pp. 91–92.

10. S. M. Lipset, *The First New Nation,* 2d ed. (New York: W. W. Norton, 1979), pp. 164–65.

11. J. Sarna, "Antisemitism and American History," *Commentary* (March 1981), pp. 46–47.

12. Lipset, *American Pluralism.* Glazer, *American Judaism.* Sklare, *Understanding American Jewry.* Hertzberg, *The Jews in America,* esp. chapter 18.

13. D. P. Moynihan and N. Glazer, *Ethnicity: Theory and Experience* (Cambridge, Mass.: Harvard University Press, 1975).

14. Hertzberg, *The Jews in America,* from chapter 18 on. Lipset, *American Pluralism.*

15. Charles E. Silberman, *A Certain People: American Jews and Their Lives Today* (New York: Summit Books, paperback edition, 1988). Calvin Goldscheider and Alan S. Zuckerman, *The Transformation of the Jews* (Chicago: University of Chicago Press, 1984). Calvin Goldscheider, *Jewish Community and Change: Emerging Patterns in America* (Bloomington: Indiana University Press, 1986). Steven Bayme, ed., *Facing the Future. Essays on Contemporary Jewish Life* (New York: Ktav Publishing House, American Jewish Committee, 1989).

16. R. Bachi in an interview with Yosef Goell, *Jerusalem Post* (August 11, 1983).

17. Avil Goldman, "Poll Shows Jews Both Assimilate and Keep Tradition" *New York Times* (June 7, 1991), p. A8; and see also the interchange on S. Lachman's and B. Kosum's "What is Happening to American Jewry?" *New York Times* (June 4 and 6, 1990).

6. Modern Jewish National Movements and the Zionist Movement

1. E. Gellner, *Nations and Nationalism* (Oxford: Basil Blackwell, 1983). B. Anderson, *Imagined Communities: Reflections on the Origin and Spread of Nationalism* (London: Verso, 1983).

2. See, for example, D. Vital, *The Origins of Zionism* (Oxford: Clarendon Press, 1975). Idem, *Zionism* (Oxford: Clarendon Press, 1982).

3. Vital, *Origins*. Eisenstadt, *Transformation of Israeli Society.*

4. See S. Avineri, *The Making of Modern Zionism* (New York: Basic Books, 1981).

5. See S. Almog, *Ziyyonut ve-Historiyyah* [Zionism and History] (Jerusalem: Magnes Press, 1982).

6. See Vital, *Origins.*

7. See Arieli, *Individualism and Nationalism in American Ideology.*

8. See Bellah, "Civil Religion in America," pp. 168–189. A. Seligman, "The Failure of Socialism in the United States: A Reconsideration," in S. N. Eisenstadt, A. Seligman, and L. Roniger, eds., *Centre Formation, Protest Movements, and Class Structure.*

9. See L. Hartz, *The Founding of New Societies* (New York: Brace and World, 1964).

10. On Zionist attitudes to territory, see E. Schweid, *Moledet ve-Eretz Ye'udah* [Homeland and a Land of Promises] (Tel Aviv: 'Am 'Oved, 1979).

11. Bellah, "Civil Religion." Idem, *The Broken Covenant* (New York: Seabury Press, 1975).

12. See Y. H. Yerushalmi, *Zakhor.*

13. On the Wissenschaft des Judentums, see, for example, N. Rotenstreich, *Ha-Mahashavah ha-Yehudit ba-Et ha-Hadashah* [Jewish Thought in the Modern Age] 2 vols. (Tel Aviv: 'Am 'Oved, 1950). S. Avineri, "Graetz: Revolutionizing Jewish Historical Consciousness," in *The Making of Modern Zionism.*

14. See M. Balaban, *Bibliography on the History of the Jews in Poland and in Neighboring Lands* (Jerusalem: World Federation of Polish Jews, 1978). I. Halperin, ed., *Beit Yisrael be-Polin* [The Jews in Poland] (Jerusalem: Zionist Federation, 1948–54).

15. See A. Mapu, *Kol-Kitvei Avraham Mapu* [From the Writings of Abraham Mapu] (Tel-Aviv: Dvir, 1947). M. B. Margolies, *Samuel David Luzzatto* (New York: Ktav Publishing House, 1969). S. L. Nash, *In Search of Hebraism* (Leiden: E. J. Brill, 1980). H. Walter, *Moses Mendelssohn, Critic and Philosopher* (New York: Arno Press, 1973).

16. See Vital, *Origins.*

17. See Ahad Ha-Am, *Essays, Letters, Memoirs,* trans. Leon Simon (Oxford: East and West Library 1946). Idem, *Selected Essays,* trans. Leon Simon (Philadelphia: Jewish Publication Society of America, 1912); Theodor Herzl, *Altneuland* (Haifa: Haifa Publishing Co., 1960). Idem, *The Complete Diaries of Theodor Herzl,* 5 vols. (New York: Herzl Press and T. Yoseloff, 1960).

18. See J. Katz, *From Prejudice to Destruction* (Cambridge, Mass.: Harvard Unviersity Press, 1980).

19. See Mr. Braslavsky, *Tenu'at ha-Po'alim ha-Eretz Yisraelit* [The Eretz Yisrael Workers' Movement] (Tel Aviv: Ha-Kibbutz ha-Me'uhad, 1962). Eisenstadt, *Transformation of Israeli Society,* part 2.

20. See Z. Jabotinsky, *Iggerot Ze'ev Jabotinsky* [Letters of Ze'ev Jabotinsky] (Tel Aviv: The Chaim Weizmann Institute for Zionist Research and Jabotinsky Institute in Israel, 1972).

21. See Kaufmann, *Golah ve-Nekhar.* S. Avineri, *The Making of Modern Zionism.*

22. Georges Friedmann, *The End of the Jewish People?* (New York: Doubleday, 1967).

23. See Ehud Luz, *Parallels Meet,* trans. L. J. Schramm (Philadelphia: Jewish Publication Society of America, 1988).

24. See A. Fischman, *Ha-Po'el ha-Mizrachi 1921–1935* (Tel Aviv: Tel Aviv University Press, 1979).

7. The Formation and Transformation of Israeli Society

1. Eisenstadt, *The Transformation of Israeli Society.*

2. Ibid., part 2.

3. A. Bein, *The Return to the Soil: A History of Jewish Settlement in Israel,* trans. Israel Schen (Jerusalem: Young and Hechalutz Department of the Zionist Organization, 1952). D. Horowitz and M. Lissak, *Origins of the Israeli Polity: Palestine under Mandate* (Chicago: University of Chicago Press, 1978). S. N. Eisenstadt, *Israeli Society* (London: Lords, 1968).

4. Simon Kuznets, "Lecture V: The Problem of Size and Trends in Foreign Trade," in *Six Lectures on Economic Growth* (Glencoe, Ill.: Free Press, 1961); S. N. Eisenstadt, "Sociological Characteristics and Problems of Small States: A Research Note," *Jerusalem Journal of International Relations*, 2 (1977): pp. 35–50.

5. Horowitz and Lissak, *Origins of the Israeli Polity*. Eisenstadt, *The Transformation of Israeli Society*, chapter 9. Y. Ben Porath, *The Israeli Economy: Maturing through Crises* (Cambridge, Mass.: Harvard University Press, 1986). N. Halevi and M. Klinov, *The Economic Development of Israel* (New York: Praeger, 1968). Mitchell Cohen, *Zion and State: Nation, Class, and the Shaping of Modern Israel* (New York: Basic Blackwell, 1987).

6. Peter Medding, ed., *Israel, State and Society, 1948–1988: Studies in Contemporary Jewry, An Annual*, 5 (Oxford: Oxford University Press, 1989). Eisenstadt, *The Transformation of Israeli Society*, chapter 9. N. Lucas, *The Modern History of Israel* (London: Weidenfeld and Nicolson, 1974). N. Safran, *Israel, The Embattled Ally* (Cambridge, Mass.: Belknap Press, 1978). D. Shimshoni, *Israeli Democracy: The Middle and the Journey* (New York: Free Press, 1982).

7. Ben Porath, *Israeli Economy*.

8. Charles S. Liebman, "The Dilemma of Reconciling Traditional Culture and Political Needs: Civil Religion in Israel," *Comparative Politics* 16 (1983): pp. 53–66. Idem, *Religion and Politics in Israel* (Bloomington: Indiana University Press, 1985). Ehud Luz, *Parallels Meet: Religion and Nationalism in the Early Zionist Movement, 1882–1904* (Philadelphia: Jewish Publication Society, 1988). See also Aryeh Fishman, "Torah and Labor: The Radicalization of Religion within a National Framework," *Studies in Zionism* 6 (Autumn 1981): pp. 255–271. Eisenstadt, *The Transformation of Israeli Society*, chapter 10.

9. Eisenstadt, *The Transformation of Israeli Society*, chapter 12. E. Krausz, ed., *Migration, Ethnicity, and Community* (New Brunswick, N.J.: Transaction Books, 1980). M. Lissak, *Social Mobility in Israel* (Jerusalem: Israel University Press, 1961). J. Matras, "Intergenerational Change in Occupational Structure of Immigrant Groups in Israel," *Jewish Journal of Sociology* 7, no. 1 (1966): pp. 31–38; S. Smooha, *Israel: Pluralism and Conflict* (London: Routledge and Kegan Paul, 1977). A. Weingrod, *Israel: Group Relations in a New Society* (London: Pall Mall, 1965). S. N. Eisenstadt, M. Lissak, and J. Navon, eds., *Studies on the Ethnic Problem in Israel* (Jerusalem: Jerusalem Institute for Israeli Problems, forthcoming).

10. N. Lorch, *One Long War* (Jerusalem: Keter Publishing House, 1976). Y. Peri, *Between Battles and Ballots: Israeli Military in Politics* (Cambridge: Cambridge University Press, 1983). B. Kimmerling, *The Interrupted System: Israeli Civilians in War and Routine Times* (New Brunswick, N.J.: Transaction Books, 1985). Lucas, *The Modern History of Israel*. Safran, *Israel, The Embattled Ally*.

11. B. Kimmerling, *The Interrupted System*.

12. M. Davis, ed., *The Yom Kippur War: Israel and the Jewish People*, Foreword by E. Katzi (New York: Arno Press, 1974). Idem, ed., *World Jewry and the*

State of Israel (New York: Arno Press, 1977). Idem, ed., *Zionism in Transition* (New York: Herzl Press, 1980).

13. Eisenstadt, *The Transformation of Israeli Society,* part 4. M. Aronoff, *Power and Ritual in the Israeli Labour Party: A Study in Political Anthropology* (Assen: Van Gorcum, 1976). E. Etzioni-Halevy and R. Shapiro, *Political Culture in Israel: Cleavage and Integration among Israeli Jews* (New York: Praeger, 1977).

14. A. Arian, ed., *The Elections in Israel, 1977* (Jerusalem: Academic Press, 1980). R. Freedman, ed., *Israel in the Begin Era* (New York: Praeger, 1982). Dan Caspi, Abraham Diskin, and Emanuel Gutmann, eds., *The Roots of Begin's Success: The 1981 Israeli Elections* (New York: St. Martin's Press, 1989).

15. Dan Horowitz and Moshe Lissak, *Trouble in Utopia: The Overburdened Polity of Israel* (New York: State University of New York Press, 1989). N. Lucas, *A Modern History of Israel.* Eisenstadt, *The Transformation of Israeli Society,* part 4.

16. Myron Aronoff, *Israeli Visions and Divisions: Cultural Change and Political Conflict* (New Brunswick, N.J.: Transaction Books, 1989).

17. Baruch Kimmerling, "Between the Primordial and the Civil Definition of the Collectivity: Eretz Yisrael or the State of Israel?" in Erik Cohen, Moshe Lissak, and Uri Almagor, eds., *Comparative Social Dynamics: Essays in Honor of S. N. Eisenstadt* (Boulder, Colo.: Westview Press, 1985), pp. 262–283. G. Aran, "From Religious Zionist to a Zionist Religion: The Origin and Culture of Gush Emunim, a Messianic Movement in Modern Israel" [Hebrew] (Ph.D. dissertation, Hebrew University, 1987). L. Hoffman, ed., *The Land of Israel: Jewish Perspectives* (Notre Dame, Ind.: Notre Dame University Press, 1986).

18. Baruch Kimmerling, ed., *The Israeli State and Society: Boundaries and Frontiers* (Albany: SUNY Press, 1989). Kimmerling, "Between the Primordial and the Civil Definition of the Collectivity."

19. Hoover Institution, *Israeli Democracy under Stress* (Stanford, Calif.: Hoover Institution Conference Papers, 1990). Pnina Lahav, "Rights and Democracy: The Court's Performance," in ibid., pp. 58–88. E. Sprinzak, "Extreme Politics in Israel," *Jerusalem Quarterly,* no. 15 (Fall 1977): pp. 40–41.

20. Aronoff, *Israeli Visions and Divisions.*

21. S. Baron, *B'Mivhan ha-herut* [Hebrew] [Steeled by Adversity—Essays and Addresses on American Jewish Life] (Tel-Aviv: Schocken, 1977), chapter 6.

22. E. Sprinzak, "Extreme Politics."

8. The United States and Israel:
An Essay in Comparative Analysis

1. Safran, *Israel, The Embattled Ally.*

2. Perry Miller, *The American Puritans* (Garden City, N.Y.: Doubleday,

1956). See also Neimart and Delbanco, *The Puritans in America: A Narrative Anthology.*

3. See, chapter 6, and also, in greater detail, Eisenstadt, *The Transformation of Israeli Society,* especially part 3. Horowitz and Lissak, *Origins of the Israeli Polity.*

4. Hartz, *The Founding of New Societies.*

5. Ibid.

6. See Bellah, *Beyond Belief,* especially chapter 9; and also, *The Broken Covenant;* Martin Marty, *Religion and Republic—The American Circumstance* (Boston: Beacon Press, 1987).

7. Arieli, *Individualism and Nationalism in American Ideology.* Walzer, "What Does It Mean to Be American?" pp. 59–65.

8. Tocqueville. *Democracy in America.* See also Lipset, *The First New Nation.* Richard Hofstadter, *The Age of Reform* (New York: Vintage Books, 1955). Huntington, *American Politics: The Promise of Disharmony.*

9. Lipset, *The Continental Divide.*

10. Lipset, *The First New Nation.*

11. See Hartz, *The Founding of New Societies.* Eisenstadt, *Transformation of Israeli Society,* part 3.

12. On the United States, see Moynihan and Glazer, *Ethnicity: Theory and Experience.* On Israel, see Eisenstadt, *The Transformation of Israeli Society,* chapter 4.

13. See Miller, *The American Puritans.* Heimart and Delbanco, *The Puritans in America.* Bellah, *Beyond Belief.*

14. Robert Bellah et al., *Habits of the Heart* (New York: Harper and Row, 1985). Michael Walzer, *Radical Principles* (New York: Basic Books, 1980). David Reisman, *The Lonely Crowd* (New Haven, Conn.: Yale University Press, 1958).

15. Rainer Baum, "Authority and Identity: The Case for Evolutionary Invariance." in Roland Robertson and Burkart Holzner, eds., *Identity and Authority* (New York: St. Martin's Press, 1979), pp. 61–118.

16. Louis Hartz, *The Liberal Tradition in America* (New York: Harcourt, Brace, 1955).

17. Eisenstadt, *The Transformation of Israeli Society,* chapter 8.

18. Ibid., chapter 9.

19. Pnina Lahav, "Rights and Democracy: The Court's Performance," pp. 58–88. Yonathan Shapiro, "Israeli Democracy," pp. 127–145 in *Israeli Democracy under Stress.*

20. Ibid. See also Ben Porath, *The Israeli Economy.*

21. See chapters 7 and 8.

22. Martin Marty, *Religion in America, 1950 to the Present* (San Francisco: Harper and Row, 1979). On fundamentalism, see Jerry Falwell, Ed Dobson, and Ed Hinson, eds., *The Fundamentalist Phenomenon* (Garden City, N.Y.: Doubleday, 1981). Grace Halsell, *Prophecy and Politics* (Westport, Conn.: Lawrence Hill and Co., 1986). Samuel Hill, *The New Religious-Political Right in America* (Nashville: Abingdon, 1982). Ernest Sandeen, *The Roots of Fundamentalism* (Chicago: University of Chicago Press, 1970). *Studies in Religious Fundamentalism* (Basingstoke, Hampshire: Macmillan Press, 1987).

23. Aran, "From Religious Zionist to a Zionist Religion."

24. Moynihan and Glazer, *Ethnicity.*

25. Eisenstadt, *The Transformation of Israeli Society,* chapter 1.

26. Kuznets. "Lecture V: The Problem of Size and Trends in Foreign Trade," pp. 89–100. Eisenstadt, "Sociological Characteristics and Problems of Small Estates," pp. 35–50.

27. R. Kent Fielding and Eugene Campbell, *The United States: An Interpretive History* (New York: Harper and Row, 1964). Richard Hofstadter, *The Structure of American History,* 2d ed. (Englewood Cliffs, N.J.: Prentice-Hall, 1973).

28. Eisenstadt, *The Transformation of Israeli Society,* part 4; Kimmerling, "Between the Primordial and the Civil Definition of the Collective Identity," pp. 262–283.

9. Concluding Observations:
The Jewish Experience in the Modern and Contemporary Eras

1. L. S. Dawidowicz, *The War Against the Jews, 1933–1945* (New York: Holt, Rinehart and Winston, 1975).

2. See Y. Tobi, J. Barnai, and R. Bar-Asher, *History of the Jews in Islamic Countries* (Jerusalem: Shazar Center, 1981).

3. L. Kochan, ed., *The Jews in Soviet Russia since 1917,* 3d ed. (London: Oxford University Press, 1978). For Leschinki's analysis see *The Jews in Soviet Russia—From the October Revolution to the Second World War* [in Hebrew] (Tel-Aviv: 'Am Oved, 1943).

4. For a very interesting comparative analysis of the different selections from Jewish tradition that developed in Israel and the Jewish community in the United States, see Charles S. Liebman and Steven M.Cohen, *Two Modes of Judaism, The Israel and American Experiences* (New Haven, Conn.: Yale University Press, 1990).

5. Davis, *The Yom Kippur War*. Idem, *World Jewry and the State of Israel*. Idem, *Zionism in Transition*.

6. Seth L. Wolitz, "The American Jew Is American First," *Jerusalem Post* (February 20, 1991).

7. J. Katz, "Accounting for Anti-Semitism," *Commentary* vol. 91, no. 6 (June 1991): pp. 52–55.

Additional Bibliographical References

The Holocaust in University Teaching edited by Gideon Shimoni.

Jewish Civilization in the Hellenistic-Roman Period edited by Shemaryahu Talmon.

Studies in Jewish History volumes I and II, edited by Joseph Dan.

Index